BOLIVIA: *The Uncompleted Revolution*

James M. Malloy

UNIVERSITY OF PITTSBURGH PRESS

BOLIVIA:

The Uncompleted Revolution

In memory of
Genevieve Delaney Malloy

CONTENTS

vii

PART IV

PREFACE

On April 9, 1952, a group known as the *Movimiento Nacionalista Revolucionario* (MNR) initiated an armed insurrection which resulted in the overthrow of the military junta then ruling Bolivia. As a result of this successful uprising, Bolivia was plunged into processes of social change and experimentation the likes of which had not been seen in Latin America since the experience of Mexico in the early part of the century. In short order the new Bolivian government nationalized mines, enfranchised its Indian population, passed a wide-sweeping agrarian reform, and downgraded the old military organization. Because of the profound effects of these changes, Bolivia was judged to be undergoing Latin America's second true revolution.

In this book I seek to analyze the "Bolivian National Revolution." In so doing I approach Bolivia as a case study in the general problem area of revolution in hopes of rendering the Bolivian experience intelligible and of drawing from it conclusions of a wider comparative significance. With these ends in mind, the study is preceded by an introductory chapter in which the theoretical framework that informs the body of the study is laid out. Chapters 1 through 13 contain my basic analysis of the Bolivian experience, and in chapter 14, I have attempted to summarize the study and draw from it a number of more general conclusions.

The basic research for this book was done in Bolivia in the years 1965–66. During that period I had the opportunity to travel widely and to speak at length with a spectrum of Bolivians who ranged from sophisticated politicians in the capital to peasants and hard-rock miners. It would be impossible to name all the people who aided me, and unfortunately the present political situation is such that prudence dictates that I not name many of my most valuable contacts. Let me say simply that my heartfelt thanks goes to the many Bolivians who directly aided me and to the Bolivian people in general whose openness and warmth taught this interloper from the north many unforgettable lessons.

I am especially grateful to Carl Beck and Richard Cottam who, as my teachers, colleagues, and friends, contributed more to the completion of this book than I am sure they realize. My special thanks also go to Cole Blasier who aided me on this book in more ways than I could enumerate. I would like to thank the following persons who read parts of the manuscript and offered valuable criticisms: John Gillin, Carter Goodrich, Murdo Mac-Leod, Steven Rosen, and Reid Reading. I owe an important debt to Herbert Klein who read the entire manuscript and whose incisive comments led me to rethink many important questions.

I am grateful to the Foreign Area Training Program whose generous financial support during the years 1964 to 1966 allowed me to spend a stimulating year at the University of California at Berkeley and fourteen exciting months of field research in Bolivia. My thanks also go to Woodrow Wilson Borah, who patiently introduced a brash political scientist to the complexity of Latin American history; David Apter, who gave a wandering special student a place to hang his hat among stimulating colleagues; and Robert J. Alexander, who most generously opened his rich collection of Bolivian materials to a young graduate student.

Most excerpts in both the text and footnotes were taken from sources originally written in Spanish. I have taken the liberty of translating these excerpts into English for my non-Spanish-speaking readers. If any errors in translation appear, they are unintentional and reflect no desire on my part to mislead the reader.

BOLIVIA: *The Uncompleted Revolution*

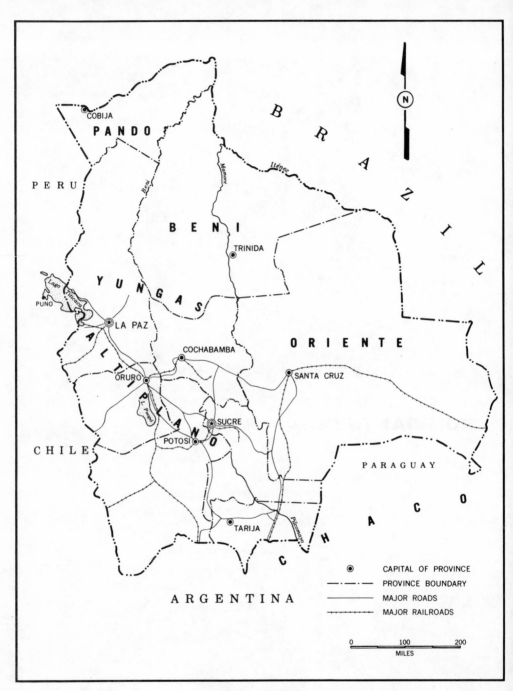

Map of Bolivia

Introduction:
A Frame of Analysis

A revolution is not an event but a process of varying duration and outcome. As I conceive it, a completed revolution (not all are completed) involves a movement from one authoritative political order, through a period when political order is in question, to a new authoritative political order. Thus, in a sense, a completed revolution is analogous to a story with a beginning, a middle, and an end.

One task of the observer of any specific revolution is to look back and unravel its plot. The task of building a theory of revolution is to seek a basic theme upon which the plots of specific revolutions are variations. In this study, I shall attempt to delineate the plot of the Bolivian Revolution of 1952 as it has been enacted thus far (it is my contention that the revolution has yet to be completed) and, hopefully, to grasp at least a part of the theme which ties it to a wider set of phenomena.

One problem in undertaking a case study of revolution such as this is that a generally agreed-upon definition of the concept does not exist. In attempting to come to a usable definitional concept of revolution, I follow those who argue that revolution should be viewed as a species of "internal war." According to Eckstein, "The term internal war denotes any resort to violence within a political order to change its constitution, rulers or policies."[1] In

3

other words, violence can be used to serve a variety of ends—from limited changes of governmental personnel (the classic *coup d'état*) to general rearrangements of all aspects of a socio-political order. The term revolution usually has been used to refer to those dramatic social upheavals which result in the more general rearrangement of the social, economic, and political relations within a society. In this study, revolution will be defined as that form of internal war that results in (a) a redistribution of the capacity of groups to influence a society's authoritative mechanisms; (b) the exclusion of groups with a previously high authoritative capacity from any future access to power; (c) the redefinition of a society's concepts and principles of authority; and (d) a redefinition of the goals which governmental authority usually pursues.

While violence is an integral part of internal war and, therefore, revolution, the amount and intensity of violence that occur can vary widely from case to case. Past experience indicates that the degree of violence tends to vary with the kinds and generality of changes at stake, that is, from a personnel-oriented bloodless coup to a wide-open revolutionary insurrection. Yet, as many have pointed out, it is also possible to conceive of a coup with limited violence resulting in a revolution. Moreover, both the degree of violence and types of changes sought can vary over a period of time. A group may begin with limited reformist goals and with a tactic of limited violence, but over time it may escalate the types of changes sought and the amount of violence it is willing to use to achieve these changes. As we shall see, this type of escalation occurred in the Bolivian experience. Also, the Bolivian situation indicates that the inclination of change-oriented groups to up the stakes and resort to more violent means varies with the degree and duration of resistance to their demands.

For purposes of this study, then, revolution will be conceived of as a form of internal war involving struggle over the four dimensions listed above. As a form of internal war, some degree of violence is inherent in the phenomenon, but the incidence and type of violence (coup, guerrilla war, civil war, insurrection, etc.) can vary widely over time. Aside from the dimension of violence, internal wars and revolutions are forms of struggle for authority and political power that are out of the ordinary or extra-legal (illegal from the point of view of the incumbents).

Part one of this study is concerned with an analysis of the Bolivian old regime, the destruction of which was the object of the revolution of 1952. The major concern here is to pinpoint those aspects of that political order which, over time, acted to predispose significant social groups to respond to appeals for radical change. In brief, the aim of chapters 1 through 4 is to stipulate the structural preconditions of the revolution that ultimately ensued.

In this section the analysis is couched, in part, in terms of the approach developed by Chalmers Johnson in *Revolution and the Social System*.[2] The major concepts in Johnson's frame of reference include dysfunction, an intransigent elite, and accelerators. Following a structure-function mode of analysis, this approach operates from the assumption that the major structural precondition to revolution is a society beset by a large number of incongruities in its social, economic, and political structures which create perceived problems for significant groups in the society— multiple dysfunctions. The nature of the dysfunctions is to be determined empirically by the observer case by case. An illustration of a dysfunctional, structural relationship and its connection to a revolution can be found in Tocqueville's analysis of the French Revolution.[3] Tocqueville points out that due to the process of centralization of power around an absolute monarch in prerevolutionary France, the landed nobility lost its major political function but continued to retain its old status privileges. Moreover, to meet its increased court expenses, this largely absentee stratum increased the economic burdens on its serfs, despite the fact that it no longer performed the "protective" role which previously legitimated such privileges. The result of this development was a weakening of the existing elite structure of the society while simultaneously creating pressure on a significant group, the peasants. As Tocqueville himself points out, there were a number of such dysfunctional relationships in the French old regime which contributed to its vulnerability to revolution.

Dysfunctionalities are manifested in part by politically relevant "protest" activities such as petitions, strikes, demonstrations, and riots. These activities are the means of articulating demands on incumbent elites for remedial action. In the face of such demands, the incumbent elite may sponsor reforms or effectively squash protest, or a combination of both. Either way it could follow an effective adaptive course of action resulting in a solidification of the status quo or a process of piecemeal evolution. In some cases, however, the incumbent elite is either incapable or unwilling to adapt. Such a situation could provide the second major precondition of a revolutionary situation—an intransigent elite.

So far in this discussion, the major preconditions which act to predispose a society to a revolutionary situation include (a) a socio-political unit experiencing multiple dysfunctions and (b) an incumbent elite or elites unwilling or incapable of carrying out an effective course of adaptive action. (Again the reasons for the existence of these situations are to be determined empirically 'case by case.)

However, though a society experiencing both these factors would no doubt be in serious difficulty, it still may not experience a revolution as such. A third element—accelerators—may stimulate a revolution. Major disconnecting social experiences such as a lost war, a major depression, or a natural catastrophe may galvanize the preconditions of revolution, causing the society to experience a crisis. Johnson illustrates his use of the concept of accelerators with the following metaphor: "the heart patient who unexpectedly contracts pneumonia—a disease that a healthy man can survive—and who then succumbs from the combined effects of the two."[4] His argument is that multiple dysfunction plus elite intransigence plus accelerators equals revolution.

I would argue that while extremely useful as far as it goes, this approach is incomplete and much too deterministic. It is becoming increasingly evident that revolutions *had* to happen only after they had already done so. In many societies revolutions appear to be imminent, but for one reason or another do not occur at all or are inexplicably delayed. In short, societies can experience revolutionary situations without experiencing revolutions, and, in contradiction to Johnson, I believe that the total sum of multiple dysfunctions plus an unwilling or incapable incumbent elite plus accelerators equals a revolutionary situation, but not necessarily revolution per se.

Revolutionary situations develop when significant segments of a society begin to conclude that an existing societal framework does not fulfill their desires or their needs. From such lack of fulfillment come demands for change. A revolutionary potential is reached when those discontented persons conclude that the existing political framework is the major roadblock to desired changes, and that they, as an organized group, must act as the agents of change. Once at this point, would-be reformers and/or revolutionaries begin to direct challenges against the government with the ultimate purpose of seizing political power. Thus, political combat is shaped around contending definitions of the authoritative institutions within which the society should be governed, and the society experiences a crisis of legitimacy. There is a tendency for the society to move into a state in which existing institutions become less and less relevant in adjudicating conflict, and force increasingly becomes the mechanism of resolving perceived differences. In other words, the society lapses into a condition of internal war. The tendency to resort to force is a characteristic of the revolutionary situation, but the degree of force is also a function of the duration of the conflict and the level of political struggle that is taking place.

Revolutionary situations are those in which legality and authority in the most profound sense are the issues. Since the competition concerns the rules themselves—rules by which differences would have been authoritatively resolved—there are no common standards to evaluate behavior or accepted means to resolve the dispute nonviolently. Struggles in a revolutionary situation are quasi-moral battles, and as time wears on, "righteousness" becomes an increasingly more important element of the equation and the resolution of differences by force, more and more the dominant "mode of politics."

The framework being proposed here rejects any deterministic cause-and-effect analysis. Analyses must proceed in terms of interacting factors developing in a potentially sequential fashion over time. There is no necessary outcome to a revolutionary situation as defined here, and its duration is indeterminate. A revolution is at all times possible, but its probability varies with the strategic context. The situation may lead to revolution but it also may result in counter-revolution, adaptive change, or it may drag on indefinitely. A revolutionary situation is defined by its qualities, not its outcome.

Parts two and three of this study contain an analysis of the revolutionary situation, which, I argue, developed in Bolivia with the close of the Chaco War in 1936. Part two (chapters 5 through 8) focuses on the period from 1936 to 1952 in which the strategic problem was the control of formal governmental power. Part three (chapters 9 through 13) focuses on the period from 1952 to 1964 when the revolutionary government of the *Movimiento Nacionalista Revolucionario* (MNR) grappled with the problem of establishing a new national political order. In my view, Bolivia was in a revolutionary situation throughout this entire period. I argue further that revolutionary situations are not terminated until a new coherent and stable political order is established; for this reason, I contend that the revolutionary situation in Bolivia continues to the present day. However, for reasons of manageability, this study concludes with the overthrow of the MNR by a military coup in November 1964.

While socio-economic factors are important in shaping revolutionary situations, the major factors determining outcomes in each of the two major revolutionary phases are the will, capacities, and orientations of the actual contestants. I analyze the unfolding of the revolutionary situation in Bolivia in terms of the interactions among incumbent elites, counter-elites and those sectors of the society which are actively drawn into the central conflict (mobilizable publics). The lines among these groups are not always clear. There can be overlap between reformist counter-elites and revolutionary counter-elites, and groups can change over time: reformist counter-elites can evolve into revolutionary counter-elites and vice versa.

In analyzing the revolutionary situation, I continue to be concerned with macro-situational factors such as economic crises and social dislocation, but my primary focus concerns the actions and reactions of the contenders themselves. A revolutionary situation is characterized by the existence of noninstitutionalized political combat. In this framework such combat is viewed primarily as a struggle between elites and counter-elites against the backdrop of a varying breadth and intensity of public involvement which, in part, determines specific outcomes of the elite struggle. Thus, one of the most important characteristics of many modern revolutionary situations is mobilization or the expansion of the scope of conflict.[5] Since incumbent elites largely control extant forms of political power (for example, office, instruments of force, wealth, and status), they will tend to seek to restrict the scope of conflict, while counter-elites, usually weak in extant forms of political power, will tend to seek new forms of power such as organized numbers, and, thereby, attempt to expand the scope of conflict. The revolutionary struggle is waged among incumbent elites and counter-elites in a limiting environment in which a critical parameter over time is the scope of public involvement. The permutations and development of important "instrumentalities" such as political organizations, ideologies, and programs are, in part, dependent variables fluctuating in this general strategic context. They are important factors in structuring and controlling the unstable relationship of critical publics to the conflict.

Assuming a successful seizure of formal power by counter-elites, the task of making a revolution remains open. The revolution comes to a conclusion only when the society is effectively redefined and reordered. The situation continues to be basically one of internal war, but again there is no certain outcome. The status quo elite has been eliminated from formal power, but its successors must face the dangers of a counter-revolution and disintegrating unity in their own ranks induced by the "defeat" of the enemy. Past revolutions indicate that political conflict becomes even more intense after the seizure of power as revolutionary movements split into rival elite factions struggling over power and over how to redefine and reorganize the society. It is the resolution of these latter questions that makes a revolution a revolution and not simply a *golpe de estado* ("blow against the state"—Latin American equivalent of *coup d'état*).

As Hannah Arendt has pointed out,[6] the era of modern revolution began in France in 1789 with the entrance for the first time into the political realm of large masses of human beings who had never before been a prime political factor and whose most basic reality was the day-to-day struggle for sheer physical survival. The social (as opposed to the political) demands of these masses became one of the critical elements of political decision-making.

It was also at this historical juncture that the notion of progress took hold, both as an article of faith and as a goal for political action. Not until the late nineteenth century, however, did the fomentation of the economic development of nation-states become systematic policy for Western countries, particularly in Germany under Bismarck. Later, when the Russian Revolution was consolidated under Stalin, rapid state-sponsored economic development for the purpose of creating a powerful state appeared as an avowed goal in what we now refer to as the underdeveloped context. Since that point, rapid economic development increasingly has become the chief goal of emergent elites in the underdeveloped world.

Thus, two factors—the mobilization of "necessity-driven" masses and the elite intention to use the state to push economic development—are defining characteristics of most contemporary revolutions and also limiting factors within which contemporary revolutionary behavior is played out in underdeveloped countries. Another limiting factor is the debilitating lack of capital, technology, and trained and organized human resources which often exists in such countries. In the modern underdeveloped context, the normative goal of rapid economic development is so pervasive that many elites are forced to base their actions and publicly posed alternatives in terms of this as a primary goal, whatever their original intentions may have been. In these countries the battle after the seizure of power eventually boils down to alternative political models for the goal of rapid economic development.

There are many conflicts in the contemporary revolutionary situation. The first involves the potential clash between a mobilized mass demanding immediate alleviation of need and the development goal of elites which demands accumulation and investment. In the underdeveloped countries, even more than the others, an investable surplus demands deferral of consumption. And the problem is even more complex, for often the only immediately available resource is sheer human energy, mobilized, organized, and pointed to the development goal; but such additional mobilization would undoubtedly spur an increase in demands for gratification.

The conflict between investment and consumption is common in all underdeveloped situations, revolutionary or not, but in the revolutionary setting it is exacerbated by the need to build support for a new political order and specific governments to run it. The task is hard enough when a functioning system exists, but, obviously, it is extraordinarily difficult where one is trying to bring a new system into being after having just destroyed the old one.

Support may be generated for a political system by the mobilization of commitment by force or by demand satisfaction. The first is the ideal, and there may be fervor within the revolutionary movement—especially in the early days—though it is usually based on anticipation of early gratification once an insurrection has succeeded. Force raises moral questions for some types of projected systems, is unstable and uneconomical over the long run, and presupposes that the government has the capacity to exercise force which it does not always have. The only remaining method is demand satisfaction, which can lead to the clash between consumption and investment in a revolutionary and, thus, far more serious context.

Another point of conflict is the question of social costs or which social groups shall carry the greatest burdens in the process of economic development. The reality that some groups bear more of the burdens of a society's gross advance seems historically undeniable and, unfortunately, unavoidable. This problem feeds the already high tendency toward violent conflict in the contemporary revolutionary situation.

Ultimately, the resolution of these questions demands the formation of alliances of social groups which provide a basis of power for the imposition of a "development solution" on a revolutionized society. Therefore, any specific political model of development will be fashioned out of an imposed solution of the problems of elite control and the allocation of social costs. However, the continuing tension between political logic (generating support) and economic logic (accumulating an investable surplus) makes such a task extremely difficult.

Bolivia provides an important example of a recent attempt to wrench a society out of extreme backwardness and propel it into modernity by means of violent revolution. Yet, this important process, for some inexplicable reason, has been largely ignored by American political analysts. Hopefully, the following chapters will begin to remedy this situation and convey to others the fascination of this exciting country and the drama of the new course it embarked upon in 1952.

PART I

1 Economic Development of Bolivia Under the Liberals

Following the Spanish conquest of the Indian populations of the New World, the area previously organized within the "Inca" imperial system was converted into an administrative unit of the new Iberian imperial system and called Alto Peru. The political center of Alto Peru was Lima, the present capital of Peru, but the early importance of the region to Spain was due to the silver deposits of the famous *Cerro Rico* ("Rich Mountain") located near the city of Potosí, which is situated in the mountainous area of contemporary Bolivia.

From the beginning of the exploitation of the *Cerro Rico* and other mineral resources, Alto Peru's main function was to extract and ship raw materials to the Spanish mother country. Alto Peru, as well as other parts of the empire, was organized to service Spain's mercantilistic needs. But the roughly hewn and militaristic *conquistadores* ("conquerors") who had, by force, subjugated the Indians were, in the main, ill-suited to the peaceful process of imperial business. In the eyes of the Crown, they posed a potential threat to the orderly flow of precious goods between Alto Peru and Spain. For this reason, the Crown sought to domesticate them with generous land grants and by giving them access to free Indian labor through the institution of *encomienda* ("Indians put in the care and trust of an appointed individual").

15

Although the ownership of the land and the control of Indian labor were initially separate legal rights, over the years they merged into the system of organizing man and land commonly known as the hacienda system. The hacienda ultimately became the basic unit of rural life and, through it, vast stretches of territory and large numbers of Indians were subjected to the control of individual families. Eventually, the hacienda units became relatively independent jurisdictional realms supporting a creole elite (persons of Spanish descent born in the New World) who became increasingly hostile to the peninsular-controlled (controlled by Spaniards representing the mother country) imperial system.[1]

Thus, a dual economic rhythm was established which, with some variations, has set the tone of socio-political realities in that region up to the present time. On the one hand was a centrally administered imperial system of extraction and export, while, on the other, a fragmented and increasingly localistic rural system organized within independent familial domains.

In the first decade of the nineteenth century the creole elite revolted against peninsular dominance and, after fifteen years of war, the Spanish Empire collapsed. Throughout Spanish America, the imperial system became fragmented, leading to the creation of a number of new independent states; Alto Peru was divided into the republics of Peru and Bolivia. But the depredations of the wars of independence and a decline in European demand for silver seriously disrupted the economic foundations of the new Bolivian state. With the flow of trade disrupted, Bolivia slipped into economic stagnation and isolation. For most of the nineteenth century, Bolivia, as well as other new Latin American states, was primarily rural and, hence, dominated by the creole landed elite. Throughout this period, politics was controlled by regional alliances of landowners led by individual strong men, usually referred to as *caudillos*.

These rival alliances struggled among themselves to control the national government and, through it, to appropriate offices, land, and power. It was the era of "the man on a horse," who through sheer personal power and magnetism ruled his countrymen until unseated, usually by force, by an even more powerful individual. These caudillos forged a legend of violence, daring, and unstructured willfulness which continues to permeate the political style of Bolivia.[2] Under these caudillos there was, in effect, a new conquest of the Indian. Through the manipulation of law and the application of force, many previously "free" Indian communities[3] were destroyed as legal entities, their lands expropriated, and their members organized as *colonos* ("one who gives free labor for a subsistence plot") within the hacienda system.

In the late 1850s and early 1860s, a new demand for silver developed in Europe creating a boomlet in silver production in Bolivia which lasted into the 1890s. With the renewed demand for silver, the old rhythm of extraction and shipment reemerged and slowly regained its former dominance in setting the national tone. Structurally, the pattern was the same as before, that is, there was a relationship in which mineral wealth was extracted from Bolivia and dispatched to service the needs of more developed European countries, with England now the major beneficiary. However, this time silver flowed to Europe, not in response to overt imperial authority, but in response to the demands of a new and more complex international market into which Bolivia was becoming integrated as a supplier of raw materials. The impersonal tie of supply and demand replaced the personal link of crown and subject. It was to become a form of dominance every bit as severe as the Castilian sovereign's will.

Extractive outward-oriented capitalism started to take firm root as the dominant mode of economic activity. Bolivian entrepreneurship began to flourish and the introduction of modern methods of extraction and organization, combined with the necessity of laying an economic infra-structure, brought forth new ancillary social types.

As commerce of any kind demands order, organization, and predictability, this relatively modern form of commercial venture, which demanded more sophisticated forms of organization, set off a call for a new state policy and style of politics. In the ensuing years, a struggle for control between the caudillo and entrepreneur developed. The battle was won by the entrepreneur who, in the new constitution of 1880, set out to solidify his position and make Bolivia safe for commerce.[4]

With the triumph of civility and business, Bolivia took a hesitant but definite step into a modern era of politics—an era in which the politics of territory, force, and personality began to give way to the politics of class, interest, and party.[5] However, first there was to be a period of transition known in Bolivian history as the era of the conservative oligarchy. This conservative oligarchy, which eventually formed a conservative party, was a curious mixture of modern, traditional, and regional interests and orientations. The modern element came from the revived importance of silver extraction for personal profit; the traditional element, from the ownership of land as a domain; the regional element, by grace of the fact that the great silver mines and land domains were located mainly to the south of the present capital, La Paz, around the cities of Potosí and the old capital, Sucre. More often than not, the owner of the silver mine and the land-holder of established lineage were one and the same.[6]

During four successive periods of conservative party rule, silver magnates directly ruled Bolivia's fortunes from the presidential chair. Under their control, the first efforts to develop economically relevant public and private works were made. The focus of these efforts was in the development of a communication and transport system which would bridge the formidable natural barriers of Bolivia and tie the mining camps to the cities and to international shipping points. The effort of these new silver entrepreneurs was restricted to programs concerning the easy flow of silver. There was no general threat to the traditional semi-feudal land system. Actually, the conservatives made a conscious attempt to meld the two into a political framework by supporting a constitution which safeguarded traditional values (including the continuance of Catholicism as the official religion).

Once started, however, the changes occasioned by the kind of development Bolivia sustained in this period were difficult to check. The conservative oligarchy was soon challenged by a different configuration of interests and outlooks, again partly modern, partly traditional, and partly regional. Traditional elements excluded by the consolidation of power of the conservative party and newer social elements brought into existence by the ancillary activities associated with silver and the city of La Paz (beginning to burgeon because of its pivotal position as the link with the outside) converged into a new Liberal party. These newer elements, including some associated with the first rumblings of a new extractive possibility, tin, were dominant in the Liberal party. They took a more aggressive, change-oriented position and were soon labeled "Jacobin anarchists" who sought to destroy the eternal verities of God and tradition.

Bolivia began to experience a titanic and essentially new kind of political struggle—a battle of party and ideology in which the stakes were the fundamental structure, organization, and definition of the country. The conservatives, an important element of the new industrial impulse, demanded a strong central state which, based in Sucre, would assure the continued dominance of traditional values and regional interests. The Liberals, on the other hand, demanded a federal system in which the newer interests of La Paz could flourish. In addition, they called for a rollback of traditional values, particularly established religion. In rhetoric, at least, the Liberals represented a demand to continue and expand the process of modernization.

The deep differences between the two parties inexorably led to civil war. The rival configurations clashed openly in 1898, resulting in a victory for the Liberals. An important reason for that triumph was the mobilization by the Liberals, through the promise of land and corporate freedom, of a powerful Indian peasant army. However, in exchange for their services, the peasant leaders were executed and a new round of land seizures around La Paz and the nearby Lake Titicaca region took place. With the defeat of the conservatives and renewed helplessness of the peasant support group, the Liberals set out to shape their Bolivia.[7]

One of the first moves by the Liberals was to do an about-face and come out for a strong central government, but one based in La Paz. This they were able to achieve, and while Sucre remained the de jure capital, La Paz became the effective capital and the pivot of Bolivian national life. The Liberals, then, consolidated their hold on the instrumentalities of government and began a reign which was to last for the next twenty years.

Liberal party governments continued and broadened the previous governmental commitment to a national economic development. Under the Liberals, the ideas of nationalism and development of economic resources were pushed as legitimatizing values. To make these values a reality, the Liberals embarked upon a policy of centralization, standardization, and the continued building of an economic infra-structure. The ideology which sustained and justified this course of action could be described as an imported, basically classical European, liberalism heavily flavored with French positivism, the former influence establishing a laissez faire market principle, and the latter, the notion of environmental control as the basic principle of administration. The chief governmental concept was the idea that the state should supply the limited essential means within which private economic domains, based on the motive of individual profit, could flourish.[8]

Liberal policies in this regard included demotion but not destruction of church influence, generation of public revenue through moderate import-export and excise taxes, the establishment of the gold standard, the formation of a central bank, and so on. The government continued the program of building transport links between the mines, the principal cities, and foreign ports. At first financed out of government revenue, the funding of these projects eventually shifted to internal and external governmental borrowing because the Liberal party policy set a limit on the use of the tax as an instrument of financing economic development.

Concomitant with the consolidation of the Liberals' power, Bolivia experienced the impact of a most important economic pattern: the last and definitive decline of silver and a boom in tin. The industrial breakthrough in Europe and the United States, spurred on by the coming world war, set off a tremendous demand for tin. Bolivia responded to this demand and a whole new cycle of mineral extraction and export trade was under way.[9]

The Liberals, not surprisingly, tied their personal fortunes, as well as the nation's fortunes, to the new source of wealth. Government policy was structured to nurture the inchoate tin industry and precious little else. Bolivia seemed to put all its faith in tin and, in the early twentieth-century context, it seemed to make sense. This policy was the result of a convergence of interests, values, and the prevailing economic and political logic of the day.

Whatever its source, a definite pattern emerged. The government encouraged the private growth of the tin industry. It chose, with the Smithian logic of the time, to catch up to Europe by specialization in the most readily available modern sector. As part of this policy, Bolivia built relatively few tariff barriers between itself and the outside, allowing an easy inward flow of manufactured goods; this was done on the assumption that favorable trade balances would more than pay the bill. Like most Latin American countries, the income tax was eschewed as a source of public funds. Export taxes on the nascent tin industry were purposely kept low.[10] The debt that accumulated by the policy of financing public works through borrowing was considered a small price to pay for the large inflow of foreign exchange which the country would hopefully eventually receive.

It was not long before the idyllic picture born of this prevailing theory was brought up short by some rather disturbing realities. Economic depressions in 1907 and 1913 were bellwethers of a dangerous overreliance on factors outside local control even though the industry bounded back each time more potent than before, and doubters were pushed aside. Significant, also, was the steady convergence of export and import figures. The country was becoming used to living off the outside—first for manufactured goods, but later for food as well—and it was relying on tin to pay the bill.[11] Conversely, local demand created by the new wealth was not being funneled into the local market, but into the international market; there was, in fact, a reduction of demands for local goods as tastes became more cosmopolitan.

As the ghost towns which dot the western United States bear eloquent testimony, extractive capitalism can drain a geographic area without sending out any positive impulses. Indeed, from the point of view of regional development around such an operation, most of its effects are negative. The outward flow feeds the raw material needs of industry in other regions. The propensity to use the local monetary inflow to buy already available manufactured

eral party rule. However, it is important to note that they were not in opposition to the order created by the Liberals. The ranks of the Republican party included dissident Liberals, representatives of the southern provincial cities, representatives of landed interests, and representatives of the urban professional groups.[13] The appearance of this party, which in 1920 unseated the Liberals by a *coup d'état,* seemed to mark Bolivia's definitive entrance into a modern political mode in which rival interests formed into parties and struggled for control of national governments. However, the existence of the two formal parties masked a more complex political game based on intra-elite faction struggles, the dynamics of which shall be discussed later.

In summary, then, during the latter part of the nineteenth century and the first quarter of the twentieth century, Bolivia underwent two fundamentally important processes. First, there was a process of political change which saw the creation of a modern centralized state oriented toward economic development and also the first outline of political conflict in the modern style in which class, party, and interest group played an important structuring role. Secondly, through the silver boomlet and then the definitive tin boom, the country sustained a strong burst of economic development and modernization which saw the progressive rationalization of economic organization, the country's entrance into the international market, the appearance and influence of new theories and values, and the emergence of new groups and interests.

However, the process of development and modernization during this time became increasingly reliant on the fortunes of the tin industry. As a result of this, the development experience of the country expressed itself in a dangerously skewed pattern. The development of the tin industry eventually detracted from and curbed the development of other productive sectors. Finally, it began to dominate all aspects of the country's development, not only as a focal point of economic organization and integration, but also as a primary cause of negative economic effects which led to stagnation in all other spheres of local activity.

National and Local Systems: "Two" Bolivias

This phenomenon of skewed development eventually resulted in a bifurcation of the country into two increasingly differentiated socio-economic systems. On the one hand, a system emerged based on the extraction and shipment of tin abroad, while, on the other, there was an agricultural system based either on subsistence farming or on very low-level, regionalized commercial activity. This kind of dual economic division was not new to Bolivia, but the nature of the tin industry and the new international market were such that a hitherto unknown wrenching apart of the country's two economic pivots was experienced.

The tin industrial system was relatively modern in tempo, urban in organization, and international in orientation; the rural or agricultural system was semi-feudal, atomistic in organization, and regional in orientation. A number of important factors quickly began to build walls between these two Bolivias.

The communication and transport links (railroads, roads, and telegraph systems) built by the mining-oriented Liberal governments helped increase the separation of the two systems. The mining camps and the major cities of Oruro, Cochabamba, and La Paz were internally connected. Due to its proximity to important tin mines, the city of Potosí was also tied to the net, but continued to hold an inferior position to the other three. La Paz functioned as the center of this system and the others as satellites.[14] La Paz, in turn, was tied by rail to Chile, Peru, and Argentina in such a manner that goods and people could flow more easily from La Paz to those countries, and then to Europe and the United States, than they could between La Paz and the vast bulk of the Bolivian interior. The flow of the transport system was such that it became cheaper for La Paz to import food from its neighboring countries than from its own internal provinces. Thus, aside from a small flow of persons and goods and some limited petty commerce between the cities and their immediate rural hinterlands, there was no sustained economic interaction between the two systems; this was particularly true in regard to interactions with the vast southern and eastern regions of the country. The only rural areas

to receive any positive feedback from the rise of tin and urbanization were the Cochabamba Valley and the region adjacent to
Lake Titicaca, located about two hours from La Paz by truck.[15]

Organizationally, the tin system tended to be closed and
dependent on the outside. In its most labor-intensive years, tin
employed no more than fifty thousand laborers, while related
activities employed even less. There were, therefore, no advancing
demands for labor which could set off a strong pull effect from
the rural to the urban semi-modern system, a factor reinforced
by the failure of a manufacturing sector to develop. Aside from
laborers and the few entrepreneurs themselves, there was a small
group of administrative, technical, and bureaucratic personnel
involved in mining and ancillary activities such as railroads. Many
of these were foreigners. Also, there were a limited number of
middle- and upper-income Bolivians who functioned almost
exclusively within the confines of the three major cities and the
mining camps.

The percentage of the population involved in the semi-
modern tin system was always small compared to the total population of the country. After a certain point, the system neither
demanded nor could absorb more. Wages and salaries were, in the
main, low and spent in urban shops and camp stores stocked primarily with imported foreign goods. Highly paid foreign personnel and foreign investors removed their share of the economy
from the country. Hence, no consumer demand of any importance radiated from the tin system to the rest of the country.[16]
Demand effect, like everything else in the system, tended to tie the
tin industry of Bolivia more firmly to the outside than to the rest
of the country.

The semi-feudal rural system accounted for the vast bulk of
the country's population.[17] Of this population, the majority were
Indian peasants organized either in haciendas as colonos or in the
few surviving "free" Indian communities dating from the Inca
Empire. Both the haciendas and the communities tended to be
closed autarchic entities. There was, therefore, little horizontal
movement among the units of the rural system itself. This already
atomized structure was characterized by strong regional identifica-

tions and localized marketing systems which further enforced horizontal isolation.

The largest part of the energies expended in agriculture went into subsistence endeavors. After a brief boom in rubber and nuts at the beginning of the twentieth century, agricultural production for export died out completely. Furthermore, due to the lack of any real manufacturing sector and the fact that those manufacturing activities which did exist imported most of their primary materials, there was no agricultural production to speak of for local industrial activities. Existing commercial agriculture was restricted to supplying some basic foodstuffs to the major cities or to the camps. This commercial activity never reached great levels and, as previously noted, it was localized in the Cochabamba Valley and the Lake area near La Paz.[18] However, this activity, especially after the growth of La Paz, did occasion the building of roads, some limited urban-rural interaction, and the flow of money into the two affected areas. Of the two regions, the most deeply affected was the Cochabamba Valley where there was some change in tenure patterns and some acculturation. Despite these important changes, the limited internal demand was generally accommodated within the hacienda framework with minimal changes in technique or rationalization of procedures. Thus, agriculture experienced no pervading modernization impulse and, even in the stimulated areas, the Indian peasant remained, in general, an outsider controlled by a patron serving as the main link between the two systems.

Both the hacienda and the Indian community functioned to isolate the Indian peasant mass from any developing national reality. Bolivia as a concept and the state as an entity were epiphenomenal to the day-to-day reality of the Indian peasant, and, hence, to more than 60 percent of the country's population. Whatever relationship that did exist was that of conqueror and conquered. Whether a comunero ("member of an Indian community") or colono, the Indian experienced the Bolivian government as an arbitrary and alien power, which when it didn't ignore him, sought to use him and nothing more. The national state and Spanish culture remained a colonial reality for the bulk of Bolivia's population.

The agricultural organization of Bolivia was not only backward, fragmented, and isolated; it also was minuscule in terms of geographic extension. A very small percentage of the arable land of the country was under cultivation.[19] The basic reason for this anomaly lay in the nature of the hacienda form. The chief input of this system is free labor. Thus, the extension of the system follows the geographic contours of a subjected population. In Bolivia this meant the bleak *altiplano* ("high plateau") and adjacent valleys where the Indian population had been concentrated since pre-Inca days. Geographically, this was only a small portion of the juridical state unit and contained the worst and most exhausted lands. Obviously, a *hacendado* ("landholder") wanted decent land, but he also sought an area where an exploitable population was available. The existence of Indian settlements as well as arable land set the limits of agricultural expansion. Given these factors, large regions of the country never felt even the minimal organization of the hacienda system nor did they have any connection with the national state that was Bolivia. The eastern region of the country, especially the departments of Pando, Beni, and Santa Cruz, were totally isolated and subjected to constant incursions by foreign states. Not surprisingly, they were areas of strong separatist sentiment.

Bolivia as anything resembling an effective state unit was restricted mainly to the altiplano and the adjacent valleys. This, properly speaking, was the limit of effective national sovereignty. Due to the contradiction between its juridical definition and effective sovereign control, Bolivia was incapable of defending its borders from its more aggressive neighbors. Brazil, Peru, Chile, and Paraguay all absorbed parts of what was originally Bolivia. The Bolivia of today is approximately one-half the size of the state which emerged in 1825.

Bolivia entered the twentieth century with all the symbolic accouterments of a modern national state. However, the national system, by its reliance on tin and the world market, became increasingly differentiated from the retrogressing and stagnating agricultural sphere around it. The Bolivian government directly touched very little of the human or geographic reality of Bolivia.

In this sense, we can talk of the development of "two" Bolivias. However, the conception that is being stressed here is that of a process of differentiation within a larger unity rather than a separation into two distinct unities. The concepts of "national system" and "local system" attempt to pinpoint an important line of internal structural differentiation, but, at the same time, attempt to recognize an important dimension of reciprocal interaction. Following the argument of Rodolfo Stavenhagen, I am trying to draw an image not of a "dual society" but of an internally differentiated unit in which the parts (or subsystems) are locked into a relationship of "internal colonialism."[20] The "national system" not only differentiated itself from the "local system," but did so at the expense of it; the backwardness of the latter was due in large part to the manner in which the former developed. For this reason, I refer to the development pattern experienced by the country as a whole as being skewed. From the political point of view, a key link between the two was an amalgamated national elite which became, in effect, the only nationwide grouping in the country and, therefore, one of the most important elements holding the two Bolivias together.

The overreliance on tin created other fundamental problems. Aside from the two depressions previously mentioned, the tin industry grew consistently until the late 1920s; 1929 was the single best year of production. After that date an entirely different pattern took hold. Instead of a steady upward push accompanied by sharp declines, the depressions of the 1930s started a steady downward thrust punctuated by periodic throes of greater dislocation. Even during World War II, when Bolivia was the sole supplier of tin to the Allies, production never reached the 1929 figure. From the 1930s on, Bolivia was not even capable of meeting the quotas assigned to her by the international tin producers' cartel. The simple fact was that the great mines were giving out. The companies failed to explore new sources, and the rate of investment in existing plants declined. Bolivia became a high-cost producer and her competitive position deteriorated rapidly.[21] The pattern of the Bolivian tin industry during that time is shown in the following table.

BOLIVIA: EXPORTATION OF TIN, 1925–1950

Year	Amount in Tons	Volume in Thousands of Bolivianos	Unit Value in Bolivianos	Value in Constant Prices—Base 1950 (Thousands of Bolivianos)
1925	32,598	27,123	832	66,114
1926	32,184	29,521	917	64,561
1927	39,972	35,684	893	79,823
1928	42,074	32,753	778	84,346
1929	47,087	37,388	794	94,456
1930	38,772	26,967	696	77,777
1931	31,637	16,257	514	63,464
1932	20,918	8,059	385	41,962
1933	14,957	12,089	808	30,004
1934	23,224	26,663	1,148	46,587
1935	25,408	28,147	1,108	50,968
1936	24,438	24,696	1,011	49,023
1937	25,531	30,363	1,189	51,215
1938	25,893	23,723	916	51,941
1939	27,648	27,843	1,007	55,462
1940	38,531	40,044	1,039	77,293
1941	42,740	48,283	1,130	85,736
1942	38,899	49,538	1,274	78,031
1943	40,959	55,188	1,347	82,164
1944	39,341	59,889	1,522	78,918
1945	43,168	60,274	1,396	86,595
1946	38,222	52,000	1,360	76,673
1947	33,777	54,615	1,617	67,756
1948	37,829	79,971	2,114	75,885
1949	34,300	72,087	2,102	68,806
1950	31,320	62,843	2,006	62,843

SOURCE: *Analisis y Proyecciónes Del Desarrollo Económico* IV (Mexico, 1958), p. 12.

Aside from some internal modifications of no great import, the industry was more or less the same in ownership, organization, and technique in 1952 as it was in 1929. However, in 1952 the industry was facing exhaustion and deterioration. During the 1920s ownership was consolidated, with over 80 percent of production coming under the control of the three giant combines of Simon Patiño, Carlos Aramayo, and Mauricio Hochschild. Of the three, the Patiño combine was by far the largest. The remaining

20 percent was in the hands of a number of medium- and small-sized operations. These smaller operations used a low level of modern technique. The truly modern element of the industry was controlled by the "Big Three."

With the consolidation of the tin industry, the basis of the entire economy was consolidated. As tin peaked, so did the effective potential growth of the country. Finally, as tin declined so did the overall economy. In the late 1920s the modernization impulse abated. The country's immediate growth potential was exhausted and the overall national socio-economic system began to stagnate and, later, to contract. With this set of phenomena, overall movement stopped and Bolivia was, in a manner of speaking, hung up: bifurcated internally, dominated by a mono-producing economy, completely reliant on external factors, and with a level of modernization rapidly becoming obsolete.

The picture was made bleaker by the fact that the agricultural system was also exhausting its possibilities of expansion. The beginning of the century saw a new round of land seizures and dispossessions occasioned by the emerging elite's desire to achieve landed status. By the 1920s, however, Bolivia was simply running out of Indian communities, on half-decent land, to be expropriated. Internal pressures were building inside the system as sons began demanding their legal rights and family holdings started to fragment. The hacienda system was progressively pushing against poorer and poorer land and the big haciendas began putting pressure on the boundaries of their smaller neighbors.[22]

Almost simultaneously, the two major motors of economic growth came sputtering to a halt. The entire unit was becoming static. A growing problem of circulation of wealth developed horizontally as well as vertically. The problem was aggravated by the fact that the two major forms of wealth—mines and land ownership—were not easily transferable. As the economic system became static, the control of wealth and status began to crystallize. Social mobility that opened at the beginning of the tin push was later closed off; lines among groups hardened. The divisible economic pie became fixed and after 1929 actually began to shrink. This was to create problems not only for those who wanted to

move up, but also for the ability of those already there or half-
way there to secure their positions.

It is within this context that we must begin to move toward
an understanding of what was to be the Bolivian National Revolution. In Bolivia, modernization was never generalized and no
self-sustaining basis of development was ever achieved. As a
result, a historical immobilism occurred within which the country
was fractured and was neither wholly modern nor wholly traditional. But neither was it transitional; for after a certain point, it
was in transit to nowhere. It was immobilized, crystallized, and
contracting. These internal contradictions led to internal pressures
which, in turn, led to louder and louder demands for change.

2 *The Old Order: Structure and Process*

In the previous chapter I outlined some of the chief dimensions of economic growth which took place in late nineteenth- and early twentieth-century Bolivia. The purpose of that discussion was to provide a basis upon which an analysis of the structure and process of the prerevolutionary social and political order of Bolivia could be made. During that discussion, an important analytical distinction was made between what I termed the "national system" and the rural or "local system": The national system was based on the tin industry, organized in the western cities and mining camps, and was dominated by the city of La Paz; the local system was, at root, traditional Spanish colonial, picking up some rudimentary modern characteristics in certain areas, as the Lake region and the Cochabamba Valley. Theoretically, the state was sovereign throughout the length and breadth of Bolivia, but effective state control tended to stop at urban limits. The state functioned mainly to facilitate the operation of the tin system. The national state and the "national system" tended to be one. They were differentiated from the local system in that the local system was effectively organized within a complex framework of official and nonofficial local authorities.

33

Class Structure of Prerevolutionary Bolivia

The national constitution reflected the general schizophrenia of the country. It stated that Bolivia was a unitary republic with sovereignty "vested essentially in the nation."[1] All persons born in the territory of Bolivia were Bolivians. But to be a Bolivian was not necessarily to be a Bolivian citizen. To be a citizen one had to, among other things, "be able to read and write, to own real estate, or to have an income of two hundred bolivianos, provided that this amount does not represent wages received for work as a domestic."[2] If one was not a citizen as defined, one could not concur in the constitution, exercise public powers, vote, be a candidate, or hold public office.

By constitutional fiat, over 75 percent of the population were not citizens of the republic of Bolivia. The entire agrarian Indian population was excluded, as were urban floaters and a good number of workers. Citizenship was primarily a middle- and upper-income group privilege. As these groups lived primarily in the cities, particularly the western complex, effective citizenship was mainly a characteristic of the "national system," thereby further reinforcing the fragmentation of the country.

A core characteristic of the prerevolutionary political system was legitimated nonparticipation.[3] One element of the history of the advancing European nation-state—the Bolivian elites' direct model—was the increasing political awareness of populations and their direct linkage to states through the advancement of the concept of citizenship. One of the clearest reasons for Bolivia's stunted growth was its open rejection of this form of incorporation into a national state community. At first, the ruling elite obviously did not want a true national base; after the development pattern described above began to jell, it positively demanded non-involvement. Increasing the scope of citizen involvement would have meant an increase in demands on resources. As the economic base began to crystallize, however, the country had enough trouble accommodating the demands of already established groups, let alone incorporating any excluded groups. One of the prerequisites of system stability, therefore, was the passivity and noninvolvement of the majority noncitizen population.

Relative to the population at large, the national political system was by definition an elitist system and was legitimated as such. The constitution assured that the simplest basis of political power —citizenship—would be monopolized by the monied, educated, and propertied. As all these characteristics tended to cluster around the middle- and upper-income groups of white or mestizo (Indian-white) racial extraction, the constitution thereby legitimated a correlation between money, race, and political power.

The twentieth-century Bolivian political elite is understandable only in relation to the relatively unbroken economic boom which Bolivia experienced from 1870 to the 1920s. The period saw a relatively high degree of social mobility. This was particularly true in the cities, such as La Paz and Oruro. The old southern conservative oligarchy, composed of an amalgamated group of silver and landed interests, was increasingly supplanted by a rising group of urban professional and administrative types. The most outstanding example of this new mobility was Bolivia's Horatio Alger, Simon I. Patiño.[4] Patiño started as a poor and despised mestizo, who, by manipulation of the growing economic opportunities, built the world's largest tin empire and became the single most important man in Bolivia, although he spent most of his life outside of the country. Using Patiño as the limiting case, the emerging new elite can be seen from two perspectives.

In the first instance, we can note the difference between the tin and the silver elites. The big silver magnates of the latter half of the nineteenth century arose from already established southern elite families. They used their financial power to enter public life directly (trading the presidency among themselves) and ruled as if by seignorial right. Of the big three tin magnates, however, only Carlos Aramayo came from this tradition. Even before the period of consolidation in the 1920s, the tin industry was owned largely by foreign (especially Chilean) financial interests who, while seeking to manipulate public policy, did not directly enter public life. Patiño, as indicated, arose from entirely new social roots and, once arrived, chose to live outside Bolivia. The third big magnate, Mauricio Hochschild, was a German Jew who came to Bolivia later (in the 1920s) by way of Chile.

Once consolidated, the "Big Three" incorporated their companies outside of Bolivia. Moreover, they all had extensive financial interests outside of the Bolivia territory. In the case of Patiño, it can be said that his Bolivian holdings eventually became secondary concerns. These new businessmen did not approach Bolivian public life from the tradition of the old *criollo* ("creole") aristocracy nor did they labor under the desires or values of seignorial right and duty to oversee the affairs of state directly. They were more or less pure modern capitalist entrepreneurs whose major interests and values lay in the pursuit of private economic power, not public political power. Their concern with Bolivian public life was that of an interest group which worried mainly about the furtherance of their private interests. They therefore played politics in the modern interest group style, content to leave actual public power to other men whom they sought to influence, when necessary. For them the state was not something to possess, but rather an instrument at times useful to manipulate. This was a subtle but important shift in the conception of public activity.

With the rise of tin, a partial split between private economic power and public political power took place. Previously, direct public power and private economic power (silver and land) were exercised and controlled by the same individual. Patiño, Hochschild, and Aramayo eventually came to control 80 percent of Bolivia's most critical economic power, but they did not directly exercise public power. They represented the beginning of modern interest group politics in Bolivia. Yet, this division of public and private power and the emergence of modern interest group politics was only partial. Again the cause was the failure of the developmental process to continue and to diversify. Landed groups continued, in part, to exercise public power directly; but it was an exercise tempered by the existence of the potent tin interest group which, as the all-powerful single interest in the country, could deflect or initiate policy in those areas of immediate concern to them.[5]

The second perspective of interest here is the emergence of a new elite recruitment pattern. The partial split between public and private power took another form. In the urbanizing centers—especially La Paz—there appeared a rising group of liberal professionals, engineers, administrators, and an expansion of that ubiquitous Latin American group, *empleados* ("white collar employees," usually bureaucrats).[6] In the old conservative oligarchy, public and private power were one. Then in the early twentieth century, 80 percent of the new pivotal private economic power, based on tin, came under the control of three men. Thus, many of the new urban elite did not start from independent and fixed bases of private power. Many rose, rather, as the *abogados* ("lawyers") of the big companies, or administrators of those and other related operations. Such a route was often facilitated by the achievement of public office through which one became useful to the private companies. Finally, the real consolidation of status came when such an individual could make the right marriage and achieve, often by questionable means, landed status.

During the period of economic growth (roughly from the 1880s to the 1920s), the effective political elite broadened. The rise of the Liberal party brought with it a new urban elite type. Although many eventually achieved landed status, their real base of power lay in being the administrators of the new tin interests and/or the direct manipulators of political office. The Liberal party pushed aside the conservative party, and in so doing, shifted the locus of state power from the traditional south and Sucre to the emerging west and La Paz. At the beginning, the rise of the group associated with the Liberals was at the expense of the old oligarchy, and, in many respects, the latter never completely accepted the changes. But as the modernization drive abated and mobility was cut off, these new elements tended to merge with the old. Although their channel of emergence was new, they did not bring with them a definitively new set of values. Rather, as the new and the old reached accommodation, the new power group progressively adopted the values and orientations of the traditional landed oligarchy.

New forms of power and organization were created by the economic development drive under the Liberals, but at the level of values and outlook, the new was increasingly co-opted by the old. Co-optation was facilitated not only by the closing off of mobility channels, but also by the fact that most of the new elite's power did not emanate from independent sources, but from the fact that they directly or indirectly served a set of interests which found the continuance of a static semi-feudal agricultural system much to its liking. The only means for the new elite to solidify its position in the increasingly static reality of Bolivia was to secure land. It therefore developed a common interest base with the old landed aristocracy.[7]

When the possibility of achieving independent economic footing in either land or mining began to disappear, the amalgamated elite tended to close in upon itself and adopt the stance of an estate. A new fused ruling group of old and new elements based upon the traditional values of wealth, pedigree, and race was formed, probably constituting less than 5 percent of the country's total population. In this study, I will call this new sociopolitical elite the "national bourgeoisie."

The most important families of this elite functioned in both the national and the local systems. In a real sense, it was the only social group with a foot in both the agrarian and "tin" Bolivian systems. The typical elite family had extensive land holdings, a respected name, and, perhaps, a member who was a lawyer for one of the big three tin companies, a senator or cabinet minister, or even a general or two. Families of this sort directly dominated politics. They produced presidents, congressmen, and cabinet ministers and also largely dominated the land and the Indian. Although this elite group did not dominate the tin industry, it did, in large part, work for it.[8] Like the society it dominated, this elite was neither purely modern, nor purely traditional. It was a rather unique amalgam produced by a partial and eventually arrested development process, which was based on an extractive industry rooted in a predominantly colonial agrarian society. It is important to note that this very small grouping was the only coherent grouping in prerevolutionary Bolivia which bridged both systems. It was, therefore, the only class or caste (depending on how the concepts are used) of nationwide character.[9]

All other groupings in Bolivia existed in sets of relationships structured by either the national system or the local system. Prerevolutionary Bolivia cannot be conceptualized in classic three-class (upper, middle, lower) terms, since there was no single class system. The country lacked a single social space in which groups could be structured systematically. Actually, given the semi-modern nature of the tin system and the semi-feudal atomistic nature of the local system, it is difficult to speak of classes at all in pre-revolutionary Bolivia.

The orientation of the Bolivian national bourgeoisie reflected a socio-political reality geared to facilitating the outward flow of metals. The liberal positivistic ideology was a European framework grafted none too comfortably onto the complex Bolivian culture. Europe, particularly France, became a model of almost slavish imitation for the national bourgeoisie of Bolivia. Imitativeness reflected itself in almost everything: the constitution, clothing, literature, art, etc. The national elite produced little or nothing which was identifiably theirs. The Europe they imitated was the literary and aristocratic Europe, not the entrepreneurial Europe. The average son of the highborn was educated outside of Bolivia and most of his lifetime was spent in foreign capitals. Bolivia for many of these people was little more than a place where one had some financial interests and personal relations to be looked after from time to time. Due to the pervasiveness of this group's power, their borrowed style became the style of Bolivia at the national level, leaving very little that was exclusively Bolivian in the "national" culture.[10] In view of this, the national bourgeoisie was closer in sentiment to cosmopolitan European circles than to that of the majority population of Bolivia. This cultural and stylistic set of identifications reinforced the deep divisions in the country. It further reinforced the negative impact of the national tin system on the integration and development of Bolivia as a whole. The fundamental orientation of the national bourgeoisie remained colonialist. They were still behaving as European conquerors ruling the savages of a new world and looking to Mother Europe for spiritual and cultural sustenance.

In revolutionary myth this national bourgeoisie (called *La Rosca*) is pictured as a semi-demonic group moving with singular will to plunder Bolivia. It must be pointed out that this elite hardly constituted a self-conscious entity of unitary purpose. A certain degree of coherence was evident; there were commonalities of interest and outlook which were strengthened when groups challenging the basic framework appeared in the late 1930s. From the 1930s to 1952, there were periods when unitary political action was almost achieved. Yet, it is hard not to conclude that one of the reasons this elite was ultimately pushed aside, as will be discussed later, was the persistence of deep and abiding divisions within its ranks. Resentment between the old and new, long-standing regional differences, and clashes among long- and short-term interests all acted to divide it internally. The long-term result of these factors was a weakening of the national elite's ability to resist opponents and an erosion of its capacity to sponsor timely adaptive changes.

Prerevolutionary Bolivia had no middle class as such. As a result of the processes of urbanization and growth discussed above, a grouping, roughly identifiable as middle on the basis of occupation and income, did appear. Due to the pattern of growth, however, this was a grouping associated mainly with the western urban centers, especially La Paz. Even more than the new elite, it was tied to the role and skill demands of the complex around tin and its ancillary activities. It was, then, a more specific product of what I have called the "national system." This grouping tended to live encapsulated in the urban dimension of the national system. With few exceptions, it did not spread into the countryside, nor was it found in the provincial cities. Unlike the national bourgeoisie, this grouping was not national in scope and did not bridge the gap between the national and local systems. Although this so-called middle class was a part of the national system, and, therefore, was associated with the state which presented itself to the world as Bolivia, it was not a nationwide class in any meaningful sense.

Perhaps the best way to identify this middle group is to call it the "petite bourgeoisie." This petite bourgeoisie was identifiable by what it was not rather than by what it was. It was not a modern middle class of small businessmen, entrepreneurs, and the like. It was not a traditional artisan group, nor was it a working-class group. By the same token, it was not a part of the national bourgeoisie, for in the majority of cases its members lacked the wherewithal to maintain the requisite style or the racial and family pedigree demanded. In numbers, it constituted somewhere between 7 and 10 percent of the population. Both socially and politically the group showed little cohesiveness or identity of purpose. For this reason, it is rather difficult to think of it as a class at all.

By and large, the petite bourgeoisie encompassed those who rose in economic status during the last quarter of the nineteenth and first quarter of the twentieth centuries, but didn't make it to the top. Occupationally, it was, in part, a lower level recapitulation of the newer groups of the national elite, for example, the less well-placed lawyers, doctors, administrators, and engineers. This "middle" also included teachers, petty traders, and low-level government and private bureaucrats. Basically, it filled out the occupational and status roles between the national bourgeoisie and the myriad "lower" groupings. Aside from a few small landowners, the people of the "middle" had little in the way of hard economic resources. In the main, the middle group was a dependent stratum living off salaries, fees, and some small commercial profits. Economically, the petite bourgeoisie was a vulnerable group, relying on the smooth functioning of the national system to secure its position.[11]

As a product of recent mobility, it was a group with aspirations. These aspirations included entrance into the national bourgeoisie which it aped in all aspects of its life style. This urban middle sector was not a focal point of change-oriented activity in the sense of modernization and development, at least in the pre-1935 era. Ideologically and aspirationally, it identified with the national bourgeoisie, an identification reinforced by its economic dependency. The link was tightened further by the fact that branches of established families often slipped to petite bourgeoisie status by dint of having failed to advance with other branches of the family or by having fallen economically backward.

A factor of growing importance to the petite bourgeoisie's life situation was the closing of mobility channels which occurred with the leveling off of economic growth. Possibilities of mobility slowly disappeared until they became almost nil in the late 1920s. The dependent urban middle stratum became trapped in the middle. Although the possibility of mobility became more remote, the aspiration to achieve upper status continued. The clash between desire and opportunity put great pressure on the petite bourgeoisie to maintain the requisite style of living fundamental to any possibility of moving up through a good marriage or political fortune. Not surprisingly, the petite bourgeoisie was, above all, security-minded, unadventuresome economically, and very status-conscious.[12]

Between them, the national bourgeoisie and the petite bourgeoisie made up the overwhelming majority of the polity of the prerevolutionary national state system. Aside from some mestizo traders, shopkeepers in the provincial towns and cities, artisans, a few workers, and shopkeepers in the major cities, the national bourgeoisie and its less privileged mirror image monopolized citizenship and, with it, political roles and power. In reality, the national bourgeoisie directly controlled major governmental offices and policy-making positions. The petite bourgeoisie monopolized the lower official positions and functioned as the electoral body which chose among competing elite groups in an often real but limited democratic process. By grace of its role as the effective electoral body of the state, the petite bourgeoisie was the real source of continuing legitimacy for the relations of authority and political dominance operative in the country. The petite bourgeoisie was the bedrock support group of the prerevolutionary sociopolitical order. This relatively small and ill-defined grouping, encapsulated in the cities and only tenuously connected with the rest of the country, was the human foundation upon which the Bolivian "national state" order stood.

The Monopoly of Private Economic Power

Public political power in prerevolutionary Bolivia was exercised by the national bourgeoisie and ratified by the petite bourgeoisie, but within the limiting framework of a monopoly of private economic power. The power potential of the tin magnates is obvious at a glance. The strategic importance of the industry to the economic well-being of the modern sector alone would have assured a pivotal position for these individuals. By 1920, tin, alone, accounted for more than 70 percent of the exports of the country. The power potential of the tin magnates' position was increased by the value of their exports, which resulted in a great accumulation of wealth in private hands. Little of this wealth accrued to the benefit of the state. Infra-structure projects had to be financed by borrowing. Export profits for much of the period were taxed only minimally and the government asserted no controls over foreign exchange, giving a free hand to private entrepreneurs.[13]

With the consolidation of the tin industry, the "Big Three" not only controlled the productive bases of the country, but also the bulk of its real monetary wealth.[14] They were thereby capable of ramifying their control throughout the private sector. Patiño, for example, besides holding interests in railroading, land, and the like, became the country's largest single private banker as well.[15] When the possibilities of foreign loans were exhausted, the government found it necessary to borrow from Patiño and the other magnates, thus increasing its dependency upon them. Hochschild also spread his control deep into the private sector. Besides his primary activities, he monopolized the activity of buying and selling the production of the small- and medium-sized mining operations. This gave him an important measure of control over the remaining 20 percent of production, and increased the amount of foreign exchange in his domain. It should also be remembered that a good part of the national elite was dependent either directly or indirectly on the companies for a large part of their income. Finally, although the appearance of tin separated public and private power and introduced modern interest group politics, the tin interest group was the only economic interest group of note. The tin group was not balanced by any other group of comparable power. They had, as a result, a clear field to influence policy outcomes and to define and raise issues upon which the national decision center focused.

It is extremely difficult to establish the extent to which a group such as the Bolivian tin magnates did or did not control government policies. Time dimensions are quite important in considering the issue. The "Big Three" did not consolidate their hold on the country's productive capacity until the 1920s. They were not, therefore, three string-pullers operating a puppet government throughout the entire period. However, it is indisputable that, from 1898 on, successive governments followed policies favorable to the interests of the tin sector. Voices were raised in opposition, but they had little effect on the government's overall thrust. Under the government of Bautista Saavedra (1921–25), taxes on tin were increased and some minimal social legislation passed, but until the late 1930s, no fundamental challenge to tin was raised.[16]

It is probably more accurate to view the developments during the first quarter of this century as the result of a developing convergence of interests and values between the liberal, positivist-minded governmental elite and the tin sector. The government pursued a pro-tin policy not simply in response to interest group pressure, but out of the logic of the day and their world view. In the first part of the century, the degree of government impingement on the private pursuit of gain was minimal. Aside from tax policy, policing, and the building of an infra-structure, governmental policy was of little interest to tin. Within the camp areas, the companies ran their affairs with sovereign-like independence.

Later, the situation began to change. An incipient labor movement started to make claims for organizational rights, wages, and other benefits. At times ambitious politicians saw this movement as a new road to power; a countervailing and hostile force was developing. Growing financial and other economic problems, which occurred with great frequency after 1925, stimulated an increase in demands for greater taxation and other controls on tin. The government began more and more to impinge on the private sector, and the companies, like any interest group, were forced to pay closer attention to the ins and outs of politics. A dialectic of mutual involvement, at times quite hostile, was developing between the private sphere and the public sphere. The career interests of an ambitious politician could often lead in directions inhospitable to the private economic interests of tin. The picture becomes more and more complex as antagonisms grew, but, on balance, it can be said that the companies did a remarkable job of using their power to defend their collective interests right down to 1952. That they did so in the face of challenge is testimony to their effective involvement in government. That they had to do so is testimony to the fact that government was no mere puppet.

A factor of major importance in structuring the tin sector's relations with governmental power was the signing of an accord in 1930 among the world's tin-producing countries. Under the accord each country was given a quota, and the various governments were given the power to allot these quotas in their respective territories. With this agreement, the Bolivian government for the first time assumed a major element of responsibility and control over the doings of the private tin sector. At this point there begins a more open and intimate involvement of the magnates in the doings of government.[17]

An important derivative of this 1930 agreement was the outbreak of an undeclared war among the "Big Three" for shares of the quota. Although there was a certain commonality of interest, rivalry had long existed among elements of the industry to increase the proportion of resources under their respective control. This rivalry was exacerbated significantly by the quota agreement.

With the appearance of the factors outlined above, the government experienced a growing direct, and not always savory, involvement of the companies in the prosecution of public business. In addition, it was subjected to the conflicting pressures of the competing giants, each seeking to use public power against the other. The tin barons, like the national bourgeoisie, could present, with sufficient reason, a united front, but internally they were deeply divided.

It seems fair to conclude that for the bulk of the formative period of the prerevolutionary socio-political order, the tin industry acted more to set the contours of national political activity than to regulate it. At the level of overall form and major policy, the government and politics of prerevolutionary Bolivia were shaped by the boundaries of the configuration of power and interest that came from the dual economic forms upon which the bifurcated system rested. The day-to-day dynamics of politics were spurred on by a derivative, but different, motor.

Political Structure of Prerevolutionary Bolivia

As a political order, the prerevolutionary system was created by the victory of the Liberal party in the civil war of 1898. Between 1898 and 1920, the Liberals ruled, and Bolivia experienced a period of unusual political stability. This stability and the conscious "developmental" policy of the Liberals allowed for the advancement of the tin industry and the modernization impulse it occasioned. However, reliance on tin led to a skewed, rather than generalized pattern of development. Development briefly opened mobility channels, and a new middle sector was created. As the impulse abated, the new and the old elites consolidated into a national bourgeoisie, more traditional than modern in outlook. At this point, the general upward movement of the so-called middle class was halted.

As the growth of tin industry leveled off and was consolidated, the overall economic growth of the country slowed down considerably. Concomitantly, the possibility of further expansion of the hacienda system (determined by the availability of land and, more important, Indians to work it) lessened. The two basic motors of economic growth had reached their peak. Thereafter, the entire system stopped growing and became static. With this crystallization of the economic system, control of wealth and status became fixed. This development created a problem of the circulation of wealth, both horizontally and vertically. When the system stopped growing, the economic pie became nonexpansive, and the elements of economic power (particularly ownership of mines or land) tended to become nonvariable in possession. This created a problem not only for those ambitious to move upward, but also for the middle and upper groups. The middle and upper groups, by natural processes, found their numbers increasing against a relatively static and noncirculating economic base.

In such a situation, political power, particularly through the holding of high office, becomes one of the few mediums through which circulation of economic power takes place. As Merle Kling has pointed out:

> [When] control of the conventional economic bases of power remains relatively static . . . an exceptional economic premium attaches to the control of the apparatus of government as a dynamic base of power. Whereas the conventional bases of power restrict mobility in economic status, control of government provides an unusually dynamic route to wealth and power. Thus the contrast between the stable character of the conventional economic bases of power and the shifting, unconventional position of government provokes intense and violent competition for control of government as a means of acquiring and expanding a base of wealth and power.[18]

In such an economically static situation, there tends to be a point when politics becomes dominated primarily by an intra-elite struggle for office as a means of securing or gaining economic power. As a common saying in Bolivia so aptly expressed the situation, *La industria mayor de Bolivia es la Política* ("The major industry of Bolivia is politics"). The struggle over office in such a situation becomes intense. One set of elite "ins" often attempts to stay in office while another set of elite "outs" attempts to dislodge them. If constitutional means fail to dislodge the "ins," the nature of the stakes are such that the "outs" quite often resort to the golpe de estado. Hence, political instability, characterized by intra-elite violence and frequent coups, is common in such countries. It has often been noted that such coups seldom lead to a basic change of the existing order. The political style of the golpe de estado employing minimal violence in which basic power relations remain intact springs from a static economic situation in which the chief political issue is intra-elite circulation of personnel.[19]

Such a political dynamic became operative in Bolivia by the end of the second decade of this century. At this time, the twenty-year reign of Liberal stability was showing severe strain. A rival

Republican party was formed by elements of the old conservative party and dissatisfied elements of the Liberal party itself—that is, the elite "outs." The Republicans finally seized power through a golpe in 1920.

Despite the passage of some social legislation, there was no fundamental ideological or programmatic difference between the Liberals and the Republicans. Political conflict became more intense and at times violent, but public debate was restricted mainly to arguments over constitutional norms, e.g., the rules of intra-elite circulation.[20]

Once in office, the Republicans proceeded to split immediately into factions. The Liberals also were suffering such splits. Although the Liberal and Republican parties continued to be distinct officially, politics became less a struggle of parties than of intra-elite factions. The notion of the formal party gave way to that of the personal clique. Personality rather than program came to dominate. The politically ambitious (this of necessity included practically all of elite status) lined up behind the individual strong man who stood the best chance of acquiring the presidency from which he could dispense coveted offices to his followers. As the presidency was the key to the vital cache of offices, it became the focal point of struggle with the personal faction becoming the basis of political division. When one faction won their man the presidency, all of the "out" factions, whatever their theoretical party affiliations, lined up against him, hedging for the day when, through a shrewd maneuver, their man could be placed in the presidential chair.

The constitution strictly prohibited a president succeeding himself, and any attempt to hang on past the prescribed period could lead to violence. When, for example, Republican Hernando Siles announced his intention (due to extraordinary circumstances) to stay in office in 1929, all the opposition united against him and ousted him by means of a coup.[21] Almost immediately the factions making up the opposition fell to struggling among themselves for the presidency and other public positions.

The basic political process in prerevolutionary Bolivia was, therefore, structured around the fierce intra-elite struggle for jobs in a nonexpansive economic environment. Questions of ideology or program became quite secondary. In this elite-dominated political struggle, the principle of division was not party, but faction. The dominant form of leadership was personal, involving the primary commitment of one's political and economic fortunes to an individual strong man. The shrewder individuals managed to flit blithely from faction to faction, depending upon the ascending or descending fortunes of various individual leaders.

The late nineteenth century witnessed the emergence of a relatively modern political system in Bolivia. However, the triumph of the Liberals in 1898, the consolidation of an amalgamated national bourgeoisie, and the eventual truncation of economic growth led to a new period of decline of party power and ideology. The rhetoric and outward form of party politics continued, but it was a shell within which an increasingly vicious struggle of intra-elite factions took place. This pattern resulted from (and later reinforced) the declining economic strength of the system. The growing economic stagnation and the tendency of the elite to close in upon itself, exhausting its energies in internecine faction struggles, led to a weakening of the elites' ability to adapt to changing circumstances. The elite became progressively incapable of acting as an agent of change.

It was not long before the accumulating tension springing from a plethora of internal contradictions began to manifest itself. In the late 1920s, rumblings emerged in reaction to the economic stagnation, immobilism, and lack of opportunities for advancement gripping the country. These basic limiting realities were to become constant factors in shaping much of Bolivia's political future. The intra-elite conflicts brought these problems out in the open and, at the same time, prevented the kind of climate necessary for their solution. The outline of a "vicious circle of underdevelopment" was drawn in Bolivia well before 1930.

3 Group Conflict and Pressures for Change

Within what I have called the "national system," the pattern of social stratification was quite complex in pre-revolutionary Bolivia. Beneath the national and petite bourgeoisie, there were a number of lower groups which, like the middle sectors, cannot be categorized, in any meaningful sense, as the lower class. However, for lack of a more coherent system of classification, a number of occupational categories embracing essentially traditional groupings, such as artisans (small-scale self-employed craftsmen), the smaller shopkeepers, market-sellers, domestics, and the sub-employed living in the loosely defined *barrios populares*, must be considered part of a lower stratum. In addition, the process of development had created a number of modern worker groups—drivers, a few factory workers, railroaders, and, of course, a growing number of miners. Previous to the late 1930s and 1940s, the only worker group to reach a high level of cohesion and activity was that of the railway workers (*ferroviarios*).

In referring to these "lower strata," we are again primarily dealing with urban groups living in the three larger western cities —groups which are mainly of mestizo and Indian racial extraction. In the provincial cities and towns, the stratification pattern remained more traditional, less complex, and without any signifi-

50

cant development of new elements.[1] The pattern of distinction between the national and local systems was mitigated somewhat at the lower levels. The growth of some commercial agriculture in the departments of La Paz and Cochabamba created a small transport sector and some commerce between countryside and city. Hence, there was a small group of truckers and traders (*comerciantes*) who moved between the two systems. In addition, there was migration from the *campo* ("countryside") to the city of people who became workers, sub-employed, or floaters.[2] These elements retained some roots in the countryside, but the rhythm of the city came to predominate. Moreover, the movement from the countryside to the city was small and not generalized in terms of sources of emigration. La Paz, by far the most complex city, drew the largest number of its new elements from the immediately surrounding countryside in the department of La Paz.[3] Oruro did the same, while in Cochabamba, movement from the countryside went mainly to the mines. In the remainder of the country, there was little rural to urban movement.

The rise of liberalism, tin, and emphasis on economic development had contradictory effects on the lower strata of the society. Through the demand for labor and new skills, essentially modern worker groupings were formed. This in itself was a modernizing process in which previously excluded Indians and mestizos were tied to the system by becoming workers. Relatively speaking, this movement offered better opportunities to the Indian and at the same time stimulated new wants and expectations. This naturally led to increased demands for economic and social advancement. New, modern, and upward-oriented groups appeared. These groups were brought into the economic cycle and, thus, were tied to the advancement of industrialization.

Development had an opposite effect on the previously established artisan and small merchant groups. In the traditional order, they occupied a well-defined and, while not affluent, at least secure place. In the first wave of growth, some of the higher level artisans and the like advanced socially into the ranks of the petite bourgeoisie. The rest, however, began to experience downward pressure. Under the relative free trade system, they lost the protection of a backward, but largely autarchic economy. A continual increase in the level of sophistication of wants among upper groups, as well as the availability of relatively cheap imports, rendered most local artisans noncompetitive. Many elements of this grouping began to be proletarianized. Unlike the proletariat, these traditional elements did not advance with economic growth but, instead, declined. Development helped the worker advance and then want more. On the other hand, it impoverished the artisan groups who struggled against being turned into proletarians, and these groups demanded their old security.[4]

The appearance of organized expressions of demands for advancement and alleviation of pressure by the lower strata came about early in the twentieth century. The first forms of organization were traditional mutual aid societies in which lower stratum groups drew together to pool their own resources to protect individual members. These organizations later switched their focus outward and began to pressure the national government directly. This early activity was mainly among artisans, such as typesetters (gráficos), who slowly emerged as a leading lower stratum organization. After 1915, this process of organization broadened and included the newly important railroad workers and other worker groups in La Paz and Oruro. This early organizing process is often referred to as the beginning of the Bolivian labor movement. However, throughout the period from 1910 to 1935, it would be more accurate to refer to this organization of lower stratum groups as an artisan-labor movement.

The Artisan-Labor Movement: Pressure from Below

The formative period of this artisan-labor movement was from 1915 to 1920. Purely mutualist activity gave way to generalized demands made on the governing elite. For this reason, the movement was developing political implications, although its focus was on economic demands more than demands for political power and control. European socialist ideologies began to emerge and there were some attempts to create socialist parties. These experiments were, however, short-lived and left little impact until a few years later.[5]

In the early 1920s the artisan-labor movement began to gather steam. Serious efforts were made to form industry-wide federations and a national confederation and to launch a class-based party. All of these efforts met with some limited success. The railway workers formed a federation which became the basis for a powerful and self-conscious organization. In 1921 local organizations met in a national conference which, although it did not produce a confederation, set an important precedent—disparate lower level groups were beginning to think in terms of widespread organization to press their demands actively and on a national level. In 1920, a local socialist party was formed in La Paz and coalesced into a general socialist party in 1921. The party managed to elect two deputies who proposed pro-labor bills, but the base to support such activity was too small and the party languished. These developments demonstrated, however, that lower stratum elements could in fact organize themselves, and, even at this early date, were looking for alternatives outside of the extant political framework.

An important factor in the movement's growth was the ascension of the Republican party in 1920 and, specifically, the emergence of Bautista Saavedra (president of the Republican government from 1920 to 1925). In the complex faction struggles which had developed, the Saavedristas found themselves in a weak position. While the bulk of the worker elements were not electoral participants, many of the artisans and semi-proletarians of the capitol were. Though small in number, they could provide a much-needed boost to a faction in intra-elite deadlocks.[6] Saavedra made a successful bid for this support by promulgating decrees legalizing the right to strike and establishing formal government arbitration of disputes. In addition, he pushed through legislation regulating working hours and imposed slightly higher taxes on the tin industry.

However, Saavedra's willingness to entertain the formation of power groups outside the intra-elite context was limited. When an attempt to win organizational rights by miners led to a strike in

1923 in the camp town of Uncía, the strike was severely repressed by the Saavedra government and the organization collapsed.[7] Saavedra moved with equal vigor and force against an Indian uprising in the altiplano community of Jesús de Machaca in the same year. While willing to use some of the more traditional lower elements of the capital as a lever in his faction battles, neither Saavedra nor any other leader was going to allow a major shift in the existing distribution of power, especially in the direction of the proletarian groups or the peasant masses.

The experience with Saavedra eventually spurred the growing artisan-labor movement and also taught it an object lesson. Due to their limited numbers and the disenfranchisement of the bulk of their members, the lower strata could achieve only very limited success by working through traditional elite parties and factions. They stood little chance of becoming a strong interest group within the system. The movement was, therefore, forced to fall back upon itself and seek alternative forms of expression. A major dilemma arose out of the fact that the same factors which blocked the interest group outlet also militated against the formation of a viable working-class party which could seek power in its own right. This dilemma presented obstacles at every succeeding stage of the movement's development.

The Saavedra episode indicated other potential developments as well—namely, that there would be an increasing temptation for elite factions weak in power to enlist aid from below. Due to the weakness and disorganization of the lower strata, the Saavedra sojourn in this direction did not fundamentally alter the extant political situation. In later contexts, however, enlisting the aid of lower stratum groups was to have more significant consequences.

An event of some importance in the developing situation took place in 1922. In a climate of intense intra-faction conspiracy and struggle, Saavedra, in a move to cut down the movement of his rivals, banned night taxi service in La Paz.[8] The taxi drivers reacted bitterly. Other groups, particularly the railway workers and graficos, seized the opportunity to press their own demands, and before he knew it, Saavedra had a general strike on his hands. The strike was remarkably effective. The government yielded, rescinded the ban on taxi service, gave concessions to other groups, and recognized the railroad federation as the official representative organization of the railway workers.[9] In this strike, the incipient movement discovered its most effective weapon. The labor movement was unable to act as an important interest group because it was too small, largely voteless, and disorganized. For the same reasons, it could not launch a class-based party. In the existing situation, it was also weak in relation to management. In 1922, however, they learned that a strike which hit the general economy and disrupted public order could achieve favorable government attention. Strikes and demonstrations aimed directly at the government became and remained thereafter the preferred instrument of struggle of the various artisan, semi-proletarian, and labor groups.

After this first success, outward artisan-labor activity appeared to dwindle, but organization continued. The concept of organizing into *sindicatos* (a kind of labor union) spread throughout the entire lower strata, resulting in a bewildering variety of organizations. The action-oriented sindicato was eclipsing the mutualist organization which remained at the margin of union formation. The general currents of unrest coursing through the South American continent penetrated the Bolivian scene, and contacts were made with Chilean and Argentine groups ranging from radical socialist to anarchist. Continued proletarianization of artisans, market-sellers, and the like, and the consolidation of true proletarian groups strengthened the movement's desire to exert pressure and its capacity to do so. During the 1920s, the final monopolization and modernization of tin took place and, in the huge camps, the basis for strong miners' organizations was laid.

However, the railroad workers remained the main proletarian group and tended to play an independent game, though in certain situations, as that in 1922, they were willing to support a common effort. These ferroviarios made up the strongest and most cohesive organization of the many groups forming. Still, in terms of numbers, there were many more artisan and semi-proletarian groups, among which the graficos were the strongest. Thus, the overall movement retained a decidedly artisan flavor and the graficos became the major representative group.

During this important gestation period, the movement continued to follow a bread-and-butter action program, but was
radicalizing significantly in ideology and rhetoric. Radical socialist
positions gained ground, but the more popular ideology in this
period was anarchism. The two positions battled each other and
hindered attempts to form a national organization. There is still
not enough data to establish the hypothesis, but the prevalence of
anarchism most likely sprang from the preponderance of artisan
and semi-proletarian elements. As such, this anarchism represented
a reaction to the ravages of development and modernization and
manifested a wish to go back to the way things were. The anarchists fought against forming a movement to achieve and use
political power and argued for union purity, the destruction of
the state through violence, and a return to previous traditional
forms of association. In any event, the relationship of anarchism
to artisan influence gains credence by the fact that, when after
1935 true labor groups achieved dominance in the movement,
anarchism rapidly died out in Bolivia.[10]

The graficos seemed to be a transition group between the
future-projected labor groups and the past-oriented artisans. Ideologically, it was split in many directions and the group never took
an official position. In action, the graficos continually pursued a
moderate socialist position. With the later emergence of organized
proletarian groups, the graficos slipped out of leadership and is
today a small, minimally influential and moderate group.[11]

In 1927, the movement's desire to form a national confederation was finally realized. A congress attended by over two hundred
delegates met in Oruro and launched an organization called the
Federación Obrero del Trabajo. The meeting adopted a platform based on the principle of the class struggle, but, due to the
anarchist-socialist rift, no international affiliations were made.
This time the confederation, once launched, gained hold to a certain extent. Despite serious internal dissension, there has been
some form of national confederation in operation since 1927.
However, this and later confederations, due to the factors listed
above and others I shall discuss later, were never more than very
loose groupings before 1952. The movement achieved a measure

of general unity, but was not able to launch a unified class-based movement.

It was also in the late 1920s that the first real contacts between the artisan-labor movement and leftist intellectuals from the petite and national bourgeoisie took place. These contacts were sporadic, and while they stimulated the launching of a number of socialist parties, no sustained linkage was yet made. The contacts did, however, leave an important ideological legacy and also pointed the way to a potentially powerful coalition.[12]

There are two basic points to be gained from the above sketch. Throughout the first two decades of the century, considerable pressure for major change was building in the lower reaches of the prerevolutionary system. The artisans and semi-proletarian groups were demanding protection from the effects of development and the government's free trade policies. The rising modern labor groups, in turn, were demanding satisfaction for their new aspirations, the ability to control their primary environment, and the wherewithal to compete for a share of the economic pie.

This kind of combined movement and pressure from below is a characteristic feature of development and modernization wherever it occurs. There are any number of studies on how particular countries did or did not adapt to the process. The dislocation of old groups and the incorporation of the new is undoubtedly one of the main political problems of the modern era. Under the best of circumstances the resolution of this problem has been difficult.

By the late 1920s, Bolivia was unquestionably not in the best of circumstances to cope with the problem. Moreover, the national elite showed an increasing unwillingness to make any basic changes in either the economic or the political order. Over the next few decades they opted to meet each more potent challenge from the lower strata with more determined intransigence. This manner of dealing with pressure from below seems to show that Bolivia's ruling elite was modern in rhetoric, but ever more traditional and caste-like in its style and action, making it simply incapable of transforming itself into an agent of basic adaptive change.

In reality, the problem went deeper than the will, or lack of it, of the elite to sponsor reform and change. The skewed pattern of development, the dependence on factors outside local control, the slow exhaustion of the tin industry, and the abatement of the development drive all called into serious question the capacity of the system to adapt. The artisan-labor movement was banging on the doors of a more and more static economic situation and a political order progressively more steeped in atrophy. Intra-elite faction politics became more intense. As pointed out above, economically, socially, and politically, the system was geared to a minimum of movement and change. This predisposition was reinforced by structural immobilism. The later political course of the lower strata is understandable mainly in view of the contradiction between segmental movement and demand for change within a general order of immobilized capacity to change by means of adjustment.

Throughout this early period of growth, the artisan-labor movement evolved on the periphery of the main political power structure of the country. There were no connecting links by which the movement was co-opted into the intra-elite faction struggle, nor was the movement able to generate enough internal strength to project itself into the struggle as an independent force. At best, it could draw attention by open assaults in the form of general strikes and demonstrations.

As a result, the movement experienced a relatively long period of independent internal development. Generally and individually, lower stratum groups were learning to organize and were building a tradition of self-conscious activity and independence. Continued exclusion and impotence fostered a growing radical orientation, a predisposition strengthened by the apparent fact that economic demands could be achieved only by aggressive assaults directed at the core of political power.

More important, perhaps, was the generation from within the lower groups themselves of a sectoral leadership stratum. These leaders, marginal to the national elite, became the main focal point of identification and commitment for the individual artisans and workers, especially the latter. All of these factors were operating to create a strong militant and alienated force parallel to the mainstream of Bolivian national politics. In addition, a potentially powerful segmental elite appeared which would not only press with vigor the particular demands of its followers, but eventually demand entrance to the realm of national power and control.

Economic Stagnation and Ideological Contradictions

As previously mentioned, a growing swell of demands from below was only one source of tension that the country began to experience in the 1920s. By this time, the national system had stopped growing. Upward mobility was cut off. The national bourgeoisie built caste barriers of race, family, and cultural style between itself and other groups. The dependent petite bourgeoisie was blocked in the middle with no place to go but dead center or down. The traditional middle estate of artisans was under economic pressure and in a state of social decline. The only dynamic element was an incipient working class growing out of the tin industry and its ancillary activities. The upward dynamism of this class, buttressed by artisan demands, brought it into a direct clash with the creeping immobilism of the general system. Negative impulses causing unemployment and other forms of dislocation were coming into play. In short, a set of multiple reinforcing contradictions was developing.

The first contradictions were those between certain key values of the liberal ideology and aspects of the objective reality. The liberal notions of equality, citizenship, and advancement by achievement clashed rudely with the operative traditional notions of caste based on race and pedigree. Through property and literacy requirements, over three-fourths of the population were denied citizenship status. In addition, the mobility drive set off by the tin boom rapidly collided with newly erected caste barriers. There was also a reverse aspect. The artisan class which continued to exist and be legitimated by persisting traditional values was being systematically pauperized by liberal principles in the market realm.

Along with the positivistic liberalism adopted in early twentieth-century Bolivia came the values of nation and systematic development. The various "liberal" governments justified their reliance on tin as the best way to develop Bolivia. These values were imbibed and used by all the active and educated sectors of the populace, but they clashed with rather fundamental realities.[13]

The original developmental impulse of tin was petering out and regression became apparent by the late 1920s. A recurring cycle of boom and bust generated by the expansion or contraction of demand in foreign centers brought home the fact that Bolivia had little control over its economy. In addition, the country lived under the constant threat of territorial loss. Vast stretches of what was legally Bolivia had no national presence. The majority of the nation's population lived outside the "national system." Thus, the liberal notions of "nation," "self-determination," and "progress" were contradicted by the reality of the Bolivia created by those who espoused the liberal rhetoric.

In a world in which nationalism, in the twin form of progress as a goal and the nation-state as the object of progress, was gaining universal ascendancy, it would have been surprising if the above anomalies did not generate dissidence in Bolivia.[14] Even so, in a healthy system such dissidence could have been held off indefinitely and been progressively ameliorated by adaptive change. There were, however, more fundamental structural imbalances at work.

As I indicated previously, by the 1920s the Bolivian economy was tied almost exclusively to the health of the tin industry. By 1925 there were growing indications that the industry was far from healthy. This basic fact began to have a severe impact on the society at large. Indeed, one can argue that, from roughly 1925 on, Bolivia began to experience a permanent state of economic crisis. This crisis became a national obsession and a matter of political perturbation. This increasingly severe economic crisis, resulting from a static economic base, was the subject of a long article published in 1927 by the La Paz daily newspaper *El Norte* which recognized the seriousness of the situation:

> The Republic is suffering at this moment a severe economic crisis which as time goes on becomes even worse,

despite all efforts at reform and formulas to alleviate its
consequences. . . . The mining industry as the principal
source of our economy can not support the progressive
increase in necessities. . . . The rising population concentrated in specific centers, the lack of means of communication, the distances that separate the regions that
could produce for the consumption centers, the absence
of large capital and the lack of industry are all tied to
and cause of our difficult economic situation. . . . With
the exception of mining, the country can rely on no
other stable source of wealth. During the last ten years
the needs of consumption and the need for social services have grown enormously. Production, however, has
not grown in relation and this disequilibrium has produced an anguishing financial crisis.[15]

This article is not an isolated statement. There is continued reference in the pages of both *El Norte* and *El Diario* during the late
twenties to manifestations of economic disarray throughout the
country. One of the problems most often mentioned is the effect
that rising prices were having on the economic situation of the
middle class and workers.[16]

An important result of the basic imbalance between the
society and the economy was the emergence of a problematic situation for the petite bourgeoisie as a whole, but especially for its
oncoming generation. The system was educating an expanded generation of individuals for first- and second-rank elite roles beyond
its capacity to provide such roles. The society was incapable of
providing outlets at a level to which background and education
taught the oncoming generation to aspire.

The educational system stressed preparation for professional
and administrative rather than entrepreneurial careers.[17] By the
1920s, the professions, serving a small and by then nonexpansive
sector, were overcrowded. The government bureaucracy was growing without functional purpose.[18] Top administrative positions in
the major industry of the country were mainly in the hands of foreigners.[19] The export-import trades were dominated by foreign

houses.[20] The kind of land appropriate for developing or expanding haciendas was becoming scarce and family holdings were being subdivided among sons. Business and entrepreneurial activities were scorned by those with traditional values.

Politics became the only outlet for the ambitious young man of the petite and national bourgeoisie. Job politics characterized by factionalism and personalism, already endemic, became more rife.[21] Intra-elite struggles became critical and vicious. To lose in one of these struggles could be disastrous for an individual's career as well as for his family. Intra-elite violence and threats of coups increased accordingly. The basis was being laid for the alienation of the entire oncoming elite and sub-elite generation.

This alienation became an obvious reality from 1925 on. Beginning in the universities and spreading through the ranks of young professionals, a ground swell of anti-system political activity arose. The dissatisfaction also manifested itself in literary activities. The situation was tantamount to the general prerevolutionary phenomenon termed by Crane Brition as the desertion of the intellectuals.[22] The generation coming to maturity in the late twenties and early thirties expressed disdain for the job-hungry dimensions of Bolivian politics and, particularly, for the lack of viable choices it offered to them. What is more, they directly linked the dismal futures facing them to an economy trapped by its mono-economic base.

One of the clearest spokesmen of the generation was the daily newspaper *La Calle,* created in 1936 by young professionals. In its first issue, *La Calle* railed against the problem of job politics. "Having concentrated the activities of the country in mining which benefits specific interests, all our governments have been beset by the problem of the lack of other sources of work which logically has forced them to satisfy their political promises by looking for positions in the budget and creating them as exigencies demand."[23] In a later article, *La Calle* returns to the problem, particularly focusing on what the situation does to the individual who enters the vicious circle of job politics.

Bolivia for many years has been given over to political groups that alternate in power with marvelous programs that they never complete until finally they have paralyzed the country in a chaos of *gradilocuente* rhetoric. The control of important public jobs was their patrimony and only under exceptional circumstances do they admit new elements, and, then, once the interest was made and the promises and the pressure applied, it ended all personality and all initiative in the new element that entered the privileged clan. Quickly he followed the current and was one more against the ignorant and uneducated mass and the authentic intellectual class that fatally and out of necessity had to serve the groups fighting for power.[24]

The generation which first raised its political banners in 1927–28 did so in a context in which it was faced with two realities. On the one hand, it was forced to contemplate the disparity between the general condition of its country and the more advanced nations, while, on the other, it personally confronted a static domestic situation which presented it with intolerable choices with regard to developing an acceptable career within the current framework.[25]

By natural process, the elite and sub-elite strata were outgrowing the economic bases of their eliteness. By the late 1920s, the process had gone so far that the old intra-elite style of faction politics was becoming a less and less viable mechanism for the ambitious and the security-minded. Before this time, Bolivia had had its dissidents and exponents of radical ideologies. However, these early elements were small and insignificant to the country's basic power structure. In the late 1920s, a steady stream of Marxist and other ideological literature entered the country and gained widespread popularity, particularly in the universities.[26] The nation's elite youth in increasing numbers were turning to new thought and action paradigms, all of which were anti-liberal and which projected either radical reform or revolution. The liberal-positivist ideology, through which the authority of the existing order found its legitimation, was losing its grip on the country's single most important group, the oncoming elite generation which would assume, in normal circumstances after internalizing the existing thought and value framework, control of the system and carry it on.

Actually, the first rumblings of a global split were making themselves felt—a split which at the elite level would drive deeper and deeper wedges between winners and losers, and which would further see the steady estrangement of the national bourgeoisie and its major support group, the petite bourgeoisie. The immediate manifestation of this fracturing of the unity of the country's dominant segments was along generational lines.

National Reformists and Revolutionary Socialists

Dissidence, desire for change, and ideological heterogenity were general after 1925, but were ill-defined and did not go much beyond the expression of deep dissatisfaction and growing alienation. In retrospect, the early division into two modes of change-oriented thought and action is apparent. One was a national reformist orientation, and the second a revolutionary socialist orientation. The lines were far from clear and much crossing and recrossing of lines took place; later, systematic positions, without too much difficulty, can be traced back to these incipient models of change which ran counter to the then-prevailing mode. From the beginning, the two tendencies evidenced not only different perceptions of the nation's dilemma, but different preferences in strategy and tactics as well.

The national reformist tendency was most closely associated with young professionals already on the political scene, mainly in La Paz. Some of the most notable names connected with this movement were Augusto Cespedes, Carlos Montenegro, and Enrique Baldivieso. The revolutionary socialist tendency, on the other hand, was most evident among university students, particularly in Cochabamba and Sucre; important individuals involved here were José Antonio Arce, Ricardo Añaya, and Arturo Urquidi Morales.[27]

The nationalist group was much looser in organization and disparate in ideology. Members of the group often referred to themselves as *la generación del centenario* ("the generation of the

centennial"). They were unclear as to the causes of their dissatisfaction or to specific remedies. The group had no specific ideological referent. One of the group's more illustrious members
reported that they knew little of Marxism and were more influenced by writers such as Ortega y Gasset and Bergson. This infor-
mant also indicated that they were stirred by the Cordoba University reform movement, the Mexican Revolution, and the Apristas
of Peru (nationalist revolutionary party formed in the early
1920s); but they reacted more to the sentiment than to the ideas
of these new movements.[28]

This nationalist group approached politics from a negative
and emotional position—a generalized emotional rejection of
what "liberal" thought and works had brought to pass in Bolivia.
Their enemy was seen as an oligarchy that operated through the
traditional parties to feed off Bolivia. "Vacilabamos entre la anti-
cultura mental y un sentimiento confuso, pero fuerte, de, la obra
negativa realizade por la oligarquía con las ideas liberales."[29] They
argued that their duty was to renovate the system so as to redis-
cover what the liberals had perverted. They saw themselves as a
new generation destined to initiate a new era through which they
would recreate the republic.[30]

Tactically, the group operated within the traditional elite
faction framework. A nationalist party was formed, but it
remained a young elitist cabal. There was no attempt to build a
sustained mass base or to tie up with the artisan-labor movement.
Following the contemporary situation, they immediately sought to
gain power by entering high government office. Hence, a leader
was sought among the existing stock of powerful national figures.

The group eventually attached itself to Hernando Siles, president of Bolivia after 1925, and one of the dominant personalities
of the Republican party. Siles himself was embroiled in a complex faction battle within his party. The hand-picked successor of
Bautista Saavedra, Siles was attempting to differentiate himself
from his former mentor and become a faction leader in his own
right. The new group of nationalist reformers provided him with
the opportunity to construct his own personal faction. He invited
the Baldivieso group to join with him in la edificación de una

neuva era ("the construction of a new era"). In return for their support, Siles identified more and more with the nationalists and attempted some reformist sallies. His flirtation with this zestful youth group turned the rest of the Republican party against him. The nationalist party became a semi-official party and Siles' sole base of support.

It was a fragile base. In the midst of economic crisis and social unrest, Siles in 1929 declared his intention to remain in office with the nationalist's support. This sin of sins in the intra-elite circulation battle sparked the formation of a united front of all other factions, regardless of party, against Siles. The opposition made its move on June 27, 1930. In a rapid coup, Siles and the nationalists were easily toppled.

However, the young nationalist-Siles alliance marked an important transition. While reformists, the nationalists were also, in part, a traditional faction which, although identified on a generational and change-oriented basis, were deeply involved in the current struggle for office and the spoils and status it brought. Given the later careers of some of these men, it is apparent that opportunism played a large role in the nationalist episode.[31] But, while it can be said that the intra-elite struggle of personalistic factions continued, a new ideological dimension was added to it in which competing groups would project and act out a drive for basic adjustments and changes in the system.

On the other hand, the revolutionary socialist tendency was, from the beginning, a more systematic, coherent, and organized thrust. Marxism and Leninism were and remained the pivot of this orientation. With little delay this group began to formulate a Marxist critique of the country's ills and to project a socialist substitution of the liberal order.[32]

The nationalists immediately and individually sought to enter office with little or no idea of what to do with the power. The growing socialist tendency, on the other hand, concentrated on developing its ideological critique and on laying the basis for a broad-based movement. Books and pamphlets reflecting a native reading and application of Marx started to circulate out of Cochabamba. Contacts were sought and made with the artisan-labor movement and the formation of new organizations and parties was discussed.

In its first stage, it was mainly a university movement. The specific and less divisive issue of university reform, then a continent-wide symbol, became the focal point around which a concerted generational drive was launched. In 1928, a meeting was held on the campus of the University of San Simon in Cochabamba. Delegates representing the entire country attended. The main issue discussed was university reform. The group represented other than socialist positions, but the major leftist student leaders and professors were in marked ascendancy. The meeting resulted in the creation of a national federation of students and teachers and the launching of a determined drive to achieve university reform.

The agitation for university reform brought the largely socialist student movement into a direct clash with Siles and the young nationalist professionals and intellectuals around him. Siles resisted their demands and instituted a policy repressing the movement. This brought students into the streets, where they joined worker and other groups in an ascending level of disorder, resulting from a severe monetary crisis and the first effects of the worldwide depression. In their tactic of encircling Siles, the traditional factions enlisted the aid of the student movement by promising university reform. The students responded by increasing the tempo and intensity of their demonstrations, thereby providing a level of social disorder which the army used as an excuse to seize the government in 1930. With Siles and the nationalists out of the way, university reform was decreed and the army turned over the government to a coalition of the traditional factions.

The traditional factions immediately fell to battling among themselves for the presidency and the offices which flowed from it; national politics reverted to the old mode. However, the world and Bolivia both were groaning under the depression. In Bolivia these pressures were spurred on by structural contradictions which, when no longer containable, made the return to politics-as-usual impossible.

The basic outline of Bolivia's political future was drawn by

1930. Growing pressure resulting from stagnation and immobilism sparked a clamor for change. In greater and greater numbers the county's oncoming elite generation was abandoning in whole or in part the value framework in which they had been raised, and committing their energies and actions to alternative counter-frameworks. From within its own elite and sub-elite ranks, the system was generating a wave of reformist and revolutionary counter-elites.

Simultaneously, the collision between the rising labor movement, reinforced by the downward economic slide of the artisans, caused demands for change from a different source. Elite intransigence, frustration arising from their inability to influence the faction battle or to mount a party of their own, and the discovery of the efficacy of disruptive action, were pushing this critical sector toward a revolutionary method of securing change. In the lower reaches of the national system; a potentially powerful public was becoming available for mobilization by counter-elites aiming at reordering or destroying the system.

4 Depression and War: Accelerators

Bolivia experienced the first tremors of the looming worldwide depression in 1927. The apparent elasticity of demand for tin by the world's industrial centers was related less to natural growth needs than to the preparation and execution of war. With the First World War over and the arming for the Second World War not yet begun, demand contracted and leveled off. As a result prices entered a slow period of decline and the earning power of Bolivian tin fell off steadily.

Production continued to mount, heading for the great 1929 peak. The overall value of exports thereby managed to be maintained and even increased. However, the meaning of the trend was inescapable. The industry constantly had to increase production simply to stand still. To push up earnings, production had to be increased greatly.[1] The lag between production and price was bad enough, but even worse factors were at work. The necessity of increased tonnage reflected not only the price lag but also the fact that the amount of saleable tin per ton of earth moved was declining. The external market was turning against the industry, as were the tiring mountains from which the metal was being extracted. The industry was caught in a double bind.

The long-range implications of the trend are obvious. The more immediate effects showed first in the realm of government

69

finance. By 1927, the Bolivian government was in mortgage to foreign banking houses. By its second year, the Siles government was in the throes of a full-blown financial crisis. The crisis was aggravated by growing border tensions between Bolivia and Paraguay which led to a sizeable increase in military expenditures. The 1929 budget bespoke the amassing financial problem: some 37 percent of expenditures was earmarked simply to service the foreign debt while 20 percent was allocated for military needs.[2] The financial situation, in balance, was dangerously weak. The government was committed to a foreign debt which demanded continual increases in budget outlays; concomitantly, government income was declining. For years the Bolivian government was living over its head, depending on the future, but "the goose that laid the golden egg" was getting old and years of accumulated debt had become too heavy for the government to bear.

Already teetering, Bolivia was hit hard by the depression and was eventually pushed over the brink. The financial structure of the country simply collapsed. The government suspended debt service and, in effect, declared itself and the Bolivian state bankrupt. Its international financial credibility wiped out, the government had little choice but to turn to internal borrowing and to the floating of paper to keep the economy going. The first steps toward inevitable inflation were taken. The collapse was not a temporary aberration created by the depression; it was the result of deep-seated structural imbalances accelerated by the depression. When the collapse came, it was definitive and set in motion financial difficulties from which the country is just beginning to recover.

As the bottom fell out of the tin industry, the financial edifice of the state crumbled. The decline of tin, too, was not simply a temporary aberration, but the culmination of deep-seated structural problems created by the country's economic reliance on the industry. The price trend which dipped precipitously was one problem, but, with the coming of the depression, the industry began a decline from which it was never really to recover. Production started an assiduous downward pace. More critically, the amount and quality of tin per ton of earth was to diminish continually, creating increasingly difficult recovery problems.[3] The cost-profit ratio became progressively skewed and Bolivia found it more and more difficult to compete. More fundamental than any of these factors was the steady withdrawal of investment in the tin industry beginning in 1929. In 1928, capital value in the industry was approximately $160 million; in 1952, capital value was only $161.2 million, indicating that reinvestment hardly went beyond the cost of maintenance of equipment.[4] Perhaps scared by the depression, perhaps because they read the trends, the barons of tin slowly began to move their capital out of the mines.

The effects of depression spread quickly through the active sectors of the "national system" economy. Unemployment became widespread and chronic, forcing the national and local governments to institute work projects.[5] Widespread layoffs were followed by rising prices and acute shortages of food and other primary goods in the cities. With the country's reserves exhausted, imports were restricted, but the local agricultural sector was not organized to fill the gap. Here again the depression did not create problems so much as expose existing imbalances and contradiction.

The worsening economic crisis reflected itself in the political sphere. Strikes, demonstrations, and civil disorders became daily occurrences. The artisan-labor movement expanded and became more radical. Student activity went in the same direction. Most significantly, there were demonstrations and marches by petite bourgeoisie groups reacting to rising prices and shortages. On occasion, these activities reached new levels of dissidence in which there were reports of quixotic attempts to carry out socialist or anarchist revolutions.[6]

The military junta which ousted Siles in 1930 quickly turned over the government to a coalition of traditional parties. After much infighting, Daniel Salamanca, the very epitome of the traditional elite, assumed the presidency. In response to the continuing public disorder spurred on by the worsening crisis, Salamanca declared all-out war on the "Communist" threat. He made it clear that under his administration no basic structural changes would be carried out and that anyone who insisted on demanding them would be dealt with resolutely.

Salamanca took few steps to ameliorate the imbalances underlying the crisis. Instead, he whipped up fear of an alien Communist threat among the people. At the same time, he began to appeal to Bolivian chauvinism as war drums began to beat. The girding for war with Paraguay became an umbrella under which repression of internal opposition was justified. By these means, Salamanca attempted to divert the growing internal pressures demanding change.

Through the use of force, political firings, blackballings, jailings, and exilings, the strike movement was broken and labor organization demoralized. The same techniques were used to quash student and radical intellectual activity. The approach was quite successful. Radical opposition disintegrated and went underground. The threats from the lower strata and political left were subdued, but the underlying grievances behind them were hardly touched.

There is a limit to how long a government in the throes of economic crisis can survive by repression, especially when the expanding crisis affects the well-being of groups which are ordinarily the bedrock of governmental support. The Bolivian crisis was hitting just those groups, as was revealed by mounting protest activity among government employees and other types of empleado groups.

Whatever his reasons, it was in this context that Salamanca chose to lead his country into a major foreign war. The issue of the war was the disputed territory between Bolivia and Paraguay known as the Chaco. This piece of arid wasteland, days from La Paz, was to be the arena in which an army consisting of Indians from the high Andes and led by urban types from the same region would test the Bolivian national honor, and by extension, the reality of any such thing as a Bolivian nation.

The Chaco War

On paper, the war was a good bet. What match could tiny, backward Paraguay prove against the relatively industrial Bolivia whose army was trained by top-flight German military advisors (hired years before by the Bolivian government)? When it became apparent that little Paraguay, backed by Argentine money,[7] had an excellent chance, the resulting humiliation for Bolivia was magnified considerably.

War was begun in July 1932 and ended in victory for Paraguay in June 1936. From the beginning, the Paraguayans out-thought, out-fought, and simply out-lasted the bewildered Bolivians, most of whom were fighting in an environment so foreign as to be another world. What was to be a fast blitz-type operation turned into a slow, grinding, dirty, and exhausting little war. Hardly a country which could provide the wherewithal for a protracted military effort, the already exhausted Bolivian economy was strained even further.[8] The government increased its internal borrowing (mainly from Patiño) and continued to issue unbacked paper.

To meet the military needs to at least hold its own in the war, the government had to embark upon a course of maximum mobilization. The Chaco War was converted into a nationalist crusade. To drive the mobilization and sublimate the sacrifices occasioned by the war, jingoism and patriotic fervor became the order of the day. The war, in reality, was Bolivia's first "national" war and, indeed, its first real "national" effort of any kind.

The spirit of nationalism, once ignited and whipped to fever pitch, tends to become the all-pervading principle of authority in the modern state. The fact that few governments and few political orders have survived defeat in a modern war mobilized through and justified by nationalism points to a twentieth-century rule of political thumb: he who uses nationalism to justify war demands and sacrifices had better be a winner. But Salamanca's Bolivia was a definite loser.

Thus, the question emerges: In a country like Bolivia, to whom could nationalism become a principle of action leading to sacrifice and perhaps death? To the Indian peasant living as a subject people marginal to all that was Bolivia? Hardly. It was the Indian who was to do the fighting, but he was a most reluctant soldier. The Indian was not drafted into the army; he was hijacked. There were regiments which did nothing but round up reluctant peasants to serve their nation. Literary accounts indicate that while in the army, the Indian remained bewildered, homesick, and hardly aware of what he was doing, let alone for what.[9]

Nationalism was hardly a potent drawing card for workers, many of whom were fresh from the land. Though the basis for a nationalist response was in them, it was not as yet formed. Many workers responded to the call, but the sizeable desertion rate indicates that they did so with little enthusiasm.[10]

Nationalism springs from a sense of identity and, therefore, presupposes some basis for that sense. In Bolivia that sense, although perhaps more widespread after the war, was, in the early 1930s, restricted to the small number of active participants in the "national system." If peasants and, to some degree, workers did not march off to the call of nationalism, there were city groups, particularly among the petite bourgeoisie, who did. Of these, the ones who marched most gladly and who returned the most humiliated were the young. The really enthusiastic supporters for the national crusade came from a large section of a generation which had already expressed considerable doubts about the makeup of their country.

This younger generation, however, was actually split on the war issue. Those who had previously begun to seek answers in the revolutionary socialist direction rejected the war both in concept and execution. Already under Salamanca's repressive guns, the young leftists who opposed the war were either driven into exile, or, if not so fortunate, were drafted into the army as privates in line outfits. This policy might well have been a mistake, for the more courageous used this opportunity to proselytize among their fellow soldiers, both in the trenches and in prisoner-of-war camps. The result was that more leftists returned from the war than had originally marched out.[11]

Those young men associated with the nationalist crusade threw themselves into the war with patriotic fervor. Most served as front-line reserve officers. During the war the split between the nationalists and revolutionary socialists widened. Still smarting from the role the left had played in overthrowing Siles, the nationalists assailed their peers as internationalists who sought to use Bolivia as a pawn in a wider game. In the years following the war, the nationalists consistently argued that only those who had sweated in the Chaco could legitimately offer solutions to Bolivia's problems.

It is difficult to measure anything as vague as the psychological impact of a war on people; but by the same token, it is clear that war, especially a nationalist war, has such an impact.

What effect did the war have on the thousands of Indians who were carted out to the Chaco? Undoubtedly, there was some effect. Veterans returning from the front brought with them at the least an awareness of a larger world. In some areas this was reflected in changing culture patterns, especially in dress, after the war. More important is the fact that after their release from service, many Indian peasants did not go back to their lands but remained in the cities, especially La Paz.[12] In the cities, they joined the swelling ranks of unemployed and underemployed. Many periodically returned to their homes where they undoubtedly told of the new life they were leading. Some entered new occupations such as truck-driving (having learned the skill in the army) and, thereby, had the opportunity to travel widely. In this group which sought the cities, it is most probable that the attraction of a new kind of life was the pulling force. But the question remains, What specific impact did the war have on the Indian and on the agricultural system itself?[13]

There is as yet little evidence of a direct impact of the war on the Indian mass. It is true that in the Cochabamba Valley what appeared to be a peasant union was formed immediately after the war. This organization sought with temporary success to redistribute land among its members. But there is some question as to whether this experiment was initiated by the peasants or by urban persons associated with the reform government of Colonel David Toro (president from May 1936 to July 1937).[14] Moreover, as I will clarify later, there were factors at work in the Valley, both before and after the war, which are of more importance in explaining the later political activity of Indian peasants in that region. The war no doubt affected Valley peasants, but mainly, I would argue, because the region was already predisposed to change. It seems to me that the war, even in such a "prepared" area, at most, resulted in the appearance of a potential leadership stratum, a stratum which did not mature politically until it had experienced a wide variety of reinforcing stimuli over the next sixteen years. In conclusion, the existence of a generalized impact of the war on the average Indian peasant seems doubtful since, aside from this isolated case of peasant union organization, no political behavior directly traceable to the war has yet been shown.

The question of the war's impact on workers and other lower groups is more confused. Immediately after the war, labor and other popular protest activity reappeared with new vehemence. Submerged organizations returned more powerful and more radical than ever before. Strikes, demonstrations, and the like broke out in all major cities and had a hitherto unparalleled political impact. A general strike precipitated the overthrow of one president and made uncomfortable the tenure of others. The psychological impact of the war no doubt contributed to the climate of popular agitation, but it should not be overemphasized. We must also take into account the economic crisis which followed the war, and that the overthrow of Salamanca by the field army in 1935 provided the opportunity for pent-up demands to be expressed. Whatever factors one chooses to emphasize as causal, the important point is that, with the end of the war, movement from below came into its own. After 1935, such movement came steadily under the leadership of more specifically worker groups. After 1936 it became virtually impossible to turn the tide.

There is no doubt that the war had a deep psychological and intellectual impact on both the left and right wings of the middle- and upper-stratum youth. Indeed, it is mainly with this already partially alienated group that any really direct connection between the war and later political behavior can be made. While it may be true that few Indians found anything as abstract as "Bolivia" in the sands of the Chaco, it is more than apparent that the young bourgeoisie of the cities discovered the Indian there. As the veritable flood of novels, books, and pamphlets which poured out after the war attests, this young generation discovered the "real" Bolivia in the Chaco; or perhaps, more accurately, they discovered the "non-Bolivianess" of Bolivia. They discovered that they fought for a nation which didn't exist. Over and over the same refrain was driven home—the glaring contradiction between what Bolivia should be and what Bolivia really was.

Before the war, this generation had manifested deep dissatisfaction with the world offered them. Aside from the leftist strain, the feeling remained a generalized sense of frustration with no clear notions of causes or remedies. With the bitter close of the war, there occurred a grand "Aha!" A sense of discovery emerged in which those who had conducted the war appeared as demons, with Bolivia the object of their foul intentions; the youth who fought the good fight were portrayed as the betrayed and used. Now tried in battle and shorn of illusion, the new generation vowed to become the agents of purification and regeneration. Nowhere was this generalized outlook more apparent than in the junior officer corps of the army which deemed itself the super victim of the war.

Desire for change stems from perceived anomalies in concrete situations, such as the desire on the part of the artisans for economic protection; that of labor to advance socially and economically; and the problem of no social or economic outlet which confronted the elite youth. This feeling becomes radical as groups become convinced that those who rule are either unwilling or unable to change that which creates these aggravating situations. There is nothing like a completely bungled war to convince groups, already predisposed to doubt, that those who rule are completely incapable, and therefore no longer justified in holding their positions. When the anomalies are so deep and the bungling as gross as they were in Bolivia, people are apt not only to reject leaders, but the system of values and institutions that they symbolize as well.[15] The elite and sub-elite youth who returned from the Chaco vehemently renewed their previous demands for change. Moreover, they now began to demand the exclusive right to carry out those changes. Thus, among this, its most critical group, the system's authority was irrevocably besmirched. Among those who had yet to be really brought into the system, no national authority had as yet been established; but now, as they approached inclusion into the system, the existing principles were less than convincing.

Beginning in 1936, Bolivia embarked on a search for a viable basis of political authority which has yet to end successfully.

The war contributed to the process of internal economic ruination since it was fought at tremendous cost to Bolivia. Over sixty-five thousand men were lost, among whom were many of the country's most skilled. Scarcely a family of the petite bourgeoisie was not touched directly, and there is reason to believe that the ranks of skilled miners were decimated.[16] The war was a great financial effort for a country the size of Bolivia and to underwrite it the government had to continue the process of internal borrowing and the floating of currency. Immediately after the war, inflation appeared and continued to grow in intensity year by year.

The returning veterans, their ranks swollen by Indians who did not want to return to the land, glutted the labor market, creating widespread unemployment and underemployment. The old problem of shortages in the cities and rising prices of needed goods became more virulent. These factors hit all groups hard, but caused particular havoc among the middle elements of the major cities and among the workers.

However, not all economic developments were negative. The cutting off of many imports and the availability of inflated capital stimulated a boomlet in manufacturing. While the rest of the economy was collapsing, this previously neglected sector was beginning to grow. Growth in manufacturing was, however, quite limited and located almost exclusively in La Paz.[17] This limited secondary growth could hardly act as a substitute for tin as the basis of the economy. Where possible, local manufacturers relied on imported primary goods and, therefore, did not stimulate local growth. In addition, this small sector was not capable of making much of a dent in urban unemployment. In its best years, manufacturing did not employ many more than twenty thousand men. Finally, the nature and extent of these operations (most were small family firms), plus the fact that they tended to be foreign-owned, hardly made the sector a viable career outlet for the oncoming elite generation. While it represented a much needed growth spurt, it was, in the end, too little, too late.[18]

The most immediate economic result of the war was the continuing monetary collapse and inflation. Inflation was a problem primarily of the major cities and had its deepest effect on consumers with fixed income. Inflation constituted a particularly severe challenge to the solidity of the world of the urbanized and dependent petite bourgeoisie. Economic stagnation had begun to pinch this vital social grouping before the war. The first to experience the effects was the younger generation. After the war, the overall petite bourgeoisie, as well as elements of the national bourgeoisie, started to experience increasing pressure.[19]

Under this pressure, which shattered security and threatened social decline, the previous identification of the petite bourgeoisie with the national bourgeoisie was slowly turned into resentment. In the late 1930s, this urban middle elite group began to add its voice to those asking for economic succor and political change. This turn of events was particularly serious, for the petite bourgeoisie was the major social support of the existing socio-political order. Between 1936 and 1939, elements of the middle elite, both young and old, became the most vocal supporters of two serious experiments in government-initiated reform.

Conclusions

It should be clear by now that a causal argument has been developing in this study, and that it is not in agreement with those who single out the Chaco War as the cause of the revolution of 1952. Causes, in the sense of concrete anomalous situations which set off demands for change among significant sectors of the population, were in operation previous to the war. These situations arose mainly from a series of contradictions derived from the pattern of skewed development and socio-economic immobilism discussed above. It is difficult to speculate where these might have led if not reinforced by events, but it seems clear that the liberal socio-political system of Bolivia was already in serious straits by the end of the second decade of this century.

The image I wish to convey is that of a society beset by a series of critical problems which were then galvanized to crisis proportions by two traumatic experiences in a time span of less than six years. The first was the Great Depression; the second, the Chaco War. These two events are best viewed as integral parts of an unfolding process which they neither started nor culminated, but accelerated to a point where revolution became not inevitable, but possible. They were accelerators, which, by aggravating existing dislocations, raised demands for change to a politically new and potentially revolutionary level. They brought the country to a revolutionary situation in which politics became structured around competing models of socio-political organizations offering varying solutions to the growing pressures at all levels of the society.

In retrospect, it can be said that the political stability of the prerevolutionary order depended on three basic factors: (a) a healthy and growing tin industry, (b) a committed petite bourgeoisie, and (c) minimal movement in those sectors consciously defined as outside the system (approximately 75 percent of the population). By 1936, the tin industry was chronically ill and not apt to get better. The petite bourgeoisie, trapped in a static social and economic climate and then threatened with the possibility of decline, was becoming progressively more alienated. Almost an entire generation of youth, ordinarily destined to enter the national elite, had lost complete faith in the authority of the existing order. Movement in the lower reaches of the "national system" was reaching a level of organizational maturity which was to establish it as a permanent feature of the national political scene. Finally, the first faint stirrings of potential movement among the agricultural Indian mass was rippling across the surface of the agricultural system.

Thus, in 1936 the preconditions for a revolutionary situation were established in Bolivia. Reformist and revolutionary counter-elites committed to new modes of ordering reality were not only in existence, but were in a position to present a serious threat to the existing order. In addition, there were developing publics, especially in the labor-artisan sector and among the petite bourgeoisie, who were increasingly available and receptive to mobilization against the system in one form or another. In short, the basis for the serious mounting of counter-movements had been laid.

The existence of these preconditions did not guarantee that a revolution would take place. Much was to depend on the responses of the status quo elite to the challenges levied at them. Of equal long-term importance was the question of the ways and means through which various potential publics were allied with the various counter-elite groups who fought among themselves every bit as ferociously as they did with the status quo elite. In Bolivia this process of unfolding revolutionary conflict, bounded politically by the relations among status quo elites, counter-elites, and potential counter-publics in an economic environment of continuing crisis was to last seventeen years. During this seventeen-year period, Bolivia was to experience bitter conflict and incipient civil war plus a wider and wider involvement in the political arena of hitherto excluded social groups.

)

PART II

5 Opening of the Revolutionary Situation

Upon the disastrous close of the Chaco War in 1936, Bolivia entered a three-year period of more or less permanent challenge and response between a number of dissident groups and the established political elite. The old order was immediately put on the defensive and was forced to respond accordingly. These years following the war saw intense but confused activity. A good deal of energy went into a search for a mode of opposition. There were interminable debates over what was wrong, who was responsible, and what was to be the solution. Above all, it was a period of ideological nit-picking. With scholastic fervor, the counter-groups spent as much time in distinguishing and defining differences among themselves as in mounting challenges to the old order. The Bolivian crucible became a microcosm of the ideological battle raging in Europe.

The period of search for a mode of opposition was initiated by the younger officers of the defeated field army. These men formed a sub-group of the alienated generation of the petite and national bourgeoisie. After the war, they faced the general problem of finding meaningful advancement within a specific carreer channel. The army, a critical institution of the prerevolutionary order, was even more static in generating new roles than the overall society. Many sons of less well-off branches of the petite bourgeoisie were ambitious lower officers. For this very reason, the established elite realized that the army was full of "climbers" (arribiṣtas) who had to be kept in check so that staff positions could remain the preserve of older, already arrived officers.

The war brought about the rapid expansion of the Bolivian army and, for a brief moment, offered unheard-of opportunities for the rapid rise of young officers, though mainly in the form of field commands.[1] However, these younger officers eventually realized that even as they were fighting the war, the oligarchical staff was planning an end to their usefulness. In the Chaco, they experienced the power of command, a role they were not anxious to give up with the end of the hostilities. They returned from the Chaco pointing an accusing finger at both politicians and the established army staff. From the beginning, personal politics poisoned the war effort. The army staff was in continual conflict with the civil leadership, while the younger officers played both sides against the middle. The bitterness of these internal battles carried over into the post-war period.[2]

Post-War Governments of Toro and Busch

Near the end of the war, ambitious army staff officers with the aid of younger field men deposed President Salamanca and placed his vice-president, Tejado Sorzano, in nominal power. Less than a year later, the army moved again, but this time it was more obviously influenced by the younger officers. Sorzano was deposed and one of the shrewdest manipulators of internal army politics, Colonel David Toro, formed a military junta. Although the public spokesman of the junta, it was rather apparent that Toro relied mainly upon the support of the junior officers. The most popular leader of junior officers was German Busch, one of the few untainted heroes to emerge from the war. These younger officers, imbued with the idealism of the self-declared victim, set out to purify the army and the state.

Although the old office-hungry politics of power factions was still evident, there was a new twist to the conflicts. The new government under Toro, while clearly seeking the personal rewards of power, also set out to undertake some basic reforms. In a sense, it embodied the new style presaged in the nationalist party that had formed around Hernando Siles. The old intra-elite, office-motivated faction struggles persisted, if for no other reason than the fact that the basic conditions which brought them about in the first place had not changed. However, a real intention to use office to carry out as yet undefined change and reform was evident. One reason for this was that growing public pressure acted to threaten with political extinction any factions that simply grabbed office and let it go at that.

The game as played among traditional elites became much more complex. Having little choice, all the elite factions, both old and new, heralded the military's ascension to power. The peers of the young officers did so with enthusiasm, but the older parties expressed guarded approval and the hope that the military would soon return the reins of power to civil elements. Other groups also threw their support behind the "military revolution," as it was popularly termed. The reemerging artisan-labor movement played a significant role in the coup which unseated Salamanca in 1935 by staging a general strike on the eve of the military's manuever. Another group of growing importance consisted of the numerous war veterans who formed the *Legión de Excombatientes* dominated by urban middle elements. This Legión provided important nationalist support (in the form of demonstrations and public propaganda) for the Toro regime.

Toro adopted a reformist socialist stance, but behind the public facade raged an intense battle among both old and new elements to influence the course of the regime. Toro's original cabinet reflected a wide diversity of positions. One of his first moves of significance was to create a Ministry of Labor for the first time. He appointed Waldo Alvarez, head of the graficos, the first labor minister. It was a significant move not only in concept, but also because it was the first time that someone not born of an elite or sub-elite group was allowed to hold a high office. Members of the pre-war nationalist party were prominent in Toro's cabinet, as was a group of moderate socialist youth associated with the old Republican leader, Saavedra. Also, under the leadership of the pre-war nationalist Baldivieso, a socialist party was formed which declared that it represented a true socialism appropriate to Bolivia, a national theory *sui generis*. Older faces associated with traditional elite interests were also visible in the government.[3]

At first Toro, under pressure from the young officers, the continuing economic crisis, and social disorder, appeared to be adopting a course defined by the nationalist youth. The line was heavily laden with both nationalist and socialist allusions. Toro announced a ban on all traditional party activity and set about to turn Baldivieso's party into an official government party called the State Socialist Party (*Partido Socialista del Estado*). A newly founded newspaper, *La Calle,* directed by the nationalists Armando Arce and Augusto Cespedes, declared enthusiastic support for the new order and developed in its pages the theory of *Socialismo del Estado.*

In essence, Socialismo del Estado was a corporate state theory in which the elements of state intervention in the economy and state responsibility for public welfare were emphasized. As such, it expressed more closely the problems of the dependent urban middle sector, artisan groups, and the moralistic young intellectuals than those of the rising labor groups. True proletariat groups, while developing fast, were not as yet strong enough or political enough to play a major role in the government itself. Of the combined movement from below, it was the artisans who played the greatest role, and even this was transitory. Hence, the Toro government was dominated mainly by elements of the national and petite bourgeoisie, be they young or old, reformist or status quo.

The attitude of the government toward lower groups, particularly workers, was paternalistic and manipulative. One of the keystones of the projected corporate state was a compulsory unionization decree which commanded all groups (worker, artisan, professional, and managerial) to form into unions (*sindicatos*) for purposes of negotiating social and economic questions with the state. An ancillary concept which never materialized was a project to create a legislature based on functional representation.

These measures were designed to remove the arbitrariness and insecurity from social relations, while solidifying the present patterns of ownership and authority. The unionization decree was a thinly veiled attempt to remove labor organization from internally generated control and to place it under state control.

This elitist and manipulative attitude reflected not just Toro's orientation but that of his nationalist (now national-socialist) supporters as well. This group was engaged in a bitter battle for control of the artisan-labor movement with the Marxist socialists (whom they labeled "infantile internationalists"). The decree was designed partially as a means to deny the Marxist radical tendency its most natural public support. The battle for control was carried out in labor conferences, socialist gatherings, and in the editorial pages of *La Calle,* where the radicals were scored daily as anti-Bolivian. Beyond this, the decree represented the deep distrust and superior attitude of the young nationalist elite toward the worker groups which they considered to be irrational and "underdeveloped."[4]

Agricultural issues were also raised by the Toro government, but they in no way constituted a central concern. The general approach was to say that the state of agriculture in the country did indeed present a problem and that the government must deal with it someday. The attitude toward the Indian peasant was even more patronizing than that adopted toward labor. The problem of the Indian was reduced to one of cultural backwardness—there were some discussions of the need to "civilize" the Indian. Isolated attempts at rural educational reform were initiated, but the state did not direct any real energy in this direction. As noted above, the government supported an experimental program of land redistribution on the hacienda of Santa Clara in the Cochabamba Valley. The hacienda was owned by a community of nuns who rented it to other landowners. There was some talk of "reforming" other such "corporate" properties but it was never followed up. In sum, the Indian and rural property relations did become, to some extent, a "national" issue under Toro, but, in the end, the question was allowed to fade and extant rural property relations were never seriously questioned.[5]

Toro himself clearly saw his public role (as opposed to personal interest) as savior rather than remaker of Bolivia. According to Toro, his aim was to bring the tin interests under state control for the first time, and to divert the alarming radical drift of labor through this alleviation of economic pressure and assertion of control. The government was neither left nor right, but national in the sense of the state acting as a social arbiter and guarantor of security.[6] In contemporary terms, it was an attempt to stop movement and carry out development while guaranteeing the continued existence of the old social values and modes, without incurring generalized social costs. It was a utopianism doomed to failure.

In conjunction with its position, the government attempted to legislate a number of other reforms. The government fixed prices and established subsidized food stores. Wages were increased and decrees for improved working conditions passed. The judiciary was reformed and both penal and civil branches established. There was talk of reforming education. A section of the Ministry of Education was set up to deal with the cultural reformation of Indian schools. Toro further established ministeries of mines and of commerce, both with the defined purpose of regulating production. Activities were also initiated to protect the small- and medium-sized mine operations from the big consortiums.

By far, the most dramatic act of the government was the nationalization of Standard Oil's holdings in Bolivia. Standard Oil was, at the time, considered to be the real cause behind the Chaco War. The war, according to the nationalists, was really a struggle between Standard Oil and Royal Dutch Shell, a struggle in which Bolivia and Paraguay were used as pawns. The expropriation of the holdings of Standard Oil was a popular act and found its real rationale in its symbolic value.[7]

The weaknesses of government policy soon began to appear. The idea of putting the state in a position where it could regulate traditional interests and deradicalize pressure from the worker groups simply did not work. Every move which pleased one group angered others. The degree of social cleavage was such that any effective government could not hope to survive without allying itself with some interests. Government could not be all things to all people for the simple reason that everyone wanted contradictory things. Moves to regulate prices for consumers angered sellers; projections in the countryside angered landlords; wage and hour decrees angered the big companies; the failure of the companies to implement the decrees brought howls from labor. Finally, all the traditional factions were disgruntled by the political influence of the younger generation. The government had to move in some direction. Toro chose to go right.

Before long, the national left figures saw their influence over Toro diminishing. Waldo Alvarez of the graficos was replaced in the Ministry of Labor by a representative of the old guard. At the same time, Toro drew closer to the tin interests, particularly to tin magnates Aramayo and Hochschild. An interesting and complex split ensued. Aramayo and Hochschild publicly cooperated with the Toro government. The move reflected a desire to temporize the reformist government, but also grew out of an attempt to use their influence with Toro to increase their share of production quotas at the expense of Patiño. The Patiño combine, on the other hand, responded to projected labor and tax reforms by threatening to curtail all production. Toro, trapped in these cross-currents, found himself assailed by the national reformers and Patiño, both of whom actively plotted sections of the military against him.[8]

The instrument of this rather complex interplay became German Busch, the young hero of the Chaco. Rallying the younger officers, Busch deposed Toro on July 13, 1937, and assumed the presidency. While Toro started from the left and moved right, Busch started from the right and later moved definitively to the national left. This shift in field not only reflected Busch's own erratic personality but also the early influence over him by the Patiño group. From the outset, Busch assumed a high-handed and personal approach to the presidency, preferring to rule with his own artificial instrumentalities, a predisposition which greatly disturbed the traditional Liberal and Republican parties which were beginning to feel the effects of the long period out of political office. The possibility of an indefinite period of military rule sparked widespread defection from the old faction leaders, although the ambitious sought to find a personal place in the new scheme of things.

The course of his government still undefined, Busch in 1938 convoked a national convention to draft a new constitution and to legalize his presidency. The convention was designed to be a broad-gauged gathering based on functional and sectoral interest representation. The traditional parties were ignored and it became obvious that Busch was out to do away with them once and for all. The convention was a very disparate affair and the entire new ideological spectrum was represented. During the deliberations, the original group of nationalist reformers and radical socialists, buttressed by a new group of independents, emerged as the most vocal convention factions. For whatever reasons, Busch moved rapidly to the national-socialist position, and a coalition similar to that of the first days of the Toro government emerged.

The convention of 1938 became the landmark of this inchoate period. The constitution it produced was the most formalized statement of the nationalist orientation to that point. The most fundamental change from the past was the adding of a long economic and social section to what previously were documents that dealt almost solely with political institutions. The new sections introduced two important concepts: (a) the economy functioned for the good of the state and therefore the state would function as the regulator of the economy, and (b) the state assumed the responsibility for the economic welfare of the general population. A further important change involved the alteration of previous constitutional provisions legitimizing the ownership of private property to that of constitutional legitimacy only if it served a social function. The constitution was followed by a general labor code which defined the rights of labor vis-à-vis management; stipulated, in minute details, rules on wages, hours, working conditions, etc.; and gave the state the authority to regulate all such matters in the future. The state, thereby, was legally placed as the pivot in labor-management relations at the same time that it was constitutionally made the organizing focal point of the entire economy. Even under future reaction governments, the essential features of both the constitution and labor code remained the law of the land.[9]

Bolivia thereby officially rejected an unfettered liberal framework and officially committed itself to being a modern welfare state. However, commitment and actualization are two different things. The elite of the liberal order was not yet dead, and even if it had been, Bolivia lacked a sufficient grade of development and economic surplus to realize such an advanced dream. The country overshot its reach. Despite the continual ratification of the constitution, the basic battles were to continue and grow worse. The new legal basis of political life was artificial and legitimated aspirations destined to frustration. The constitution guaranteed that every social and economic question would immediately become a major national political issue.

Once committed to the national left course, Busch moved with alacrity and determination. To the popular forces growing stronger and more radical by the day, Busch assumed an attitude similar to Toro's. Through artificial means, he attempted to bring them under firm state control, both to deny them to the radical socialists and to buttress his own regime. In this endeavor, he experimented erratically but tended to rely mainly on the Legión de Excombatientes. His personal magnetism and his policies won widespread popular identification, but the emergent labor sectoral elite resisted attempts to reduce their personal power or to destroy the independence of the movement. His attempts to launch an official support party from above ran into the same obstacles. Busch took an openly hostile attitude toward the tin barons. He went so far as to threaten to shoot them personally if they interfered with his program. When his program failed to gain results as fast as he wished, Busch blamed it on the recalcitrance of vested interests and declared himself dictator. This maneuver was resisted by the socialist left and the old factions, but was rammed through by the national left and independents with a definite assist from the young sector of the army which hovered in the background. Assuming total power, Busch brought the nationalist reformers and independents into his government.

With this small group of young reformers, he set out to change the face of Bolivia.

Busch was a dictator without an apparatus, and neither he nor his small coterie of intellectual reformers had any structural links with the population at large. Busch attempted to realize his development dreams by harnessing to the state the profits of mining (now not all that high). He created the *Banco Minero* ("Mining Bank") which provided that henceforth the state, not Hochschild, would buy and sell the produce of the small- and medium-sized mine operations. The aim was to liberate this sector from the control of the combines and to bring it under the state's wing, especially with regard to foreign exchange. Control of the bank was given to young independents, Víctor Paz Estenssoro and Walter Guevara Arze, both of whom were embarking on what were to be long and important political careers.

The bank measure was followed by the most radical measure conceived by a government to that date: on June 7,1938, Busch decreed that henceforth 100 percent of the foreign exchange (*divisas*) earned by the "Big Three" would be sold to the state at an exchange rate defined by the government. It was a popular decree among the urban petite bourgeoisie, who had already begun to blame their problems on the big capitalists, as well as among the lower groups. But Busch had no way to translate this popularity into a sustaining basis of support. The companies, of course, threw all their strength behind the scenes to reverse the action. Tremendous pressure was brought to bear on the young dictator from all directions. Before the struggle had an opportunity to play itself out, however, Busch ended his political career as explosively as he began it by shooting himself in the head on August 23, 1939.

Busch's death, popularly believed to be a murder authored by the tin magnates, set off a wave of popular demonstrations led mainly by the young nationalist reformers. Street demonstrations were to no avail. The old elite moved with speed to end this bizarre period of experimentation by what they believed were young upstarts and madmen. Baldivieso, Busch's vice president, was denied the presidency and a junta dominated by older army staff officers assumed caretaker power. The old parties regrouped and coalesced to assume joint power in a united front called *La Concordancia*. Bolivia's first modern period of experimentation in radical reform was over and a period of reaction or "restoration" was underway.

Political Factions in Post-War Bolivia

During this first post-Chaco War phase, there were four primary elements of counter-movement in Bolivia: (a) civilian petite and national bourgeois youth, (b) the junior officer corps of the army, (c) the inflation-threatened, dependent bourgeoisie of the cities, and (d) the artisan-labor movement. The bulk of governmental and ideological activity was carried on by the first two groups against the backdrop of agitation and protest generated by the latter groups. Personal factions pursuing the immediate rewards of office continued to structure national political activity, but a significantly new ideological commitment to new general forms of organization was added.

This period of conflict and change was brief, lasting only about three years (1936-39), but despite the brevity of its duration, it saw the rapid development and maturation of all elements of the political equation. Among the civil counter-elite youth (now called *la generación del Chaco*) there were, as indicated before, two basic tendencies: (a) a nationalist reformist and (b) a revolutionary Marxist. In the first flush of socialist rhetoric following the war, there were attempts to form a united left socialist movement. The attempts floundered and the two movements continued on their separate ways.

The Marxist revolutionary tendency received a great morale boost after the war with the return from exile in 1936 of Gustavo Navarro, better known as Tristan Marof. One of the few Bolivian intellectuals of international stature, Marof had moved widely among revolutionary circles throughout Europe. A writer of considerable talent, his works began to have a great impact among Bolivian students previous to the Chaco War. Although weak theoretically and showing a strong tendency to favor the rule of a strong personalistic leader, works of his, such as *Justicia del Inca,* became the books upon which many university students cut their first Marxist teeth.[10] In *Justicia del Inca,* Marof coined the phrase which became the rallying cry of the Marxist revolutionaries, *Minas al Estado, Tierra al Indio* ("Mines to the State, Land to the Indian"). Marof returned to Bolivia in the late 1920s and helped launch a number of ill-fated socialist parties. During the Salamanca repression, he fled to Argentina where he became the center of a group of revolutionary leftist exiles. It was an important period during which the exiles hobnobbed with Argentine radicals. Many of these exiles were influenced by Trotskyites.

On his return to Bolivia in 1936, Marof was received as the leader of Bolivian revolutionary socialism by the leftist youth. Marof in person, however, turned out to be a disappointment to those who had been living off the Marof myth. His flamboyant personal style and his obvious desire to become the caudillo of the revolutionary left clashed with the more conspiratorial and organization-minded youth who had initiated the university reform movement of 1928. In a 1938 call for a united leftist socialist party, Marof revealed his basic personalistic approach to politics.

> As I have told you comrades there exists in this moment spontaneous socialism and love for the leader. Why not take advantage of this opportune moment over other parties to create our own on solid bases and adapt ourselves to the Bolivian environment in which circulate personal influences and sympathies and leave theory aside.[11]

Marof's call was immediately attacked by Ricardo Añaya, one of the young leaders of the 1928 movement. Añaya accused Marof of caudillismo and opportunism and argued that a party founded on such principles would divide the socialist movement and lead the masses into the trap of reformism. Marof's party, Añaya argued, would fall into the hands "of the petty bourgeoisie of people wishing to be functionaries who in the ultimate analysis are seeking only public offices."[12] Añaya made his own call for a class-based party rooted in Marxist-Leninist theory. The student left split with Marof and pursued the course outlined by Añaya and another, even more important, Marxist leader, José Antonio Arce.

Marof continued his attempts to form a broad-based united socialist movement. His continued preference for a party based on his own undisputed personal leadership engendered further trouble in his own ranks. In the fall of 1938, a battle broke out between Marof and the popular José Aguirre Gainsborg. The issue was Marof's desire to launch a party organized from above (elitist-controlled), aimed at a multi-class base and oriented toward legal electoral activity. Aguirre Gainsborg argued for a small conspiratorial elite party mainly aimed at class propaganda. The two split, leading to the formation of two of the first socialist parties of any note.

The bulk of the group stayed with Marof and formed the *Partido Socialista Obrero Boliviano* (PSOB). But Marof, the leftist caudillo, was hardly a match for the flamboyant Busch, who dominated the national scene. Like the Busch government, the PSOB never built real structural links with particular publics to retain factional support. Thus, after a brief flicker, the party, with Marof at its head, went into decline. In the early 1940s, the PSOB disappeared and Marof, left standing alone, ended his career wandering all sides of the political fence, looking for a base he never found.

The Aguirre Gainsborg faction formed a small cabal which called itself the *Partido Obrero Revolucionario* (POR). Shortly after the break with Marof, Gainsborg was killed in an accident, but the POR remained a small sectarian elite group. Eventually, the POR openly adopted the Trotskyite line, affiliated with the Fourth International, and began to attack the student left, Arce-Añaya group as Stalinists.[13] Maintaining its small and conspiratorial form, the POR started assiduously to pursue meaningful links with true labor groups, especially in the mines. During the early 1940s, it met with some success and, as a result, proletarian elements began to achieve importance in the party alongside original middle- and upper-group intellectuals.[14] Although it remained fairly insignificant throughout this period, the party was eventually to gain a greater influence in the mines, through which its impact on the course of events would be considerable.

In the student Marxist camp, centered around the original student leaders of the 1928 university reform movement and concentrated in the city of Cochabamba, José Antonio Arce became the most dominant personality. Forced into exile by the reformist military, Arce took up residence in Chile where he made important contacts with Chilean Marxist groups. While in exile, Arce formed a group in 1939 called the *Frente de la Izquierda Boliviano* (FIB).[15] The FIB propounded a platform which was profoundly revolutionary. The organization gained immediate recognition and support in Cochabamba at a leftist unity conference held the same year. The FIB, with the help of various student federations, backed Arce in the presidential elections of 1940—to the surprise of many, he did quite well. Following the dictum of the need for a strong, class-based revolutionary party, the FIB, after a number of conferences, converted itself on July 26, 1940, into the *Partido de la Izquierda Revolucionaria* (PIR). The PIR was the first new, truly modern party to emerge from the ferment begun in the late 1920s and accelerated by the depression and the war. It was a direct descendant of the 1928 university reform movement and represented the strongest and most general expression of the Marxist-Leninst revolutionary tendency long gestating among the alienated oncoming elite generation.

The PIR followed a style and orientation evident from the first days of the leftist revolutionary movement. The group was elitist in background, but in a specific sense. The position of the group was that, due to uneven economic development, the Bolivian proletariat was weak in numbers and consciousness. However, it rejected the approach of the nationalists or the Marofists who held the same basic hypothesis. Instead of the Marof desire to launch a multi-class party organized from above, the PIR projected the long-term creation of a revolutionary movement from below to be led by radical intellectuals; that is, a proletarian revolution led by a consciously radical elite sprung from the middle bourgeoisie.

The PIR, while never affiliating with the Third International, did follow a roughly Stalinist position. Its long-range view gave primacy to economic development (especially industry) which was deemed necessary for the survival of a socialist state. At the same time, it argued for the necessity of passing through certain developmental stages—the notion of a permanent revolution, either national or international, was rejected on the grounds that before socialism could be established, Bolivia would have to pass through a full capitalist developmental stage. These concepts were not completely spelled out in 1940, but the outlines were there.[16]

Tactically, the PIR eschewed immediate entrance into political office. Instead, the party sought to build a sound basic organization, while keeping up a continual ideological barrage against the traditional elite and what the PIR called the "false reformist" national counter-elites. In this way, the PIR was the first major counter-elite group to act directly on the artisan-labor movement in an attempt to radicalize and politicize it.

The first major organizational success of the group which was to become the PIR was the formation of a national confederation of teachers in 1936. This powerful grouping eventually became a PIR stronghold. Although more a petite bourgeoisie than a proletarian group, the confederation adopted a radical stance and gave the PIR some influence in the country's primary and secondary schools as well as in various isolated groups. From the very beginning, the party maintained an abiding interest in educational theory as part of its intention to revolutionize Bolivia. Its control of the teachers' confederation gave it an opportunity to experiment with its theories and to leave still visible marks on succeeding younger generations.[17]

The group also sought to place itself at the head of popular movements from the lower strata. In this, it had some success. Links were made with various artisan and labor groups, and the PIR became the dominant influence in the national labor confederation (*Confederación Sindical de Trabajadores Bolivianos* or CSTB) formed in 1936. The PIR gained footholds in all major labor groups including that of the miners. The group least influenced by the party was the just-forming factory workers *(fabriles)*, while that most influenced was the well-established railway workers federation.

The PIR was able, for a brief period, to succeed in making itself the national political representative of the movement from below. However, as later events were to show, this leftist revolutionary counter-elite group never really melted into the artisan-labor movement enough to create a true labor party. A permanent gap remained between the two so that the PIR continued as a radical bourgeois elite group allied with certain labor groups. Thus, the PIR had a great deal of influence in accelerating and directing the activity from below, but never reached a position of real identity and control.

The people who eventually formed the PIR were also the first to explore the possibility of the formation of an agrarian political movement. From their base in Cochabamba, radical students and teachers probed sore points among the Cochabamba Valley Indians. Radical teachers were on hand during the reform in Cliza, and they also staffed positions in the *campesino* ("peasant") school built in Ucureña in 1937. Although the activity was sporadic, the PIR was the first organized group to plant notions of using organized pressure for change among the Indian mass.[18] All in all, the PIR—which included radical students who achieved university reform—agitated, organized, and eventually launched a potent Marxist party and played a critical role in preparing the ground of the developing revolutionary situation.

The other youthful counter-tendency which I have labeled "national reformist" went through a similar set of permutations in this critical three-year period. As Marxism appealed to one branch of this generation, the other was pulled toward the less systematic set of ideas associated with corporatism, fascism, and the like, then current in Europe. Evolutionary socialism and various vitalistic positions also had their appeal. The concepts of most general appeal seemed to be anti-liberal capitalism, anti-imperialism, statism, and the single leader principle. Nationalism and a variant of racism often referring to the Indo-American race were more or less generic orienting points of this entire spectrum.

A good number of these concepts were brought together in the theory called Socialismo del Estado.

A variety of small groups, some frankly Nazi, made a brief appearance but, in the main, three sub-tendencies emerged. The first durable new party to emerge was the *Falange Socialista Boliviana* (FSB). The FSB modeled itself after the Spanish Falange (Fascist party in Spain) and adopted the outward symbols of similar Fascist groups of Europe, complete with white shirts and military posturing. In its early days, the FSB was the nationalist tendency's sectarian counterpart to the POR (Trotskyites). It remained a rigidly small group based on a strict leader principle. The FSB avoided standard political action and mainly appealed to younger (high-school age) bourgeois youth and to various regional and separatist sentiments. It adopted a conspiratorial and violent approach to politics and jealously guarded its ideological and political purity. Moralistic in tone and tactically oriented toward violent action, the FSB remained until recently a quixotic group more interested in the bold and heroic gesture than in the serious pursuit of power.[19]

On the other side of the nationalist reform spectrum were the evolutionary socialists. Most were young professionals and many of this group had previous experience in politics, mainly with the Saavedra faction. Individual moderates such as Gabriel Gosalavez and Pedro Zelveti Arce played important roles in both the Toro and Busch regimes. In the main, however, this group, although part of the general indulgence in socialist rhetoric common to the day, was out of step with the rest of its generation. After a brief flirtation with minor reforms, this group began to find its traditional sectoral roots and slowly realigned itself with the old elite; they rejected the more radical positions and, during the period of La Concordancia, joined the restoration effort. In 1946, they formed a "socialist" sector of a front formed among regrouped fragments of the old Republican party known as the *Partido de la Unión Republicano Socialista* (PURS). After 1946, they became a reformist wing of the status quo elite in support of the traditional order, but counseling reform, before gathering revolutionary pressure swept all of this away.

Between these two there was a more or less identifiable nationalist mainstream tracing its heritage to the nationalist party of Hernando Siles. This was the Cespedes Montenegro group of young professionals associated with *La Calle* and identified with early Toro, late Busch, and the theory of Socialismo del Estado. Ideologically, the group was confused, but continued to pursue its notion of a Bolivian socialism *sui generis*. In 1938 the group of independent deputies of the Busch constitutional convention joined them. Together, the two backed Busch and used him to pursue their confused goals, some of which found general expression in Busch's constitution.[20]

Throughout this period of military-based experimentation, the core nationalists continued the tactical preferences they manifested under Hernando Siles. Their basic approach was that of fairly radical reform imposed from above by a small statist elite. Thus, unlike the PIR, this group sought immediate entrance into high political office. These nationalists experimented with political party formation but essentially remained a faction. They supported attempts to submit the movement from below to state control. However, they did not build any sustaining links between themselves and artisan or labor groups. They relied, instead, on the strong leader who would seize the executive post, surround himself with members of their group, and impose reform. They were a kind of platonic intellectual elite anxious to get on with the job and not disposed to build bases for the future. They were young, from the upper and middle bourgeoisie, and clearly elitist. Their attitude toward the lower strata was manipulative, paternalistic, and distrustful. It was from this small nationalist reformist and elitist cabal that Bolivia's most important modern party, the *Movimiento Nacionalista Revolucionario* (MNR) eventually was to form. At this point, however, the group was still a product of and deeply involved in the old political process based on factionalism and personality.

The young military counter-elite deserves special mention for, although it was part of the general alienated generation, it began and continued as a self-consciously distinct group. The military counter-elites began to organize themselves around a number of secret societies (*logias*). The most well known of these was called *Razón de Patria* (RADEPA). Its orientation was most directly influenced by the various corporatist, Fascist, and statist doctrines of Europe and Latin America. The touchstone of its view was nationalist and statist. Its members spoke of themselves as victims of the Chaco War who, by dint of fighting the good and pure fight, had not only a right but a kind of transcendental duty to seize the state and use its power to purify and purge Bolivia. Their view was quite romantic and projected itself in moralistic, vitalistic, and virile symbols and language. Beyond this vague orientation and set of predispositions, they had almost no program. Tactically, they leaned toward a direct seizure of the state by a coup, with the purpose of using the state to cleanse the existent mess. They were elitist to the core and authoritarian as well. They made little attempt to court openly a mass base, and only reluctantly negotiated contacts with other counter-groups of their generation. To the extent that they thought of popular power, it was from the perspective of organizing the social machine from the pinnacle of state power through such devices as Toro's compulsory syndicalism or Busch's national dictatorship.[21]

While the counter-elite groups of the urban bourgeoisie struggled among themselves and with the status quo elite, agitation continued at the non-elite level. Driven in part by continuing environmental dislocations and in part by contradictory stimuli coming from above, practically every sector of the population of the "national system" was being drawn directly into the national political fray. The power of non-elite groups was demonstrated in the general strike which helped topple Sorzano in 1936 and in activist bodies such as the Legión de Excombatientes.

Previous to the war (1927), the artisan-labor movement had succeeded in reaching a degree of national coherence through the *Federación Obrero del Trabajo*. In 1936, this ability was confirmed when a third national conference resulted in the formation of the *Confederación Sindical de Trabajadores Bolivianos* (CSTB). The CSTB marked the highest stage of general unity the movement was to reach before 1952. It was a tenuous unity racked by ideological splits and troubled by the particularistic orientation of its constituent parts, but, in the Bolivian situation, it was enough to mark the movement as a serious political force for the first time.

Originally, the CSTB reflected the same ideological mixture of bread-and-butter unionism, anarchism, and radical socialism as the previous national organizations. Immediately after the war, "economic" unionism still predominated and the movement was willing to remain the passive recipient of reforms instituted from above. Aside from the brief tenure of Waldo Alvarez (head of the Ministry of Labor), no major labor leaders held particularly important posts during the period. However, the socio-political drift of the country, summed up in the Busch constitution and labor code, helped politicize labor, though the intention of the reformers was just the opposite. Many factors made the politicization of labor almost inevitable.

In the first instance, the appetite of the labor groups was whetted as they began to glimpse the possibilities for a better life. The deference paid to the movement by the post-war reformers conveyed a new sense of their power to influence the flow of events. Furthermore, the very fact that desired changes originated in the governmental apparatus and that the state was made the future pivot of the economy assured that, henceforth, unions would bypass bargaining with management and bring their demands directly to the seat of governmental power.

Within the movement itself, important internal changes were taking place. The railway workers, always strong, reached a new height of organization and the previous railroad federation gave way to a working national confederation. The final industrialization of the mines took place in the 1920s and was now bearing fruit in the first real outlines of potent miners' organizations. In La Paz, the boomlet in secondary economic activities was creating a new proletarian group of factory workers. Hence, although it was a grafico (Waldo Alvarez) who was given a head post in the Toro government, the influence of the artisans was fading. Leadership of the artisan-labor movement was passing to worker elements and converting it into more of a labor-artisan movement. With the decline of artisan leadership, economic unionism and anarcho-syndicalism began to give way to a political unionism predisposed to radical socialism.

As I pointed out previously, the movement of both artisan and labor groups developed, for the most part, independently of the national intra-elite struggle. Under Saavedra there was a brief attempt of an elite faction to enlist wider support from below, but it was short-lived. However, post-war counter-elites followed the Saavedra example and widened the power spectrum. The reformers attempted to co-opt the movement from above, while the leftist revolutionaries sought to push it on with themselves at the head. By 1939, events had progressed to such a point that there could be no turning back to the old Saavedra formula; once the arena of conflict had widened, it was to remain so.

There was a drawing together of the two levels of activity. At first, the movement from below followed, to some extent, the reformers' lead. But the attempt to establish *sindicalismo dirigido* ("state-controlled labor organizations") and the failure of the private companies to implement legislated reforms pushed the movement toward the leftist revolutionary counter-elite.[22] By 1938, the Arce-Añaya group had made such significant inroads among the ferroviarios and the CSTB that Busch felt obliged to attempt a purge of leftists and officially to substitute the Legión de Excombatientes for true labor organizations. Busch exiled Arce and a number of labor leaders. Although the labor-artisan movement accepted in large part the political lead of the radical leftist intellectuals, it did so with caution. In 1940, the CSTB declared its intention to remain independent of any specific political party, and, in doing so, revealed its deep distrust of the entire spectrum of young intellectuals, be they nationalist reformers or revolutionaries.

> In Bolivia as in all the world intellectuals have never demonstrated sincerity, affinity and spirit of fight with the masses; always they carry a secret intention, a calculation to traffic with our strength; always they try to take over leadership positions without consulting the base, without identifying with the base, without sharing its pains, anguish and sense of rebellion.[23]

The statement reflects not only the distrust of one previously excluded grouping for the youth of the national elite and sub-elite estate, but also the intention of the emergent labor elite to guard jealously their leadership and control of the movement. The labor movement was, on one side, a focal point of contention by counter-elites seeking to influence and control it, while, on the other, there was resistance by the labor leadership itself to any takeover by bourgeois intellectuals, no matter what their ideology.

The labor-artisan movement had, over the years, developed an independent thrust with its own organizations, orientations, and leaders. It entered the post-Chaco War period in the same fashion and continued to move along its own trajectory. While it became a public more and more available for reformist and revolutionary activity, it remained an independent motor force acting to radicalize the national political scene. Labor was still mainly predisposed to concrete economic programs and to political activity couched in socialist symbols, but not to any specific variant of socialism. The movement drew closer to the contending young counter-elites, but still maintained its identity. Contacts were in the form of alliances between the young bourgeois elites and the emergent labor sectoral elite. Labor strove to keep its alliance options open.

Another potential revolutionary public also started to gestate in the post-Chaco War confusion—the broader petite bourgeoisie. Inflation, increasing in intensity yearly, began to remove the solidity of the bourgeois world. It is well known that the middle class, especially a dependent middle class, as in Bolivia, is one of the hardest hit social segments in a relentless inflation. The economic and status security that the middle class tends to prize so much is slowly sucked out of daily life.[24] Its greatest fear, slipping backward, becomes a tangible possibility. The once comfortable, if not satisfied, Bolivian bourgeoisie, after 1936, began living with this significant environmental problem, first intimated in the late 1920s. To the degree that the old system was deemed responsible for it and incapable of alleviating it, the bourgeoisie became restive at first. Then it became more and more an available base for counter-system activity.

The turn of events was critical. We have already seen that the petite bourgeoisie was the bedrock of the old liberal regime. Thus, unlike the artisan-labor movement which was a comparatively new development, the dissatisfaction of the bourgeoisie meant, at the very least, the weakening of the internal base of the liberal order. In Bolivia, the alienation went deeper than passive rejection of the status quo. The dependent urban-middle segments became an increasingly important support public for counter-elites, especially those of the nationalist strain.

The receptivity of the petite bourgeoisie to counter-activity was rooted in a frame of reference different from that of labor's (although it did share a certain commonality with the artisan's), since the major referent of the middle elements was their previous position. Labor, previously excluded, sought to win a new place by either adjusting, expanding, or ultimately destroying the old order. Actually, in the long run this labor movement was an increment in the composite threat to the petite bourgeoisie. The latter identified with and shared the values of the old order. Although it was effectively blocked from full participation in the things valued by the system, it previously had been afforded a guaranteed place and, at least, the illusion of upward movement. The petite bourgeoisie gave its support to the old order in exchange for security at a certain level and at least a faint possibility of upward movement.

However, inflation was eroding the basis of this exchange. The petite bourgeoisie, therefore, began to manifest resentment toward the "big" man who lived the life that he, the "little" man, desired and strove to emulate. Basic to the middle sector's problem was the fact that the economic basis of its ability to maintain a specific life style was withering away. The remembrance of things past and the existence of the national bourgeoisie as the chief stylistic reference group set the limits to the type of counter-political proposals that the dependent middle was apt to follow. State corporatism and a brand of nationalism spiced with racial and anti-internationalist allusions was the most immediately appealing idea syndrome to the middle sector. The activities of Germany and Italy were looked upon with new interest and talk of international capitalist, Masonic, and Semitic plots became common items of conversation.[25]

Unlike the labor movement, the dependent middle had no real tradition of independent group or "class" action. Its political experience was restricted to providing a legitimating audience for intra-elite faction battles and to the pursuit of minor bureaucratic careers. Hence, when threatened, the middle tended to look for a great leader for salvation. Lacking any internal political structure other than the old factionalized parties, the middle was the main social segment available for direct mobilization in the the new organizations which the youthful counter-elites were beginning to bring into existence. The middle, so used to relying on elites from higher stations to provide a secure world, possessed a closer affinity to the style and value system of the bourgeois counter-elites, especially the nationalists, than to that of the worker groups.

By 1940, the major contours of the revolutionary situation were defined. The status quo elite factions had been driven to a semblance of internal unity by a situation which, from their point of view, was getting out of hand. The formation of La Concordancia drew the line of battle between old and new in terms of implacable and incipiently violent hostility. It opened an era of challenge and reaction, violence and counter-violence, which poisoned political dialogue and destroyed any basis of common understanding.

The most significant factor of the brief period from 1936 to 1939 was the steady expansion of the scope of political conflict and the creation of new bases of political power. In the halcyon days of the old regime, political power and conflict were the preserve of the thin national bourgeoisie. The dependent petite bourgeoisie provided a passive audience for the intra-elite drama, but was not a part of what went on behind the scenes. The rest of the population was constitutionally blocked from playing even this passive role. In the 1920s, the growing thrust from below made itself felt, but did not essentially affect the framework of power and authority.

Now all that had changed. The petite bourgeoisie was wrenched from its passivity and forced to attend to the flux of national conflict, if only to shout hurrahs for the young caudillos. The labor-artisan movement was pulled into the central arena of conflict where it levied demands and flexed its considerably enlarged muscles.

Previously, elites discussed in private great affairs of state while the passive audiences concerned themselves with the problems of getting a local plaza or the like.[26] Now each governmental issue was a general public issue. Every move of the government was perceived as having great general impact, and each group openly demanded public time and attention for its demands. The activized publics pressed around the national center of decisions, pulling each issue into the realm of public clamor, and infused national decision-making with a tone of continual crisis.

Contending political elites, when weak in the primary power struggle, did not hesitate to go to the public encouraging involvement so that they could wave public passion at their opponents. Power in the old days rested upon the control of economic resources, troops, status, and office. After 1935, the power of organized numbers became, for the first time, a permanent factor in the equation of national political struggle. Opposing elites then had to struggle among themselves to harness this new power to their respective goals. Thus, the period saw experimentation, not only in social and economic relations, but also in forms of political organization. The old types of organization were incapable of structuring this new fluid phenomenon. Artificial organizations created from above and the magnet of a personal hero were, in the long run, no more successful.

The demise of Busch, who embodied in his erratic and volatile personality the contradictory pressures wracking the Bolivian body politic, brought home to all the need to forge new mechanisms and to mobilize on a sustained basis the new power of numbers. An awakened public, especially among those of the middle sector, might well look to a hero for salvation, but as the successful reaction of La Concordancia showed, this kind of relationship hardly provided a sustaining base for a regime of change. The personal caudillo approach practiced by Toro and Busch and espoused by Marof proved rather ineffective. In the next round, national political conflict would have to operate within the limits imposed by the politicization of the labor, artisan, and petite bourgeoisie publics. Both the status quo and counter-elites would have to find ways to cope with that situational reality.

6

The MNR:
From Faction
to Party

In March 1940, a transitional military junta headed by General Quintanilla conducted elections for a new government. La Concordancia ran another old guard general, Enrique Peñraranda, for the presidency. At this time, no real opposition parties existed. Peñraranda's only opposition for the presidency was José Antonio Arce, running in the name of the Students Federation of Sucre and backed by the FIB and other leftist student groups, all of which were to be consolidated into the PIR just a few months later.

The election was an attempt to reconstitute the legitimacy of the pre-Chaco War political order. Under the existing system of legally limited participation, only 60,000 votes were cast. Thus, despite the greatly increased breadth and intensity of public involvement in national political affairs, the status quo elite was seeking to base a regime upon the old, very limited electorate.

Peñraranda carried the election definitively with around 50,000 votes, but the outspoken young Marxist, Arce, with no machinery to speak of, polled over 10,000 votes. The winning of 10,000 votes from an almost completely petite bourgeoisie electorate by an open radical like Arce was an important barometer of the growing disaffection in the middle sector and the further narrowing base of support for the status quo. Actually, the anti-system inroads into the critical base of the old order were even greater. In the congressional balloting, counter-elements did quite well. Arce's supporters placed a sizeable delegation, the Marofists gained a few seats, and six individuals running as independent nationalists won clear victories. One independent, Rafael Otazo, polled 6,000 more votes in La Paz than Peñraranda.[1] It was evident that a substantial part of the critical middle sector had expressed themselves in one way or another against status quo politics. The portents for La Concordancia's ability to reconstitute Bolivian political life in the old mode were far from impressive.

During the first year of its existence, the Peñraranda regime attempted to roll back most of the reforms instituted under Toro and Busch, both in law and, more important, in practice. However, the regime did not return completely to the pre-1930 world. The divisas decree was set aside and enforcement of the labor code was allowed to lapse, but other measures, such as the establishment of the Banco Minero and the nationalization of oil, were not changed. La Concordancia had co-opted into its ranks many of those associated with the Baldivieso socialist party and most of the young Saavedrists. In doing so, the old guard leaders had captured a branch of the alienated young generation committed to some moderate reform. They did this on the theory that, to save itself, the system would have to bend with the times. However, internal pressure related to the continuance of job politics and a new political crisis began to cause problems for the new government.

Opposition elements in the congress (primarily nationalists) maintained a steady attack on the Peñraranda government. Under Peñraranda, Bolivia identified itself with the Allied cause in World War II. As the Japanese expanded their control in Southeast Asia, Bolivia became the only predictable source of tin for the Allied war effort and, thereby, assumed great strategic importance. The local industry, in turn, experienced an upswing due to inflated war demands. Despite its market monopoly, Bolivia contracted to sell tin to the United States at forty-eight and one-half cents per ton, although the world price was fifty-two cents per ton. This contract became the first big issue of disagreement between the opposition elements and the new government. The opposition flayed the government for "giving away the national wealth" (un gobierno entreguista). An important by-product of the debate was a growing concern in United States diplomatic circles regarding possible pro-Axis sympathies among the "nationalists" who led the attack.

The first year of the restauración was an important period in which the various young counter-elite groups were forced to pause and ponder their long-range situation. The leftist revolutionaries were the first to act by formalizing their views through the formation of the PIR. On the nationalist side, the picture remained confused. The experience of the two youth tendencies thus far had been quite different. The PIR was the logical culmination of the orientation and tactic followed by the leftist revolutionaries from the beginning. The nationalists, on the other hand, had already experienced a taste of governmental power, only to have the rug pulled out from under them when Busch committed suicide. They continued to have a foot in the door but, given their previous style, were somewhat at a loss as to what to do next.

As one prominent member of the group related: "We found ourselves in 1940-41, unlike the PIR, with no mechanisms to mobilize the masses."[2] Without a Busch to place them immediately in power, they were forced to think about creating a more predictable power base from which to work. The group, therefore, began to consider a broader realm of support, particularly among the clase media ("middle class") and the proletariado incipiente ("white collar workers, the new fabriles, drivers, and the like").[3] The value of aroused numbers had become apparent, and the group started to consider the possibility of stimulating wider public involvement. The key target groups were to be the restive middle sector and the more inchoate sectors of urban workers.

To this end, the Cespedes-Montenegro group of Siles nationalists held meetings with the group of independent deputies who had backed Busch. Following the PIR's lead, the conferees decided to solidify their political capital by launching a joint organization; on August 25, 1941, the MNR (*Movimiento Nacio-nalista Revolucionario*) was formed. The purpose of the group was to be "a patriotic movement with a socialist orientation aimed at affirming and defending the Bolivian nation."[4]

With the founding of the MNR, a new political era was under way in Bolivia. The change was comparable to that which took place at the end of the nineteenth century. In that period, Bolivian politics entered, for the first time, the modern dynamic of class, ideology, and party. The parties founded then were capable of changing the face of Bolivia, but were incapable of finding an internal flexibility whereby they could expand and adapt to changes around them. Instead, from the perspective of party development, they regressed to the pre-party from of personalistic elite cabals. In this regression they reflected the general nonexpansiveness and nonflexibility of the liberal order.

After 1930, this form of political organization lost its viability. The old parties lost their appeal to the elite and sub-elite youth who embarked upon a period of experimentation. Similarly, the old parties were never able to integrate aroused publics into their support structures. The older parties deteriorated and managed to survive only by drawing together into an unstable coalition. In their first experiment, the nationalist counter-elite youth flirted with new mechanisms, but relied mainly on the strength of single personalities. The fragility of this tactic and the undeniable need for means to control and direct newly awakened publics forced them to pursue new political means seriously.

The formation of the PIR and MNR, therefore, reflected many things. First, it reflected a move away from the erratic politics of personalism to that of impersonal organization and ideology. For the first time, two parties formalized in a coherent manner the two youth counter-tendencies that had been gestating at least since 1927. It reflected, also, an organizational transcendence of the old order. Despite the use of different tactics, both the PIR and the MNR started to pursue a power base among elements consciously excluded from the existing legitimate political order. Bolivia was entering the era of "mass politics" for the first time.

At this time, one of the most important aspects of politics became the expansion of the scope of conflict; that is, the degree to which publics are or are not involved directly in the national political struggle. Controlling the degree and manner in which publics were involved became the critical tactical problem of Bolivian politics. Previously, politics had been a game elites played with each other, but now it was a game that elites played with publics as well. The creation of broadly oriented parties reflected the progressive emergence of publics as a pivotal feature of political power. In the end, the prize would go to those who could best call forth and maintain public support on a variety of active levels.

From this perspective, the PIR was the more advanced of the two new organizations at first. In spite of its formalization, the MNR remained a cabal of young intellectual elitists, aware of the relevance of broader support, but not really inclined to construct institutions capable of organizing support on a sustained basis. The MNR had few or no mechanisms to maintain contact between elections. By way of contrast, the PIR, although not able to break through all the barriers, did attempt to establish a day-to-day impact on its supporting publics.

In orientation, the MNR continued to seek elite-sponsored, manipulative reform from above; the PIR continued to build for an elite-led revolution from below. Ideologically, the MNR gained considerable coherence, but, programmatically, it remained vague. The intellectual framework became Marxist but it was, according to MNR theorists, Marxism as a method rather than as a dogmatic program. More important, they claimed it was a type of Marxism used by Bolivians to understand Bolivia, and had no international aspects whatsoever. The great failing of their PIR opponents, the MNR argued, was their uncritical commitment to dogmas conceived in realities irrelevant to Bolivia. The PIR retorted, in turn, that the MNR members were pseudo-Marxists and bourgeois reformers unwilling to make the basic changes Bolivia needed.

Given its programmatic obtuseness, it is difficult to say what the goals of the early MNR were. In public, they adopted a xenophobic stance and attacked everything international, from imperialism to the Masons to the Jews. They created images of grotesquely powerful big men such as the tin barons and referred to them as the super-state. The MNR claimed that the barons (La Rosca) used Bolivia to enrich the already bulging pockets of international financiers while the Bolivian little man starved. The MNR constantly pointed to the decline of and threat to the middle class, which it summed up in the concept of *clase media empobrecida* (the "impoverished middle class"). They pointed out that not only did foreigners control the economy but they also held all the good jobs. The MNR demanded the use of Bolivian workers in Bolivian jobs.

The MNR called for support from the *obreros* ("workers") and *campesinos* ("peasants"), but mainly from the *artesanos, propietarios de la tierra, profesionales, pequenos industriales, pequenos comerciantes, estudiantes, artistas* . . . ("artisans, landowners, professionals, small industrialists, small commerce, students, artists").[5]

The party also proclaimed a series of catchy slogans:

Contra la falsa democracia—"Against false democracy"
Contra el pseudo-socialismo—"Against pseudo-socialism"
Con el Movimiento Nacionalista Revolucionario—"With the MNR"
Por la consolidación del estado y la seguridad de la patria—"For the consolidation of the state and the security of the country"
Por la liberación económica del pueblo Boliviano—"For the economic liberation of the Bolivian people"[6]

In the latter two slogans, the two prime concerns of the original MNR are evident. In the first instance, the question of the power of the Bolivian national state in a world of nation-states was raised. In the second, they argued for the subjection of the local economy to state control in order to increase the power and dignity of the state. Above all else, the MNR was concerned with the control of the Bolivian economy and the power of the Bolivian state. Nationalism was the symbolic and expressive link between these two primary, interrelated goals. At this point in time, there was little systematic discussion of programmatic means to these goals other than references to (a) restricting foreign involvement in the local economy, (b) making the state the economic regulator, (c) allowing some state control of tin profits, and (d) obtaining some kind of "justice" for the Indian peasant. The PIR, in contrast, unequivocally called for a nationalization of the mines and a thorough agrarian reform.[7]

Its xenophobia and increasingly strident anti-Semitism led to the charge that the MNR was Fascist and pro-Axis. In the case of some individuals associated with the MNR, the charge is probably accurate. In the main, however, the MNR's stance reflected its overwhelming concern with the local situation. To achieve its end, it was willing to seek help from whatever quarter, much as contemporary neutralists play both ends of the cold war. The MNR stance on the tin contract grew mainly out of a desire to capitalize for once on a favorable market position. In the long run, the MNR undoubtedly planned to hedge its bets and maneuver for a good position with whoever won the war. It wanted to be out from under Allied control, but not to become an Axis satellite.

The question of anti-Semitism was more complex. Anti-Semitism was and remains a strong force in most of Latin America. In the late 1930s, Bolivia nonetheless opened its doors to Jewish exiles fleeing from Germany. The incoming Jews were expected to become agricultural colonists in the virgin lands in the East. The majority, however, remained in the capital and became competitors, functioning at the same level as the petite bourgeoisie. The question of Jewish immigration took a bad turn when it was found that members of the diplomatic corps were selling illegal passports to the fleeing Jews. Pressed by inflation, the Bolivian petite bourgeoisie, like their German counterpart, looked for scapegoats; and, as in Germany, the big capitalists and Jewish internationalists were singled out. The image of an international conspiracy involving Jews and capitalists gained superficial plausibility by the fact that the powerful tin baron, Hochschild, was a German Jew. For these reasons, the Bolivian petite bourgeoisie, always latently anti-Semitic, became, at that time, actively anti-Semitic.

Aside from what may have been the personal feelings of individual members, the party itself was functioning in a tactical environment in which it primarily pursued the electoral support of the petite bourgeoisie. Therefore, anti-Semitism espoused by the party did not grow out of any particular attachment to nazism, but rather to a somewhat cynical manipulation of the fears current among the Bolivian dependent middle sector.[8]

The immediate strategy of the MNR was to fan the intensity of public involvement in national political conflict and to garner electoral support through rhetoric. Congress became the MNR's platform and its congressional delegation, its main action instrument. In the 1942 election, support for the MNR increased and the congressional delegation swelled to twenty. The party shrewdly used every opportunity to present its explanations of Bolivia's overall problems. The MNR spent a good deal of time raising and defining issues. In this rhetorical process, Víctor Paz Estenssoro stood out as the party's most effective spokesman. Paz soon became the unofficial head of the parliamentary delegation and ultimately became the chief of the party.[9]

The continuing air of crisis allowed the MNR to turn almost every debate into a discussion of great national issues. Tin experienced a recovery with the war demands but it was not enough to alleviate the repercussions of the country's anomalous economic structure. Inflation, shortages, etc., continued unabated and the position of the dependent middle sector deteriorated accordingly. The desire to meet war contract demands led the government to take a hard line with labor, which, in turn, was increasing the intensity of its demands for bargaining rights and wages. It was at this point that the ruling elite of La Concordancia made one of its most fateful moves in handling the labor movement.

In the first three years of the 1940s, the labor force in the mines grew rapidly from thirty thousand to fifty thousand. The reason for this quick rise was twofold. First, there was the sharp increase in demand due to the war. The now apparent policy of minimal capital reinvestment by the companies, plus the fact that the Allied countries could not ship machinery, led to massive hiring to fulfill production needs. In addition, the level of the quality of mined ore had fallen to a point where an increased labor input was more efficient than machinery. Thus, the industry was in the process of shifting from the capital-intensive operation it had been to a relatively labor-intensive operation.[10]

With the growth in the labor force, there developed a concerted drive to unionize the mining population. The companies resisted the organizing efforts and followed a policy of union-busting. The companies also attempted to quash the growing leftist political influence in the camps. Resistance was particularly acute and high-handed in the Patiño organization.

In 1942, as part of an organizing drive, the sindicato of Cataví Siglo XX (a Patiño camp and the largest single operation in Bolivia) presented a list of demands to the company. The demands were resisted and the union took its claims to the government, which did not respond. Under the threat of a strike, the companies asked for government help and a strong military force was sent to Cataví. In November, the situation grew tense and the company, in an effort to bring the miners to heel, closed down the camp store, the miners' main source of food. In December, the miners went on strike. On the twenty-first of December, the strikers and the occupying troops clashed. The troops fired on the strikers and scores were killed. The strike was finally broken, but shock waves from what was called the *Massacre de Cataví* were felt as far away as Washington.

The opposition groups flayed the government and public opinion was outraged. The situation was so grave that the United States government dispatched a high-level study mission to look into the conditions in the mines. The commission's report was highly critical of working conditions and commented particularly on the resistance of the companies to the legitimate organizational and economic demands of labor.[11] The MNR and PIR seized upon the document to launch fresh attacks.

In interpellation after interpellation, the MNR and PIR turned the events into the greatest cause celebre since the Chaco War. The *Massacre de Cataví* was considered to be the second great symbolization of the bankruptcy of the old order. In the mines themselves, syndicalization actually speeded up. The PIR increased its influence significantly. Holding high the list of martyrs, the mine camps swiftly became the bastions of the country's strongest and most radical labor organizations.

There was a certain inherent contradiction in the strategy the MNR had publicly adopted since its founding. While obviously increasing its popularity, the chances of the party's attaining power through election were quite slim. By the same token, it had not bothered to lay the organizational groundwork for a mass insurrection. As a party, it was little more than a small group of intellectuals stirring up all the fuss they could. The question arose, To what end?

However, this contradiction between ends and means was only superficial. Behind the scenes, the MNR was quietly pursuing old faction tactics to forge a direct route to the top. While the public battle of words raged, the MNR was engaged in protracted discussions with the young officers of the military. Discussion ripened into an alliance between the MNR and the *logia* ("secret society") RADEPA, an organization of young disgruntled military reformers. Before long the alliance became a conspiracy. The alliance was based on the fact the MNR needed the RADEPA's military power, and the officers wanted the aura of civil legitimacy and support that the MNR could give a military regime. On the morning of December 20, 1943, the civil-military alliance of young counter-elite staged a classic coup which succeeded without bloodshed.

The government secured, the rebels placed the previously unknown army major, Gualberto Villarroel, in the presidency and formed a cabinet with Paz Estenssoro and other Movimientistas in key economic appointments. Another period of military-based strong-man experimentation had begun. The nationalists appeared in their familiar role as high-level manipulators and advisors to the strong man. Yet, the scenario had changed a bit with the times. Villarroel had neither the manipulative flair of Toro nor the overpowering personality of Busch. The Movimientistas, in turn, were no longer starry-eyed idealists, but battle-hardened politicians. Moreover, the MNR entered the government as a small but tightly knit group used to working together, rather than a loose collection of ambitious individuals as was evident under the previous military governments. Finally, in a situation of crisis and intense public awareness, the MNR had at least the beginnings of a popular base.

Although far from pleased with the Peñaranda government's embarrassing labor policies, the Allies were, to say the least, upset with the combined MNR-RADEPA government and they refused to recognize it. After six months of lengthy diplomatic maneuverings, the Allies finally acceded recognition, but on the condition that the MNR leave the government. The provision was met, but after a cooling-off period, Paz and other MNR notables found their way back to top positions. The ousted Concordancia played up the Fascist ties of the government and tried to convince the world that theirs was the cause of democracy; a cause threatened by the Bolivian counterpart of Nazi barbarism.

The PIR at first explored the possibility of entering the Villarroel government, but was rebuffed, thereby becoming an opposition force. Eventually, its members joined the ousted Concordancia in a grand "democratic" front against the *dictadura Nazi-Fascista* ("Nazi-Fascist dictatorship").

In the Villarroel government itself, all was not well. A strong wing of the RADEPA had not wanted civil participation in the coup, particularly not that of the MNR. Partly out of personal ambition, partly out of a long-standing civil military antagonism, this group wanted to seize and use power alone. Pro-MNR officers had prevailed in the ensuing debate. The none-too-dynamic Villarroel represented a compromise choice between the powerful personalities on both sides of the issue. The anti-MNR wing, however, continued seeking to minimize MNR influence in the new regime.[12]

Villarroel at the outset played a role similar to that of Busch during the first year of his presidency. The government declared itself reformist, but in a rather vague manner. His classic statement of intention was, "We are not enemies of the rich but we are more friends of the poor." After the MNR pulled out of the government, Villarroel constituted a more widely based regime, perhaps in an attempt to regain United States confidence. In any event, during its first year and a half, the government changed little. This did not stop the opposition (ousted parties and the PIR) from mounting at least two serious coup attempts indicating that, issues aside, job faction politics was still an important factor in the dynamics of the situation.

In January 1945, the MNR returned to the government with Paz Estenssoro in the Ministry of Finance, Julio Zuazo Cueca in the Ministry of Agriculture, and German Monroy Block in the Ministry of Labor. The return of the MNR coincided with the promulgation of a new constitution which returned to the principle of the Busch document of 1938. It again affirmed the state's role as regulator of the economy and declared the interest of the state to be higher than any individual or sectoral interest.[13]

From the start, the Villarroel government followed a strict regimen of financial austerity and succeeded in stemming the inflation.[14] With the economy more or less in control and the MNR back in top economic positions, the regime made its first reformist sallies. In April, an executive decree provided that the companies would have to sell 60 percent of their foreign exchange to the government at a fixed price. At the same time, export taxes were raised. A tax was also levied on dividend payments when made in foreign currency.

These measures were followed by a set of pro-labor decrees. Under the so-called *Fuero Sindical* decree, firing without cause and transfers without consent were prohibited. The decree was important for labor's organizing efforts and was aimed at protecting organizers from company retaliation. Decrees providing for layoff benefits and a variety of bonuses were also promulgated. An important reinstated measure, promulgated originally in the Busch code but ignored thereafter, provided that after eight years of service, a worker could quit his job with the right to one month's salary for every year worked. These decrees had wider application than to the labor sector alone; they also applied to all empleados. Therefore, many sectors of the urban middle sector received benefits as well. Other measures striking at particular companies, especially the Aramayo combine, were passed.

The government also took a favorable position toward the

nascent manufacturing sector. Protective tariffs designed to improve local efforts were established. However, this measure was in part, negated by the battle against inflation which included tight restrictions on credit. The austerity program, though blocking inflation, created important and powerful enemies. Finally, for the first time, a national plan for the diversification of the economy was proposed. However, the measures included in the plan were resisted by local vested interests and the project did not materialize.[15]

The most radical experiment of the Villarroel government was the convocation of the first national Indian congress on May 10, 1945. Campesino representatives from most of the country attended. Previous to the congress, government organizers appeared in various parts of the campo ("countryside") where they encouraged local Indians to organize.[16] A national *Federación de Campesinos* was launched under the leadership of Francisco Chipana Ramos, an Indian from Sicasica in the department of La Paz.

Preceded by much fanfare, the convention raised for national discussion the profound problem of the relation of the Indian peasant population to the Spanish "national" society. Significantly, the issue of land reform was neither raised nor acted upon. Instead of examining property relations in the countryside, the convention restricted itself to the question of labor relations. At its end, Villarroel's convention issued two decrees: one abolishing gratuitous personal services known as *pongueaje;* and the other instituting the principle of wage labor into the agricultural system.

As radical a departure as it was, the convention indicated that the level of "nationalist" elite thinking about agrarian problems was still quite restricted. No one was proposing an agrarian revolution. Since Toro, the issue of agriculture and the Indian had been a national theme. But the national viewpoint, except for the Marxists, remained liberal in essence. The agrarian problem was viewed mainly as one of labor relations in which there was a need to transcend static feudal labor forms and to introduce modern contract labor forms. The Indian was looked upon as a backward being who had to be civilized in terms defined by the dominant culture's values and this problem continued to be viewed mainly as one of education. Perhaps the most significant reflection of the then-current thought on the problem, even among reformers, was the fact that the 1945 constitution maintained the concept of a restricted definition of citizenship based on literacy in Spanish.

Be that as it may, even these mild measures brought deep consternation to the landholders and disquiet to the petite bourgeoisie as well. Previously, reformist efforts had been restricted to bringing the big companies and the "national" economy to heel. This was the first time that possible changes in the vast agricultural system were seriously raised. Given the deeply ambivalent relationship which, structured by tones of racial and cultural inferiority, existed between the small dominant Spanish culture and the vast subject Indian culture, deep fears were bound to be aroused by any hint of collective movement among the Indians.

In the end, the Villarroel decrees never took effect. The landlords, by and large, simply ignored the provisions and went on as before. The real significance of the congress lay in the fact that no matter how limited in scope, reformers were contemplating basic changes in the agricultural system. More significant yet was the fact that, for the first time, reformers were exploring the possibilities of the Indian mass as an organized power base. Up to this point, the rapid extension of public involvement in political conflict had been restricted to the society's powerful but small active sectors; now the drawing of the previously inert Indian masses into the central arena became a distinct possibility.

The attention paid the Indian was only one aspect of the government's exploration into the realm of creating organized bases of support. During its parliamentary period, the MNR had become increasingly aware of the potential power of organized labor. In debates such as that on the Cataví strike, the party courted labor verbally, but in comparison to the PIR, still had no great influence on labor. Once in power again, the MNR had to face the fact that one of its principal opposition groups (the PIR) had this important support. To head off the threat of opposition from labor, the party encouraged pro-labor legislation. In addition, it began a concerted drive to dislodge the PIR from its position and to bring the labor movement under MNR control. It was another attempt, similar to that of Busch and Toro, to use political office to establish *sindicalismo dirigido* ("unions under governmental control"). The MNR initiated a policy to push the PIR out of the labor movement, although it concentrated its efforts on the more flexible and volatile mining camps.

Under Villarroel, a vicious and often bloody battle began between the two counter-elite groups for control of the labor movement. The MNR used all the resources at its command to pressure its opponents. Not unexpectedly, such persecution strengthened the PIR's resolve to aid the traditional factions in their plotting to bring the civil-military reformers down. The MNR had some success in dislodging the PIR, but it by no means completely diminished its influence. The MNR apparently had its greatest success in organizing the miners. In 1944, under MNR sponsorship, the first miners' federation—*Federación Sindical de Trabajadores Mineros de Bolivia* (FSTMB)—was formed.

The new secretary-general of the FSTMB, Juan Lechín Oquendo, had been a political unknown previous to 1944. Lechín was of Arab extraction and as such, he was the first leader of national prominence to come from a background considered to be somewhat lower than the young counter-elites who had held the spotlight since the war. After high school, Lechín gained some notoriety as a football player and later took a position as a minor government functionary in the the Cataví Siglo XX complex. In early 1944, he publicly resisted a blatant company bribe. Lechín became an instant hero to the miners. On the basis of this popularity, the MNR chose him to head the new federation. Once in a prominent position, Lechín's star ascended rapidly and he soon became one of the most powerful labor leaders in the country. Lechín had not been a member of the MNR and joined only after assuming control of the FSTMB. As part of a new political breed, Lechín quickly solidified his own power base and made it quite clear that neither he nor the FSTMB would be mere puppets of the MNR core elite.

Before the labor policy, or any other of the features developed under Villarroel could mature, the regime found itself in serious trouble. The coalition allied against the government was made up of widespread and potent forces in the society. Long-standing antagonisms between the civilian and military components of the regime weakened its internal unity. Some members of the government were actively plotting with the opposition. In July 1946, street demonstrations organized by PIR students and teachers created confusion and havoc in La Paz. PIR supporters among labor joined the demonstrations, increasing their intensity. In the face of the mounting threat, many of Villarroel's supporters openly abandoned him. On the morning of July 21, 1946, the hapless leader was trapped inside the palace, virtually stranded by a street mob. Villarroel concluded his presidency on the end of a rope attached to a lamppost in the central plaza.

With Vilarroel dead and his supporters, including the *Movimientistas,* banging upon the doors of the nearest foreign embassy, the "democratic" front again seized power and began a second "restoration." Once again, the MNR nationalist reformers had touched power by grace of backing a strong-man president. Once again, the strong man went down and, with him, the MNR.

7 The MNR: From Party to Revolutionary Movement

In MNR martyrology, the years from July 21, 1946, to April 9, 1952, are known as the *Sexenio,* the period when the faithful were persecuted, killed, and driven into an exile from which they ultimately were to return triumphant. The Sexenio marks the definitive ripening of the revolutionary situation in Bolivia. Opposition forces were moving inexorably toward violence as the major arbiter of political difference. After 1946, the incidences of violence increased to such an extent that the country entered what was essentially a state of civil war. The possibility of solving the country's basic problems within a revised edition of the old system, previously a real possibility, was diminishing daily.

On the occasion of its fall from power, the MNR was a small but relatively well-knit group of reformers. The party had demonstrated an ability to garner popular support, especially from the middle sector. It had achieved some contact with labor leaders, and it had developed a pro-labor image among workers. But none of this popular support was coherently organized or tied to the MNR on a sustaining basis. As a result of PIR and, latterly, POR inroads, there was suspicion and hostility toward the MNR in many labor quarters.

127

The grisly circumstances of Villarroel's fall indicated that accumulated bitterness was now forming into a generalized desire for vengeance. The desire for revenge carried over into a concerted attempt by the new government to crush the MNR once and for all. Following a predictable logic of conflict, this intense reaction by the second "restoration" government reflected the extent of the new threat which the MNR as an organized counterforce posed. Within the general effort of the status quo elite to crush the MNR challenge, the PIR, as part of the government, was also manipulating state instrumentalities against the MNR organization.

The PIR seized the opportunity to get a certain amount of revenge for its previous persecution by the MNR, and, at the same time, to reestablish its ascendant position with labor. There was, therefore, a double thrust against the MNR, springing from different and contradictory motives, and, perhaps for this reason, the attack was more severe. Most of the MNR leadership fled into exile; the less fortunate went into hiding. For the moment, the MNR disappeared from the political arena.

The ruling front was hardly a united or oligarchic affair. Deep splits arising from the old dynamic of job politics and post–Chaco War ideological differences plagued the governing council. The PIR obviously intended to use the opportunity to seek some basic changes. The Republican socialists, while not radical, did see the need for change before it was too late. The traditional factions and interests, however, clearly wanted to stop further change and curb that which had taken place. As the threat of MNR intervention was apparently diminished, the facade of unity broke down. In anticipation of elections to be held on January 3, 1947, the old Liberal-Republican split reappeared with a Republican coalition of factions known as the PURS girding to do battle with the Liberals. The PIR, essentially a pariah to the coalition—although a useful one—temporarily entered an electoral alliance with the Liberals (of all people).

The PURS won the election by a hair. Its candidate, Enrique Hertzog, received 44,700 votes to the Liberal candidate's (Luis Guachalla's) 44,300 votes. The total vote cast was 105,000. These results put into stark relief the anomalous state Bolivian politics had reached. In a situation of incipient civil war with the scope of public involvement in political conflict broadened and intensified, a government was being constituted on the base of 44,700 votes.[1] The entire traditional elite represented, at best, 89,000 votes; if we subtract the PIR's contribution, it is even less. The politically active population was not huge, but the big three of labor alone—*ferroviarios* ("railway workers"), *fabriles* ("factory workers"), and *mineros* ("miners")—represented close to one hundred thousand persons. The Hertzog government, starting from a pitifully small base, attempted to pacify and restore. In a real sense, the government was simply irrelevant in this context.

The PURS, as I pointed out, was a hodgepodge party formed of classical Republicans, Saavedrists, and that branch of *la generación del centenario* which was disposed to seek change, but unwilling to go the route of either revolution or radical reform. Hertzog's government was even more disparate. Perhaps sensing the need to broaden his base by including the labor sector, he invited the PIR to participate in his cabinet. The PIR, toying with notions of using progressive sectors of the bourgeoisie and having tasted the rewards of high office, made the mistake of accepting.

In MNR demonology, the PURS, which governed from 1947 to 1951, is lumped wholesale with the Liberals and the two are pictured as a united oligarchy devoted to the return to pre–Chaco War Bolivia. While such a characterization may have a tactical political utility, it obscures certain factors of interest to the observer of the revolutionary process. The record shows that the PURS thought of itself, and to some degree attempted to act, as an enlightened elite determined to salvage the system by limited reform. In one of its documents, the PURS advanced the interesting thesis that no revolution is necessary and that revolutions occurred because of the failure of the ruling class to adapt. The PURS period of rule was to become a proof (negative from their point of view) of the partial validity of this thesis.[2]

The government of Hertzog adopted a reformist public stance promising to deal with economic problems, take pressure off social groups, and maintain order. The Villarroel constitution was abrogated, but its replacement, drafted in 1947, differed only in detail and contained the same economic and social principles current since Busch. Few of the reforms made under Villarroel were openly rescinded. The truth of the matter is, however, that in practice the pressure was partially taken off the great companies, and many of the acts favoring labor were ignored.[3]

The major weakness of the PURS regime was that it was incapable of mounting a coherent policy in any one direction. The party was split deeply between reformers and old guard elements. The PURS constantly threatened to fall apart. The Liberals, in turn, took a very hostile line toward the Hertzog government. The liberal-oriented paper, *El Diario,* assailed the government for its anti-liberal policies and intimated that it was a statist and socialist regime. The status quo elite was badly split and seemed determined to weaken its ability to resist the gathering pressure for radical change.

Due to these and other factors, the PURS government was highly erratic. One day it seemed to be meeting labor's demands, but the next day was openly attempting to smash labor organizations. On one occasion the government would appear to be the puppet of the tin companies, while on the next it appeared determined to bring them to heel. Hertzog's successor, Mamerto Urriolagoitia, for example, in 1951 revived the Busch decree demanding that the companies sell 100 percent of their foreign exchange to the government. In reality, the Urriolagoitia effort was even more onerous than that of Busch, due to the fact that the rate of exchange designed for the transaction was lower than the market rate. The companies put great pressure on the government and Urriolagoitia backed off. The interchange was more or less symbolic of the PURS style: a public attempt to bring the old interests to heel, followed by humiliating public capitulation. Thereby, the image was created that despite its words, the PURS always bowed to the vested tin interest, who by now were being attacked in many quarters as the source of all of Bolivia's problems.

Continual vacilation severely weakened the already small PURS base. Sectors of the old elite came to view the government as a potential threat, partly because of its policies, partly because of its sheer incapability. At the same time, its erratic policies failed to gain any countervailing popular support. The PURS, which tried to be everything to everybody, ended by alienating everyone and putting itself in the middle to be crushed.

The PURS situation was not helped by the fact that economic crisis, partly stemmed during the war, reappeared after 1946 with new intensity. The price of tin began to drop again and, with it, government revenues. To meet its much increased obligations, the government again resorted to borrowing and the use of the printing press. Inflation picked up where it left off and grew steadily worse. High prices, shortages, speculation, etc., again plagued the major cities, setting off cries from all quarters for action.[4] More important, the companies wishing to cut production costs set out to thin down their war-inflated work forces. Unemployment and all the questions of compensation around it became nagging national questions of crisis importance.

The government brought in the PIR in an attempt to win labor support. This tactic was backed by a drive against "nonlegitimate" labor organizations and leaders (e.g., the FSTMB and other organizations associated with either the POR or the MNR). This attempt to quash popular leaders, combined with the government's erratic policies, set off an interchange between the government and labor characterized by increasing bitterness. The propaganda potential of the declared reforms of the PURS was nullified in the process. In the end, PURS bumbling in the use of violence and its open attempt to control labor was the final straw pushing labor into a revolutionary frame of mind.

The first series of clashes began in January 1947, when the Supreme Court chose to interpret the voluntary retirement clause of the labor code in such a way as to nullify the originally intended employment compensation. In protest, labor staged a wave of strikes and demonstrations beginning on the twenty-fifth of January when fabriles stoned the presidential palace. The government responded with arrests and the accusation that the MNR was behind the disturbances. The identification of the MNR with the protest was a propaganda mistake the PURS was to make with infallible regularity. In so doing, the government played into the MNR's hands by always putting itself in violent opposition to labor demands while openly identifying the MNR with those same demands. The government, in a sense, became the MNR's press agent with the labor movement.[5]

On the twenty-ninth of January, protests against the Court decision broke out in the big Hochschild mine outside of Potosí. The government ordered the arrest of the union leadership. The miners responded violently and the government moved in troops. It was 1942 all over again. Again, striking miners were shot down by government troops and a new symbol was created. The PURS became for labor *el gobierno asesino* ("the assassin government"). Agitators held up the action as further proof that when all was said and done, La Rosca was one oligarchic force: a force that would slaughter the worker before giving in to his demands.

When government troops fired on the miners, the supposedly revolutionary PIR found itself in the uncomfortable position of occupying positions in the Ministry of Labor. This was the first of many occasions which would find members of the PIR in the forefront of government anti-labor action. Naturally, anti-PIR labor leaders did not miss the opportunity to point out the contradiction between the PIR's ideology and its actions. By 1949, the PIR's critical labor support had disappeared and this once-potent counter-elite group was eliminated as a serious contender for power.[6]

In 1947, the government and labor clashed again. This time, the scene was the historic Cataví Siglo XX complex. During the war, the labor force at Cataví had been augmented considerably. In the face of declining world demand and changing technological problems in the mine, the Patiño company sought to reduce the labor force drastically. Due to the static nature of the economy, the miners resisted the layoffs as a threat to their economic existence. A derivative issue of no little importance was the fact that FSTMB organizers and leaders were the first scheduled to go. As usual, the government was placed in the middle, between labor and the companies, and again it chose to back the companies. The layoffs were enforced and a very large number of miners were denied their jobs.[7] Agitators, by now well skilled in symbol manipulation, created a new title which stuck in the public minds—*masacre blanco* (the "white massacre").

Almost daily, dramas of this nature were played out between the PURS government and labor. The next major confrontation again took place in Cataví Siglo XX—by this time, the focal point of labor resistance. In May 1949, a number of strikes took place in which the miners demanded cost-of-living increases, collective contracts, and organizational guarantees. Determined to break the FSTMB, the government deported a number of mine union leaders. The same tragic situation reoccurred; the miners reacted violently and the government replied with bullets: another massacre, another symbol, another inducement to public violence.[8]

In 1950, the script was the same but the location had changed. By this time, the labor movement was the most coherent radical force in the country. Reacting out of fear, the government attempted to break up May 1 celebrations in La Paz. The highly politicized labor leadership seized the opportunity and called a general strike which was clearly political in inception and goals. The government responded as usual with arrests and repression by troops. The affair resulted in street combat between factory workers and government troops in the workers' district known as Villa Victoria. Eventually, the government put down the strike. The troops subdued the workers, killing many in the process. The price of the government victory was a new labor symbol, *la inmolación de Villa Victoria* ("the immolation of Villa Victoria").[9] By 1950, it was obvious that there was absolutely no basis for agreement between the government and labor. The two were in a permanent state of war.

While this dialectic of ascending violence was played out between the PURS and the labor movement, a similar dialectic was in operation in another sphere. In early 1947, most MNR members came out of hiding and the MNR was back in open operation, plotting with anyone available and using every opportunity to foment social unrest. The government gave them plenty of opportunities. The PURS government responded to the revived MNR challenge with characteristic erratic violence. From the point of view of self-preservation, the government had reason to crack down on the MNR, but it made the mistake of seeing the MNR behind every social disturbance. The PURS did little to solve the real problems of social and economic dislocations generating unrest, and only provoked the public further through repression and attack against the MNR.

Every disturbance became an excuse for violent crackdowns on the MNR cadres. The MNR played on traditional norms against excessive violence towards one's political opponents and gained great public sympathy. A particularly shrewd tactic developed in the battle by the MNR involved the use of women. After one particularly severe crackdown, scores of MNR militants were hustled off to prison camps throughout the country. The next day a large numbers of wives and mothers of the arrested men crowded into the Palace of Justice and declared their intention not to eat until their men were released. The government attempted to ignore the maneuver, but after a few days, a number of women became ill and had to be rushed to hospitals. When it became apparent the women were going to hold out and that public sensibility had been deeply moved by them, the government had little choice but to capitulate.

It was a great moral victory for the MNR and a serious blow for the government. The female hunger strike became a permanent part of the MNR tactical arsenal and was used on many occasions to great effect.[10] To this were added other dramatic devices, such as public commemorative masses for the party's fallen heroes. Beyond this, the MNR simply kept its name alive and prominent. Every crackdown was followed by some grandstand tactic which proved to the public that, despite pressure, the MNR lived. The overall effect was to call the morality of the government into question and to give the MNR the image of being invincible.

As Machiavelli pointed out, violence is a dangerous mechanism to use against one's enemies; but if violence is to be used, it should be used with quick, ruthless efficiency, for a brutalized but still functioning opponent is the most dangerous opponent of all. The PURS government used violence quickly and ruthlessly, but hardly efficiently. Indeed, its style of violence offended the sensibilities of many, even among the old guard elite.[11] In 1951, a PURS minister of government (Ciro Felix Trigo) felt impelled to resign his position and publicly protest arbitrary and violent police procedures. The use of violence, therefore, had the expected negative impact on the PURS public image, but did not achieve the primary aim of destroying the victim of repression.

Between 1947 and 1951, the same cycle was continually repeated: first, there was an effort at violent repression that would set off a wave of public indignation, then, in the face of the negative public reaction, the government would declare amnesties and pardons of political prisoners. When the political climate softened a bit, the MNR would again begin to harass the government. The government, in turn, would again resort to violence, and so went the cycle. In repression, as in almost everything else, the PURS government was highly ineffective.

These multiple processes of challenge and response were played out against a backdrop of continuing economic crisis which the PURS was powerless to alleviate. By 1949, the country was in social, political, and economic chaos. The PURS regime had, by then, developed three public images; (a) one of incapacity in the face of economic crisis, (b) as implacably anti-worker, and (c) as a perpetrator of erratic, ruthless, and seemingly pointless violence.

Faced with a breakdown in public order, Hertzog fled or was pushed from the responsibilities of his office and his vice-president, Mamerto Urriolagoitia, assumed the presidency. On August 26, 1949, a nationwide revolt exploded in which all opposition groups took part. The country was in a state of open civil war. Rebel forces had remarkable success and seized control of every provincial capital and mining camp, but they failed in La Paz. Demonstrating that La Paz was still the key to political power, loyal government troops used it as a base to suppress the rebels, province by province. In two weeks, rebel resistance collapsed. Although successful in this clash, it took no fortune-teller to realize that the Urriolagoitia government was in deep trouble, as was the entire system.[12]

Internal Workings of the MNR Organization

The violent fall of Villarroel in 1946 was a traumatic blow
to the fledgling MNR. Twice the group of nationalist reformers
had been on top, and both times they were toppled (for some, as
Cespedes and Montenegro, it was three times). After 1946 a
serious rethinking of party tactics began among the exiles and
party remnants in Bolivia. Two basic lines emerged: an accom-
modationist line associated with Rafael Otazo, sub-chief of the
party; and a new revolutionary line associated with the party
chief, Víctor Paz Estenssoro.

The Otazo faction argued for a slowing down of the party's
pace and counseled a *modus vivendi* with the restoration government. Otazo expressed his sentiments to the party remnants in a
letter from exile, in which he urged an end to anti-government
activities and the fomenting of strikes by the MNR.[13]

Paz argued that there could never be an accommodation
between the old elite and the MNR. The only course left open to
the party was to plan for violent revolution. The Paz faction made
one critical point, namely that the MNR previously had confused
formal power with real power. The MNR had twice achieved
formal power, but with La Rosca in control of the mines and the
land, real power was in their hands and they could use it to
nullify the MNR reformers' efforts. It appears that at least Paz
and some others were now thinking in terms of more profound
changes—changes that would emasculate the power bases of the
status quo and thereby allow the MNR to get on with the
declared task of building a new powerful Bolivia. How many
shared this radical view and how far even the Paz group was
thinking of going is impossible to establish. The only thing that
can be said with confidence is that a large number of party cadres
made the decision to come back to power by any means available; and once there, they aimed to make sure that they would
not again be vulnerable to a coup.

This internal battle took some time and bitterness to settle.
It was not until the party convention of 1948 that the defeat and
expulsion of Otazo and his supporters was finally confirmed.

Meanwhile, leaders in the country had already begun to convert the MNR into a conspiratorial organization girding for violent revolution. Under the new line, and particularly after 1948, the MNR consciously sought to build a mass base. In the process, it was slowly converting itself from an elite faction oriented toward reform from above into an elite-led movement pursuing revolution from below.

The major tactic of the new offensive was to fan the intensity of social conflict and draw wider and wider sectors of the populace into the political arena. The task was undoubtedly made easier by the bumbling of the PURS government and the growing economic crisis. The growth of the MNR in this period is complex and must be looked at in terms of social sectors as well as phases.

The first MNR step in the new direction was the creation of a nationwide party organization. The new command organ of the party was the *Comité Político Nacional* ("National Political Committee") located in La Paz and staffed by old-time party members. Between 1946 and 1952, membership in the Comité varied little. The Comité's social composition in this period was almost exclusively middle- and upper-bourgeois professionals and intellectuals. Beneath the central committee was a system of regional and local commandos; below these was a system of party cells in which the members were theoretically unknown to each other. The little evidence available indicates that the commandos were likewise made up of urban bourgeois types, but often of lower status. In addition to this main network, there were special sectors, such as the *sector femenino* ("women's sector"), the *sector militar* ("military sector"), and the *sector obrero-artesano* ("worker-artisans' sector").[14]

The latter sector was definitely more artisan in membership than worker. In 1947 and 1948, the MNR made organizing sallies among taxi drivers, truck drivers, and other similar groups. Some contact was also made with fabril leaders, but they were very tenuous and, in some instances, fraught with hostility.[15] In 1951, the sector obrero-artesano evolved into what became known as *Los Grupos de Honor* ("The Groups of Honor"). Los Grupos were a series of paramilitary cells located mainly in La Paz and

Cochabamba. They had their own executive body, some members of which belonged to the national committee; this new organization, however, numbering between five hundred and eight hundred, acted, in the main, independently of the national head. Near the end of the Sexenio, Los Grupos began to evolve into the terrorist-type bodies so common to revolutionary situations of long duration. The social composition of the organization was mainly lower middle, artisan, less well-organized workers of small factories, and elements of the *clase popular* (an unclassifiable urban lower group).

In the early period (1948-49) the overall party was widespread, but its commando groups were small. Tactics were very poorly coordinated and intra-party communication was almost nil. The national committee was the major source of activity, but operated largely by itself. At times, coordinated efforts were made but the party was still essentially a bourgeois elitist cabal in terms of effective action.[16]

Aside from organizing efforts, the party girded for battle in a variety of ways. Over the years, it accumulated as many weapons as possible and built a substantial arsenal. The national committee maintained continual conspiratorial contact with the FSB (right-wing nationalists) and young military groups. In coordination with these groups, innumerable abortive Villarroel-type coups were attempted. In addition to these contacts, possible alliances with disgruntled elements of the old elite factions were also explored. Throughout the period, although broadening its base, the leadership demonstrated its continuing preference for the old shortcut to power (that is, a coup in alliance with almost anyone willing).

The loosely knit cellular structure under a central committee made up what can be called the MNR primary system of operation. Throughout the late 1940s it grew rapidly, probably reaching its high point around 1951. This party system was substantially different from anything the MNR had been previous to 1946. The party had indeed become a movement with a sustaining base. In addition, the principle of a seizure of power through widespread violence was accepted and attempted in 1949. But the old intra-elite faction style did carry on into the new period.

If possible, a coup which would make the MNR a partner in a new reform coalition government was still preferred.

The MNR primary organization was still rather restricted in social scope. It was mainly a city phenomenon which primarily incorporated the petite bourgeoisie, artisans, workers in small factories, and the sub-employed. In other words, the primary party system was a focal point of mobilization for those social elements heretofore unorganized either economically or politically. The primary system gathered those elements progressively alienated due to inflation, scarcities, and unemployment, but who had no previous outlet for their frustrations. These elements made up the main MNR membership in a psychological as well as organizational sense.

The MNR and Its Relationship with Labor

The MNR's relations with the labor public during this period of permutation were complex and difficult to grasp. Governments in which the MNR had participated had adopted pro-labor stances, but the MNR elite always showed a preference to approach labor from a position of power, rather than to use labor as a means to power. MNR contacts with labor had always been in terms of creating government-sponsored organizations. As a result, in the labor movement, there was a certain suspicion toward the MNR elite. In many quarters they were considered bourgeois reformers who only wished to co-opt labor into a system of government-controlled unions. Given the MNR's style of operation, the suspicion was well founded.

After 1946, those in the MNR who adopted the revolutionary line began to think of labor for the first time as a mobilizable base from which to pursue power. However, the labor movement, which by the late 1940s had gone through a long period of internal growth, had its own leaders with independent ideas regarding political power and its uses.

In 1946, there were three dominant labor groups: railway workers (ferroviarios), miners (mineros), and factory workers (fab-

riles). Due to the time sequence of their appearance as groups
and the organization of their respective work activities, these
groups evolved separately and were largely isolated from each
other and the society at large. The ferroviarios were the first
proletarian group to appear and to reach organizational maturity.
They played an important role in the pre-Chaco War artisan-
labor phase. After the war, all railway workers were consolidated
into a strong national organization.

Socially, the ferroviarios were made up of well-acculturated
Indian and mestizo elements. By and large, they were social types
already associated with urban areas and the national system before
being transformed into workers. The ferroviarios traveled widely,
but, in the main, lived in barrios around the major railheads or
encampments along the lines. This pattern made for strong group
cohesiveness, but also created strong particularism.

The fabriles were the last labor group to be organized. As
a group of any consequence, they came into being after the war,
along with the small boomlet in manufacturing. Socially, the
fabriles came from previous urban marginal groups and the urban
influx of Indians after the war. On the whole, they were less
well acculturated by the national system. Fabril organization was
much more primitive; sindicatos were in operation at the factory
level, but a functional federation only came into existence on the
eve of the 1952 uprising. The fabriles were, therefore, a much
less politicized group, a factor reinforced by the fact that most
worked in small traditional-type factory operations.[17]

As over 70 percent of the country's manufacturing activity
was located in the capital, the fabril group was, in the main, a
La Paz phenomenon. They lived in separate barrios in the city's
upper reaches. A fairly large concentration lived in the factory
town of Viacha located on the altiplano near La Paz. Besides
living in such barrios, there was a tendency for workers of a factory to live and socialize with each other. Thus, although in the
city, they lived relatively isolated lives, and formed small groups
with traditionalistic life styles. Particularism was also strong among
these workers.[18]

By far the most isolated group was the miner. The pattern
of the miners' development was also distinct. The ferroviarios

and fabriles were formed out of previous semi-urban types with a high mestizo admixture. The miners were formed by the direct conversion of Indian peasants into workers. The miner is traceable to the old Spanish form of forced labor imposed upon the conquered Indian population. Out of these forced drafts, over the years a small but identifiable group of miners evolved, working mainly in silver extraction.

When the tin industry got off the ground in the late nineteenth century, the original corps of workers was drawn from the small coterie of silver miners. As the industry progressed, the original workers were supplemented by contract labor recruited among the Indian peasants. Most of the contract laborers came from the Quechua people of Cochabamba and Potosí. The contracts were usually short term. There was, therefore, a floating population of peasants who worked for a few months and then returned home. Over the years, increasing numbers remained in the camps and the resident population grew.

During the late twenties and early thirties, the tin industry was consolidated and the big operations rationalized. Although surrounded by a sea of labor, the advancement from pick and shovels to the use of machines demanded a higher level of skill than contract peasant labor could provide. The companies, therefore, sought, through a variety of means from inducement to coercion, to create a stable population of skilled personnel. The use of floating labor continued, but the major camps began to settle into complex and fairly stable communities. These camp settlements increased substantially during the labor-intensive phase of World War II. In the big camps, a large and relatively self-conscious proletarian population began forming in the 1920s and consolidated itself in the early 1940s. Contacts were kept with home areas, but the miner as a separate social type was created.[19]

The mining camps, especially the large ones like Cataví Siglo XX, were, in reality, isolated individual societies. Given the means of his recruitment, his job, and his living pattern, the miner, although an integral productive component of the national system, had little real contact with it. The camps had their own stratification structure which ran from company administrative and technical personnel (upper class) through low-level empleados (middle class) to the workers (lower class). The miner worked for the company, which at the same time acted as his effective government. The companies controlled administrative, judicial, and police functions. The camps were a kind of third sociopolitical system. The miner experienced national authority mainly as a kind of foreign ally of the company.

The organization of these three labor groupings reflected the general compartmentalization of prerevolutionary Bolivia. We can speak of labor groups which in one way or another related to the national system, but we cannot speak of a working class as such. The so-called labor movement was, in the first instance, a mix of semi-traditional groups and more modern ones. In the pre–Chaco War phase, the orientation of the former dominated, while, in the post–Chaco War phase, the latter struck the dominant tone. Throughout, there was a strong tendency toward particularism and the pursuit of perceived group interests before "class" interests. The social composition mix and the tendency toward particularism plagued attempts to form industry-wide federations, let alone class-wide confederations. In 1936, the CSTB was formed and persisted until 1952, but it never established itself as anything close to the singular voice of Bolivian labor.

An important characteristic which set off the more specifically modern proletarian groups from the more traditional artisan groups and the urban middle was the forward thrust of their basic orientation. While the artisan and urban middle groups were reacting to and opposing the modernization impulse, the worker was becoming an integral part of it. The worker's lot was hardly pleasant, but, in most cases, it was a distinct improvement over floater or peasant status. At the least, it brought the worker into a qualitatively different world where, often for the first time, he experienced a money exchange system and the complexities and possibilities of modernism. To the extent that Bolivia experienced the phenomenon of "rising expectations" associated with modernization, it was found mainly among the worker groups. The workers experienced a taste of this kind of advancement and demanded more. Indeed, it seems that the better off the group was, the more radical it tended to be. The United States commission investigating conditions in the mines after the 1942 Cataví slaughter concluded that, though the conditions were bad, the miner was relatively better off than any other worker group.[20]

The laboring groups were not driven by poverty alone. They were pushed more by the persistence of relative poverty after the possibility of better things had been offered and experienced. The movement radicalized and became political when its upward drive clashed with the stagnation and regression gripping the system. After 1940, labor was demanding more of a dwindling pie, and at the same time, trying to safeguard what it already had from the perils of inflation, layoffs, and the like.[21] The middle and the artisan groups reacted mainly to the losing of a world, while labor reacted mainly to the possibility of gaining a world. The former responded to anarchist, corporatist, and the gamut of state nationalist appeals, while the modern labor group responded to revolutionary socialist appeals which projected a totally new order in which the worker would be ascendant.

The early artisan-labor push was strong enough to push through some "social" legislation under the Republican party government of Bautista Saavedra (1920-25). The same government, however, smashed attempts by miners to organize in 1923. The artisan-labor movement became stronger after 1925. Also, there were short-lived attempts to launch "socialist" parties. Strikes and labor agitation bloomed significantly between 1929 and 1932, but like everything else, disappeared with the war. After the war, activity reappeared at a new and stronger level. Between 1935 and 1940, the movement was still dominated by artisan and employee groups; neither miners nor factory workers were as yet dominant factors. The movement was largely "nonpolitical," and mainly sought to pressure the middle-class military reform governments to pass pro-labor legislation. These governments did so out of the fear of a leftward shift by labor, and in an attempt to harness labor to some kind of corporate state.

Between 1940 and 1945, the most significant development was the appearance of the miners as an organized force. The character of the movement changed drastically. Leadership shifted definitely from artisan to worker groups—specifically to the min-

ers and ferroviarios. From the political point of view, this was
the movement's real formative period. The period was marked
by labor's first sustained contact with middle-class counter-elites.
Through the PIR and the POR, a new political orientation was
shaped, and it was in a revolutionary socialist direction.

With the fall of Villarroel, the definitive revolutionary push
began in Bolivia. It was marked by a drawing together of a basically middle-class reformist movement epitomized by the MNR
and the advancing revolutionary labor movement.

In retrospect, the politicization and radicalization of the labor
movement is tied to two basic factors. First was the collision
of the upward drive of labor with the stagnating Bolivian system.
Economic reality was such that it would have been difficult for
management to meet labor's demands even if the will had been
there. In point of fact, the demands were resisted assiduously by
the companies. In this deadlock between labor and management,
the role adopted by the government became critical. A definite
pattern appeared: under Salamanca, the government allied with
the companies and smashed labor; under Toro and Busch, labor
prospered relatively; under Quintanilla and Peñaranda, the government again aligned with the companies and viciously attacked
labor; under Villarroel, the government was again pro-labor; in
1946, a new round of anti-labor reaction was again setting in.

Between 1935 and 1946, labor advanced in absolute terms,
but the advance was punctuated by sharp reactions. Both advancement and reaction was influenced by government. Labor learned
that its advancement depended on the existence of friendly governments. It also learned that, in the existing context, governments friendly to labor were vulnerable to overthrow. It became
clear, therefore, that the development of labor as political power,
a changing of the political context, and some control of the state
by labor were the *sine qua nons* of labor's future status in Bolivia.
Given this knowledge gained from experience, the Marxist theory
of politics made sense to the labor movement. Labor, therefore,
expanded its bread-and-butter demands into demands for political
control.

After 1940, an important factor in the politicization of labor
was the beginning of its first sustained contact with young bour-

geois counter-elites. These contacts were mainly with members of the PIR and POR, and, together, they shaped the new political orientation in a revolutionary socialist direction. This wing of the alienated young generation left a lasting impression on labor with its use of rhetoric, symbols, slogans, and programs. After 1946, the PIR was compromised and lost its influence on labor. The POR, in contrast, since 1940 had been converting itself into a group with heavy proletarian influence. The POR concentrated mainly on the miners, where it bored deeply into local sindicato organizations. By 1946, the POR was firmly ensconced in the mines. Although the FSTMB had been an MNR-sponsored effort, members of the POR were prominent in its executive committee.

In 1946, then, the labor movement was highly politicized and functioning in a revolutionary Marxist framework. Although strong due to its strategic economic position, Bolivian labor was neither large enough in size nor developed enough organizationally to carry out its own revolution. The many abortive socialist parties proved this. When the PIR compromised its credibility, labor was left without a national political instrument. The POR, although influential, was too localized to fill the gap. The movement's leadership, including those of the POR, realized that a more viable vehicle was needed.

At the same time, the bourgeois-based MNR had also learned it could not go it alone. The ground was laid for a drawing together of the basically bourgeois reformist movement epitomized by the MNR and the advancing revolutionary labor movement. The motors pushing the two movements were fundamentally different and potentially contradictory. The two approached each other with mutual suspicion and caution; within both there were elements which counseled against the marriage. The active period from 1935 to 1946 was one in which young bourgeois elites, backed by an inflation-threatened middle sector, pressured for reform from above. Then, labor played the role of pushing from the outside and limiting action. After 1946, labor began to join the central struggle directly. Labor became the ascendant factor pushing the nation along the path of revolution.

Aside from the less organized sectors of the fabriles, labor was not directly integrated into the MNR primary structure.

The various major worker groups had their own organizations and segmental leaders. For the organized workers, the fulcrum of identification and their day-to-day lives were shaped by their sindicatos and their chieftains. Between the MNR elite and the labor public stood the local sindicato, the functional federation, and, to some extent, the national confederation. The labor movement remained an independent force, the sectoral elites of which were consciously exploring the possibility of an alliance with the MNR elite. Within labor, there were powerful centrifugal tendencies based on specific occupational clusterings rather than on class. The MNR never, in any meaningful sense, achieved control of its key labor groups. Instead, the MNR became the chosen national political instrument of the labor leadership.[22]

Some further differentiation must be made. As I noted before, many artisan, empleado, and semi-proletarian elements did enter the party directly and, for them, it became the focal point. The powerful ferroviarios, on the other hand, maintained a strict distance from the party and, despite the political demise of the PIR, their leaders were always considered to be basically PIR-istas. When they found it tactically advantageous, these leaders cooperated with the MNR.[23]

The relationship with the miners was even more confused. The MNR had gained a foothold in the mines in 1944 through the FSTMB and the affiliation of Lechín. The MNR fell with Villarroel, but Lechín did not fall as leader of the FSTMB. His power in the mines was based on worker organizations, not on the stability of the MNR. During the period of MNR reorganization, Lechín was isolated and forced to operate on his own. At this time, he pulled close to the POR which controlled many of the sindicatos affiliated with his federation. Lechín formed an alliance with the POR, and its influence obviously became greater than that of the MNR in the FSTMB.

In 1946, the FSTMB drafted its first ideological statement, known as the *Tesis de Pulacayo*. This document was written by the Trotskyite leader of the POR, Guillermo Lora. The central concepts of the document contradicted those of the MNR. The MNR called for a movement based on the notion of "nation" versus "anti-nation"; the *Tesis* projected implacable internal class conflict. The MNR projected a multi-class movement led by the middle-class elite; the *Tesis* spoke of the necessary leading role of the proletariat in any revolution. It also differed from the MNR on numerous other important points.[24]

The MNR, which had some influence in the mines through Lechín, was, to this extent, always rooted in an alliance (often an uneasy one) with the POR. The alliance was based on the fact that the MNR needed labor might, while the POR labor leaders saw the MNR as the only more or less pro-labor group which stood a chance of gaining governmental power. The aim of the POR was to use the MNR nationally, while pushing it in a more and more radical direction.[25]

The Villarroel interlude created a favorable sentiment toward the MNR among the rank and file of workers. In national elections, especially in 1951, this sentiment was often expressed in the casting of the workers' ballots—due to restrictions there were not many—for MNR candidates. In the crucial sindicato elections, on the other hand, followers of Lechín and members of the POR dominated. The MNR leadership never called the shots in the mines or in the other chief labor organizations.[26]

Even after striking an alliance of sorts, the MNR central leadership and the FSTMB leadership operated independently of one another. The MNR attacked every anti-labor act of the PURS to its favor, but, at the same time, it entered into pact after secret pact with the FSB and the military logias to seize power without direct labor aid. Likewise, Lechín and other nominal MNR union leaders followed their own tactics, quite often ignoring directives from the Comité Político Nacional of the party. An important factor inhibiting closer contacts between the miners and the MNR leadership was the isolation and working conditions of the mining camps. It was not the style of the MNR bourgeois elite to spend any considerable time in the mining camps, or in any non-urban place for that matter. The MNR milieu was the capital and it was there that they preferred to live and plot.

The problematic nature of the relationship of the MNR elite with labor was apparent in a number of ways. Previous to the 1947 elections, the MNR national committee sent party slates to Lechín and his group. The slates were ignored. The FSTMB did not even run candidates under the MNR name, but, rather, formed a *bloque minero* ("miners' bloc"). The candidates elected by this block were Lechín, Mario Torres, and the POR leader, Lora—other PORistas also were elected.[27] In the La Paz municipal elections of 1947, the party approached local fabril organizations and asked them to run candidates; the groups refused and disavowed further contact with the MNR.[28]

In September 1947, the bank employees and the fabriles went on a concerted strike for cost-of-living increases. The MNR contacted the leaders and encouraged the strike. At the same time, it plotted with young officers and police officials to mount a coup. The plan was to use the strike as a screen from behind which to grasp power. The entire plot failed when the government called in the bank employees to meet their demands; whereupon the bankers went back to work.[29] The fabriles, left alone, had little choice but to return to work, having gained nothing. The case was typical of the situation. It showed that the MNR could not control labor activity to its own political ends. It also demonstrated the particularism among labor groups and the easy way in which one group could be played off against the other.

Another aspect of importance was the fact that the Comité Político Nacional and other top directive bodies of the MNR did not include, until very late in the game, any labor leaders; even then never more than a few were named. The same names representing the original MNR elite composition and orientation occur over and over in the leadership lists. Clearly, the old-line MNR elites guarded their top positions jealously. They were willing, if necessary, to use labor, but they had no intention of allowing the labor sector elites to achieve control positions. They would have much preferred to come to power without labor and they tried to do so any number of times with their old military allies. Of necessity, they talked revolution, but they still acted as elitist reformers. However, the times were changing and national conflict was becoming generalized. The MNR elites' ability to control the flow of forces and events was slipping.

The first major joint effort of the MNR and labor was in the civil war of 1949. In that action, the hard-fighting miners proved their worth and strength beyond question. Likewise, in the general strike of 1950, the power and importance of labor was proved. Even as labor demonstrated its power, the incessant coup failures began to call into question the viability of the MNR's old techniques and allies. In 1951, the MNR actively set about to build a mass base, and labor was the key to its stepped-up efforts.[30]

The government called elections for May 14, 1951, and the MNR decided to enter. The MNR used the occasion not only to court votes, but also to win the support of those elements excluded from the electoral process. It sought not only office, but generalized legitimacy. In the campaign, the impact of the labor-left axis on the MNR became evident. Openly and secretly, the MNR sought alliances on the left with the POR and a new-born Communist party formed by disaffected PIRistas (*Partido Comunista de Bolivia* or PCB). More important, the party for the first time publicly committed itself to a specific program which included nationalization of the mines, agrarian reform, and universal suffrage. The MNR had, in effect, adopted the program of the revolutionary socialist tendency now being pushed mainly by a labor-left axis.[31]

As later events would demonstrate, the adoption of this program was primarily a tactical move for most of the in-country MNR elite. Actually, the party leadership was split on many questions: some were against one or all of the measures, while others who might have been for the concepts in principle had somewhat less than radical ideas as to what they would entail. However, the fact remains that the MNR leadership had embarked on a rhetorical road from which it would be difficult to return.

The MNR had decided after 1946 to broaden itself into a mass-based movement. Apparent success in this tactical move meant that the party became more reliant on the ascending power of the labor public. With each new increment in the scope and intensity of public politicization, labor drew closer to the MNR, but the price was the increasing radicalization of the party. In the 1951 campaign, it was evident that the new mass-oriented MNR was adapting to, rather than controlling, the motor forces of the ongoing revolutionary situation. At that point, the strongest force intensifying and radicalizing conflict was the Marxist-programmed, miner-dominated labor movement.

8
The Insurrection

The MNR's decision to participate in the elections of May 14, 1951, turned out to be a master stroke. The old elite factions were incapable of creating a united front for purposes of the election. Urriolagoitia called for an alliance of the PURS and Liberals in a democratic front to stave off the MNR challenge, which was now painted as being both Nazi and Communist. The Liberals refused, choosing, rather, to berate the PURS for leading the country to bankruptcy. Within the PURS organization itself, dissension had become bitter and open. The party broke into warring factions on the issue of a presidential candidate, and the party began to crumble. Not an infrequent charge on all sides was that of crass office-seeking. Finally, a large block, under the leadership of the prestigious Demitrio Canelas, withdrew from the PURS to form an electoral front called *Acción Civica* ("Civic Action").

The months preceding the elections were chaotic. The remnants of the PURS were attacked viciously from every quarter—left, right, and center. In editorial after editorial, the liberal-oriented *El Diario* painted a picture of economic chaos, police brutality, and total governmental absurdity. The mining association, dominated by the "Big Three," took full-page ads accusing the government of unwarranted intervention in the economy and

151

capitulation to leftists. The association of manufacturers followed suit, blasting the government for giving in to "Communist" union demands. Rumors of coups sponsored by the tin companies were rife. There was also widespread talk of military intervention.

A similar din was raised on the left. Strikes were daily occurrences, as were demonstrations by students and civic groups. On some occasions, the government gave in to popular demands, while on others it carried out widespread arrests and deportations. *El Diario* charged that never had so many Bolivians been forced to live outside their country. In characteristic fashion, these crackdowns were followed by amnesties, and a number of important leaders, including Lechín (exiled after the civil war of 1949), returned. There were more reports of coup plots by a bewildering array of left-right combinations.

On the left itself, the picture was one of confusion. The newspapers speculated daily on new electoral alliances, formulas, and splits. The MNR one day was said to be in league with the Communists, and, on the next, dissident elements were said to be negotiating with the PURS. As it turned out, there was a left-right split in the MNR. The right wing was seeking a moderate electoral alliance, but Paz threw his weight in support of the leftist. The MNR worked out an agreement so that both the PCB and the POR could support its presidential and vice-presidential candidates.

Amid violence, mutual recrimination, and disorder, Bolivia went to the polls. On the eve of the 1951 election, a small drama epitomizing the contradictions in the PURS approach was played out. After following an erratic labor line for years, the government made a last-minute bid for miner support. It decreed a 32 percent salary increase and corresponding raises and fringe benefits. The companies, through the mining association, openly defied the government. They refused to obey the order and actually threatened to reduce salaries if the government persisted.[1] In the face of this open defiance, what was left of the PURS limped rather feebly into the electoral fray.

When the vote was in, to the surprise of all and the chagrin of most, the MNR had won. The MNR polled 54,049 votes, while the PURS, its nearest rival, turned in a weak 39,940 votes. The once-dominant Liberals gained only a humiliating 6,441 votes. To the extent that the PURS was known as a reformist and mildly socialistic party, the vote indicated a complete repudiation of a pure liberal system and a generalized desire for some kind of reform and change. If we remember that the vote reflected only the sentiment of the upper and middle bourgeoisie, artisans, and a few workers, the results take on a profound significance.

Looking into the results more closely, the situation becomes even more interesting. The MNR took La Paz definitively with 17,501 votes compared to the PURS's 10,667 votes. It also triumphed in Cochabamba, Oruro, and Potosí. In all other departments, it lost. The indication is that the MNR carried active "national" Bolivia while dropping the more isolated and traditional regions. Given the critical nature of the capital and the ancillary cities of the national system, the MNR showed its strength where it counted. The party could obviously claim wide support among the key social bases of political legitimacy.[2]

Assuming that a large part of the PURS was really a reformist wing of the traditional elite, when we combine its votes with the votes of the Liberals and *Acción Cívica,* we get a total of 52,941 votes, representing support for the broadest definition of the status quo. Alone, the MNR beat this total figure, which reflected the combined strength of what had been La Concordancia of 1940. The PIR, it would seem, had been a most important element in the democratic front's seizure of power in 1946. Now following an independent line, the discredited PIR received only 5,170 votes. Realizing that the POR and PCB supported the MNR, we can get a rough estimate of the center-left sentiment in the country by adding the votes of the PIR to those of the MNR for a total of 59,219 votes. Thus, taken purely on its own terms of definition, the extant political system was completely polarized; the center-right represented 52,940 votes and the center-left, 59,219 votes. If we then take into account the excluded, but obviously leftist sentiment of labor, the drift away from the old order is patent. Within this polarized and left-drifting situation, the pivotal role held by the MNR in the dimension of civil politics was unmistakable.

Having failed in this last attempt to defend itself by the legal rules of the game, the elites and interests associated with the old order turned to the military. Although the MNR polled a plurality, it did not achieve the needed majority to immediately assume power. According to the constitution, the election should have then gone to the congress. Given the disarray of the traditional factions, however, what would have come out of any such polling was anyone's guess. Rather than take the chance, the military, supported by the tin companies, the Liberals, and sectors of the PURS, forced Urriolagoitia to turn over the government to a military junta.

The junta, headed by General Hugo Ballivian, declared that their action was not a coup, but an assumption by the military of its duty to protect democracy and freedom from a combined Communist-Nazi menace. A state of seige was declared, strikes were made illegal, and leftist political and labor leaders were arrested. A document purporting to reveal a pact between the MNR and the PCB was made public. On the basis of the document, the MNR was declared illegal until such time as it broke relations with the Communists.

The military's biggest selling point was that they would impose order, reintroduce efficiency, and solve the country's economic problems. Its first vigorous decrees indicated that it might well be able to supply the tranquility so dearly wished for. Pledges of support came from all directions. By all odds, the junta had an auspicious beginning. However, unless the military was willing to make basic structural reforms, it was questionable as to what exactly it could do, aside from forcing the population to accept a situation which, in the main, it evidently rejected. Basic reforms were not in the junta's mind, however, and soon there was social, economic, and political chaos, as usual. Support rapidly turned into opposition and, before long, the junta was reeling from the same kind of blows which bloodied the PURS. The junta's reaction was the same: erratic stumbling from one crisis to the next.

The economic situation continued to deteriorate. The three

old evils besetting the economy since the Chaco War were at work: inflation, unemployment, and scarcities. Behind these continued the structural problems of a bifurcated economy, a sick tin industry, and a bankrupt government. The absurd fiscal situation of the country became clear in 1950 when Bolivia resumed the servicing of its foreign debt; the single largest budget item became the payment of the interest on the debt. Of the little remaining, the single largest amount went to national defense; indeed, in its projected budget the new military junta earmarked more for defense than for servicing the debt.[3] *El Diario* assailed this budget as sheer idiocy and blasted the junta in the same style it had used to beat the PURS over the head.

The 1952 budget, like those in the late 1920s, was earmarked mainly to meet debt obligations and the demands of the military. In the interim the government had assumed a raft of welfare obligations deriving from the Busch, Villarroel, and Hertzog constitutions. With little more government income now than in the 1930s, these obligations could not be met. As a result, labor set off a new wave of strikes which demanded wage increases as well as the meeting of promised social security obligations. Financially, the country was again in a state of collapse.

As if all of these difficulties were not enough, a new spectre arose. The United States government announced a general rollback of the price it would pay for tin, and its further intention to reduce stockpiles accumulated during the Korean War. The entire country reacted violently. The military government claimed the United States action was nothing short of a mortal blow to the Bolivian economy. The total economic dependency of Bolivia on tin and of tin on the United States was never so evident, and the left sat back with a satisfied, "I told you so." Charges of economic warfare, imperial aggression, etc., long the stock phrases of the MNR, were raised now by the old factions and the companies.[4] Negotiations with the United States over the price of tin became the single biggest issue of public concern. After months of negotiations characterized by bitter acrimony, the United States relented a bit, but tentatively fixed a price much below what Bolivia had demanded. The junta had little choice but to accept.[5]

The outcome of the price negotiations was a serious blow to the prestige of the junta. By all accounts the interchange confirmed the criticisms of the economy sounded by the counter-elites since 1935. The junta's capitulation, after months of whipping up nationalist sentiment, was humiliating in the extreme. Moreover, who could any longer believe that a government so feeble in protecting the most vital aspect of the national economy could really do anything to solve the full range of economic and social problems grinding away at every sector of the population?

Like the PURS before it, the junta was soon encircled by both leftist and rightist groups, probing for the softest place to strike. After Ballivian made some ominous statements that the military might have to rule for perhaps twenty years, the traditional civil factions began trying to reformulate a Concordancia-type "democratic" front. The MNR, as might be expected, began plotting day and night with everyone and anyone looking for a formula to power.

Also, like the PURS before it, the junta was falling apart internally. Ballivian was in open conflict with the chief of staff of the army, General Torres Ortiz. Rumors were circulating that Torres would not be loath to fill the presidential seat. Behind the scenes, other ambitious members of the junta were plotting as well. One, the minister of government, General Antonio Seleme, opened protracted negotiations with the MNR Comité Político Nacional.

By early spring, the question was not whether or not the junta would fall, but when it would fall and by whose hand. The MNR was determined that it would be the agent of Ballivian's political demise. The contacts with Seleme were stepped up and a coup plan formulated. Simultaneously, negotiations were begun between the MNR and the FSB and General Torres. One formula promised that Torres would be president and the FSB strongly represented in the cabinet. At the last minute, Torres backed out and the FSB hesitated. Fearful of exposure, the MNR decided to go ahead with Seleme and moved the date of the planned coup from April 15 to April 9. The original formula was for Seleme to become president in a united MNR-military cabinet. There was also strong sentiment on the MNR right to cut out Paz Estenssoro and make Hernan Siles Zuazo, then sub-chief of the party and leader on the scene, vice-president.[6]

On the morning of April 9, MNR civil elements (*Los Grupos de Honor*) of La Paz, in conjunction with the national police (*carabineros*) under Seleme's command, initiated an insurrection. The uprising involved relatively few people and was restricted to La Paz. After some initial success, the rebellion began to lose steam. The bulk of the military remained loyal and moved to crush the rebellion. By the end of the first day, the insurrection appeared doomed and Seleme sought asylum.

However, Siles and other leaders refused to capitulate and rallied the party. By afternoon of the second day, the rebellion had caught on and was spreading. Heavy action took place in Cochabamba, Oruro, and Potosí. Captured weapons were distributed to fabriles in La Paz. Armed workers from the nearby factories of Viacha also began moving toward the capital. The tide was dramatically turned when armed miners from the Milluni mine seized the railroad station above the city, capturing, at the same time, a munitions train. The final step occurred when armed miners encircled the city of Oruro, thereby cutting off possible reinforcements for the capital. With armed miners above the city and rebels controlling the center, the capital troops were trapped without hope of reinforcement. After a final heroic but pointless stand by students of the military college, the government fell. On April 11, 1952, the MNR found that it possessed its long desired prize, and for the first time, nominally at least, on its own hook.

While all the details are far from clear, it seems safe to say that the MNR discovered itself in control of formal power under somewhat unexpected circumstances. The original plan smacked strongly of a Villarroel-type formula, that is, a rapid coup involving little civil participation, followed by a military-civil coalition government. There is some reason to believe that this was a conscious decision on the part of some leaders, due not just to tactical exigencies, but also out of a desire to diminish the role of labor in the coup and its influence in any following government. This rationale was probably behind the desire to put Siles in the vice-presidency rather than Paz, who had become known as a bit more radical. In other words, there are good reasons to believe that the in-country MNR elite was aiming at establishing a Villarroel-type reformist regime in which labor could have a secondary role, at best.[7] What would have transpired if the original time schedule had been maintained and if the miners had not entered into the fray is impossible to say; but after three days of strong fighting which led to progressively broader social involvement, the MNR, which had for years been a party of reformers, was about to become the sponsor of Latin America's second "great" revolution.

Before examining the revolution itself, it would be well to take a closer look at the structure of the party which assumed governmental authority on August 11, 1952.

Structure of the MNR as a Political Party

Between 1946 and 1952, the continuing economic problems of the country and the erratic and ineffective policies of the PURS fostered a steady growth of the MNR. As a result of its significant showing in the 1951 elections, the party established itself as the major national contender among the various counter-elite groups in gestation since 1935. Not unexpectedly, its electoral success redounded to the generally strong image of the MNR. The party quickly became a magnet, attracting the various public and elite counter-groups looking for a winning political vehicle.

It would not be unreasonable to argue that after 1951 there were, in fact, three MNRs. The first was the primary system, made up of the Comité Político Nacional, the commandos, the cells, and Los Grupos de Honor. The second, the labor-left faction, centered around Lechín and the FSTMB, and it included other labor and student leaders. The third grouping was the MNR exiled group in Argentina headed by Paz. Although there were some major exceptions, the three represented basically different orientations regarding aims, style, and tactics. The first had a generally rightist reformist approach; the second, a revolutionary socialist approach; and the third, a pragmatic nationalist approach.

The primary party system was the most direct descendant of the original MNR. It was made up of the in-country remnants of the previous second-level party elite (secondary leaders who became important after 1946) and embraced within its structure the original MNR clientele—what was called the *clase media empobrecida* ("impoverished middle class") and the *proletariado incipiente* ("incipient proletariat"). The two most active elements of the primary structure were the small bourgeois elite central committee, which kept the party alive during the rough days of the Sexenio, and after 1951 Los Grupos de Honor, which carried out the bulk of the party's almost daily sallies against the government.[8]

The "rightness" of this primary group derived from the essential petite bourgeoisie nature of the leadership and most of its organized following. Into this apparatus were drawn, in the main, those reacting to the destruction of a once secure but dependent existence. The first to react was the leadership which found no future in the old system. They were followed by wider elements of the petite bourgeoisie and declining national bourgeoisie who found the substance of traditional status positions disappearing. In a sense, these social elements were the most debilitated by the contradictions of the system. They held system values, but found their ability to realize them increasingly more difficult. They felt the need of change, but this desire arose from images of the past rather than the future. The artisan social element was experiencing essentially the same problem. The "popular" elements of the party were basically lumpen groups, frustrated by their marginality but with no tradition of self-organization for group ends.

One of the most striking aspects of the primary party system, leaders and followers alike, was a lack of clear goals and programs. In its early days, the MNR had a fairly well-worked-out idea of what was wrong with Bolivia, but it was quite lacking in program other than the blandishment of vague symbols of national dignity and collective self-determination. Even its image of the opposition was drawn in vague terms, e.g., La Rosca, the anti-nation, and the like. One of the most consistent characteristics of this primary group, especially Los Grupos de Honor after 1946, was an orientation to action and an involvement in what one MNR leader calls *la mistica de la revolución violenta* ("the mystique of the violent revolution").[9] They were more interested in the seizure than the use of power. Once having embarked on the revolutionary road, they had little idea of where they were going, beyond the hope of gaining a place in the political sun.[10]

Within this primary party system, the response was mainly to abstract and emotive concepts such as "nation," "harmony," *dignidad nacional* ("national dignity"), "anti-Semitism," and the like; that is, the stuff of which the original Fascist image of the MNR was made. Despite the changing public image of the MNR after 1949, these concepts, symbolized by uniforms and secret rituals, held the elements of the primary organization together. One thing that can be said with little fear of contradiction is that, although lacking a program, it expected to be clearly on top once power had been achieved. We can say that many in the party core saw the problem of political power mainly as a personnel problem—i.e., a problem of substituting themselves for those holding office. The simple desire for political jobs was still quite strong.[11] For this reason, the primary party leaders preferred, when possible, to work with elites from their own social milieu rather than with the more radical labor-left leaders.

As I pointed out previously, after the initial attempt to create a state-controlled union system under Villarroel, contacts between the MNR center and the FSTMB lapsed significantly. Lechín became more deeply involved in the sectoral problems of labor and became progressively under the influence of the POR. Relations with the MNR were reestablished after 1946, but in day-to-day matters, Lechín worked more closely with leftist union leaders and PORistas.

The social types around Lechín were quite different from those in the official MNR leadership body. There were some radicalized intellectuals, but they were primarily surrounded by proletarian and semi-proletarian types. Lechín worked with the sectoral elite which had emerged during the long evolution of the labor movement and was now coming into its own as a political power group.

What started out as a small group of mine leaders around Lechín, grew into a rather coherent labor-left faction. Two factors played important roles in the growing coherence of the faction. The first was the exiling to Chile of Lechín and other labor leaders in 1949. While in Chile, this group spent a good deal of time together planning for the future. At the same time, they participated in and were influenced by Chilean radical left groups. They returned to Bolivia as a strong cadre whose acknowledged leader was Lechín. The second factor solidifying the group into a coherent faction was the rush to join the MNR after the 1951 elections.

In the wave of political newcomers there were a number of rightists who were affiliated with the MNR primary party system, but most of these newcomers were leftists. The newcomers from the left included former PIR members, post-Villarroel leftist youths, and PORistas. In some cases, these newcomers actually joined the MNR; in others, previous party identifications were kept, but the individuals worked with the MNR. These new leftist elements associated mainly with the Lechín labor-left faction, and in so doing made Lechín one of the dominant political figures in the country.

The influx of leftists into the ranks of the MNR both before and after 1952 is referred to in Bolivia as *entrismo* (loosely meaning "infiltration"). The pre-1952 entrismo and the rising political significance of the labor public resulted in a definite shift of internal power in the general MNR movement toward the labor-left faction. It became increasingly difficult to ignore the more and more commanding figure of Lechín. A final increment strengthening the leftist position was the formation of a radical MNR student wing known as *la avanzada universitaria* ("the advanced guard of university students"). After 1946, new blood was usually leftist, or, at the least, center-left.

Unlike the right, the left leadership was clear on its goals and program, and its labor base was well-schooled in Marxist rhetoric and slogans.[12] The original position of the labor-left faction, which included a presumed ultimate clash with the MNR bourgeois leadership, was set forth in the previously mentioned *Tesis de Pulacayo*. The leftist *entristas* and collaborationists aligned with the MNR after 1951 on the theory that it was a progressive sector of the bourgeoisie, and the most likely countergroup to succeed. Their task, therefore, was to radicalize the party from within and push it in a socialist direction. The MNR electoral platform adopted in 1951 indicated that this was a rational course of action.

The pragmatic nationalist center was made up of many of the original major leaders of the party such as Paz, Guevara Arze, Hernan Siles, and Augusto Cespedes. Most of this group spent the duration of the Sexenio in exile, although a few, such as Hernan Siles, managed to slip back into the country. In comparison to the in-country primary party leadership and the relatively new labor-left wing, the pragmatic nationalist center had no institutional basis of power. Their influence derived in large part from the mystique of Paz and a leadership in exile that was created by the other two wings to maintain coherence, unity, and legitimacy. This group also modulated differences between the right and left wings.

Most of the original party ideologues were in the pragmatic center. A curious aspect of the Sexenio was the fact that most of these party thinkers were in exile. Those who remained in the country were, by and large, men of action. As intellectuals, the center group took a longer view of things than many of the in-country leaders. During their enforced exile, they had an opportunity to think more deeply into the causes of the party's 1946 fall. In addition, certain exiled figures, such as Paz and Guevara Arze, had always been known to be more radical in their approach, although few of their original programs showed up in official party documents.[13]

Ideologically, the pragmatic center functioned within Marxist intellectual categories reshaped by nationalist values. Its ideological orientation was basically national-developmentalist: its primary goal was the creation of a developed Bolivian nation-state. Its stance was more an attitude than a clear program, and over time many conflicts arose within the group. However, one area of agreement was that whatever the road to development, this progressive elite sprung from the bourgeoisie would be the chief leaders. Although from the same social milieu as the rightists this elite differed in terms of primary commitment, perspective, and willingness to adjust to new power situations. It was mainly the pragmatists who argued for the conversion of the party into a broad, mass-based movement, sustained contact with the left, and urged the adoption of a radical platform in 1951. For these and other reasons, there was growing resistance to Paz among the in-country rightist leaders.[14]

Tactically, the pragmatic center also differed in orientation from the other two wings. The right was oriented toward violent action and the attainment of political power and office; the left wanted to shape the organization of mass action to specific socialist goals; the center had a more manipulative approach to tactical problems. It was attuned to and willing to adapt to the shifting realities of inter-group power. As labor emerged as a major driving force, and the left wing of the MNR became a critical intra-party power faction, the pragmatic center adapted. It shifted left, but not without projections beyond pure immediate power. As was to become clear, it always sought to co-opt the left, blunt its drive, and hook it to the national-developmentalist framework. It always remained a bourgeois intellectual elite bent on harnessing social forces for the purpose of creating a Bolivia in its image.

In sum, the pragmatists like Paz differed from the MNR right wing in that they were more futuristic and had a developmental image in mind. They differed from the left wing in that socialism was not a primary concern. They had no intention of relinquishing leadership to the emergent labor sectoral elite beyond what was necessary for given tactical realities.

The MNR, which led the insurrection of 1952, had come quite far since the first stirrings of young elitist reaction in 1927 and 1928. Along the way, it permutated from a small reformist faction to an elitist party to a mass-based popular movement. It was, however, hardly a coherent unified movement. Rather, the MNR of 1952 was a multi-cephalic, multi-organizational alliance of disparate and potentially antagonistic social groupings.

Beyond this, the MNR was specifically a product of what I have called the tin-based "national system." The movement, both in terms of elites and major publics, was formed out of the diverse sectoral reactions to the contradictions of the "national system." The party developed and adapted over time to the changing tactical realities posed within the tin-based complex. Counter-elites directed most of their thought to the problem of tin.

The MNR's relationship with the Indian peasant, a major potentially revolutionary public, is quite cloudy during this period. The MNR, as well as other parties, maintained contacts with more advanced peasant leaders. By and large, it was the leftist MNR faction and the leftist parties which moved through the countryside testing support. It seems fairly clear that within the MNR right wing, there was definite resistance to any involve-ment of campesinos in projected revolutionary activities. During the civil war of 1949, for example, MNR leaders in Cochabamba refused to elicit peasant support, although there is reason to believe it was available.[15] If anything, the MNR rightists had a more profound fear of a peasant uprising than of a labor threat. In part, this fear derived from the fact that many rightist leaders were small- and medium-sized landowners. In addition, there was a general bourgeois resistance to emerging groups which might supplant them in status. More profound were the deep feelings of inferiority and superiority born of the essential colonial rela-tionship between the "civilized" Spanish Bolivia and the "savage" Indian Bolivia. As a minority culture existing by grace of con-quest and subjugation, there had always existed among the Span-ish cultural group a deep fear of a massive uprising of revenge-seeking Indians. At best, their plans for the Indian involved "civilizing" him and making him into their image. The idea of Indians running around loose as a revolutionary force was a most terrifying prospect.

Although the MNR was a mass-based popular movement and the insurrection, a major popular effort, action was restricted to the major urban areas linked and organized for the shipment of tin to the industrial United States. Indian peasants played no role in the insurrection of 1952. Even with the significant expan-sion of the scope of conflict, the insurrection involved on all sides only a small part of the actual population of Bolivia.

PART III

PART III

9 The Revolution—Phase I: The National System

The extent of the rebels' victory came as a surprise to everyone, including the MNR. As might be expected, confusion was the order of the day. In many parts of the country, MNR commandos took control of local governmental outposts and police duties. Simultaneously, armed units of miners established themselves as controlling bodies in the biggest mine camps and the towns bordering them. Within days, MNR units, or groups acting in its name, had established their authority in all departments and major population centers of the country.

In La Paz, Hernan Siles Zuazo assumed the presidency in the name of the MNR. Despite pressure from certain quarters in the party to hold on to the office, Siles declared himself provisional president only. He avowed his intention to transfer power to the party chief, Víctor Paz Estenssoro, as soon as he could arrange his return. Paz, meanwhile, negotiated frantically with the Argentine government to arrange his safe exit.

As part of his interim duties, Siles appointed a provisional cabinet. The cabinet reflected the full range of party opinion. Besides old MNR stalwarts, it included three designated *ministros obreros* ("labor ministers," official representatives of the labor left): Juan Lechín, minister of mines and petroleum; German Butron, minister of labor; and Nuflo Chavez Ortiz, minister of

167

peasant affairs. Although this formula was a clear concession to the power of the left, most cabinet and sub-cabinet positions went to leaders of the party's primary organization, and, thereby, reflected a good deal of anti-left sentiment.

Víctor Paz returned on April 17, 1952. He received a tumultuous welcome which began at the El Alto Airport, and continued as his motorcade wound its way down through the center city to the presidential palace. Throughout the long trip, the crowds repeated the same refrains: *"Viva el MNR!" "Viva Victor Paz!" "Nacional-ización!" "Reforma Agraria!"* By all accounts it was an impressive sight and did not fail to impress the leader, returning to his country after six years of isolation and exile. Paz received the presidential chair from Siles, who, in turn, assumed the vice-presidency. The provisional cabinet was reaffirmed by Paz. Bolivia had a new government.

Most significantly, Paz and Siles claimed their right to govern on constitutional grounds. They claimed they were merely assuming the powers delegated to them by the electorate and denied unjustly by the military in 1951.[1] In other words, the armed action of April 9 through April 11 of 1952 returned the legitimacy abrogated in 1951. They were, in fact, the country's constitutional officers. This line was not simply a verbal tour de force, but reflected deep elements of the MNR old guard's orientation toward the relationship between political power and the socioeconomic problems of Bolivia.

We will have cause to delve into this attitude more deeply at a later time; for the moment, the significant point is that the MNR justified its existence not only through revolutionary action, but mainly by dint of the continuity of constitutional legitimacy. At the formal political level, there was no conception of a radical break with the past. It is more than coincidental that the revolutionary government did not draft a new constitution until 1961. Thus, although the new government expressed a revolutionary or at least reformist intent towards the social and economic spheres, it based its authority on traditional political norms and the extant constitution.

Aside from major reshufflings in the judicial and administrative branches of government, the only formal political change introduced by the MNR was the granting of universal adult suffrage. Undoubtedly, this was a momentous move and has proved to be a critical factor in the contemporary scene. The enfranchisement of close to 75 percent of the population was bound to have repercussions in the political sphere. However, if this had been the only revolutionary act, its implications would not have been as great, for a peasant vote controlled by hacienda owners would have been quite possible. Hence, the real significance of the vote came with the agrarian reform which broke the existing patterns of control in the agrarian system. At that moment, the vote reform was not really a revolutionary act in terms of the previous political norms. Rather than changing the existing political institutions, the vote was an amplification of the citizen body that would participate in them. The MNR was still, in the political dimension at least, very much part and parcel of the liberal world view.

There was no attempt in Bolivia, as in most other modern revolutions, to create a new political community with its own conceptions of legitimacy, institutions, definitions, etc. It was, rather, a broadening of the existing political community. A total break with the past was not proclaimed.

A common characteristic of most modern revolutions, beginning with the French Revolution, is an effort to break totally with the past in political concept as well as in social and economic deed. Also, there is usually an attempt to create a new conceptual and institutional order. Central to the process is the advancement of new concepts of legitimacy and authority. The new order is usually endowed with legitimacy by the nation, the act of a charismatic leader, or, most recently, a revolutionary party. In Bolivia, however, the process was reversed. The core revolutionary party did not set out to legitimate a total new order of things. Rather, it sought to legitimate its claim to make cerain changes by means of the old political norms. It drew upon the past for its right to rule, and never claimed to be a source of right in itself.

For an understanding of the Bolivian revolution, the implications of this fact are many. In the first instance, it indicates that no matter how revolutionary it may have become in deed, the old guard MNR (I am not speaking of the labor left) remained in spirit and political orientation essentially reformist. In other words, as one of the revolution's most prominent figures has said: "We did not aim at making a social or political revolution but an economic revolution."[2] This aim, especially as it was to be carried out by the group I have called the pragmatic nationalists, was to be a source of great semantic confusion which exacerbated the inevitable conflicts that arose within the revolutionary camp. The spirit of the old guard MNR (both right and center), if not in its official words, was bound to rub against the well-developed Marxist thrust of its labor-left allies. Similarly, the MNR put itself in a position in which, first, remnants of the status quo, and, later, its own right wing, could assail various government actions by pointing to the contradictions between latter revolutionary acts and the norms upon which the party claimed legitimacy.

In the first days of the revolutionary epoch, a kind of official normative schizophrenia was introduced into Bolivian public life and was to tear at the insides of the MNR and weaken its ability to reorganize the country. There was a serious contradiction between the MNR's tying of itself to old norms and institutions and the often violent process by which the social and economic foundations of those norms and institutions were dismantled. Quite often, the violent abrogation of official norms was carried out by groups who acted in the name of the MNR, but who were actually beyond party control. In such cases, the party leadership, unable to make these important social groups conform to their declared norms, was forced to legitimize their actions after the fact by lame references to "revolutionary justice."[3]

Instead of claiming the advent of a totally new era which, through revolutionary action, would define and legitimize its own normative world, the MNR harked to a past understanding of right, while presiding over a process that aimed direct attacks at the heart of the past. Thus, official justice and revolutionary justice collided, resulting in a situation in which there was neither justice nor any understanding of what would constitute justice. Justice became a thing to be defined locally through power, more often than not by force; as effective power came to vary widely throughout the country, so too did notions of the just or the right. Such a situation is, almost by definition, intrinsic to those processes we call revolution; in Bolivia, this was exacerbated by an official clinging to a set of abstractions in the face of a reality that was violently sweeping away the solidity which underpinned them.

Like it or not, the MNR, through action, put itself in the position of being the only institution that stood a chance of pulling the country into a coherent whole. To have carried out this task, the MNR needed, at some point at least, a cohesion of organization and unity of purpose that it was never able to achieve. The party remained divided on what it was doing (was it building a new Bolivia or salvaging the old?) and never defined a clear basis for intra-party judgment. Eventually, the MNR became stalemated, with no wing of the party able to impose its concepts on the party organization, let alone the country at large.

The degree of the MNR core's identification with past norms and styles was evidenced in ways other than the formal maintenance of the constitutional facade. Aside from a few basic words and concepts generated mainly by the labor left, the MNR did not bring a new revolutionary language into existence, a process which is usually pervasive in other revolutionary contexts. Nor were there any attempts to forge new religions, foment a new cultural pattern, or adopt distinctive styles such as beards, uniforms, and the like. The guns of the insurrection had not stopped firing before the victorious party led a traditional Good Friday procession to the cathedral. This was followed by other MNR-led ritual connections with other critical institutions and values of the past. In their own personal, essentially bourgeois, life styles, the MNR members made no change. The common phenomenon of revolutionary puritanism did not occur in Bolivia: puritanism as a style was common only among the far left groups, such as the POR. A final manifestation of the spiritual, psychological, and orientational identification of the MNR core with the past can be seen in the presidential portraits of Paz, and later Siles; attired in tails and sash with the seal of the republic about their necks, they fit neatly into an unbroken line of Bolivian presidential portraits. At best, the MNR core was a reluctant band of revolutionaries.

In the early days of the revolution, however, these expressions of continuity shared the stage with the more radical cries couched in a new language that was emanating from the left. The result was confusion and an air of anticipation, which some contemplated with joy, others with deep trepidation. Anticipation was heightened by the quick appearance of deep dissension among the revolutionaries. Paz made speeches cast in generalities dealing with national unity, economic independence, and justice. But, from the left came demands for specific action in the form of a rapid completion of the 1951 electoral promises. Leftist leaders spoke ominously of reactionary cliques in the MNR and counseled their followers on the need for continued revolutionary vigilance. Through various propaganda organs, the left cranked out leaflets putting forth demands and attitudes that jarred with official MNR style. In reaction, the MNR right wing put out its own propaganda, attacking the left in tones previously reserved for La Rosca. The long-standing voice of the Comité Político Nacional, *En Marcha,* openly declared the right wing's limited view of the revolution and its firm commitment to a Christian past. Simultaneously, it warned of a "Communist" attempt to seize and pervert the "national revolution."[4]

It soon became impossible for the government to delay taking decisive reform action any longer. There was talk of examining the feasibility of an agrarian reform, but little was done in an official way to make the talk concrete. Not unexpectedly, the first really decisive steps were taken in the context of the previous "national system," and aimed attacks at its two most discredited institutions: the tin companies and the army.

The first decisive assault on the economic bastion of the "Big Three" tin combines occurred on July 2, 1952, when the MNR government established a state monopoly on the export and sale of all minerals. The agency that was delegated this gigantic function was the Banco Minero, originally established under Busch. Actually, this decree was an extension of the earlier Busch concept. The original purpose of the Banco Minero was twofold: (a) to bring under government control foreign exchange earned by the country's small- and medium-sized mine operations, and (b) to weaken the economic power of Hochschild and other *rescata-dores* ("middlemen") who had incurred significant hard currency profits by operating as selling agents for the smaller operations. By extension, the original measure aimed at strengthening the smaller sector of independent holders by releasing them from the control of the big private rescatadores and by putting them under what was assumed to be the more benign wing of a state agency. The Busch measure, therefore, did not strike against private property in any way, but rather sought to protect the small independent operator from monopolists.

This train of thought, aimed at strengthening the little man as a private operator and increasing the state's dollar ingress, was part of the MNR core's view of the country's economic difficulties. A part of this fundamental view also included the idea that the reason for the stagnant and truncated growth of Bolivia was the failure of mine profits to be reinvested in the country. The cause of this failure, in turn, was monopolization and an elevation of liberal international market principles over the principle of national development. The activities of all the reform governments in which the MNR was either a direct or indirect participant indicate that the goal was never a socialist one in the sense of challenging the principle of private property itself. The state moved into the economic sphere, mainly mining, to guarantee reinvestment in one way or another. This was to be done by increasing taxes and by getting control over all or part of the mineral-earned foreign exchange; thus, the Banco Minero, the Busch foreign exchange decree, etc.

The decree of July 2 was obviously in this spirit. If the decree had stood alone, its effect would have been to guarantee dollars to the state while leaving the principle of private property inviolate. There is strong reason to believe that a significant number of the MNR core wished to restrict its punitive action toward the "Big Three" to this extent.[5] At the time, the rumor was that Paz was lukewarm at best toward nationalization and that he leaned toward the restricted view expressed in the July 2 decree.[6]

However, much had happened since the MNR's early flirtation with state power. One of the most important developments was the radicalization and politicization of the labor movement and a drastic change in the composition and organization of the MNR. The labor left made it abundantly clear that, in its view, property relations were at the core of the issue and that they would tolerate nothing less than nationalization. The rumors of strong anti-nationalization sentiment in the MNR core group and Paz's supposedly lukewarm attitude set off ominous grumblings and threats in leftist circles. As a counter-move the leftists proposed an immediate occupation of all mining operations by the miners themselves, to be followed by total *nacionalización sin indemnización* ("nationalization without indemnity"). An intense debate took place behind the scenes on the issue of policy toward the mining sector. Throughout the spring and early summer of 1952, the labor left, now formally organized into the *Central Obrera Boliviana* (COB) under the leadership of Lechín, sponsored a steady stream of parades and mass demonstrations in which the demand for nationalization was repeated with increasing vigor. Although the exact contours of the issues were often blurred, it was evident that the MNR core and the labor left had fundamentally different conceptions of the root economic problem, as well as differing visions of the nature of the revolution and of what a new Bolivia should look like.

Also at work in shaping the outcome of the debate on this issue were certain unavoidable aspects of the MNR core's own political experience. Twice, members of the MNR had held power and attempted to reform the mining sector, twice they had been unseated. The question of the mines, therefore, presented itself not just as an issue of public policy, but as one of concrete political power. With reason, most MNR leaders were convinced that the tin magnates had been the moving force behind their previous overthrow. What then was to prevent them from doing the same in the future? Upon what basis could even a reformist regime be assured of its safety in the face of this super-state? It was not difficult for some to argue that they could never be safe as long as such tremendous economic power remained in the hands of a few men, for at the very least, the companies could wipe out reform by perverting the party with money. Whatever the economic logic and the decisions about property, a political logic also existed which had expressed itself eloquently in the past. When the more pragmatic elements of the party core began to weigh the factors of power, the need to pull the political teeth of the barons became more evident. Thus, principles aside, the need of some form of nationalization became apparent: their strategy demanded interim tactics adjusted to situational realities. Resistance made insurrection necessary, and now the need to neutralize that resistance became imperative.

It was in this context, both ideological and situational, that the MNR moved toward nationalization, a move which many in the core party took with reluctance. A commission to study the question of nationalization was constituted. Despite this gesture, the labor left manifested its distrust of the MNR core by maintaining "revolutionary vigilance" in the form of continued strikes, demonstrations, and political delegations. By the fall of 1952, the movement toward nationalization was irreversible. On October 2, 1952, a state mining corporation, *Corporación Minera de Bolivia* (COMIBOL), was formed and given the task of exploiting, commercializing, and administrating state-owned mines. On October 7, the operations of Patiño, Aramayo, and Hochschild were interrupted by the state. On October 31, the nationalization decree was signed.

In final form, the nationalization decree represented a consciously engineered compromise between the conflicting positions in the MNR: the rightist position was concerned primarily with state control of dollar profits and reinvestment; the leftist was concerned mainly with property relations and a new social distribution of economic and political power.

In the first place, the scope of nationalization was restricted to well-defined limits. The only property to be affected was that of the "Big Three." Small- and medium-sized operations, including some owned by foreign private capital such as Grace and Company, were not affected. Indeed, the government committed itself through the Banco Minero to foster the growth of this private sector. The decree did not strike at property as such nor, for that matter, at foreign capital as such. The government paid oblique homage to the notion of private property by providing for indemnification of the dispossessed companies. Besides the distaste for nationalization on the part of many of the MNR core, limited action and repayment provisions were made with a wary eye toward Washington. In December 1952, the MNR ambassador to the United States expressed the position of the MNR core on the restricted meaning of nationalization, and for that matter, the national revolution itself:

> 1) My government subscribes wholeheartedly to the principles of democracy; 2) The nationalization of the properties of the Patiño, Aramayo, and Hochschild groups represented a special case. Nationalization of private property is not the policy of Bolivia; 3) Nationalization of the tin mines did not mean confiscation of the property. We intend to pay the former owners of the properties every cent that is due them; 4) The government of Bolivia realizes the part which private capital can contribute towards the development of its resources and hopes to attract that private capital.

MNR Ambassador Andrade went on to argue that it was the specific action of these three specific companies that forced nationalization.[7] In short, nationalization was in no way a basic principle of the MNR core's approach to matters of political economy. It was an isolated, almost aberrant action, and not part of an integrated view of revolution and social change. The commitment to democracy was to that form embodied in Bolivian "liberal" constitutions since 1880, but limited in scope due to franchise restrictions.

The "official" MNR position comes out even more clearly in the nationalization decree itself and deserves quotation at some length.

> That the great companies, ignoring the superior interests of the country, subordinated the national strength to the exclusive exploitation of their mines.
> That in contrast to the rapid enrichment of the magnates of tin the country was gradually impoverished.

That to implant and sustain their system the three companies through trickery, bribery, and intimidation came to dominate the personnel and powers of the state.

That the system of work imposed by the great companies is so inhuman and oppressive that the average life of the interior miner is barely 27 years.

That the cultural expression of the country also suffered from the domination of these privileged interests since no spiritual force which was not in their service had hope of finding support or stimulus.

That the national victory of April, the culmination of a long historical process, has made possible the realization of the irrevocable decision of the Bolivian people.[8]

The point of most interest and relevance to an understanding of later political developments is what the decree did not speak of. This indictment is a bill of particulars leveled at three specific operations. It does not speak of a general concept of nationalization or of a general socialist thrust. To the extent that there are any general principles, they are that the general interests of the country are superior to the private interests of individuals; that the country's interests are expressed by the state and manifested in its wealth; and that when private interest threatens the general interest, the state intervenes on the nation's behalf. By implication, a derived principle is that the state shall interfere with private property and interests only when they challenge the general interest. In short, it is an expression of pragmatic nationalism measured in terms of the wealth and power of the state, which is seen as the locus and expression of the nation. The original threads of the MNR orientation which separated it from other counter-tendencies were showing remarkable persistence despite the vicissitudes of changing tactical realities.

While the subtleties of conception probably reflected more of the center-right MNR view, as did indemnification, the implementation of the decree was to reflect more the power of the labor left. The major concession to the left was the provision known as *control obrero con derecho al veto*—"worker control with a right to veto." Under this provision, two of the seven directors of the COMIBOL were to be worker-designated representatives. In reality, this meant that there would be two members designated by the FSTMB which was now the singular voice of the Bolivian miner.

Of more importance was the provision for the election in each mine of a *control obrero* ("worker controller") who had, in addition to an advising and decision-making capacity, the power to veto decisions deemed inimical to the interest of the mines and the miner. The effect of the provision was to create in the mines a new independent locus of power under the control of the union organizations. The implications for the administration of COMIBOL and the long-term distribution of political power in the country were momentous.

While MNR lawyers carefully worked out a bill of particulars against the "Big Three" and Ambassador Andrade assuaged the fears of Washington (perhaps his own as well), certain concrete realities were clashing hard with their rhetoric. Appropriately enough, the nationalization decree was signed in the mining camp called Maria Barzola, located near the imposing Cataví Siglo XX complex of Patiño. On his arrival, President Paz was greeted by a salute of twenty-one blasts of dynamite, a tool of the miners' work which quite often had been converted into their major weapon of struggle against the companies and the hated army.

The actual signing of the decree itself took place in the open air in full view of thousands of miners who expressed their pleasure by discharging round after round from their newly acquired rifles and machine guns into the thin Andean air. The first to sign the decree was Víctor Paz Estenssoro, president of the republic and *jefe maximo* ("top chief") of the MNR. Beneath the name of Paz was placed the confirming name of Juan Lechín Oquendo, minister of mines and petroleum, secretary general of the COB, executive secretary of the FSTMB, and *lider Maximo de los obreros Bolivianos* ("top leader of the Bolivian workers"). Lechín's signature on the document reflected much more than the legal nicety of the counter-signature of the appropriate state officer. It spoke of a reality comprehensible at a glance: the disparity between formal and concrete power.

The MNR and the Military Institution

Since the days of Toro, the military was a pivotal institution in the orchestration of the revolutionary process. Throughout this period, the army was bitterly divided, mainly along generational lines. This division played an important role in the declining strength of the status quo elite, vis-à-vis the challenges posed by counter-elites. Undoubtedly, one of the most important elements leading to the success of the April 9 insurrection was the disarray, mutual suspicion, and ideological division within the army officer corps.

Be that as it may, the MNR came to power through an insurrection during which large segments of the populace fought the army. Moreover, the insurrection was aimed at unseating a military government. In this, the final expression of the resistance of the old regime, it was the army against the people. This fact, when added to the memories of 1942, 1947, and 1949, generated a ground swell of sentiment in favor of destroying the institution once and for all. The COB nurtured the swell and tried to turn it into a tidal wave.

Within the MNR core, the feeling toward the military had always been ambivalent. The Chaco War and the many battles since then led to an abiding distrust and disdain for the man in uniform. The sentiment is still apparent in MNR circles where, although Busch and Villarroel are publicly canonized, they are privately pictured as ineffectual blunderers. Nevertheless, the MNR core had long-standing ties with the young officers of RADEPA and, no doubt, many personal friendships existed. Beyond this was the simple question of whether or not the party could afford to do away with the army completely. Again, there was a right-left split on this issue and, again, the pragmatists engineered a working compromise. The compromise not only sought to ameliorate right-left conflict, but reflected a definite pragmatic approach to the issue. As in the case of the big companies, the pragmatists felt that they could not trust the army as it was, but, at the same time, they did not want to lose that symbol of sovereignty completely. The answer was in reorganization.

In point of fact, a good deal of the problem was being solved by the spontaneous disintegration of the military institution. Field officers in fear of reprisals often sold off equipment and ran. As they did so, soldiers deserted and untold numbers of weapons found their way into civilian hands.

It can be said with some certainty that the Paz wing primarily wanted to reorganize the army and make it a loyal servant of the MNR. Still, the pressure from the left was such that it was all the ruling group could do to avoid bloody reprisals against the military. In dealing with the military, as with other groups, it is very important to keep in mind that Bolivia is the only modern case in which widespread revolutionary changes were made without massive bloody reprisals. Behind that singular fact lies the essentially reformist attitude of the MNR and the skill and ability of Víctor Paz and the pragmatic nationalists who surrounded him.

In any event, the MNR policy, counter to leftist wishes, evolved in the following manner: In the first instance, the officer corps was thoroughly purged. The purge was carried out by a military tribunal which dampened leftist criticism by demonstrating an intent to punish (a large number of officers were relieved of duty). An element of legality derived from the fact that the purge was conducted by a military tribunal, not a revolutionary court. This procedure was further proof of the MNR's basic commitment to the institution itself and to extant legality. Obliquely, the army was allowed to cleanse itself and, thereby, save itself. Institutionally, there was never a break between a "old" and a "new" army. During the purge, some five hundred or more officers were relieved of their posts. Some served short jail sentences but most eventually went into exile. In some cases, officers previously deemed hostile were "rehabilitated," brought into the party, and allowed to resume their duties.[9]

As a general rule, all remaining officers at one point or another swore allegiance to the party and joined the military branch of the MNR. The act of conversion and the joining of the military branch, however, were purely paper phenomena. To keep one's post or win a promotion, one had to be a member of the MNR, so one became a member of the MNR and made the appropriate pledges. Again, unlike other revolutionary situations as in Russia, Cuba, or China, political cadres never penetrated the military and gained control of it. The shrewder officers passively accepted the army's reduction in size and influence, but strove to maintain its institutional independence. Among less politically ambitious officers, a strong institutionalist orientation developed. The first post-revolutionary commander, Colonel Innofuentes, and later generals such as Molina, followed a policy of accepting revolutionary direction while, at the same time, keeping out of the public and, especially, the political limelight. They sought to retrench and build quietly for a later resurgence of the military institution. For the moment, they were content to fade into the background. They did this with so much skill that many outside the country thought the army had been definitively destroyed.

Another governmental step against the military, more dramatic than real, was the closing of the military academy which had been the last center of resistance to fall before the rebels. As early as May 31, 1952, however, a new air force academy was founded in Santa Cruz, meaning that the military had actually acquired a new branch. In early 1953, the La Paz military academy was reopened and named the *Instituto Coronel Villarroel*. As part of the new approach, the academy's doors were thrown open to a wider social spectrum, including lower-class mestizos and educated Indians. Exactly what impact this had on the social composition of the officer corps, I was not able to establish. But there is general agreement, partially confirmed by visual observation of racial types in officers' uniforms, that the officer corps now includes many new lower-stratum elements. The significance of this in political terms is difficult to measure.[10]

At the heart of the MNR's approach to the military was a redefinition of its primary functions. The major change was based on the concept of an *ejército productora* ("producing army"). The idea was to take an institution, which in the past did little beyond lose wars, repress strikes, and intrigue politically, and turn it into a controlled instrument of national economic development.

The new role of the military was outlined on June 5, 1952, by Colonel Innofuentes. In his statement, Innofuentes lamented the fact that the army had been used by La Rosca as a tool to further its own interests. He went on to compare the pre-1952 organization to a navy sailing without a destination and, therefore, never reaching a port. The responsibility for this functionless condition belonged to the old generals and La Rosca. But under men like himself, the army had discovered its proper duty. It would become a sort of *organismo de Producción* ("organism of production") within the general plan of national advancement. To do this it would train itself in all the necessary skills of history, sociology, and economics.[11]

After this statement, little was heard of the military. The fact is that a much reduced army did transform itself into an armed labor brigade. The Bolivian army became the first Latin American example of the new and now fashionable "civic action" military. At first, it mainly cleared land and built roads. In later years, these functions were increased to include school construction, food distribution, and any number of tasks. A great stimulus to this expansion of function derived from the early flirtation and eventual commitment of the United States to the idea of "modernizing militaries." A most important function acquired later was that of educating the Indian mass in "the three Rs" and basic technical skills. The story of civic action programs in Bolivia is an important one; but for our purposes the point is that the military survived the revolution of 1952. The price of survival was reduction in size, redefinition of purpose, and temporary eclipse. But from "humble beginnings big things often grow."

Political Impact of the Revolutionary Government

For the moment, we are interested mainly in the political impact of the actions of the MNR government discussed above. What was the effect of these actions on power relationships in the old "national system"? From the political point of view, major changes in the economy and in society are important. However, the crux of the issue of revolution lies in the fact that political means are used consciously to pursue such social and economic changes, and more important, that changes occur in the composition of those political groups which exercise the capacity to control and rule.

In Bolivia, the most immediate change in the pattern of control and rule after 1952 was the dramatic emergence of labor as a key power group. The advancing power of labor became most apparent after 1946. Partly through its own internal development and partly through external stimulation, labor, led by its own sectoral elite, moved into the center of the political equation. The significance of this development was reflected in the changing organizational nature of the MNR and the progressive radicalization of its public rhetoric. Behind this shift in the power equation was the fact that the parameter of and force behind political struggle was the accelerating process of mobilization and the ·expansion of the scope of conflict. In this context, the sectoral elite associated with labor became the group with the highest ascending power potential; that of other elites was either declining or leveling off.

This trend was reinforced by the insurrection itself and the structural changes introduced by the revolutionary government. The original coup was narrow in scope and intent. Its success would have meant a minimum destruction of existing structures and institutions, particularly the army. The unanticipated generalization of the action and the dramatically critical role that armed workers played in its success led to a wider and more profound defeat of the status quo elite. Symbolic of the depth of the defeat was the besting of the military by a ragtag force of civilian irregulars. This defeat set off widespread degeneration and demoralization of that important national institution.

One of the most significant results of the insurrection was the rapid dispersal of weapons and equipment to the civilian population. Armed civilian groups sprang up throughout the country. It was these groups which seized local governments, police stations, and the army garrisons in the name of the MNR. Through such seizures they increased the amount and kinds of weapons in civilian possession. On the whole, the spread of weaponry was sporadic and spontaneous, but in working-class districts, especially in the mining camps, the process was quickly organized. The speed of organization is indicative of more than a little anticipation and planning on the part of labor-left leaders. Local leaders immediately declared the existence of militias in their areas. Some five days after the termination of fighting in La Paz, a national system of workers' militias was already in existence.[12]

While it is evident that the MNR core sought to redefine rather than destroy the army, the military was drastically emasculated as a fighting organization. Concomitantly, the elements of force shifted to the population at large. The first and strongest newly organized expressions of this atomized force capacity to emerge were the workers' militias. Theoretically, these militias were part of what was to become a system of MNR militias under the authority of the central party organization. However, in fact, they remained autonomous and under the effective control of the labor-left sectoral elite. Indeed, even the control of the national labor leadership over individual militias was problematic.

This development had profound implications for the future of power relationships within the country. As Max Weber pointed out, one of the essential characteristics of the modern state is its ability to claim effectively a legitimate monopoly of the capacity to use force within its boundaries. Of all the functions that the state accumulated in the historical process of rolling back intermediate jurisdictional realms, one of the most critical was that of organizing and controlling the ability to use force.

As I have indicated, from the beginning the MNR core was oriented toward the idea of national development to be measured in terms of an increase in the power of the Bolivian state. This commitment ran especially deep in those I have referred to as pragmatic nationalists. In carrying out the "revolution," the MNR core strove to keep the existing state structure intact and the basic concepts of authority associated with it. They strove for continuity at the formal political level and were, to a large degree, successful in this goal. But, while formal continuity was maintained, an all-important functional prerequisite of the operational reality of formal power was slipping away from the formal state structure. The capacity to organize and use force was devolving to intermediate bodies whose relationships with both the state and the party were, to say the least, problematic.

The appearance of well-organized workers' militias drew added significance when, eleven days after the insurrection, the Central Obrera Boliviana (COB) came into existence. Previous to 1952, nationwide confederations had existed, but they were weak, at best, and were constantly challenged by member federations and rival confederations. National coherence in the movement was quite rudimentary. The founding of the COB marked a significant change in this pattern. As the FSTMB consolidated itself as the singular legitimate voice of the miners, the COB in theory and, to a remarkable degree, in practice established itself as the general voice of Bolivian labor. It embraced in its formal structure all organized expressions of "working" Bolivia from true labor groups, to white-collar organizations, to artisan groups.

Only those groups affiliated with the COB were allowed to exist. Previous organizations such as the CSTB and the anarchist FOL (*Federación Obrera Local*) atrophied and disappeared. Under considerable pressure in some cases, all sindicato groups lined up behind the COB. The COB demanded and received official government recognition as the legitimate representative of Bolivian labor. At the same time, all the left-wing political groups flocked to the COB. Thus, although the COB officially identified itself with the MNR, it expressly defined itself as the voice of the labor left. It pointedly recognized the right of leftist parties such as the PIR, POR, and PCB to exist officially in its midst.

From the beginning, the COB asserted its affiliation with, but basic independence from, the MNR.[13] Simultaneously, it openly attacked "reactionaries" in the MNR, and indicated its deep distrust for the MNR as a whole. By extension, it rejected the MNR thesis of a harmony of interests among the segments of the movement and adopted a position based on the idea of essential conflicts of interest between the MNR "bourgeois" leadership and the "working class" which it represented. The purely formal affiliation of the labor left with the MNR became clear when the COB demanded *co-gobierno* ("co-government"). In both theory and practice, the COB did establish its co-government status.

One theoretical pillar of *co-gobierno* was the old medieval Spanish concept of *"Fuero Sindical."* Based on this concept, the COB asserted the jurisdictional autonomy of labor within the functional realm of its primary interest. In effect, this meant the entire economy. "Co-government," in turn, was further based upon two concessions. The first was a guaranteed number of labor ministers in the national cabinet. At first, the number was three but was later pushed to five. These labor ministers were chosen by the COB and functioned as its representatives in the official state government. The COB also received guaranteed representation in the party's executive organs. The second concession of importance was the granting of control obrero in the mines, which gave the COB a powerful voice in the management of the economy.

Crucial to the significance of the formal position accorded to the COB was its ability to effectuate and increase its real autonomous status. The nationalization decree was important in this fact over and above the question of control obrero. Previous to 1952, the companies, not the government, were the real source of power and authority in the great camps. As indicated before, they functioned as governments in their own independent, sovereign-like realms. The elimination of the companies removed effective authority from the camps. By the time COMIBOL organized itself to administer the camps, the sindicatos had already made themselves the real centers of power and authority—a power backed up by the existence of the militias attached to the sindicatos. Subsequently, the authority of COMIBOL and, hence, the government was more nominal than real in the camps. The mine manager may have had formal authority, but everyone knew that it was the head of the sindicato and the control obrero who really ran the show. In fact, their local power was such that, as later events would show, they could act independently of the COB as well as of the MNR if they so chose.

Thus, in the old national system an important divergence developed between authority and power. Through the COB, the labor left became a government within the government. In some respects, it was a more powerful government. The COB had an independent base of support superior to that of the party of which it was officially a part. What actually transpired was that the MNR officially assumed the power and responsibility of state government, but the COB constituted itself as an unrivaled center of initiative and veto power. It had governing power, but not responsibility.

A final element of labor's new power position was its strategic location in the Bolivian economy. To shut down the mines was, in effect, to shut down the entire economy. Leaving aside questions of force capacity and managerial rights, the threat of a mine strike alone was enough to increase the force of labor's demands. The COB actually became the real government of Bolivian labor, and, through it, the economy. Indeed, it had all the symbolic and functional characteristics of a sovereign-like entity, including executive, deliberative, and judicial organs; a defined area of authority and constituents; and most important, armed forces. The COB allied itself with the MNR, but from a basis of independence, and only in return for guaranteed corporate status within the official state government.

It should be stressed that the COB was not a monolithic entity. Lack of unity perhaps explains why it did not simply take over the revolution immediately—as some Trotskyites urged. There were conflicts between the different member groups, e.g., workers, empleados, and artisans. There were ideological divisions involving the left wing of the MNR, the PIR, the POR, and the Communists. As pointed out before, there were also strong particularistic dividing lines between the working groups themselves, particularly between the railway workers (long close to the PIR) and the miners (long close to the POR). These divisions were later to shake the COB apart. However, in the immediate post-insurrectionary period, the COB, under Lechín's leadership and by means of internal compromise, was able to present a united front to the MNR core on the large issues concerning the direction in which the revolution was to go. Lechín secured a firm hold of the COB and because of this, became second only to Paz in shaping the revolution. The basis of his power was his control of the FSTMB and the emotional identification of the miners with him personally. The FSTMB, in turn, was the most powerful and radical group in the COB, and when all was said and done, the most powerful single group in the entire immediate configuration of power and interest.

10 The Agrarian Revolution

A striking aspect of the revolutionary process in Bolivia up through the insurrection of 1952 was the fact that it was confined almost exclusively to the tin-based "national system." With the old elite unseated and new power relations coming into play, the revolutionary drive began to break out of its previous socio-political confines. In the late fall of 1952, the first reports of peasant protest activity reached La Paz. Throughout the late fall and early winter of 1953, sporadic protest became a generalized peasant drive against the existing rural order. By January the pressure was uncontainable, the need for fundamental reform, unavoidable. On January 20, 1953, a commission to study agrarian reform was created by the Paz government. The revolution was clearly spilling over into the agrarian "local system."[1]

There had been resistance to the idea of the nationalization of tin, especially if it connoted an attack on the principle of private property itself. Yet, for years in both elite and counter-elite circles there had been a growing awareness that something had to be done about tin.[2] Hence, when political logic was added to economic logic and it was clear that only the "Big Three" were to be affected, many, including elements of the status quo elite, found nationalization a bitter, but swallowable pill.[3] However, agrarian

188

reform, especially in the context of open peasant protest and violence, was an altogether different matter.

In the first instance, agrarian reform went directly to the heart of the issue of private property. By far the greatest amount of real property in Bolivia was in land. The sanctity of these property relationships had been enshrined in every Bolivian constitution including that upon which the MNR was tacitly basing its claim to rule.

The only qualification put on that right to own property was the notion that, after 1936, property should perform a "social" function. Such a notion, however, obviously did not necessarily imply dispossession of an entire social class and the devolution of property rights to the mass of Indian peasants.

Property was not the only issue. Also at stake was a complex system of values and a way of life traceable to colonial times. The relationship between patron and colono, between master and servant, was a model pattern of man-to-man relationships and concepts of authority which pervaded the entire value system of Bolivia.[4] Reform could not help but destroy this traditional form of social and political relationships.

In Bolivia the possession of land was fundamental, almost mystical. It was through land ownership that one anchored himself in the world. It was through land ownership that one's name gained solidity. By passing land down through the generations, the family name would gain historical permanence. Land was the basis of economic security in an insecure environment. The working of colonos upon the land strengthened its economic value, while simultaneously conferring prestige and creating an arena in which the prototypical role of señor or *caballero* ("gentleman") could be played out. To be landless was to be dependent and subservient.

To speak of a prerevolutionary elite in Bolivia, to speak of an upper class, is to speak of land ownership—land organized in a way that is devoted to the economic and social underpinnings of a style of life, a total way of approaching the world.[5] The growth of tin occasioned the rise of a new elite, often from lower and landless social origins; but, once merged, this new group made its peace with the old, adopted its values, and strove, often ruthlessly, to possess land and the Indians living off it.[6] One simply was not accepted as a member of the elite until one had consolidated one's professional and political status—both of which could fluctuate radically—with the solidity of land. Race and name defined status, wealth gave the means to the requisite life style, and land and the colonos functioned as the anchor of it all.

The values associated with landedness and the life style on which it was based were not restricted to the upper-class clique called La Rosca. The petite bourgeoisie took La Rosca as its reference group, and aspired to the same landed status. Few actually achieved that status, but some did make the necessary sacrifices to secure a small hacienda with a few Indian colonos upon it. For the middle sector, a good number of whom supported the MNR and had a specific understanding of *La Revolución,* land was also a goal and a symbol of a valued way of life.

Behind these factors were questions of real power. Many, both in and out of the MNR, could look upon the passing of Patiño and the rest after nationalization with resignation if not joy. For some it would create hardships, while for others, perhaps an opportunity for advancement, depending on the individual and his ability to maneuver. Nationalization weakened La Rosca, but surely did not destroy it. A fundamental change in land tenure, on the other hand, not only would destroy the social and economic base of La Rosca, but, depending on how it was implemented, would threaten a number of the MNR petite bourgeoisie as well.

The other side of the land question was that of the Indian. The Spanish-speaking urban culture of Bolivia, if not based completely on the exploitation of the Indian, did, at the least, demand his relinquishment of the ability to posit a different culture in the geographic reality of Bolivia. The Spanish-speaking ("civilized") culture was born through conquest and continued by means of subjugation. The relationship of the national Spanish culture to the local Indian cultures continued to be one of colonialism. As in all such cases, this relationship was pervaded with mutual hate, distrust, and fear projected in racial terms. *Indio* ("Indian") was a word which conjured the image of a subhuman (uncivilized) being, locked in ignorance and bent on violent revenge.[7] Given their extreme minority status in terms of numbers, those of the Spanish culture, both urban and rural, white and mestizo, undoubtedly lived in fear of Indian mass action that would sweep them away in a paroxysm of revenge. One of the most prominently displayed paintings in the La Paz City Hall portrays the city under seige by an Indian horde. This obvious fear, moreover, was not unfounded. On enough occasions, Indians had risen in protest either in a mass or in isolated groups.[8] Fear was based on an accurate judgment of the violent potentialities of the situation. There is enough evidence to conclude that the majority of the dominant culture saw the city as the repository of civilization and the hacienda, its rural outpost. To destroy the hacienda would be to return the countryside to barbarism and to leave the city surrounded by these barbaric elements.[9]

Given these facts, it is no wonder that there was stubborn resistance both within and without the MNR to the idea of a generalized land reform. Again the internal party picture is neither clear nor monolithic. The internal party drive for a wide-ranging reform came mainly from the COB-dominated left. Resistance came principally from the bourgeois right, lodged in the party primary system. In some cases there was resistance to the reform itself. On the whole, however, the right wing of the MNR was willing to accept a limited reform based on the idea of giving the colonos title to their small plots, while preserving the existing owner's title to the rest of the estate in question. In other words, there would be devolution of legal rights to the peasants but no expropriation as such, and the agrarian power structure would remain relatively intact.[10] Individuals in the political center leaned in one direction or the other, depending on personal inclination. Víctor Paz, and to some extent Guevara Arze, both of whom since the 1930s had evidenced a more radical attitude on agrarian questions, inclined more to the leftist position. Positions on this issue within the party elite were not static. They tended to fluctuate as the tactical context changed over the fall and winter of 1952–53.[11] The major factors in this changing tactical context were the entrenchment of the labor left in the COB and mounting pressure emanating from the Indian mass itself.

There is perhaps no aspect more important, but less understood, than the Indian peasant's role in the Bolivian revolutionary process. The reason for this unfortunate position lies in the vastness of agricultural Bolivia and the tremendous regional and intra-regional variation within it. This variability of the rural system has led to an equal variability in politically relevant Indian peasant behavior. Since 1952, a number of excellent studies have been made which have helped dispel our ignorance, though the general picture is still very far from complete.[12] Studies of this type, however, cannot sidestep an immediate confrontation with the Indian as a political actor. It is, therefore, with trepidation that I embark upon the following presentation of my understanding of historical fact and interpretation regarding the Indian and the revolution. The analysis is based upon a reading of secondary materials, examination of the skimpy written record available in Bolivia, and personal interviews and observations.

The Indian Under the Hacienda System

Certain gross statistics give at least a general picture of the land situation previous to 1952. In the Agrarian Census of 1950, it was calculated that 8.1 percent of landowners controlled 95.1 percent of the land cultivated. All of these holdings were over five hundred hectares (ha.) extension (one hectare equals 2,471 acres). Medium-sized properties (from approximately thirty-five to five hundred ha.) made up 3.8 percent of land owned. Small properties (from approximately three to thirty-five ha.) made up 0.7 percent of land owned. *Minifundios* (less than five ha.) made up 0.2 percent of land owned.[13]

As stated before, the dominant rural institution was the hacienda. The owner of the hacienda functioned as the locus of power and authority in the countryside. The *hacendado* ("landholder") was also the critical link between the national system and the local system of multiple, independent, and, to some degree, self-sufficient realms. The Indian colonos were tied directly to the hacendado. On the whole, two types of relationships held sway: the colono relationship, by which the colono received a plot of land for a certain number of days' work on the hacienda lands; and the *pongo* relationship, by which personal service in the patron's hacienda or town house was extracted from the Indian and his family.[14] The operating details of both forms varied from region to region. In addition, there were a few surviving "free" Indian communities which, while legally independent in internal affairs, were subjected to the labor and economic demands of various official and nonofficial figures located near them. Thus, in one form or another, the vast number of Indians were under the effective control of the dominant Spanish system as manifested in a small number of domineering figures. The world of the average Indian was structured by the personality and idiosyncracies of the hacendado, and, therefore, it was inherently arbitrary. Much Indian behavior reflected a defensive reaction to the exploitive reality of "national" Bolivia.[15] The dominant system, for its part, demanded a certain degree of labor and a high degree of passivity from the Indian.

Passivity was the major day-to-day emotional theme of rural life. Yet, neither passivity nor submission was total. The history of the Andean region is punctuated by Indian uprisings, often of considerable size. Most such uprisings were short-lived, anomic outbursts, but some were well-organized, well-led movements. The most famous included the late eighteenth-century uprisings of Tupac Amaru and Tupac Katari. In the civil war of 1898, an internally led Indian army, responding to promises of land, was the decisive factor in the Liberals' victory. In typical fashion, the Indian was repaid by the slaughter of his leaders and a whole new round of land expropriation. The army of El "Temible" Willka demonstrated that the Indian was capable of organization and that the promise of land could call forth movement. Whether these uprisings were organized attempts to secure land or anomic attempts to seek vengeance, they indicate the Indian's awareness of his conquered status, and his desire to secure a basis for independence and withdrawal from the conquest culture.

Jumping ahead for a moment, one statement can be made with a high degree of certitude: whatever the history of protest activity, the Indian played no role to speak of in the insurrection of April 1952. However, shortly thereafter, protest activity spread with incredible rapidity throughout the countryside, and the Indian quickly became a political actor of the first magnitude. In attempting to account for the factors which brought this about, and in order to understand the subsequent political implications, it seems useful to point out some of the environmental influences which brought the Indian into close contact with the conquest culture.

In the first instance, it should be remembered that, while post-insurrectionary protest activity ranged throughout rural Bolivia, it was particularly intense and well organized in the Cochabamba Valley and the area immediately adjacent to the world's highest navigable water mass, Lake Titicaca. By late 1953, the towns of Ucureña in the Valley and Achacachi on the Lake became the unofficial and often rival centers of the campesino movement. Therefore, some background material on these two areas may prove worthwhile.

There are many dissimilarities between the two regions. The Cochabamba Valley is a temperate lush area located to the southeast of La Paz, and some seven thousand feet lower. The Lake is less than two hours north of La Paz and lies in the middle of the high, barren, and unyielding world of the altiplano. The Valley is peopled by Quechua-speakers (close to 60 percent of the total Indian population), while the Lake and the rest of department of La Paz is inhabited by Aymara-speakers. Despite these and other differences, which shall be gone into presently, the areas also have a number of important common features.

Within the realm of the hacienda system (very small in relation to the total land mass), these two areas represented some of the best available land: Cochabamba, because of its altitude and climate, and Achacachi, because of the beneficent effects of Lake Titicaca's fresh water. As a result, both had been areas of high population density since the days of the Incas. As might be expected, both were prime targets for the establishment of haciendas. Cochabamba and the areas south of it were organized into haciendas much sooner and more thoroughly than the Lake region since, previous to the twentieth century, "national" life was located in the south with Sucre as the capital. There is reason to believe that the establishment of new haciendas and the expansion of old ones around the Lake increased markedly around the turn of the century.[16] This phenomenon is related to the Liberal political triumph, which brought about the shift of the pivot of "national" life from Sucre and silver to La Paz and tin, and the concomitant growth of the city of La Paz.

Historically, Cochabamba was the breadbasket of Bolivia. With the growth of La Paz, there was reason to develop agriculture around the Lake, which is only two hours from the capital by truck. Thus, what little commercial agriculture there was in Bolivia was centered mainly around the Lake and the Cochabamba Valley; there was also commercial agriculture in the semi-tropical valleys near La Paz known as Yungas. The geographical differences between the two areas allowed for some regional specialization. The markets of both were based on supplying La Paz, Oruro, Cochabamba, and the mining camps with perishable goods. However, the demand of these outlets was in the end highly inelastic and no thoroughgoing commerical operations developed.

Furthermore, there is reason to believe that the regimen of the colono was significantly harsher in these regions than in the rest of the country. The old Sucre-based elite was by and large an elite of independent means deriving from the ownership of silver mines. They acquired land primarily for status reasons and it was not a critical element of family wealth.[17] The newer elites which rose with tin, on the other hand, were often high-level professionals who owed their positions to posts with the companies and/or to political success. Therefore, they were more economically dependent than the traditional elite groups. In the Valley, a history of some commercial farming had created groups who lived off the proceeds of their land. While it is true that, in general, the Bolivian hacienda system served to support an accustomed or aspired life style and was not simply a means to accumulate capital, there is reason to believe that, in these two areas, landowners did rely on their land as an important source of income. For this reason, as well as for increasing their social status, the newer elites strove to acquire land. In these two areas, then, there was some commercialization and there was also a desire for and possibility of profit-making. Therefore, there was a growing tendency in these areas to push the large low-cost labor input (colonos) harder so as to increase saleable surplus. In addition, the peasants were often forced to sell whatever small surplus they generated off their plots to the hacendado, who then disposed of it through his own commerical channels.

There were also other factors which set these two areas off from the rest of the country. Owing to the fertility of the soil, historically both were areas of high population concentration and density.[18] The tendency of the hacendado to follow good land and available Indian labor reinforced this factor. Rural Indian populations were locked into these areas and grew over the years, creating serious problems of man-land ratios, soil exhaustion, and property fragmentation. Man-land ratios and fragmentation were particularly serious in the Valley.[19]

To a much greater degree than in other parts of the country, these two areas were linked to and dominated by their respective regional capitals, La Paz and Cochabamba. Geographical propinquity and market structures occasioned a flow of people and goods between the countryside and the city. This flow was particularly marked in Cochabamba where the distances were less, and the city was visibly and structurally more a part of the area. La Paz, on the other hand, was less a part of the area around it and, due to its cup-shaped location in the middle of the altiplano, it was literally invisible to the countryside.[20] However, in the 1920s, arterial and feeder roads were stretched between La Paz and the Lake. In addition, the Lake area received stimulus from movement across the Lake to Peru and from the provincial capital, Achacachi, which was fairly large.

It is interesting to note that the Valley, which became the area of strongest post-1952 peasant activity, was also the region of the country where, previous to 1952, cultural boundaries were weakest and where the Indian was by far the most mobile. In addition to the flow of Indian populations from countryside to city, there was also heavy movement from the countryside to the mines. Many Valley Indians worked in the mines; some remained, while others returned to the land, bringing their experiences with them. Valley Indians also engaged in the transport and sale of salt and wood. Many Valley Indians, as a result, had money and, in some cases, managed to become small independent landholders before the agrarian reform.[21] A small but real peasant class of Indian landholders was developing and differentiating these Indians from the uniform state of vassalage experienced by their racial brothers. Still, it is very important to note that these mobilized Indians did not become citified, "cholofied," or "mestizofied." As Patch has convincingly shown, an entire new pattern of acculturation was already under way in the Valley before 1952.[22]

A very important factor in the makeup of the Valley was the fact that the entire picture of man to land, man to man, and culture to culture relationships was more complex than in any other part of Bolivia. There was a much higher spread of land tenure patterns which included large traditional haciendas, smaller white or mestizo holdings, Indian-owned minifundios, and a variety of tenant and sharecropping arrangements. Land operations were more commercial in the Valley, and landowners—particularly those with medium- and smaller-sized holdings—took a more direct hand in overseeing their operations. Finally, *pongueaje* and other forms of humiliating personal servitude imposed on the Indians were more prevalent and onerous in the Valley.[23]

Another interesting aspect of the Lake region and the Valley was the existence of large non-hacienda schools dating back to the 1930s. In 1931, a most interesting educational experiment was initiated in the town of Warisata, which is located near the Lake and quite near Achacachi. The founders of the Warisata school were radical intellectuals imbued with the *indigenismo* ideology current then in Mexico and to a lesser extent in Bolivia.[24] The school was frankly pro-Indian and utopian-socialist in orientation. Its founders defined their role as that of raising the Indian to a higher status. Shortly thereafter, in the lakeside town of Huatahata, Canadian evangelists established a mission school aimed at imbuing the Indian with new social and religious values. Actually, it seems that throughout the Lake area evangelical Protestantism became a rather potent force. In 1936, a peasant school was established in Ucureña, modeled to some degree on the Warisata school. Many of the original and later staff of the school were members of the PIR, as were most of the country's teachers after the Chaco War.

It is difficult to measure what impact these schools had. It is clear that the landowners of the Lake region saw the Warisata school as a threat, for the Rural Protective Association (set up to protect the interests of the landholders) lobbied against it assiduously. In 1943, their efforts were successful and the school was closed. Finally, it seems significant that of the handful of peasant leaders who reached national status after 1952, many were alumni of one or the other of these institutions.

I believe that the post-1952 protest activity of the peasants in these two regions is at least partially explainable in terms of the environmental factors outlined above, all of which brought the Indians of these areas into more sustained contact with the conquest culture. Such contact allowed them to learn the possibilities of the dominant culture more vividly, while, at the same time, experiencing a greater degree of personal repression from it. Yet, this could hardly be the whole story behind Indian resurgence. We must also relate the peasant to the great events and the process of political struggle which began to wrack Bolivia after 1930.

Political Effects and the Start of the Agrarian Movement

Earlier I took up the question of the Chaco War and argued that we must be careful not to overemphasize its direct impact upon the Indian peasant mass. Thousands of Indians went to war, but the use of press gangs and the high desertion rate leads me to question any discovery of the "national" reality of Bolivia among the vast bulk of the Indian conscripts. The relative post-war quiet of the countryside lends strength to the view that the direct effect of the war on the Indian as a political actor should be downgraded. As argued previously, there was no doubt some effect, but it was mainly in those areas in which Indians, due to the confluence of environmental factors described above, had already developed predispositions toward new behaviors. Even then the effect was mainly one of creating potential leaders. In the late 1930s, such potential leaders were few and isolated, and could well have regressed if it had not been for other factors operative in the "national" arena which reinforced incipient and localized rural trends.

As has been pointed out above (chapter 5), the first harbinger of what was to come took place, significantly enough, in the hacienda of Santa Clara, adjacent to Ucureña. That experiment, supported by the Toro government, contained in miniature the outlines of the key post-1952 rural ingredients, that is, devolution of land in small parcels to peasant holders, and the first organization of peasants into something akin to the sindicato of today. No doubt the scuttling of the experiment by surrounding landlords occasioned bitterness and a covert desire to try again, but here again this predisposition could have atrophied without other reinforcing factors.[25]

Although the tin-based national system and the agrarian local system were separated by many barriers, it would be difficult to believe that the seventeen years of agitation and civil strife conducted at the national level did not have a feedback effect on the countryside. No doubt this effect was more important in the areas where acculturation was already taking place. An important factor assuring spill-over was the fact that agitators from the various counter-elite groups did make periodic political sallies into the countryside. The majority of these sallies were into the Valley, but the altiplano around La Paz was also affected. The reinforcing stimulus of outside agitation hit mainly the two prime areas around the Lake and in the Valley; other areas received little such stimulus. The reason was basically logistical. The cities of La Paz and Cochabamba were the main centers of anti-system activity. Lack of roads and other barriers prohibited any widespread radiation of activity outside these centers. Thus, those who sought to stir up peasant movement were forced to restrict their activities to the relatively accessible immediate hinterland around La Paz and Cochabamba. A similar dynamic took place between Oruro, another center of anti-system activity, and its hinterland; but the dispersed living patterns in that arid region made such tasks much more difficult and basically unrewarding.

During the late 1930s and early 1940s, agitation in the campo was carried out almost exclusively by the PIR and the anarchist FOL. The PIR worked out of its Cochabamba center, the FOL, out of La Paz. Again it is difficult to measure, but there is evidence that the PIR had real impact on the Valley.[26] The Ucureña school no doubt played an important role. Many of the later top peasant leaders in the Valley, including the once all-powerful José Rojas, received their first political education by the PIR. It is impossible to guess what effect the FOL had on the altiplano. It is enough to say that in the late 1940s, the anarchists laid claim to over twenty thousand Indians organized in FOL-affiliated unions, though there is little trace of these organizations today.[27]

Penetration of the campo by political counter-elites increased during Villarroel's brief and tragic tenure. In preparation for the congress of 1945, government agents (including members of the MNR) went into many regions encouraging organization and choosing delegates.[28] This preparatory activity was probably the MNR's first real contact with the countryside. The *Congresso Indigena* of 1945 marked the first high point of national counter-elite cultivation of a rural base. Such cultivation, especially as far as the MNR was concerned, declined significantly after Villarroel's fall. Unfortunately, there is no real basis from which to measure the impact of this congress on the countryside. Some scholars and at least one contemporary Indian leader of note feel that the congress, more than any other previous factor, marked the shift from sporadic and isolated protest activity to a real potential for a broad-based movement. It did so, they argue, by heightening and broadening contacts between peasants and national counter-system activity.[29]

After 1946, both the PIR and the POR worked to gain influence in the Valley, with the latter gaining some ascendance. The exodus of the top MNR leadership weakened that organization's links with the countryside. Some MNR connections did remain, but as their failure to seek peasant support in 1949 indicates, it seems as if their attempts were vitiated by resistance on the part of MNR urban commando units and by leaders in the MNR primary party organization.[30] Agitation in the countryside was heightened

after 1946 by the increasing political activity of the new generation of students who, whatever their party affiliation, opted for a
more radical left line. Such students supported agrarian reform and
helped ply the troubled waters of the rural areas. The two prime
areas of post-1952 protest activity were subjected to more and more
outside agitation as the deadlock at the national level continued
into the post-1946 period. Again Cochabamba received the bulk
of the stimulus. On the whole, such agitation activities, both
within and outside of the MNR, originated from the radical left.

In 1947, the Valley received an additional impulse. As key
political actors such as the first minister of peasant affairs, Nuflo
Chavez Ortiz, argue, this stimulus gave the final push to convert
the Valley into a prime area of potential peasant political activity.
We recall that in 1947, the Cataví Siglo XX complex was the scene
of a socio-political crisis which has gone down in Bolivian labor
history as the *Masacre Blanco*. This refers to the mass layoff of
miners in the Patiño operation (estimates go as high as several
thousand) following the reduction of the war demand for tin
and a shift in technique used in the mining operation. Denied
work in the mines, many returned to their home regions, which in
most cases was Cochabamba. The political significance of this
influx was heightened by the fact that, in an attempt to head off
agitation, the companies used the layoff as an excuse to cull out
the strong leaders and the more political miners. Thus, many of
those laid off were members of the POR and the PIR and followers of Lechín. For this reason, the Valley was infused with a
large group of highly political ex-miners with a well-developed
tradition of organized protest.[31]

Previous to 1952, three factors were operative in the Lake and
Valley regions: (a) a general process of exposure to the conquest
culture, combined with increasingly onerous pressure; (b) the creation of potential leaders as a result of the war; and (c) a continual set of reinforcing stimuli coming from the feedback of
the struggle going on in the "national system."

Probably, the basis for a campesino movement was well established before April 1952. However, it must be emphasized that the
Bolivian government fell at this time without the aid of the Indian

mass. In any event, the nature of the government's defeat should be considered a factor in later peasant activity. It was an across-the-board defeat for the old elite, and, throughout the country, the system of power and authority of the old order was in retreat. Simultaneously, new centers of power bent on pushing the revolution into all spheres of socio-economic activity were springing into existence. To the more aware peasant leaders, the situation must have appeared as a unique opportunity to redress old wrongs. At least so it would seem, for the first Indian uprisings in the Valley after the insurrection were obviously motivated as much by a desire for revenge as for land or power. These first activities were quite violent, especially where landowners had been hard and unsympathetic taskmasters. Hacienda houses were burned and looted, while their occupants were beaten and often killed. In some cases, the drive for revenge was turned against the church; buildings were desecrated and priests manhandled.[32] As the movement gained momentum, it took on tones of a racial, or at least cultural, war. Whole towns were surrounded and menaced. In some cases, invasions and pitched battles took place.[33]

Foreign observers have often wondered whether the movement was spontaneous or directed, and whether the MNR encouraged or discouraged it. Actually, the movement took place in an extremely confused context. The general system of state authority was crumbling and many stimuli and counter-stimuli were hitting both the urban and rural realms. Moreover, the MNR was not the only revolutionary force in operation, and it must be remembered that the party was far from unified. There were parts of it which wished to carry the revolution to the coutryside, while others were determined to resist such attempts.

Indian leaders may well have decided to move on their own, but there is no doubt that they received help and ecnouragement from the left. After the insurrection, COB organizers went into the Valley, as well as into other regions, to bring the word that a revolution had indeed taken place. They exhorted the Indian peasant to move before the "reactionaries" succeeded in stalling the revolution. By most early accounts, the POR was particularly active in the first Valley uprisings. At the time, most peasant organizations were considered to be under the influence, if not the control, of the POR.[34]

The Valley movement, which originated in Ucureña, came from roots which gave it certain spontaneous characteristics. The lightning spread of the movement throughout other rural regions was another matter. The demonstration effect of events in the Valley most likely stirred Indians in other regions. Yet, in a country like Bolivia which lacked all but the most primitive means of communication, the revolution and the Valley uprisings could have occurred without the knowledge of most of the rural population.[35] However, the populace did know and someone had to carry the word.

The word was carried to the campo by the left wing of the MNR and the non-MNR left. The COB played a most important role in exhorting the peasants to rise up and seize their lands. Perhaps the most important organization in spreading the movement, however, was the ministry of peasant affairs under the control of COB member, Nuflo Chavez Ortiz.[36] Under the leadership of Chavez, a semi-official campaign to organize the peasants into sindicatos was put in operation. Organizers fanned out across the campo and Chavez himself traveled the countryside bestowing ministerial approval on sindicato after sindicato. One of the areas most receptive to the efforts of the COB and Chavez was the Lake region. The town of Achacachi quickly became as notorious for its violent uprisings as Ucureña.

As the sindicato form of organization spread, so too did land seizures, rural violence, and pillage. In retrospect, the reports of violence were probably exaggerated. Still, the movement was a violent process which stirred general revulsion and fear in white and mestizo Bolivia. Landowners, administrators, and the townsmen of rural areas began to flee the countryside, bringing tales of Indian vengeance to La Paz.

The rural structure did not collapse without resistance. Some landowners fought back or attempted to crush unions before they started. Townsmen likewise organized for defense and engaged in bloody clashes with peasant unions. The MNR split deeply over rural violence. In some cases, local police were sent to aid landowners resisting peasant land seizures.[37] Often, the local MNR commando was the basis of the townsmen's resistance to peasant demands. The party right wing backed open resistance to the peasants, while the political center took an equivocating position. In the early days, the tone of the center's position was one of disapproval of peasant violence, which it said was due mainly to Communist instigation. The picture then, both in the campo and in MNR official circles, was confused and pervaded with contradictory statements and actions.

Early in 1953 an official line began to emerge. It is best described as one of bowing to the inevitable. The party's political center made the decision to pursue a land reform in an effort to keep at least some hold on the rural situation. Hopefully, by meeting peasant demands, peasant identification could be shifted from the left to an official MNR position. At this point, the MNR officially became a supporter of the sindicato.[38] An extensive reform was promised and the sindicatos were declared legitimate. Local commandos were reshuffled and rightists were replaced with party men more sympathetic to the peasants' goals.

The commission empowered to draft the agrarian reform was called on January 20, 1953. The membership of the commission reflected a general leftward shift in the configuration of power. It included not only left MNR members but also the well-known former PIR member, Arturo Urquidi Morales, and the prominent Ernesto Ayala Mercado of the POR. The calling of the commission did not bring an end to uprisings, land incursions, and rural violence. These actions actually increased and rural pressure continued down to and past the signing of the actual reform decree on August 3, 1953.

The issue of what form the agrarian reform would take dominated the national scene during the winter and spring of 1953. Alternative projections were struggled over behind the closed doors of the party and openly in the meeting halls of the COB. Elements of the party's right wing and center pushed for a minimal reform which would give the colonos their small plots, but maintain the integrity of the traditional hacienda lands. In addition, they argued strongly that all dispossessions should be compensated. Elements of the left-wing MNR and the POR, on the other hand, pushed for complete expropriation without indemnification. In addition, they demanded the definition of mechanisms which would provide the basis for at least minimal forms of collective operations.

The position which steadily gained ascendance was that put forth by Urquidi Morales and the final decree bears considerable resemblance to his plan.[39] To this extent the reform can be said to be based on the original PIR approach to the agrarian problem. The original agrarian position of the PIR was based on a determinist stage concept of history, the essence of which was that socialism could not be achieved without the previous passage of a society through a well-developed capitalist stage.

The PIR as well as other leftist groups had always held that Bolivia was a "combined" society; that is, a society with a semi-modern capitalist sector alongside of a larger semi-feudal sector. Given this, the progressive move for Bolivia was not to go directly to socialism, but to break the feudal chains and thereby allow a state-controlled emergence of capitalism. The aim, therefore, was not one of socialistic revolution, but of a *revolución democrática burguesa* ("democratic bourgeois revolution"). This approach was held to be particularly important for an agrarian solution.

Urquidi's plan based itself on both economic and political logic, with the former clearly dominant. The aim of the reform was first and foremost to provide a rational basis for agrarian economic development. Secondly, the reform was to aim at making the peasant a "motor" force and protector of the revolution. The first aim would be achieved by bringing capitalist forms of production to the campo; the second, by meeting the peasants' demand for land and by organizing them into unions and militias attached to the revolutionary party.[40]

In theory, the reform was to realize its economic aim in the following manner. The prime target would be the *latifundios,* ("large holdings based on peonage with a low ratio of capital to labor input"). By destroying the latifundio, the basis of the feudal structure would be shattered, freeing both land and people for more rational forms of relationships. The Indian would achieve mobility and at the same time, by grace of becoming a landowner, be able to become both a producer and a consumer. The decree differentiated the latifundio from small holdings (individual peasant holdings), medium-sized holdings, and agricultural enterprises (*empresas agricolas*), which were large holdings with a higher ratio of capital to labor input. These latter forms would be protected, and through rural credit and extension services, actually be encouraged to flourish as private, profit-motive-driven operations. Finally, owners of latifundios would be allowed to maintain a certain portion (size to be determined by the case) of their holdings as medium-sized enterprises. The size of the various categories was to be determined according to the ecological and demographic characteristics of each region of the country.

The reform decree or Agrarian Reform Law of August 3, 1953, incorporated all these principles and provided for indemnification based on twenty-five year bonds. It provided for the devolution of land to colonos, hacienda workers with no plots, and to descendants of originally dispossessed *comunitarios* ("members of free Indian communities"). Types of landholdings were defined and size ranges laid out region by region. As the POR accurately pointed out, it was a liberal revolution based on establishing the individual, the profit motive, and modern private property as the basis of the agricultural system. However, this induced capitalism was based on the previous general proviso that original claim to all soil, sub-soil, and water belonged to the state and that all private property had to serve a useful function for the national collectivity. Land was then theoretically held in usufruct, development aims overrrode individual profit, and the guardian of the economy was the state. Although the MNR had not previously proposed a detailed reform, we can see that the reform adopted generally squared with its early predispositions to state-sponsored national development, using a modified capitalist system based on the little man.

The signing of the agrarian decree, like that of the nationalization decree, symbolized the dynamic shift of power relations which was under way in the country. To sign the decree, President Paz journeyed to Ucureña, by now the symbolic center of *el movi-*

miento campesino. There, on an open air platform surrounded by thousands of armed Indian peasants, the land reform became law. The bystanders showed their pleasure and their new-found strength by firing round after round of ammunition into the air.

The signing of the decree did not bring an end to uprisings, seizures, and violence. Over the next few months, the pace actually increased. The peasants, unaware of the fine points of law and theorizing, were now anxious to claim land. Likewise, many still sought to right old wrongs and to extract, where possible, violent redress. The post-decree violence, however, began to take on new characteristics. The anomic character of the earlier incursions gave way to more organized and purposeful action. The struggle to control formal and real agencies of power was under way.

At first, it appeared that by extension of the party commando system, the campo would be effectively linked to the central state structure through the MNR. The COB also made a strong bid to extend its independent control to the campo by providing sectoral representation for the peasant sindicatos. In those first days, the leftists seemed to have the edge in the campo. The Valley sindicatos were considered to be under POR influence. The first national representative of the campesinos before the COB was Nuflo Chavez, and the first national representatives of the sindicatos of the department of La Paz were non-peasant COB members.

These national ideological colorations masked a deeper independent momentum building in certain regions. Before long, departmental federations of peasant sindicatos were formed. These regional organizations were followed by the establishment of a national confederation. In short order non-peasant types were pushed out of leadership positions and true peasant types, or at least people associated with the campo, took over. POR influence declined quickly in the Valley. On the altiplano, identification with Lechín and the COB was maintained, but local leadership declared its effective independence. In sum, what previously had been a potential situation had become real. The movement began to develop its own leaders and identity. The peasants (at least in some regions) were being converted into an independent segment of political action now in the process of groping for a course.

Like the workers, the campesinos armed themselves and formed into militias.[41] These units were also nominally under party command, but in reality were controlled at lower levels.

The most immediate effect of the reform and the spreading peasant movement was the collapse of the pre-existing agrarian structure. There was a general decline of control structures followed by a withdrawal of "civilized," i.e., Spanish, cultural influence. Hacendados and administrators fled. Despite the theoretical right to hold a medium-sized plot, peasant organizations prohibited the return of their former patrons. In those cases where the owner returned anyway, he was often harassed and menaced. Concomitantly, there was an exodus of mestizo shopkeepers and traders from the small rural towns. Hence, the previous market structure also collapsed.[42]

The areas outside the major cities were, in effect, left to the Indian peasant. The links between the pre-1952 national and local systems were broken. The gap created by this process of disintegration was plugged almost immediately by the sindicato. With the exception of the persisting *comunidades* ("communities"—as used here, "free Indian communities"), the sindicato became the nucleus of social, political, and economic organization throughout the countryside. For the first time since the conquest, the rural world became Indianized. In the heavily organized areas such as the Lake region, the sindicato began to rule the town as well as the campo. Indians began moving into the pueblos, which in many cases became basically campesino towns.[43] Mestizo traders and government officials entered the campo, but, by then, a new stratum of peasant leaders, by controlling local organizations, became the new human links between the national system and the rural Indian peasantry.

Having said all this, it must hastily be added that the picture in the campo, as in other dimensions of Bolivian life, was one of overall confusion. The centrifugal tendencies operant in other sectors became even more readily visible in the campo. The National Confederation of Campesinos never reached the degree of control over its sectoral constituency as the COB did over labor. It became and remains an ill-defined organization, the influence of which waxes and wanes with changing national and local circumstances. The leadership of the confederation has most often reflected fluctuating alliances of powerful regional leaders. Therefore, it has seldom been unified internally and generally has been incapable of projecting a coherent political line. The confederation has always been more of a council of local bosses than an institution with a life and substance of its own. Decisions of the confederation have had effect only to the extent that regional bosses were willing to accept them.[44]

The underlying problem of bringing coherence to the campo was the previous existence of the hacienda system. The countryside had been divided along the myriad lines of these previously independent realms. After 1953, local jealousies, boundary disputes, and the absence of a sustained tradition of common offensive or defensive action led to a strong drive toward atomization. Accentuating the process was the tendency of the individual peasant to seize his land and opt out of the general political picture for the security of subsistence. Personal defense against the arbitrary actions of the dominant Spanish society had shaped the peasants' outlook for centuries. In this framework, land appeared as the needed base within which to withdraw from a hostile surrounding world. The majority of the campesinos, once land was assured, were no longer ready nor able to act as a collective national force. The campesinos' first reaction was one of defensive withdrawal.

After the flurry of reportage preceding and immediately following the reform, there was a steady decline in national news coverage of campo activities. The decline reflected, first of all, an abatement of violence. Secondly, it indicated a decline of peasant activity as a day-to-day influence on national decision-making. This is not to say that activity disappeared, but rather that it was not of a kind to demand day-to-day national reactions in the manner which labor activities did, for example. This period of relative national eclipse lasted until the late 1950s.

Rural Organization: The Sindicato and the Central

During the post-insurrectionary period, there began in the campo a process of gestation into units and types of organizations reflective of the different environments. No single pattern held sway throughout the vast complex of rural Bolivia. The sindicato became the formal unit of rural organization, based on the boundaries of the previous hacienda. However, the nature of the sindicatos varied widely both among and within regions. In one ex-hacienda, a sindicato organization might be very strong, but the neighboring one could well be very weak.

In some areas, such as the Valley and Lake regions, the dominant trend was toward the strengthening of individual sindicatos and, then, the consolidation of groups of sindicatos under powerful regional centers of command. In other areas, the sindicato took root as an important communal form, but with fewer political overtones and without the tendency to regional consolidation. In still others, the sindicato became little more than a name, and more traditional forms of control actually were operative. The major dividing line depended on whether the head of the sindicato achieved command status or became a traditional headman capable of achieving joint action only on the basis of mobilizing community consensus. In some cases, sindicatos went through a cycle of growth, centralization of command, and politicization, only to be followed by regression in the form of decentralization, decline of the command function, and depoliticization.[45] The relative strength of the sindicato usually depended on pre-existing conditions, and on the strength and personality of local leaders.

An example of a community in which the personality of a leader played a large role in the growth cycle is the Cinti Valley of southern Bolivia. This Valley is famous in Bolivia as a wine center and as a producer of the beverage Singani (the Bolivian equivalent of pisco, a white brandy famous in Peru). The area had certain similar characteristics to the Cochabamba Valley and the Lake regions, particularly because it had some previous commercialization of agriculture. After the reform, one sindicato of note emerged in the Cinti Valley. The leader of this sindicato, Juan Chumacero, was a powerful personality, and, under his prodding, other sindicatos became strong. The area then began to move toward a higher level of consolidation and centralization of command under the leadership of Chumacero. At this point, however, Chumacero was killed under mysterious circumstances. After his death, the process reversed. Coordinated effort ended and, shortly thereafter, the individual sindicatos began to decline. Within a year, organization had completely regressed. The only organization of any note was the original sindicato and, even this only shadowed former organizational effectiveness.[46]

The Cinti Valley was by no means an exceptional case. It appears that the emergence of strong consolidated centers of organization was more the exception than the rule. Such centers became and remain critical political factors, but we must resist the temptation to generalize from them to the totality of rural Bolivia. At the same time, it is well to keep in mind the critical variable of individual personality and leadership. Where the local and regional organization became powerful, it was under the aegis of a dominating individual. The fortune, or lack thereof, of peasant political activity since 1952, must be studied, in large measure, through the activities of a number of well-known *caciques* ("peasant bosses") who have emerged since the revolution.

The decline of the sindicato as a center of command did not mean that the state or other instrumentalities moved in. On the contrary, it usually indicated a further withdrawal of the community into isolation from the national reality. Considering that national integration has been one of the big issues in Bolivia since 1952, this isolation factor is rather important. In vast areas of Bolivia, the Indian, from the point of view of the state, regressed to passive subsistence or at least to minimal involvement in a "national" Bolivia. The Indian en masse was not becoming the wished-for producer-consumer so critical to national elite development plans. The degree of withdrawal could go so far as to be completely anomic from the national point of view. In northern Potosí, for example, two local Indian groups—the lymies and the jucumanes—used the new situation to reopen a historical feud. Violence and wholesale inter-tribal war continues, even today, defying all attempts at pacification.

It was precisely in those areas where the sindicatos grew and became consolidated and well organized that the peasant mass began to evolve as an active element in the national arena. As indicated before, the two areas where such developments had most success were the Cochabamba Valley and the Lake region. Here, individual sindicatos were consolidated into strong, centrally controlled groupings. Consolidated power, at times, reached the level of the departmental federation, but mainly tended to even off at the level called the "central" (from twenty to thirty sindicatos tied to a command center located in or near a town). Between the individual sindicato and the central was an intermediate level of consolidation known as the sub-central. In both regions, a number of strong centrals developed. In the Valley, Ucureña, Cliza, Punata, and Totora were among the most important centers, while on the altiplano, Achacachi, Warisata, and Huarina became potent centers. These centers were associated with strong personal leaders, caciques, who have continuously struggled among themselves for regional power and jurisdiction. The power of such individuals has fluctuated on the basis of their ability to bring their own and other centrals under their personal control. The struggle has been so intense and the stakes so high, from the caciques' point of view, that both regions have never been far from intra-campesino civil war.

In fact, both areas have had what can be called civil wars. The most serious conflict convulsed the Cochabamba Valley between 1957 and 1961. Two caciques, José Rojas and Miguel Veizaga, battled it out for singular control of the Valley. The Lake also saw such violence among caciques. The most notorious incident occurred when one cacique, Felipe Flores, was killed in a gun battle on the steps of the Ministry of Peasant Affairs. These conflicts involved personal rivalries, but also involved questions of outlook and national factional disputes.

In those areas where organization really took hold, it was imposed essentially from above, often by means of coercion.[47] These sindicatos, especially the centrals, became independent and sovereign-like units. The central took on the characteristics and performed most of the functions of a miniature state. Through the militias, it monopolized force in its area. In some cases, this went so far as to establish barracks financed by compulsory levies on member sindicatos. The central leaders collected taxes and imposed fines on members. With these independent sources of finance, they often bought new arms and ammunition and paid the salaries of permanent staffs. Within their regions, they made laws and punished transgressors. Failure to heed a directive could result in a fine, jailing, a beating, or even death. The sindicato organization put itself between the individual peasant and the larger society, acting as his broker with the national state. It was often the sindicato which pressed land claims and oversaw distribution.[48]

Although there were twelve offices in a sindicato, real power resided in one man, the secretary-general. These individuals, in turn, were coordinated with and took orders from the sub-centrals and centrals. The secretary-general of the central or department federation was often the undisputed cacique over a wide territory which could include thousands of campesinos. Of the many caciques who appeared after 1952, the two most prominent were Toribio Salas, who at one point controlled almost the whole of the department of La Paz from his headquarters in Achacachi, and José Rojas, who controlled the bulk of the Valley and came close to being the single most powerful peasant boss in the entire country.

These caciques could, on command, turn out an army to ward off a counter-revolutionary blow or, if they preferred, threaten the MNR government. They could block off all roads and bring traffic to a halt, which would threaten La Paz or Cochabamba with starvation. In their realms, they were the law, and no one, including the Bolivian president, entered without permission. In reality they were inviolable to state law. In November 1959, for example, a minister of asuntos campesinos, Vincente Alvarez Plata, was shot down after attending a department-wide campesino meeting. It was common opinion that Toribio Salas (the cacique of Achacachi) was author of the murder. Not only was he never punished, but was never even brought in for questioning. Case upon case could be cited of state law and state personages being flaunted, insulted, or menaced by these powerful bosses.[49]

The confederation meetings became a kind of big power parley where the big two or three or four caciques, depending on the situation, sat down to discuss what stance they should take to the state and on what issue. Thus, the pre-1952 links broken, the campo slipped out from under the effective sovereignty exercised by the Bolivian state. On the one hand, there was a reversion to more primitive kinds of community organizations in which large areas and numbers reverted to atomized isolation. On the other, powerful baronies under personalized control were created, functioning as small states warring with each other and, often, with the nominal national state.

We cannot overstress the complexity of the situation in the Bolivian campo since 1952. Every generalization is immediately confronted with exceptions. Situations varied by region, within regions, and over time; what was true of an area one year could be completely untrue the next. Temporarily at least, we can point to the existence of the following types of situations: (a) in northern Potosí, there was a total divorce from the modern Bolivian reality; (b) there were great areas of passivity and subsistence withdrawal; (c) there were large and important areas of autonomous growth and development of the campesino into a national political actor under the tutelage of powerful regional caciques.

Another pattern of importance has recently been described by anthropologists working in the Yungas valleys near La Paz.[50] In this region, the situation appears to be analogous to the situation which existed in the United States when there were big city political bosses and ward healers. In the Yungas valleys sindicatos have developed, but not into totally independent bodies or into structures based completely on command. From an early period of high politicization, often leftist-influenced, the sindicatos have become depoliticized, but they have remained organized. Secretary-generals have become important, but still have to mobilize a consensus before major actions could be undertaken. State authorities have entered into the affairs of the area under the sindicato but usually only by invitation. Yet, the sindicatos have been inclined to seek the aid and support of authorities in settling disputes. By the same token, they have been aware of the relevance of state and national politics, especially as a source of help in the form of schools, electricity, etc. They have pressed their desires for these things not directly by command, but by manipulation of the party structure and other entrees into central authority. The desire of the sindicato organizations for that which only the national center could give, and the lack of the will or ability to openly command it, has led to a greater reliance on structures of manipulation. This has resulted in their gradual integration into the formal and informal network of the national system.

Previous to 1964, the major mechanism of integration was that of the MNR party and the local political boss (distinct from the independent cacique). At least in the one detailed case reported, the boss emerges as a new social type. He is not the secretary-general of the sindicato nor is he a formal representative of the party. He is a man of some economic consequence in the area and reputed to have an "in" with the powers that be. He acts as the recipient of party favors to be distributed in his area. He receives such favors because he guarantees the votes and stability of the area. His ability to produce politically, in turn, springs from the acceptance of his role by the campesinos because he produces results for them. His personal position is based on some attributes associated with the cacique, for example, strength, fearlessness, and a willingness to use sanctions against opponents. He could probably arrange beatings, but his sanctions derive more from an ability to manipulate economic and political structures controlled, in the first instance, by others. While the cacique is an independent representative of autonomous semi-governmental authority, the boss is a true broker, filling an interstice between two converging structures. Like his counterpart in other world contexts, the boss, by functioning as the dependent nexus between the two structures, contributes, in the long run, to their integration.

In more than a literary sense, then, the real Bolivian revolution has taken place in the countryside. For all their importance, the changes in the old "national system" do not match in profundity or long-range implication those changes in the campo. We will delve more deeply into some of the political implications of the changes in the local system, as well as those in the national system, in subsequent chapters.

11 *Group, Faction, and Personality: 1952-1960*

Given what we know of revolutionary situations in general, it would have been quite unusual if the MNR had entered the post-insurrectionary period as a unified monolith. Faction feuding and disagreement over which direction to take the revolution were to be expected. In the Bolivian case, the ideological and orientational differences within the movement were so great that the resultant post-insurrectionary struggles were particularly fierce. The reason lies in the curious set of circumstances which, after 1946, made the MNR a magnet, attracting every counter-tendency from left to right, from reformist to revolutionary. By 1951, the movement was a farrago of contradictory orientations and positions. The MNR, which led the insurrection of 1952, was a shaky alliance of mutually suspicious groups doomed to internal struggle once the common foe had been eliminated.

Fast upon the heels of victory, the first rumblings were heard of the coming battle among the revolutionary elites. The three basic groups described previously formed into factions within a right-left spectrum. The right wing was made up of the primary party leadership which had organized and carried the brunt of the in-country fight between 1946 and 1952. The leaders of the faction were middle-level professionals and intellectuals. Its support, likewise, derived from middle elements and the unorganized

216

urban *clase popular*. Directly opposed to this group was the socialist labor left. The left wing first appeared as a party faction after
1946 and had grown to considerable size as a result of the party's
efforts to mobilize labor during the Sexenio. The faction was further buttressed by increasing defections to the MNR from the
PIR and POR. Victory predictably led to another round of defections, formal or informal, to the MNR, swelling the leftist ranks
even further.

In between these two political wings stood what I term the
pragmatic nationalist center. This group was made up of the origi-
nating notables of the party, most of whom spent the period from
1946 to 1952 in exile. Within this group, individual sympathies
varied. It gained a kind of coherence, however, from a common
desire to avoid open clashes in the party and its willingness to
demur to demonstrable internal party power.

The gathering internal party struggle was complicated and
partly shaped by pressures emanating from non-party elites. On
the right was the possibility of counter-revolution springing from
two sources. The first was external to Bolivia and involved the
threat of an externally supported invasion by exiles and/or by
financial sanctions from the international tin community. Intimately related to the external threat was the question of what attitude the United States would adopt. From the earliest days, the
MNR pragmatic core had argued that no Bolivian revolution
could go so far as to alienate the United States or to threaten
too deeply Bolivia's immediate neighbors, particularly Peru and
Argentina. This line sprang not only from fear of direct intervention—anticipated more from Peru or Argentina than the
United States—but also from the fear of United States economic
retaliation; as Bolivia relied on the United States to absorb her
tin and provide imports, this could be disastrous.[1] These considerations immediately led to counsels of moderation from the MNR
center and a crash diplomatic effort to reassure the United States.
These diplomatic factors undoubtedly contributed to the evolutionary tone built by Paz around his first government (he stressed
the limited nature of the revolution and the need for continuity
with the past). Be that as it may, the efforts to soothe the United

States were successful, and the Eisenhower administration adopted a cautiously favorable stance to the "Bolivian National Revolution." This and other factors helped to diminish the possibility of an outside threat, and on this side at least the rebel's flank became secure.

The second source of counter-revolutionary threats from the right was in the form of internal opposition (opposition within Bolivian borders) with some external help. This threat continued and actually became stronger. Groups outside the MNR organization, threatened by the emerging revolutionary program, began to look for a political vehicle. They found it in the rightist FSB. Although the oldest surviving post—Chaco War party, the FSB had until 1952 been little more than a cabal of young romantics with little or no political import beyond being an element of added harassment for the status quo elite. Having missed its chance to participate in the revolution, the FSB now had to find a constituency or face extinction at the hands of the mushrooming MNR. The FSB made itself the voice of those sectors of Bolivia about to be deposed by the revolution. True to its past, it adopted a conspiratorial and violent political style which won it a certain amount of sympathy among those pushed aside after 1952. The old Liberal and PURS groupings completely lost their bases—never really large anyway—and the FSB became the major counter-revolutionary opposition to the MNR. Throughout the following decade, the FSB was to present itself as a constant threat to the MNR. The Bolivian Falange staged many coup attempts. The FSB and the MNR became locked in an exchange of violence which plagued Bolivia until 1960. The FSB also became a symbol of counter-revolution cultivated by the MNR center to keep dissident elements of the party in line, lest internal division weaken the revolution's ability to resist. The FSB, therefore, played a most important role in setting the framework within which post-insurrectionary politics was played out.

Not all the threatening thunder came from the counter-revolutionary right. The non-MNR left also posed a serious problem to the party. Ominous rumblings of "permanent revolutions" and of threats to seize power from bourgeois hands presented important tactical problems to the MNR leadership as it confronted the future. Given the distribution of real physical power, the possibility of a leftist coup had to be taken seriously by the party center. In sum, the new governors, in addition to the myriad problems of pulling the society back together, had to find a way to maintain the integrity of MNR control in the face of coherent anti-party threats from both the left and the right. Only in this context do succeeding events begin to take on form and meaning.

The MNR labor left emerged from the insurrection most able and willing to lock horns on the issue of the shape of a new Bolivia. From 1946 on, one of the key elements in the revolutionary drama was the socialization of conflict in both scope and intensity. As this process mainly concerned the mobilization of the lower class and labor groups, each increment of expanding power redounded to the benefit of the labor left. Before the actual insurrection, it had been the party group with the most obvious ascending potential. In early 1952, the fullness of this potential had as yet to be realized.

The dynamics of the insurrection itself fed the expanding power of the labor left. The open defeat of the army and its consequent disintegration put a primacy on the political meaning of organized irregulars. The quick appearance of workers' militias, therefore, takes on added significance. The submergence of all union activity, excepting the COB, and the ability of the COB, in turn, to bring under its tutelage the bulk of nominal party militias, must also be considered. Within an amazingly short time, the labor left stood as the largest organized and armed grouping in the country.

An intangible but important factor in the power equation was the relative ideological coherence of the party left wing and its operative tactical assumption of inevitable battle with the MNR "bourgeois" right. Since the famous *Tesis de Pulacayo,* penned by Lora and adopted by the Lechín-controlled FSTMB in 1946, the labor left operated in a framework defined by the goal of creating a true socialist society. Operative to the goal were notions of class conflict: first, in the context of a front of progressive sectors against the status quo elite; second, in the inevitable clash of revolutionary labor and reformist middle interests. Within the goal of a socialist state, therefore, was the operational goal of an eventual emergence of labor to a position of national leadership.[2] Both elements of this model were unacceptable to the MNR center as well as to the MNR right. These original predispositions were reinforced by leftist defections to the MNR in the late 1940s and immediately after the insurrection. This phenomenon, previously called *entrismo,* was rationalized by the following logic: the left could not come to power alone; the MNR stood the best chance of seizing power; hence, the left should join the MNR and drive it in a radical direction. This radicalization, however, presupposed a previous defeat of the MNR rightists.[3]

The party right wing, by contrast, emerged from the insurrection largely disorganized and localized. However, it did have two important factors in its favor. The first was its relative control of the primary party organization. However, this control was problematic. During the Sexenio, the problem of internal party organization was formidable. The contacts between local commandos and the Comité Político Nacional in La Paz were sporadic at best. Hence, the Comité functioned partly in a vacuum, and local units were left to their own devices. The problem of coordination and control was, if anything, more severe after the breakdown occasioned by the insurrection. In the attendant confusion, the national leadership core in La Paz could hardly manipulate the diffuse party structure to its liking.

Beyond this, the second important factor in the rightists' favor was the availability of Los Grupos de Honor, a major organized base of force. No doubt these were potent groups, but their numbers were small and the units were localized to the cities of La Paz and Cochabamba. The party right wing developed a kind of unofficial command post in the La Paz City Hall which, under the mayorship of Jorge Rios Gamarra, was staffed with rightists. The La Paz *municipalidad* was hardly a base from which to rival the COB.

Ideologically, the right wing was also diffuse. The rightists advanced the concept of "nationalism" but infused it with precious little futuristic content. Beyond gradiose statements of economic independence and the like, they had no real image of a "new" Bolivia. Theirs was a reaction in terms of an increasing inability to realize the goals and values of the old system, images which were defined largely by La Rosca. Their nationalism, early anti-Semitism, and latent xenophobia spoke of blocked career channels, monopolization of economic possibility, and the use of non-Bolivians in important jobs.

A romanticization of the national revolution developed among the rightists. There was an implied belief that the violent blow alone would relieve pressure and solve their problems. Long years of bitter conflict and suppression led to a certain glorification of violent action in and of itself—*la mystica de la revolución violenta* ("the mystique of the violent revolution"). This predisposition was particularly strong in Los Grupos de Honor. Secrecy, elaborate rituals, in-group signs, the bold and daring blow in the night—this is what was nurtured, lived on, and, to a degree, became obsessive. Still today, many members of Los Grupos look back on the Sexenio wistfully as a time of purity, honor, and solidarity. The rightists had been ready to fight, but having won they were not ready to use their power to build.[4]

The concept of a pragmatic nationalist center as I have advanced it is post hoc and, to a degree, speculative. The notion gains some operational validity, however, from the fact that both the left and right wings perceived such a center. The left saw Paz and certain individuals around him as different from the right and susceptible to the kinds of pressures the left could bring to bear. The right, on the other hand, regarded Paz with suspicion, fearful of his selling them out.[5] For this reason, some urged Siles to hold on to the presidency after the insurrection. A curious fact which may or may not have meaning is that, although the insurrection was secure on April 11, 1952, Paz did not make the ten-hour plane trip from Buenos Aires to La Paz until April 17.

The pragmatic nationalist center was by all odds the smallest and weakest group from the point of view of power bases. Structural weakness was counterbalanced by the mystification of the image of Paz during the Sexenio, and the need to maintain a focal point of party unity. There was a desire on all sides to avoid an open showdown, the results of which could have led to reaction. Both sides preferred to bring pressure within the party and thereby maintain continuity and confer legitimacy on their positions. Paz and the party center were needed, therefore, to buffer the intra-party battle and to provide a symbol of the strength and coherence of the revolutionary party.

The pragmatic nationalist center did not hold its position simply by being a midpoint between two poles. I would argue that, in the case of Paz and a few like him, a commitment was held to a certain image of a future Bolivia. In these early days, the operational details of the image were still vague, but certain primary values were apparent. These values can be summed up in the concepts of "nation," "state," and "development." Reacting to the national state models of Europe, the pragmatic center, from the beginning, showed an overriding involvement in the desire to create out of the disparity of Bolivia a modern, developed nation-state, and to do it fast. Moreover, there was an obvious desire on the part of this elite group to direct that enterprise. They saw themselves as the only group willing and able to complete the task. Their pragmatism sprang from a flexibility as to which specific institutionalized means could be used to achieve the general goal.

Their earliest predispositions had been to impose reform from above. In this pursuit, they were willing to use a variety of means and to flirt with often contradictory ideological appeals. Changing tactical realities forced a variety of adjustments, including the transformation and radicalization of the MNR. However, to them the party was a machine, and its constituent parts, factors of production, both of which they, the elite, would fashion to the developmental task. To fulfill the task, they were willing to make the adjustments tactical realities demanded and to fall back in many areas, but they always strove to keep the situation within certain broad boundaries defined by them.[6]

The first shots in the post-insurrectionary battle came, predictably, from the left. They seized the initiative and forced both the right and center MNR factions to react. Lacking a coherent alternative image of a new Bolivia, the rightists, in the face of demands for nationalization, agrarian reform, universal suffrage, and destruction of the army, found themselves, in effect, defending the essential institutional structure of the old order. The center, on the other hand, was presented with a challenge to its role as the initiating and defining elite of a new Bolivia.

The left wing played its first card on the day of Paz's return. They presented Paz with the spectacle of the new power he had helped create after 1946: the power of the street, the factory, and the mine, a power now essentially out of MNR control. In this manifestation, the left used a tactic it was to hone to finer and finer precision in the next few years. Working on the assumption that Paz and those around him had aims at variance with theirs but that being pragmatic would respond to demonstrable power, the left set out to keep its power ever present to the pragmatic center's view. Cognizant that their power lay in organized numbers, the left set out to assure that the scope of conflict, greatly expanded between 1946 and 1952, would be even further expanded and kept at a high pitch. Mobilization became the watchword of the left wing.

Every major decision was either initiated in the streets or dragged from the private confines of the party into the public arena, where the weight of numbers would bear heavily on outcomes. In reaction, the party elite sought to keep the conflict a private party matter by stressing the need for party unity, discipline, and leadership. The left responded by demanding that the voice of the people be heard: party democracy and labor independence became their persistent slogans.

The spilling over of the revolution from the national to the agricultural sphere greatly magnified the weight of publicly mobilized numbers. The immediate effect, therefore, was to strengthen the position of the left, although this was to change drastically later. To the din of armed and marching workers was added that of armed and, often rampaging, campesinos. Demonstration after demonstration was held throughout the country, and always with the same refrains: *"¡Nacionalization!" "¡Reforma Agraria!"*

Beyond mass demonstrations, the labor left drove home the reality of its power by repeating over and over a simple drama.

Almost daily a delegation of workers or peasants would arrive in La Paz to make a courtesy call on the president. In the official reception that followed, the disparity of the situation would become apparent. In the majesty of his chamber, the white, urbanized intellectual, Paz, dressed in presidential tails or a business suit, would receive the Indian or mestizo delegation foreign to the city and dressed either in the helmet and boots of the miner or the poncho of the peasant. Proudly displaying their arms, they would pose with the president for an official picture. Then, in all solemnity and with a vividness made real by the weapons in their hands, they would declare faith and allegiance to *La Revolución Nacional* and their undying commitment to defend it to the end. Simultaneously, they would present a petition of demands which urged the government to *profundizar* ("make deeper, more profound") the revolution, making it clear that the critical support offered by the one hand was contingent upon the satisfaction of the demands pressed by the other.

To the popular pressure on the MNR center, a barrage of extremely radical statements was added, emanating from the COB's organ *Rebelión*. In an early statement of principles, the COB laid down the gauntlet to the party. The statement said, in effect, "Either make our revolution or have it taken away from you."

> Experience has demonstrated nevertheless that workers'
> representatives in a bourgeois cabinet cannot achieve any-
> thing for the proletariat no matter what good intentions
> they have. . . . The aim should not be to put a worker
> in a capitalist cabinet, conserving the economic order
> untouched, but to take all power for the working class
> and change the capitalist structure, completely substitut-
> ing for it one that meets the needs of the people. . . .
> The working class cannot trap itself in the officialist
> policy of any government which isn't of the workers.
> Controlled unionism has proved itself most dangerous
> for the working class. . . .
> Against speculation and manipulating exchange the

workers and the COB demand the total monopoly of commerce by the state. . . .

The COB plans the occupation of the factories and mines by the workers as the only means to prevent the sabotage of the revolution and unemployment. . . .

Nationalization without indemnification and under worker control. The workers will accept no other form of nationalization. . . . The Bolivian people cannot be put under the weight of heavy indemnities.

The mobilization and direct action of the masses is the only guaranty that the revolutionary program of the working class will be realized. . . . Manifestations, assemblies are the only means by which the masses can express their fight against capital.

The destiny of the revolution is intimately tied to the destiny of private property that can only be surpassed by the revolutionary action of the masses. No other method can liquidate this cornerstone of capitalism.

The program of insurrection can only be realized in its purity by the workers and peasants in power. . . . This power cannot be other than worker and peasant who will organize the society on the basis of collectivism.

The national congress of workers is a step toward obtaining a workers' parliament which will transcend the democratic bourgeois juridical framework and open the road to a government of workers and peasants.

Thus the anti-capitalist and anti-imperialist fight that begins in the national sphere will become more profound in the national sphere and also be extended to the international, acquiring a permanent character in both senses. The valid slogan is for a Socialist United States of Latin America.[7]

This extreme statement forced the type of right-wing reaction that was hoped for by the COB. On September 18, the right, charging like an enraged bull, issued by means of the old official organ of the party, *En Marcha,* its views on the revolution and its opinion of the COB.

In the periodical *Rebelión* of September 12, 1952, there is published a declaration of principles openly Communist and in the name of the COB, a fact that is grave for the country and the future of the national revolution and therefore the MNR is obliged to declare before the public both national and international the following:

That the MNR is in its essence a national party and therefore is against international communism.

That the noted program of the COB is contrary to all nationalist sentiment and to all Bolivian workers especially those who are Bolivians, nationalists, and have a profound sense of Christianity and therefore are enemies of atheistic communism.

That ninety percent of the workers are nationalists and belong to the MNR; on the other hand, the leaders of the COB are mainly international Communists, from the POR, PIR and PCB.

That the problems of Bolivia have a national character and are not those of class conflict which is a Communist principle.

That the program of the MNR posits nationalization of the mines, railroads, and all public services . . . respecting international law and the right of property.

The MNR believes that the country should develop a spirit of enterprise among Bolivians, and also foreign capital. . . . Consequently, it does not accept the desire of the COB to suppress commerce and private enterprise. . . .

That contrary to destroying the army as the leaders of the COB demand, the MNR sees the need to reorganize a national army.

That the leaders of the COB are following an international line attempting to develop an anti-Bolivian policy in favor of Russian-Soviet imperialism
. . . The MNR reaffirms its position as completely against all imperialisms that seek to enslave Bolivia and sees its historical duty as a national party to be against all foreign interference.[8]

After this public exchange there could be little doubt that the MNR was split internally in the most fundamental sense of the word, and that the chasm separating right from left was unbridgeable. In an effort to head off any further open clashes and remove the ideological battle from public view, the Comité Político Nacional of the MNR under the directorship of Paz issued the following statement:

> The National Political Committee notifies all members of the party that the only organ authorized to publish manifestos, votes and other documents in the name of the MNR is the National Political Committee, being absolutely prohibited that members, groups, departmental commandos or special groups make statements aside from within the internal confines of the party. Violation of this order will result in the application of punishment as defined in the by-laws of the party.[9]

In that context, the political committee's statement amounted to a veiled attack on the right wing. The labor-left document spoke in the name of the COB, not the party. Under the rules of the co-gobierno game, the COB could continue to issue its independent statements. The rightists, by contrast, spoke through a party organ and in the name of the party. The Comité in effect, was telling the rightists to hold off and be patient. The aim was to deescalate the public dimension of conflict and to deny ammunition to the non-MNR left, which was pushing the COB in a more extreme direction by warning that the rightists planned a bourgeois counter-revolution.

It seems to me that the statement of the Comité reflected the pragmatic center's awareness that if the party was split, so too was the COB—and indeed it was. There was a plethora of positions in the COB that defy any neat right, left, or center categorization. Generally speaking, it can be said that the white-collar organizations, of which there were many, held to a basically middle-class position, but one tempered with an immediate desire for redistribution in their favor. They were much more economically than politically oriented. However, the POR, PIR, and new PCB

(Communist party), based on the more specifically obrero unions,
were by definition more interested in long-range political questions. Among themselves they were bitterly divided and still fighting the old personal and ideological battles of the late 1930s and
1940s. Yet, each in its own way faced a serious set of problems, as
to what stance they should take toward the MNR, and whether or
not they should resist the temptation to attempt to take the revolution away from the MNR. To many, the temptation was irre-
sistible and voices demanding an immediate socialist revolution
were raised.

In the midst of it all stood the all-pervasive personality of
Lechín, buttressed by the powerful FSTMB and by his old POR
allies, many of whom were moving away from the core POR position toward Lechín's "realist" position. The Lechín position was
based on the old entrista argument: The Bolivian proletariat was
neither large enough nor developed enough in consciousness to
seize and use power alone. If it moved precipitously, it would be
destroyed and the rule of the petite bourgeoisie assured. The best
course of action, therefore, was for the left to build its base for
use within the MNR to push it further left. The task would be
made easier by the existence of the pragmatic center which would
respond to leftist prodding. In the long run, the left would become dominant. The government would naturally pass to the
left's hands and with the objective conditions then in existence,
socialism would be established.[10]

Lechín and his allies carried the COB with little difficulty.
The signal that the COB leader was willing to sustain the MNR
and was willing to bargain was sent out publicly by the COB central directorate under the signature of Lechín and Butron, the
COB-approved Minister of Labor.

> The executive and general secretaries of the COB declare
> that the document entitled: "Posición Ideológica de Los
> Trabajadores de Bolivia," published in the periodical
> *Rebelión,* is only a proposal prepared by a commission and
> does not represent the official thought of the COB, which
> will be decided in the next congress of that organization.[11]

In effect, the MNR pragmatic center and the COB core in their respective statements declared their intention to avoid an open break by keeping their mutual dissidents in line and entering into negotiations with each other. The game for the moment was defined by Paz and Lechín. But as the above COB statement makes clear, the hard line put forth in *Rebelión* was not the official COB position, but could well become it.

The situation of the MNR center was obvious. The COB's support against counter-revolution was needed while, at the same time, the non-MNR COB dissidents presented a separate threat. The MNR had to be certain of the COB's loyalty. To gain that support while simultaneously isolating the non-MNR left, Lechín's dominance in the COB had to be reinforced. To achieve that aim, the party would have to bend to the left's will, because Lechín's desires were sincerely leftist, and to prove that the logic Lechín expounded to hold the COB to the MNR was, in fact, accurate. The first faint outline of what was to become a center-left axis built around Paz and Lechín was emerging.

In the statement of the Comité, co-gobierno, and Paz's friendliness to Lechín, the rightists saw the materialization of their earlier fears regarding Paz. This apprehension began to stiffen into opposition. In internal party circles they began to warn of the danger inherent in the rising star of Lechín and the COB. As the days passed, the weakness of their position vis-à-vis the COB became more and more patent. As one of this group later reported, a key element in the shift was Paz's response to the public pressure put on the MNR by the COB and its militia.

> The COB organized and staged two or three large parades in which Lechín shrewdly used the revolutionary euphoria of the workers. Immediately we noted that President Paz Estenssoro was completely won over to the side that was going to communize the MNR and its government. . . . He was not going to look for problems with the workers.[12]

Even before the power of the labor left showed itself at the policy level, it was manifested at the level of political office and party structure. A number of prominent rightist leaders who had impressive credentials drawn from the battles of the Sexenio were replaced in key posts by COB members whose MNR credentials were far from impressive. The rightists reacted bitterly to the supplanting of tried and true revolutionaries with Johnny-come-latelies. Behind this reaction was not only anger at losing key power positions to the leftists, but also the simple loss of jobs. Job politics, as pointed out earlier, was an important element of Bolivian political dynamics during most of the twentieth century. The insurrection did not change the basic economic realities which fed this tendency. Thus, to the ideological issues which separated left from right was added the equally bitter issue of jobs. Based on their *bona fides* as long-time MNR members who stuck with the party through thick and thin, the primary party people felt that the top jobs were theirs by right. This sentiment of the "old-timers" feeling themselves pushed aside by a wave of last-minute opportunists went all the way down to second-, third-, and fourth-rank patronage positions.[13]

In the early fall, another major blow was delivered to the rightists. For whatever reasons, Paz disbanded the periodical, *En Marcha*. With the loss of *En Marcha*, the right wing lost its only authoritative means to put its case before the public. In the place of *En Marcha* a new official newspaper, *La Nación*, was formed. From the right's point of view, the new editorship of *La Nación* was leftist. The rightists perceived themselves as the subjects of a policy of systematic isolation and emasculation.

By the late fall of 1952, right-wing leaders were talking among themselves of the need for drastic steps. They found sympathy among disgruntled army officers and police officials smarting from the decline of their institutions and the concomitant rise of worker and party militias. At the same time, the campo was beginning to rumble, and fear of a general peasant uprising was troubling the imagination of the urban middle groups. Agrarian reform became the big and volatile issue in the party. After initial vacillation and some sporadic attempts to stop peasant land incursions, the party center began to shift toward a favorable stance on all-out reform. Things were going too far: the right wing felt impelled to make its move.

On the morning of January 6, 1953, the minister of peasant affairs was kidnapped as a prelude to a general *coup d'état*.[14] By noon it was open knowledge that a number of the party's most prominent names, in conjunction with army and police officers, were in revolt. The *golpistas* (Bolivian slang for "those making a coup") declared that their aim was to forestall a Communist takeover, reverse the power of the COB, and return to original nationalist principles. By late afternoon, it was apparent that the attempt was doomed. In a last-minute attempt to protect their positions, many plotters defected and declared their loyalty to Paz. The rightist forces had failed and the leftists moved in for the kill.

The COB called for a nationwide mobilization of worker and peasant militias. On the morning of January 7, a massive COB-sponsored demonstration was held. The demonstrators demanded an immediate, far-ranging agrarian reform. It seems not at all coincidental that after months of foot-dragging, the commission to draft a reform was constituted on January 20.[15] The demonstrators also called for the heads of the golpistas. Through the COB roar came the voice of the hard-line POR, demanding a total destruction of the army, the complete arming of the population, and the declaration of their long-time formula of a *gobierno obrero-campesino* ("government of workers and peasants"). Paz and his coterie were in trouble, and they knew it.[16]

To head off the non-MNR leftist threat, Paz moved against the rightists, but with a restraint that can be explained only by admitting deep reluctance on his part. While willing to cultivate, and indeed to co-opt, the left, Paz had no desire to be completely in its hands. Despite the calls for blood, Paz held the line at a benign purge. Los Grupos de Honor were disbanded and many prominent conspirators were downgraded or exiled. However, no blood was drawn and the involvement of some key figures in the coup attempt was covered up. Likewise, Paz continued to resist demands to destroy the army completely.[17]

As a result of the coup failure, the right wing went into temporary eclipse. The incipient center-left axis became a functioning reality. In a real sense, the driving force of the revolution at this point was the labor left. The first four years of the post-insurrectionary period belonged to the COB and the workers. To the great reforms that favored the workers was added an array of measures passed in response to their demands, in hopes of securing their support for the MNR. The measures included wage increases, bonuses, protection from layoffs, rent controls, price ceilings, subsidized stores, an array of social security measures, and numerous other "consumption" features. In addition, workers who had been laid off were rehired and the government intervened on labor's behalf in wage disputes with management. Labor leaders advanced into important party and governmental positions. The peasants also benefited greatly (perhaps more) through protection from taxes, rural investment, and the like. But during this period, and up till 1956, labor and the COB rode the wave. Through government solicitation and news coverage, labor learned that after years of denial and obscurity, it was they—their problems, their demands, their power—which dominated the national consciousness of Bolivia. So potent was their image that the figure of Lechín expanded to proportions rivaling that of Paz. Between the two of them, Paz and Lechín symbolized the revolution and dwarfed all other former or potential leading lights.[18]

Within the post-coup context, the pragmatic center of the MNR—Paz's image notwithstanding—had all it could do to hold onto its formal position of power in the government and in the party. A good deal of the center's energies were now devoted to keeping at least a loose rein on the left so as to keep it from running away with the party completely. The remnants of the MNR core assumed a Jacobin stance, radical in rhetoric, but building for the day when the drive from below would abate and become controllable. For the time being, their position was analogous to a man on a runaway horse who elects to hang on until his mount tires rather than risk the perils of leaping off.

The Jacobin role sprang not only from the fear of an unbridled leftist push, but also from the need to build a defensive base against counter-revolution. Carrying with them the experience of Siles, Busch, and Villarroel, the MNR core remembered full well the vulnerability of any change-oriented government not securely anchored in a mass base. Since they did not directly control such a base, they had little choice but to hold it in line by meeting its rank-and-file demands for gratification, as well as the leadership's demands for power and the benefits accruing thereto.

As the threat of outside intervention dwindled (the spectre to be raised again by the Guatemalan affair, in which the leftist government was overthrown by U.S.-supported exiles), harassment by the Bolivian Falange increased. The credibility of the FSB threat and the need to rely on the COB for support increased throughout the early 1950s. It was driven by one of those curious dynamics of conflict which permeate all revolutionary situations. Having started as a reform movement led and supported by the urban petite bourgeoisie, the MNR now watched with dismay as this primary support base wavered and then began to shift either to passive hostility or to open support of the FSB.

The first reasons were essentially those which motivated the coup of January 6. The depth and nature of the changes being carried out went far beyond the expectations of the middle class. The radical position of the COB, the growing image of its power, and the effectiveness of its demands, posed a threat of major proportions to the world of the dependent clase media. Furthermore, the spectre of an engulfing Indian wave was threatening. Finally, revolutionary Bolivia was gripped by an inflationary spiral which dwarfed all that had come before.[19] The combination of all of these factors drove the middle sector away from the MNR in search of a mechanism to stop the revolutionary push.

Once in motion, the dynamic followed its own logic. The counter-revolutionary threat forced the MNR core to rely more and more heavily on the left. In a literal attempt to scare the opposition into acquiescence, the MNR center left COB axis staged demonstration upon demonstration of its armed might. Miner and peasant militias were continually trucked into the capital where they paraded before the populace, discharging their rifles wildly. With their hands raised in the MNR victory salute, they hurled threats to all who harbored thoughts of turning back the revolution. The sight of thousands of armed *Indios* and workers may well have struck the desired note of fear, but it hardly reawakened the urban middle's loyalty to the regime.

The government supplemented these threats with a concerted

attempt to control counter-revolutionary activity with force. The most persistent anti-revolutionary newspapers—*La Razón* and *Los Tiempos*—were sacked and destroyed by COB-led street mobs. The building of the *La Razón,* owned by the Aramayo family, was symbolically converted into the Ministry of Mines and Petroleum. After an FSB coup attempt which included an assault on his home, Paz established openly a "state security force" (*control politico*) charged with squashing rightist rebellion.[20] Plotters were ferreted out and imprisoned or exiled. Detention centers, which the opposition labeled "concentration camps," were established. In those early years, they seldom wanted for occupants. Mutual violence, often resulting in assassination, became the rule.

Although justifying itself by the extant "constitutional" tradition, the MNR and the COB harassed all opposition groups, and, for all intents and purposes, established single-party rule. Counter-revolutionary control was often indiscriminant, touching the innocent as well as the guilty. Often, political charges justified the settling of personal vendettas. Such conditions of life seldom appeal to a security-minded middle class—especially when it has no real means to defend itself.

Such features, tragic as they are, should come as no surprise to the student of revolution. Given the degree of change carried out and the relatively short period in which it was carried out, not to mention the accumulated store of hate poisoning the country, the surprise lies in the relative benignity of this revolutionary process. Although counter-revolutionary violence was met with violent suppression, Bolivia had no reign of terror. Neither the opposition nor whole social classes were systematically liquidated or driven from the country. Repression was confined mainly to active plotters, and even these were only temporarily incarcerated or exiled. The authoritarian aspects, real though they were, never became the declared norm. The norms of constitutionality, legitimate opposition, the possibility of succession, etc., were adhered to as standards of public rhetoric. No party, not even the FSB, was denied legal existence.[21]

To the extent that the MNR center had a hemispheric revolutionary model, it was Mexico. As one leader put it: "We want to make a Mexican Revolution, but without ten years of Pancho Villa."[22] Violent though the situation in Bolivia was, until now at least, the country has avoided anything approaching the pestilence of violence that tore Mexico apart.

At some points a Mexican-type blood bath did threaten. Worker and peasant militias on occasion carried out their own unauthorized revolutionary justice. At one point, COB militiamen charging, not incorrectly, that the universities were centers of counter-revolutionary activity, seized control of practically all the country's university centers. The COB sought to convert the "oligarchic" universities into "popular" universities. A few such popular schools were established, but in the end, the MNR center helped reestablish university autonomy and the universities continued to be centers of counter-revolutionary activity.

These actions of restraint toward the MNR right wing, toward the opposition, and toward constitutional norms were not mere happenstance. They were matched, as pointed out before, by an equal restraint in the brandishment of symbols of legitimacy, style, form, and rhetoric. The failure to develop a complete revolutionary style in Bolivia can be related to many factors; undoubtedly one of the main reasons lies in the fact that when all was said and done, the original MNR members were not enthusiastic revolutionaries. There was and remains a basic contradiction between the facts and the style of the Bolivian National Revolution. The continuing disparity bears witness to the fact that, despite the ascending power of the COB, the MNR center was able to keep the revolutionary thrust within certain bounds. And from the vantage point of hindsight, we can see that the continuing thrust of the labor left would have had to clash eventually with the developmental goals of the middle-class, reformist MNR elite. There was a limit to how far the pragmatic center could and would give way.

The National Revolution: 1956–1960

In the development of the national revolution, 1956 was an important year. Following its inclination not to break totally with the past, the MNR sought to constitutionalize the revolution within the old liberal democratic political framework by calling elections. The major difference was that in the old system, voting was restricted, while these elections would allow total adult participation. To be sure, the MNR stacked the cards in its favor and never seriously contemplated losing. Still, opposition parties including the FSB were allowed to present candidates for all offices, and were allowed relatively free room to campaign. The MNR was willing to establish itself as a semi-official party, but manifested a strong reluctance to embark upon the road of a personal or party dictatorship. As expected, the MNR swept the elections, but the FSB scored heavily in all major cities, indicating a certain veracity to the proceedings. More important, the FSB vote confirmed the shift of the bulk of the urban middle class away from the MNR.[23]

The right-left split in the MNR, only temporarily muted by the abortive coup of 1953, broke open again in the pre-election party convention, this time with particularly disturbing portents. Walter Guevara Arze, one of the party's prominent leaders and previously not associated publicly with the right wing, made an open attack on Lechín, the COB, and the FSTMB. He accused them of being leftist adventurers leading the revolution to ruin.[24] It was a bad choice of battlefield. Lechín and the COB controlled the convention and were able to ram through an official party motion condemning Guevara and forcing his resignation from the ministry of foreign affairs.[25] The party threatened to break apart, this time with a considerable portion of the MNR center splitting off.

In a bid for unity, the leadership fashioned a compromise program, nominating Hernan Siles Zuazo, the party's second in command, as the presidential candidate and Nuflo Chavez, minister of peasant affairs and a high official in the COB, as the vice-presidential candidate. Siles was generally considered to have rightist sympathies, but, above all, he was considered to be a unifying force in the party.[26] Chavez, a former POR member, was pushed as the representative of the labor left. The fact that a known COB member was made the vice-presidential candidate was an obvious bow to the power of the labor left. In addition, the COB, was able to arrange the congressional lists so that they were guaranteed a COB majority in congress, and they also increased their representation in the party hierarchy. It was only a last-minute threat by Siles to resign that guaranteed at least some congressional and party posts to hard-line MNR members of the center and right factions. Siles publicly declared his intention to institutionalize the revolution; that is, to move it from its destructive, more or less anarchic phase to a constructive, more ordered phase. Siles was, thereupon, inaugurated as president, and Paz left to take up an ambassadorial post in London.

Even before Paz bowed from the scene, it had been decided that the major task confronting the MNR was to stem the economically and socially corrosive inflation. The MNR turned for aid in this task to the International Monetary Fund (I.M.F.) and the United States government. Both sources of funds indicated that any aid would have to be based upon Bolivia's acceptance of the recommendations of a joint United States–I.M.F. commission. The terms were accepted and a stabilization program based on the suggestions of George Jackson Eder, U.S. representative of the I.M.F., was drawn up. Siles, faithful to his word, announced the acceptance of the plan immediately after his inauguration. In so doing, Siles set off a battle which raged throughout the entire period of his presidency.

The plan was, in essence, based on two principles: (a) a strict freezing of wages and fringe benefits, and (b) a return to the principles of a free economy. The COB, unwilling to be characterized as supporting inflation, announced cautious approval of the plan, provided that adequate wage increases were given previous to its implementation. Once in operation, however, it became apparent that the plan would bite deeply into the benefits piled up by labor during the previous four years. The government announced its intention of removing subsidies from foodstuffs and of doing away with government-supported stores (pulperías).[27] This latter move would have had particular impact in the mines where such pulperias constituted a significant element of the miners' real wages.[28] Once aware of the full dimensions of the

238 •   BOLIVIA—Part III

plan, the COB reacted violently and the MNR was pushed into
its most severe internal crisis since 1953.

Under the threats of work stoppages and a general strike, Siles
resorted to a variety of defensive measures. Capitalizing on his
tremendous personal popularity as the man who had led the fighting in 1952, he made an impassioned and effective appeal for revolutionary discipline and sacrifice. He backed this up by a series
of personal hunger strikes and threats to resign. No one wished to
contemplate the results of a presidential resignation, and, hence,
these tactics kept his opposition off balance and fearful of forcing a showdown. At the same time, Siles moved to divide the left
wing and break Lechín's personal power over labor. In this he was
remarkably successful.

Playing on old-standing personal and ideological differences
between members of the PIR and POR, Siles drove a deep wedge
into COB unity. Through shrewd manipulation of the workers'
ministries, he enticed a number of top COB figures to eschew
Lechín. Of much help in these manipulatory tactics was the fact
that the economic stabilization did not have a uniform impact
across labor groups. The miners had gained the most between 1952
and 1956 and it was they who stood to lose the most after 1956.
The other groups discovered that they would be relatively unhurt
and could derive some positive advantages. The COB split, as a
result, into a Lechín-POR axis based principally on the FSTMB,
and a pro-Siles–ex-PIR axis based mainly on the railway workers
and part of the factory workers. The latter group called itself
the *bloque reestructuradora del COB*. ("bloc for restructuring
the COB"), and mounted a systematic attack on Lechín. At this
point, there were, in effect, two COB's.

Siles generalized his attack on Lechín's base after the failure
of a call for a general strike by Lechín on June 1, 1957. Utilizing
the ministry of government, presided over by the statist-minded
José Quadros Quiroga, Siles used the same dividing tactics in the
mines themselves. Siles-sponsored leaders and organizations were
set up in a government-supported attack on Lechín and his followers. This led to an anarchic situation in the mines which saw
widespread violence and death. After a particularly bitter struggle

in 1959, Siles withdrew a bit from the attack and persuaded Quadros to take a diplomatic post. Some have argued that in doing so, Siles missed his chance to give the *coup de grâce* to the considerably-weakened Lechín.[29] Be that as it may, Siles himself, probably fearful of the wide-open split, pulled back and even gave in somewhat to the miners' demands for wages and the maintenance of the pulperia. However, it was clear that he was not withdrawing all the way since he substituted Guevara for Quadros in the critical ministry of government.

The reappearance of Guevara in a top post was not fortuitous. It was part of a general rehabilitation of leaders labeled by the COB as rightists, including some who had figured prominently in the coup of 1953. Luis Peñaloza and Jorge Rios Gamara, for example, regained top party and governmental posts. Many of these old-line party people formed themselves into an official party faction called *La Defensa del MNR* ("The Defending Group of the MNR"). This faction, plus the anti-Lechín bloc of the COB, formed the backbone of Siles' struggle against Lechín and the more radical COB members. The tactic demonstrated apparent success in 1958 when the Lechínists were maneuvered out of both congressional and party control.[30] In response, the leftists fell back on their support from sindicatos and local party organization.

The political upshot of this maneuvering under Siles was a definite rollback of the power and influence of the labor left, especially that associated with the miners and the long-standing Lechín-POR axis. Concomitantly, there was a shift to a center-right axis in the party. Although this new coalition was officially strong, it was by no means dominant. Rather, there was more of a stabilization of political power. The result was a right-left standoff. The situation was somewhat similar to that which immediately followed the insurrection of 1952. Again, the left began looking toward Víctor Paz for a solution.

One unanticipated result of the battle was a definite resurgence of hard-line Trotskyite and Communist (PCB, not PIR) influence in the major mine centers. Lechín and his coterie of ex-Trotskyites were being assaulted from behind as well as from the front. A good deal of the radical posture adopted by Lechín in this period is attributable to this rear-action erosion of his traditional base of power. Indeed, Lechín found himself in the position that he had often put others in before, that of being pushed from below along a radical course, primarily to hold his official position. The fear that with Lechín gone, the miners would break from the MNR may have been behind Siles' decision to lighten the pressure on him.

There were other notable aspects to the battles of the Siles period. First was the attempt by Siles to win the major areas of peasant support from the left. This matter is complex and will be discussed later. For the moment, it is important to note that Siles had considerable success in the all-critical Cochabamba Valley. It was Siles who appointed the first campesino to national office by making José Rojas minister of peasant affairs. With this, the Cochabamba unions took an increasingly anti-COB line, and, for the first time, the government threatened to use peasant militias to break unauthorized strikes. Under Siles a growing split appeared between the worker as a political force and the campesino as a political force, with the two increasingly at loggerheads.

The second move of import was Siles' decision to rebuild the army. With United States aid, the army began to grow again in size and efficiency.[31] More important, Siles again gave the army a political police function when in an effort to halt a campesino civil war in the Cochabamba Valley, he declared it a military zone. Still not strong enough to pacify as such, the army, in effect, intervened on the side of José Rojas, thereby establishing him as undisputed leader of the Valley.[32] The phenomena of the emergence of the campesino as an aggressive national political actor and the reemergence of a political military were intimately connected.

Finally, under Siles, the nature of the MNR's relation to the counter-revolutionary groups changed. With the passage of time the outward threat to the revolution had diminished to insignificance and opposition was reduced to the disgruntled within Bolivian borders. But, by the late 1950s, there were few even inside Bolivia who thought the revolution could be turned back. The issue then became the direction of its advance. The relative honesty of the 1956 elections and the good showing by the FSB opened the possibility to the rightist opposition of participating in power, to some degree, by nonviolent means. Such hopes were strengthened by Siles' center-right shift. Siles himself, disturbed by the loss of middle-class support began courting rightist opposition groups. The economic stabilization was one of the keystones of the wooing. Under Siles, political repression was muted, and there was a general liberalization of the political climate. Except for one final quixotic coup attempt, the FSB moved toward a *modus vivendi* with the MNR.[33]

During the four years of the Siles presidency, we can say that, measured by leftist standards, the revolution was brought to a halt, and there began a Jacobin reaction. The hallmark of the Siles period was stabilization. The leftward push was stopped and there was an attempt to initiate a new center-right thrust. Counterrevolutionary opposition abated and the threat of a serious anti-revolution golpe diminished. In sum, a rough equalization of political power was created.

The delicate balance of forces struck under Siles was immediately called into question during the jockeying for position previous to the 1960 presidential election. Guevara made it obvious that he wanted the presidential nomination and that the party right wing and a good many of the center group were behind him. The labor left, unwilling to force a split, called upon Paz to run again, with Lechín as his running mate. The left-wing was essentially that of 1952. Reacting to a new center-right threat, the COB was able to establish most of its previous unity. Paz accepted the call and reassumed party leadership. Actually, he was the only one behind whom the bulk of the party could align themselves. The battle then boiled down to who would assume the vice-presidency.

In the pre-convention maneuvering, it became apparent that Lechín's power had far from disappeared. Both Paz and Siles, in fear of a left-wing split, vetoed Guevara for the vice-presidency as well as for the presidency. This was testimony to the fact that the labor left still had teeth.[34] Guevara, convinced of a new leftward shift, bolted the party and formed his own *Partido Revolucionario Auténtico* (PRA). Most of the party right wing and many of the center group joined Guevara. During the PRA convention, the dissidents accused Paz of again wanting to sell out the true MNR to the socialist left.[35] With Guevara gone, the Paz-Lechín formula passed with little difficulty. One prophetically jarring note marred the new coalition. Paz threatened to resign unless he had the major say in drawing up the congressional lists. Unlike 1956, Paz made sure that the COB would not be stacking everything in its favor.

The MNR swept the elections but again did poorly among the urban middle.[36] With the elections over, about a year passed during which the power standoff of the Siles period persisted. The leftist faction of the party, confident of its position, declared continuously that Lechín would receive the presidency in 1964, and, with that, the revolution would move to its final phase.

12 Structure and Process of Post-insurrectionary Politics

The success of the insurrection of 1952 was due less to the power of the loose revolutionary coalition than to the political bankruptcy of the status quo elite and the fragility of the order upon which it stood. Built upon a precarious economic base and assuming a society with minimal movement, the old order had, since 1935, pushed its adaptive capacities to the breaking point; in the face of this final challenge, it collapsed. The insurrectionaries did not seize power in any real sense; rather, they confirmed the demise of organized "legitimate" power. The great revolutionary measures of 1952–53 continued the process of destroying this power, and, in doing so, sundered the tenuous bonds by which Bolivia had been held together as a collective reality.[1] Now that the drama of revolutionary destruction was drawing to a close, the MNR counter-elite holding the symbols of state power faced the dilemma of revolutionary construction.

An insurrection, such as the MNR successfully conducted between April 9 and 11 of 1952, is neither the beginning nor the end of a revolution; it is, rather, one moment—perhaps the most dramatic—in a larger process. As a composite process, revolution begins when a society enters what I choose to call a "revolutionary situation."

In this book's introduction, I conceived of this process as one

243

which has two distinct phases. The first I called the "insurrection-ary phase" which coincides with what is usually thought of as the seizure of power; that is, the point at which revolutionaries over-throw the status quo elite and destroy the power and system asso-ciated with it. The second phase involves the redefinition of the country's image and the construction of a revolutionary order which, if successful, becomes a new status quo. An ideal revolu-tionary is both a destroyer and a creator. He not only seeks to destroy old power but wants to create new power so as to remake the society in his image.

The revolutionary situation, therefore, continues beyond the insurrectionary or destructive moment. With a successful insurrec-tion, the old elite and old power structure are largely pushed from the field of combat. However, conflict continues among revolu-tionary elites and their differing alternative definitions of the new order. At each point there is tension between the demands of power and the preferred values and images; thus, as tactical situa-tions change, ideologies permutate, as do intergroup coalitions. The revolution continues until a new status quo, i.e., a new authoritative matrix, within which differences are adjudicated, is established.

With the close of the Chaco War, Bolivia entered what I call a revolutionary situation. Year by year, the institutional matrix of liberal Bolivia became less and less relevant in adjudicating inter-nal social conflict. Counter-tendencies, at first inchoate, began to take form. By at first manipulating existing instrumentalities of power, such as parts of the army, and, later, by mobilizing the new power of numbers, counter-elites became progressively more credi-ble as threats. The status quo elite responded with greater and greater increments of force; by 1949, the country was in a state of civil war. When in 1952 the already splintered military split fur-ther, the regime faltered and fell. The successful insurrection of 1952 brought the disparate coalition known as the MNR to formal power. Immediately, the various counter-elites began to struggle over the shape of the new Bolivia. At this point, the second and most critical phase of the revolutionary situation began and it continues to this day.

A successful revolutionary insurrection usually leads to a thorough destruction of state-level authority, control, and order. Revolutionary elites thereby are faced not simply with the task of reordering the society in particular images and the pursuit of particular concrete goals, but, more immediately, they are faced with the problem of achieving order per se. The first problem is that of sovereignty. In this case, the issues were (a) the integrity of the Bolivian state in a world of nation-states, and (b) the power and authority of the state government vis-à-vis the various internal components of the state.

The problem of sovereignty is intimately connected to the question of the preferred goals revolutionary elites will try to define for the country; these goals set demands on the extent of power and control that minimal order will have to achieve. In pre-revolutionary Bolivia, for example, a juridically recognized state entity existed. As a mono-producing servicer of the industrial center, however, the "national" state system had interest in actively governing only a minimal portion of the geographical entity of Bolivia. The largest portion of the population was only tenuously tied to the national system. Aside from certain demands on their time and energy, the system mainly asked acquiescence and passivity from this general population. Beyond this, the governing of the masses was left to local patrons or customary systems which could vary widely between and within regions. Large expanses of the country were almost completely untouched by the Bolivian governmental state. Thus, as a functioning reality, the Bolivian state was small and largely epiphenomenal to the geographical entity Bolivia. It was only when the Chaco War brought home the glaring contradiction between the realities of Bolivia as a state entity and Bolivia as a geographic unit that the internal extension of state sovereignty became a burning national issue.

Arising out of that upsetting discovery was the desire on the part of young counter-elite groups to bring Bolivia as a sovereign state and Bolivia as a geographic entity together as a whole. This desire was reinforced by the growing commitment of various counter-elites to the general collective goal of rapid economic development. In confronting the post-insurrectionary problem of establishing internal order per se, the revolutionary elites faced the imperative of making it a truly "national" order: that is, an order in which the state would be the regulator of law throughout the length and breadth of Bolivia. In a sense, those nationalists who took "control" in 1952 were in a position common to nationalist elites in many underdeveloped countries today: they held the trappings of state power, then they had to find a "nation" in which to anchor it.

In this chapter, we will consider the problem of a new sovereignty. The question of preferred images and new forms will be considered in the next chapter. However, it must be stressed that strategic value goals set basic imperatives regarding the scope of sovereignty, and, hence, the two questions are intimately connected. For purposes of analysis, we shall look at the process from the perspective of the problems confronting the MNR core elite as it sought to establish its authority and redefine Bolivia in terms of its preferred image. Right or wrong, it is clear that this elite group saw themselves as the builders of a new and modern Bolivian nation-state with the basic conceptual values of nation, state, and development. They, therefore, sought to impose a new and truly national sovereignty upon Bolivia.

The Problem of Making a National Order

The great revolutionary measures sponsored by the MNR were the product of political pressures, but they were also seen by many as the necessary prelude to the construction of a stronger, more integrated, truly national Bolivia. The immediate effect of the measures, however, was clearly the opposite. The tendency to atomization inherent in prerevolutionary Bolivia was given free rein and a powerful centrifugal movement set in.

In previous chapters it was shown how the MNR as a "national" political force split into three major elite groups almost immediately after the insurrection. Concomitantly, a deflation of national power took place, and the country reverted to "lower" forms of organization.[2] Effective decision-making power became localized and/or segmented. As the power of nonauthoritative local decision centers grew, the power and effectiveness of the national authoritative center declined significantly. The insurrection led not to a "seizure" of state power, but to a destruction of it.

The centrifugal process was most immediately visible with the formation of the COB. Under the theory and practice of co-gobierno, in effect, two governments were established—the authoritative state government and the COB. Especially during the years from 1952 to 1956, the state government had the authority and responsibility to govern, but it did not have the power. The COB, on the other hand, had the power, but neither the authority nor the responsibility.[3] The process of the dispersion of effective power, however, rapidly went beyond this simple dichotomous split.

When the power of the national state deflated, so too did the control of the MNR national elite. As power diminished, local and segmental elites emerged. After a certain point, these local and segmental elites monopolized effective control over relevant behavior within the limits of their respective fiefs.

The centrifugal process occasioned by the destruction of the national bourgeoisie and the shattering of the previous institutional framework was reinforced significantly by the disappearance of the state's legitimate monopoly of the use of force. During the insurrection, the national army was definitively defeated by untrained popular forces, and immediately thereafter was drastically reduced in size and potency. Conversely, during the long prelude to the insurrection, arms steadily found their way into the hands of the civilian population. During and after the insurrection, this dispersion of weapons to the civilian population continued even more rapidly. At first, weaponry was mainly in the hands of the middle class and labor adherents of the MNR, but as the revolution spread to the countryside, there was an arming of the general peasant population as well. By the 1960s, one source reported that fully two-thirds of the country's male population were armed in one fashion or another.[4]

It is difficult to exaggerate the importance of the appearance of this armed populace. As an extra-institutional process, struggling over the fundamental matrices which will define legality and justice in a society, revolution of necessity tends to make force the major arbiter of social differences. This fact is not changed with the demise, no matter how complete, of the old elite and its power structure, for the issue of how the society will be reorganized is still wide open. In a society like Bolivia which has strong inclinations toward particularism, the problem increases in severity.

The devolution of the capacity to exercise force is a phenomenon which takes on added significance in the modern "developmental" context. Bolivia is a country of extremely limited resources available for developmental investment. In the best of circumstances, therefore, an elite pursuing economic development would have to make significant demands upon the society and its willingness and capacity to sacrifice in the name of a collective surplus for investment. The mobilization occasioned by the revolutionary struggle, however, was based, in large part, upon the articulation of demands arising out of the real and perceived needs of the mobilized groups. As a result, there was an inherent tension between the demands the development-oriented elite would have to make on the populace and the demands the latter would make on the elite and on the society's available resources. With the dispersion of the capacity to use force, the mobilized groups could, if necessary, back their demands with threats of force, but the development-oriented elite could not do the same. The consequences of this fact will be discussed at length later.

The centrifugal process was further reinforced by the terrible, debilitating inflation which gripped post-insurrectionary Bolivia. (The value of the boliviano fell from 60 to the dollar in 1952 to 1,200 to the dollar in 1956.) Inflation was hardly new to Bolivia, but the intensity of the post-1952 spiral was unprecedented. The long inflation debilitated the country's economy and further ripped the delicate socio-psychological fabric holding the society together. The wild fluctuation of the monetary system poisoned the tone of collective life. The society became bereft of predictability, bringing deep insecurity to all social sectors. Individuals and groups were thrown back upon themselves and a struggle of each against all set in. Self-defense became everyone's primary public stance. Defense set the tone of group relationships with the state and with each other. In such a situation, the individual comes to rely upon the strength and leadership of primary organizations because they are the most readily available weapons with which to fight the internecine battle. The individuals least capable of organizing themselves in this fashion were those who made up the urban middle class, and they suffered accordingly. Labor and peasant groups had class-based or segment-wide organizations to defend them. However, as the economic pressure increased, even these lines were breached and these groups were forced to fall back on more local intra-class organizations.

Whatever fund of community feeling that derived from the common effort of 1952 was shattered by the inflation. Efforts to alleviate the pressure on one group only fed the fire by alienating those who were not helped. The pre-existent tendencies to atomization, therefore, were heightened considerably. The various groups and sectors of the society came to view each other with hostility and as potential threats, and they watched the government with a suspicious eye for any signs of favoritism toward other groups.

The cleavages which accompanied the centrifugal process cut along three general lines: regional, class (or perhaps, more appropriately, segmental), and intra-segmental. Regionalism had always been a powerful focal point of loyalties in Bolivia. The immediate reason for this was the geographic and ethnic diversity of the country. The three main regions of the country—the mountainous altiplano, the inter-mountain valley region, and the tropical plain which runs to the east—are set off from each other by formidable natural barriers. These regions were organized into nine departments, each with its own capital. The capitals dominated the surrounding regions economically and politically. Although they were tied to the center by a Napoleonic-type administrative structure, municipal governments were independent and locally elected; these local governments tended to wield the real power in their respective regions.[5]

The regional capitals, dominated by strong municipal governments, were for many the pivot of public identity and terminal loyalty. The operative notion in all regions was that outlying towns and villages belonged to the departmental capital. The degree of regionalism was such that we can fairly say that until 1952, no national central government had ever really established effective sovereignty over the entire geographic Bolivian unit. The single most eloquent proof of this is the fact that Bolivia today is about one-half the size it was in 1825. Furthermore, regional rivalry was always strong. Each departmental capital demanded all the accouterments of the others. For example, although small, sparsely attended, and poorly staffed, all regional capitals except Cobija and Trinidad have their own universities. All capitals relied heavily on central government outlays to run institutions such as these. There was, therefore, strong regional competition for central funds, and deep resentment when one region apparently advanced at the expense of another. The national capitals, first Sucre and later La Paz, were often looked upon merely as rival department capitals using their positions to advance themselves at the expense of the others. This kind of sentiment played an important role in the civil war of 1898 which occasioned the shifting of the capital from Sucre to La Paz.

Congressmen and senators were really sent to La Paz not to worry about international tin prices and the like but to wrest an appropriation for a local plaza, and so on. This division between national and local concerns in the central congress helped those with more global concerns (for example, the tin companies) to shape general policy in their favor. The communication grids laid down to service the tin industry began to pull La Paz, Oruro, and Cochabamba together, but increased the isolation of the other areas. Only since 1954 has there been an effective road link between the capital of Santa Cruz and the rest of the country. Even today, the departmental capitals of Pando and Beni are reachable only by air or on horseback.[6]

Since 1952, regionalism has plagued the revolutionary governments. Throughout most of the country, regional pressure, although strong, is submerged in the more complex segmental and intra-segmental divisons and conflicts. This regional cleavage has been most apparent in the lush and potentially rich but sparsely populated eastern departments of Santa Cruz and Beni.

These regions, especially Santa Cruz where separatism was rife, presented very serious problems of control to the MNR.[7] Lacking national institutions with which to link these regions, the MNR attempted to achieve this linkage through its own party mechanisms and the departmental party commandos became supreme. The difficulty was that the national party soon lost control of its local organizations. MNR organization had never been well developed in these regions. Since they were isolated from the governmental center, these local organizations drifted away from central control into the hands of local caudillos who maintained only a fictive identification with the national party.

After a few years, these immense isolated regions became, in effect, the personal fiefs of two rival caudillos: Ruben Julio Castro, who controlled Pando and most of Beni, and Luis Sandoval Moron, who controlled parts of Beni and Santa Cruz. Since the MNR was kept busy with the struggle to govern the rest of the country, and these local chieftains had already established at least a nominal party link with these vital regions, the MNR left them alone. It is difficult for a twentieth-century American to grasp the situation: fully 40 percent of the country was the indisputable domain of two individuals. These men controlled the local economies, maintained personal armies, made laws, and dispensed justice. They were, in reality, modern princes. The power of the two became such that they, at times, warred with each other as each tried to extend his control into the isolated regions of the major departments like La Paz. The two became potent figures in the national party and in the government. They were strong enough to exercise initiative and veto power over policy of interest to themselves and their regions. They negotiated on an independent basis with the national government, for, in the end, national decisions were translated into local policy through their will, not that of the state, the government, or the party.

The second major cleavage was that along class or segmental lines. MNR ideology states that the party is the instrument of liberation for the oppressed nation. This oppressed nation was divided socially into three major groups, all of which shared a common national interest because they were equally oppressed: the middle class, the workers, and the peasants. The nation was oppressed by the industrial center, which exercised economic imperial control through its local agents, La Rosca. Through these verbal gymnastics, the MNR reduced a highly complex multiplicity of parallel stratification systems into one grand dichotomy between oppressors and oppressed. It was a formidable theory on paper, but was to prove unrealistic as an operative basis for post-insurrection Bolivian policies.

In the previous chapter, I pointed out the almost immediate split between the middle-class elite and the labor elite segments of the MNR. Labor rapidly made it clear that it did not really accept the MNR theory of the "nation" versus the "anti-nation." Labor organized itself to pursue its own "class" interests. The COB demanded and largely got the same kind of initiative and veto power in domains of concern to it which Sandoval Moron and Ruben Julio achieved in their domains. COB ascendancy and the gruelling inflation alienated the middle class, which shifted loyalties to the counter-revolutionary FSB, creating new problems of effective governmental control.

Labor as an interest group would have been one thing, but the ascendance of the COB as a semi-state-like entity was clearly another. Here again fictive MNR party links superficially masked a devolution of effective power from state to segmental instrumentalities. Through co-gobierno, control obrero, and militias only nominally under party control, the COB defined itself as, and effectively was, a sovereign entity. Lechín, like the chieftains of the east, became a caudillo who negotiated with the state government from a basis of sovereign-like independence. Again decisions of interest to the COB realized themselves only through the will and grace of the COB. The major limiting factor of COB power, itself a "national"-level organization, was that the centrifugal push was so strong that it soon began to lose control of its own constituent parts. The COB state also came to face a severe internal problem of sovereignty.

The third component of this segmental split was the Indian peasant. Seen from the long-range point of view, the conversion of large sectors of the peasantry into potential political actors of the first magnitude was the most important result of the revolution. Following the general fragmenting tendency, the campesinos likewise came to view the other sectors as competitors rather than as allies in a national movement. Where they did not revert to political withdrawal, the peasants were consolidated into peasant mini-states under the control of caciques, which like the COB and the caudillos of the east, monopolized segmental force, ruled territory, taxed, commanded, and, on occasion, exercised independent sanctions over their members.

Thus, the three great pillars of the revolution were divided among themselves and pursued particularistic notions and segmental interests. They came to view each other as threats and later as enemies. The battle was not one of rival interest groups. The deflation of national power, the dispersion of force, and the spontaneous organization of the unit around local concrete power made it (especially where labor and the peasants were concerned) a struggle among fragmental sovereignties.

Within this regional and segmental set of divisions, there were also intra-segmental divisions, particularly during the inflationary period. Ruben Julio battled with Sandoval Moron for territorial control. Toribio Salas challenged Rojas for control of the national peasant confederation, while in their respective areas, both had to use force to fend off challengers from rival sindicatos. Finally, during the battle with Siles, the COB began to fall apart. At one point, fragmentation was so deep that one mining camp was openly battling with another.[8]

From the point of view of a viable national state order, Bolivia was reverting to an anarchical situation. The state as a formal power structure became less and less relevant as an organizational focal point. Beneath the national elite faction struggle over formal power, an informal power structure evolved which negated formal instrumentalities and, with them, the state. In fact the Bolivian state began to wither away.

Elaborate organizations and bureaucracies were created to administer the agrarian reform and the nationalized tin industry, but their authority was challenged at every turn, and these realms of formal authority were actually run by norms that were dictated from below. The elaborate judicial system had little relevance beyond the boundaries of the major cities. Throughout most of the country, law was determined either by consensus based on custom or by the will of a cacique.

On the surface, Bolivia more or less functioned as a single party state, a common model to underdeveloped countries. But the pragmatic party center of would-be nation-builders found themselves presiding over a disintegrating party and a disintegrating state. By 1956, the MNR's original and only direct popular support group, the urban petite bourgeoisie, had, under the pressure of inflation and resentment at the expanding power of other groups, turned against the MNR and its revoluiton. Therefore, a very narrow middle-class elite ran the national government, but their continued stay in office was dependent upon the support of autonomous, organized, and armed groupings over which they had little or no direct control. In other words, by capitalizing upon and furthering the expansion of conflict and the mobilization of wider publics, the original MNR elite was able to "seize power," but thereafter, they became the prisoners of the groups they sponsored. The problem from the perspective of the state was not the disintegration of the power structure as such, but the specific kind of structure that emerged in its place.

Structurally, the MNR national political elite was a very thin stratum with almost no direct links to the society at large. After 1952, no effective national leadership groups existed. Therefore, the national system has been even less meaningful in contemporary Bolivia than in the past. The groups which formerly made up national Bolivia (the national and petite bourgeoisie) were either eliminated or progressively alienated from the official national structures without a more effective base to take their place.

Thus, for a number of reasons related to the structure and organization of prerevolutionary Bolivia and the manner in which specific groups, such as the Indian peasants and miners, entered the post-revolutionary system, there developed in Bolivia a steady dispersal of the effective decision-making capacity into local non-authoritative decision-making centers such as labor unions, peasant sindicatos, etc. Concomitant with this dispersal was the emergence of a series of distinct local elites who had a monopoly of legitimacy in their particular sectors, and, hence, had a practical monopoly of control over the politically relevant behavior of the subgroups of the system. As a result of the downgrading of the military and the arming of the population in 1952, they also had a virtual monopoly of force. There was no integration of these localized centers vertically or horizontally. The result was a structure characterized by a thin national elite in nominal control of national decision-making centers, having no direct structural links to the majority of the total population. At the same time, the revolutionary process heightened both the political awareness and the expectations of significant social groupings, creating a political atmosphere of intense demand articulation from all sectors of the country.

To express the hypothesized situation in more formal terms, it would perhaps be useful to employ two of the variables used by Kornhauser in *The Politics of Mass Society* and compare the structural situation posited for Bolivia to that which Kornhauser posits for a mass society.[9] Utilizing the variables, elite and mass, Kornhauser posits two important dimensions of a mass society: (a) an exposed elite, and (b) an available mass—particularly for anti-system activity. Utilizing the same variables, the structural situation in Bolivia can be expressed as follows: (a) an exposed national elite, and (b) a mass which, while not available for direct mobilization by the national elite, is available for direct mobilization by local sectoral elites. With this structural view in mind, I would like to turn now to an analysis of the exceedingly complex game of political combat which developed in Bolivia after 1952.

Economic Pressures and Political Conflict

Even in the most extreme case, a revolution does not obliterate all the norms and patterns of behavior which preceded it. In the case of Bolivia, where the MNR revolutionaries showed a definite reluctance to tamper with extant styles, symbols, and forms of rhetoric, we can expect a heavy persistence of pre-revolutionary patterns. This expectation would be even more justified if it could be established that previous patterns were connected to conditions which, for one reason or the other, did not essentially change with the revolution. In Bolivia, certain basic aspects of the prerevolutionary political situation not only persisted after 1952, but were, in fact, generalized and intensified. This was a negative phenomenon from the point of view of those wanting to establish a new order that would be hospitable to state-sponsored economic development.

In prerevolutionary Bolivia, a clear correlation existed between economic power and political power. Political power was dominated by the national bourgeoisie (La Rosca) which, economically, had one foot in the semi-feudal agricultural system and the other in the semi-modern, tin-based system. This structure was supported and legitimated (as democratic) by the dependent middle class which identified with and aspired to national bourgeois status.

Intra-elite, office-seeking faction politics, as previously described, derived not only from the existence of a static economic base, but also from the fact that group mobility was minimal and that stratification lines were rigidly drawn. The elite could indulge in this game precisely because no groups were raising credible challenges to the socio-political order itself. There were, however, dangers in the situation. To bolster their intra-faction position, the Saavedrist Republicans, for example, sought support from the inchoate artisan-labor movement. The support was given and partially rewarded by the passage of some of Bolivia's first social legislation. At the same time, Saavedra severely repressed a miners' strike in 1923 as well as an Indian uprising, indicating clearly that he was not willing to entertain any movement from below which might have unbalanced the basic structure. The relative weakness of non-elite groups at this time made this policy of selective flirtation with lower segments to bolster the faction's position in the primary struggle viable. Still, a pattern was established. When weak in the primary conflict, elite factions would seek non-elite support. In later contexts, this was to have fundamental repercussions.

A critical transition period in Bolivian politics was the late 1920s and early 1930s. At this point, the contradictions inherent in the static order began to make themselves felt with new intensity. By natural processes, the elite group was growing and putting increasing pressure on the economic bases so necessary to the maintenance of the elite status life style. As a result, factions proliferated and the intra-elite struggle escalated in intensity.

The group to feel the pinch most directly was the oncoming middle- and upper-class younger generation. The possibilities of them finding good professional positions or effective political connections were dwindling. Contradiction accelerated into a crisis when the country was racked first by the depression, and, immediately thereafter, by the Chaco War. At that time, the economic bases were not only static, but contracting. The previous pinch became a squeeze on growing numbers of the middle class and on certain branches of the upper class as well. Under this pressure, desires for basic changes in the existing order were articulated with increasing vehemence by the oncoming generation. A global split began at the elite level between winners and losers, and between the national bourgeoisie and its main support group, the urban middle. The first expression of the split manifested itself along generational lines.

With this, an ideological dimension was added to the political dynamics, bringing questions of basic changes in the order into the battle. Concomitant with upper-level divisions in elite and subelite circles was the mounting pressure from below, especially from the ascending labor groups who were prevented from climbing the desired social and economic ladder. Following Saavedra's lead, the post–Chaco War period saw a growing tendency on the part of dissident upper groups, now counter-elites, to elicit the aid of the lower non-elite groups in their intra-faction battles. The internal development of these non-elite groups was such in this period, however, that they could no longer be used and then discarded. Indeed, the degree of their involvement began to set the contours of the arena of political conflict. Bolivia entered a period of ideological conflict driven by the process of involvement and mobilization, in breadth and depth, of the system's non-elite groups.

Personal factions evolved into modern parties, and, ultimately, into a broad multi-class movement which toppled the system.

The thread of the old job politics dynamic ran throughout this process. As I pointed out before, during much of this period, dissident elite groups used the old personal faction mechanism as their preferred instrument of struggle. They still used the strategy of placing a leader in the presidency so that, through him, they would gain the immediate occupancy of high office. Be it a civil faction or military cabal, or an alliance of the two, reformist elites showed no hesitation to seize and use coveted offices for personal gain, while projecting and trying to implement change. Given the fact that the basic problem of elite circulation and outlets had not altered, but, in fact, worsened, a dissident elite, no matter how pure his intentions, had little choice but to indulge in the old job game.

If anything, the persistence of this dynamic probably intensified the deepening ideological divisions. There is no doubt that it heightened the bitterness of the post-1952 ideological faction battle within the MNR itself.[10] Thus, although serious ideological questions were raised after 1935 and continued to shape political conflict in Bolivia, these fundamental issues have often been clouded by the old problems of jobs and *personalismo* (in general, "system of putting demands of personal ties above duty to abstract concepts and principles"). A clarification of the ideological struggle—what the new Bolivia is to be—has been made more difficult by the sustained process of non-elite mobilization during the long revolutionary struggle. Partly through their own drive, partly due to mobilization from above, all of the previously submerged groups have entered the central arena of political conflict. With them has come a plethora of demands pressed with an urgency born of long years of frustration and marginal existence.

Political conflict is always contextual. A truism no doubt, but one worth repeating; for in any given case, there are certain inherent contextual features which are simply unavoidable for the actors and the observer alike. In Bolivia, one major such feature was the establishment of the country upon an economic foundation that, after reaching a peak of expansion, has been contracting for the last thirty-odd years. This has raised a serious problem of meeting the demands of internal groups, as well as of accumulating an investable surplus. This factor has been an underlying constant and was a major cause of the revolution; since 1952, it has plagued all attempts to terminate the revolution in a new socio-political national order.

This constant of aggravated scarcity has manifested itself in political conflict at two different levels: first, there has been a continuing intra-elite struggle for jobs and offices deriving from a desire to maintain or achieve certain higher level life styles; secondly, there has been a clamor from below on the part of emergent groups for an alleviation of immediate economic pressure, and for the ability to advance. While the issue at the elite level is maintenance of aspired styles, that from below is tied to the more profoundly immediate problem of tolerable levels of subsistence. At one level, style of existence is at stake, while, at the other, existence itself is the issue.[11]

Since 1952, there have been two basic kinds of political conflict in Bolivia. In the first instance, there has been an ideological struggle in which the issue was and remains, since the old order was destroyed, what the new socio-economic reality of Bolivia is to be and who is to play the largest role in redefining and remaking it. This has been mainly an elite struggle and has been at the root of the right-left-center division in the MNR and the internecine struggles carried out among these wings between 1952 and 1964.

The second kind of political conflict has been a generalized struggle over conflicting demands on the country's resources; the classic battle over who gets what, when, and how. While analytically distinct, the two kinds of conflicts have been intimately intertwined in Bolivia. Through this conflict, the would-be national elites have been brought into close contact, often fraught with tension, with the various publics mobilized by the revolution. Elites have fought mainly over redefinition of the society, but also over the immediate distribution of the revolutionary spoils. The mobilized publics have been mainly concerned with the distribution question, but as any new order would entail, in the end, a formalization of some pattern of distribution, they also have had to concern themselves with the alternative orders projected in the competing ideologies.

In sum, the situation immediately after 1952 involved the emergence of two fundamental kinds of conflicts in an environment characterized by extremely limited resources for immediate demand satisfaction, and by the rapid entrance into the political arena of new groups pressing an increased quantity and quality of demands on these same resources. Ideological conflict, mobilization, an increased volume of demands, and a limited distributable surplus were the immediate problems of the post-insurrectionary national political scene.

The MNR and the Continuing Revolution

Putting aside questions of ideology for the moment, the picture of government in Bolivia after 1952 was that of a thin and structurally isolated MNR elite, itself the product of a historically non-national class, seeking to achieve a basic nationwide order. The party was split badly, with the pragmatic center attempting to work out a viable ruling coalition in which it could retain its pivotal position of guiding and setting the tone of the unfolding revolutionary process. Beneath the level of contending elites was a society in almost total movement: the major groups of which were nominally parts of the MNR, but structurally split along segmental and other lines into mutually hostile warring camps. The task of the MNR leadership was to convince these groups to accept the state which the party nominally controlled as their basic reference point and the legitimate arbiter of social differences. The party needed these groups to generate enough loyalty, support, or acquiescence to allow the MNR government to reorganize the society on a national basis.

An intriguing aspect of the Bolivian Revolution was the degree to which the MNR was able to bring practically all the society's basic groups at least nominally into its orbit both before and immediately after the insurrection. While the motives which brought about the revolutionizing of these groups were undoubtedly complex, there is little doubt that one of the chief factors was denial of gratification under the old system. In fact, it was the demands which arose out of this denial that the MNR elite articulated and used to direct these groups against the old order. In so doing, the MNR throughout the struggle sharpened the expectations of its support groups and accumulated a rather large debt to them. The debt was greatly increased with the rapid entrance of the Indian peasant mass into the political arena after 1952. The insurrection completed, the various groups began to cash in their claims. The MNR was now directly confronting the demands it had so skillfully directed against the old elite and its order. But it was difficult to imagine where the MNR could find the means to meet its constituents' consumption demands and, at the same time, direct economic development.

Contemporary systems theorists have pointed out that one of the basic elements of political stability is the ability of government to strike a balance between demands pressed on the system and supports offered it. Support can be generated either through force, demand satisfaction, or political socialization. The latter mechanism involves the maintenance of affective commitment to the system through the inter-generational transmission of the symbols, norms, and myths of the system. It is, ideally, the mechanism employed by a fully developed system which already has an accumulated store of affective support and elaborate mechanisms to transmit it to oncoming generations. In a revolutionary situation as in Bolivia, however, we are dealing with the conscious attempt to bring a system into being in a climate in which sharp differences exist over what the system should be. There is no tradition born of long years of governmental success to pass on. The only tradition associated with government is one of failure. Aside from some emotional bonds created in the struggle against a common enemy (immediately weakened with its absence), and the ability to manipulate certain ideological symbols (which primarily express demands), the would-be builders of new systems such as the MNR elite, have little accumulated emotional capital to rely on. Likewise, with the basic institutional fabric of the government shattered, they are short on means to transmit this emotional appeal.

The revolutionary elite, therefore, has force and/or demand satisfaction as its most immediately available mechanisms. As we have already seen, the devolution of the capacity to exercise force and the tendency of the country to organize itself segmentally and locally left little force capacity at the state-national level. The thin national MNR elite, unless willing to use the organized force of one segment ruthlessly against one or more of the others, was denied this mechanism. The MNR did use force against the old elite and counter-revolutionaries such as the FSB. However, despite the tales of horror, its use was restricted to the accomplishment of major revolutionary objectives, and to ward off counter-revolution. There was never a root and branch elimination of these elements and they persist today as important aspects of the political equation. More important, until the latter part of the Siles period, force was never used in any real way to bring any of the original revolutionary publics into line.

In facing the problem of generating support for a national order, the MNR elite, bereft of any real ability or will to apply force and threatened by autonomous organized sub-units which had a virtual monopoly of force, had to rely on the mechanism of demand satisfaction. The reliance on this mechanism was strengthened, partly by the desire of the MNR elite to maintain the myth of the three-legged mass movement based on a harmony of interests among the country's three oppressed "classes." Once the process of meeting demands was started, however, appetite increased and harmony gave way to dissonance. Each social segment (eventually groups within segments) pressed its own demands with increasing exclusivity. Entering into the process and calling into question its ultimate effectiveness was the inescapable fact that the means available to satisfy the demands of the disparate revolutionary family were limited in the extreme.

Thus, with little choice left open to it, the MNR governmental elite attempted to gain support for itself and the revolutionary state by meeting the immediate and long-range demands of its major support groups. They set out to buy loyalty and compliance. A complex market system developed in which support for national leadership became a negotiated item, with immediate concrete reward acting as the medium of exchange. As the situation unfolded, it became apparent that local and segmental, nonauthoritative organizations were growing stronger, while the national authoritative center was weakening. By 1957, one observer could note accurately that "the sindicatos could live without the party, but it is doubtful that the party could survive without the sindicatos."[12] The MNR national elite needed the various lower level autonomous organizations more than they needed the MNR. Therefore, it became a seller's market and the price of support increased accordingly.

The great revolutionary reforms involved deep ideological considerations, as well as others; but the manner in which they were implemented puts them squarely in the context under discussion. Nationalization of the mines as a means of guaranteeing state control over the economy was one thing, but the hiring back of thousands of laid-off miners (some 7,000 laid off between 1946 and 1952 were rehired), their indemnification, the issuance of bonuses, and the implementation of control obrero was clearly another. The FSTMB leadership made it obvious that whatever long-range economic function the state considered a national mining industry to have, they considered it, first and foremost, to have a social function.[13] The Agrarian Reform Law, in like manner, could include all kinds of qualifications and references to optimum size of production units and who would or would not get land, but in certain areas the MNR reformist elite merely ratified what local groups had already done. We see the beginning of a pattern in these measures. National leaders projected measures in relation to national goals. In certain areas they could even begin to implement them, but, in those areas where local organizations were strong—usually the most important areas—national measures invariably conformed to local demands and goals. In fact, many were at variance with the higher level goals.

For example, the Agrarian Reform Law considers in detail the question of the size and nature of agricultural operations. Theoretically, the law most directly concerns latifundios, large land holdings which are operating in a non-modern way and are therefore unproductive. The law provides for the continuance of medium-sized holdings and large modernly operated holdings (agricultural enterprises). In the vital Cochabamba Valley, however, properties in both these latter categories were either directly taken over or parceled out to the peasants over the years due to sindicato pressure. Where the local peasants did not directly take such lands, they often refused to let their owners work them, thereby nullifying the national-level rationale. Such cases were more the rule than the exception.[14]

When the basic revolutionary reforms were more or less completed, the process of balancing demands and supports shifted to a more specific and, from the national point of view, virulent form. Throughout the first years of the revolutionary regime, there was a day-by-day increase of the volume of specific demands for wage increases, bonuses, subsidies, etc., pressed directly on the national government and, where possible, directly on the president. Each such demand was pressed with an immediacy growing out of the truly problematic daily situation most groups faced. The demands were always backed by all the strength each segment or group could muster. Moreover, each demand was invariably presented as a burning national issue which had to be dealt with immediately. Governmental mechanisms for dealing at lower levels with sectoral, group, or local demands either did not exist or were circumvented. Thus, everything from wage problems in an individual factory to space problems in a specific school became issues of national import. After a time, it seemed that there was no issue too small that could not demand the time, energy, and attention of high-level officials and possibly threaten the government with a crisis.

It was not unusual for the Bolivian national government to be directly involved in such matters as defining wages and prices. Petitioners had always sought to bring their requests directly to the government and, most particularly, to the president. However, after 1952, the process was generalized and intensified. The number of petitioners increased astronomically, as did the volume and kinds of demands. The revolution had made this style unavoidable. With the patron gone, to whom could the peasant sindicato go for help; with the private mine company gone, to whom could the miners' union go? Moreover, each group could argue with some legitimacy that they had helped to make the revolution or were essential to its maintenance and now expected their promised reward. Through the party, through the COB, through the peasant organizations, or through individuals directly, the demands poured in.

In the first wave, the demands were mainly for immediate economic advancement, guarantees, and security. In a burst of unparalleled social legislation, the government responded with decree upon decree providing wage increases, bonuses, working conditions, holidays, housing programs, family subsidies, and so on. Of more than minor interest is the fact that most of these decrees dealt not with classes of problems, but with specific group problems: houses for railway workers, a bonus for the San José mine, a pay increase for teachers, etc. This policy style reflected the particularistic approach of the demand groups and the ad hoc problem-by-problem, crisis-by-crisis response of the government. These decrees, plus the more general provisions in the areas of education, health, and public welfare, gave Bolivia, on paper at least, one of the most advanced batteries of social legislation and systems of public services in the world, not to mention a tremendous strain on the national budget.[15]

The tremendous financial outpouring occasioned by these measures and the impact of other government policies began to feed the already chronic inflationary tendencies built into the economy. The inflation quickly grew completely out of control and the value of the boliviano plummeted downward. With the inflation, there arose a second cycle of demands born out of the fear of being wiped out by inflationary pressure, or of losing advantages gained by the revolution. Demands, not unexpectedly, were pressed on the embattled governing coalition with increased stridency. The government's propensity to make ad hoc responses to crises was reinforced.[16]

The government was soon stumbling from crisis to crisis and public support split into a myriad of competing groups, all demanding to be defended from the inflation. The demands were backed by threats which constantly materialized into mass demonstrations and strikes. Bowing before the pressure put on it, the government would give in to the demands of one group, whereupon others demanded equal treatment. Failure to respond could close the schools, stop a vital industry, or turn the streets of La Paz into a battleground. In this crisis atmosphere, the ability of any group to break through the din and force the government to attend to its particular demands depended on the size and credibility of the threat it could pose if offended.

As previously mentioned, the group least capable of presenting an immediate threat was the amorphous and poorly organized urban middle. The laboring groups, due to their organization, their weapons, and the vital nature of their activities, could and did threaten the government all too credibly. Between 1952 and 1956, the middle group lost ground steadily, not because of any conscious MNR policy, but because of their inability to fight the kind of social war Bolivia was going through. The laboring groups, on the other hand, were protected from the inflationary push through cost-of-living increases, subsidized stores, prohibition of layoffs, and a variety of other devices. This protection was not spread equally. Elite groups such as the miners were much more effective in defending their position than less potent groups such as the construction workers.[17]

Labor's ability to defend itself set off hostility and bitterness among other sectors of MNR support. It was not simply out of jealousy. Labor's gains often involved direct deprivation for other groups. Rent controls, price stabilization on vital commodities, and government food distribution programs meant that some groups were doomed to fixed incomes while prices in other areas climbed inexorably upward.

While laboring groups, particularly the miners, were the more obvious beneficiaries of the situation, the less visible peasants also came out rather well. The land reform, of course, brought an immediate and massive redistribution of wealth. Secure in land possession and often capable of providing themselves with most goods, they were not hit by high food prices and the chronic shortages in the cities. Indeed, in some cases, as provisioners of critical goods, they drew direct benefits; the biggest gainer in this respect was a rapidly developing new commercial stratum of Indian middlemen, moving into the vacuum of trade between the city and the country. The rural sector was also the target of heavy government investment in a variety of spheres.[18] Finally, the peasant became the recipient of a number of public services, the most evident being a crash program of establishing rural schools.[19] Hence, during this period, the peasant was awakened to the possibilities of satisfying a number of previously undreamed-of needs. At the same time, he was taught, by example, how to use organized strength to bargain and threaten. A measure of the peasant's gains and a proof of his bargaining ability is the fact that despite many attempts, no government since 1952 has been able to levy a direct tax on him or to induce him to pay the price the Agrarian Reform Law stipulates he should for his land.

If we look at the peasants, the urban petite bourgeoisie, and labor groups as distinct sectors, we can see that they were being pulled apart and forced to fight among themselves during the first four years of the revolution. At first, the struggle was primarily about the distribution of valued public worth; but as inflation gained a firmer grip and the overall production of the country began to decline, the clash became more centered on the question of how to distribute losses. Government decrees protected most of the laboring groups, but directly injured the urban middle groups, and helped feed the inflation. The variety of investment programs in the rural sector for the purpose of economic diversification redounded to the benefit of the peasant, but drew off from the other sectors. This was especially true with the national tin industry, which was progressively decapitalized to finance such investment. The first casualty of this inter-segmental war was the urban middle group, and it responded by throwing its support behind the counter-revolutionary FSB. As the FSB during this period was functioning as a conspiratorial group mounting many coup attempts and encouraging separatism in Santa Cruz, the strengthening of its hand by middle sector defection hardly aided the MNR's attempt to establish a viable national order. The MNR was losing control in the all-important cities, and, at best it could only expect passive acquiescence. The party was constantly afraid of fast coup attempts in the capital.

By 1956, the country was in the constant throes of both political and economic crisis. The two components of the crisis were intertwined and mutually reinforcing. The economic crisis was reflected in the steady decline of the country's economic product. Behind this decline were three major factors: (a) heavy losses in the state mining enterprise (COMIBOL), (b) a precipitous decline in agricultural production, and (c) exhaustion of the country's meager gold supply. The economic picture however was not all dark. There were positive economic trends, and while the economy was poorly organized, it was at least dynamic.[20]

From the long-range point of view, the general redistribution of wealth was, at the least, alleviating poverty and it was also creating a potentially larger consumer's market. The government was making a concerted effort to build a developmental infra-structure in roads, transport, and communication. In addition, the first steps to diversify the economic base of the country were taken by developing new agricultural lands and by stimulating the long-dormant oil industry. The crux of the difficulty lay in the tension between the government's wealth distribution policies and its economic development policies. Given the minimal resource base, it was practically impossible to carry out both policies at once. The first obvious negative result was the inflationary spiral brought on by a spurt in buying power, a drop in production, and the financing of development projects by the use of the government printing press, by borrowing, and by the use of multiple exchange rates.

By manipulating exchange rates, the government systematically siphoned off COMIBOL's profits for use in welfare and development spending. This tactic was a logical outgrowth of MNR thinking dating back to the 1930s, for example, to use tin profits to diversify. However, the problem was that the industry in the 1950s was a pale shadow of its former self. The quality of the ore had declined severely, plants and equipment were decrepit, and most of the foreign technical staff had left after nationalization (about 170 out of 200). In addition, the price of tin on the world market declined steadily after the Korean War (to a low of 90 cents a pound). Finally, the rehiring of thousands of laid-off workers, the raising of wages, and a series of social welfare programs (schools, hospitals, pensions, etc.) had run COMIBOL's operating costs up astronomically (costs rose to $1.25 a pound by 1960). COMIBOL itself was in need of capital investment, and the government, after a point, was not siphoning off profits as much as decapitalizing the operation. The long-range effects of this policy of "sowing" tin was threatening to kill the goose that, theoretically, should lay the golden eggs.[21]

The reasons for the government's attempt to follow consumption and investment policies at the same time were many, but the root cause was the political situation described above and the resulting conflict between political and economic rationalities. Political rationality in that context demanded that the government meet the demands of its critical support groups, for example, facilitate income distribution and consumption. Economic rationality in that context, on the other hand, demanded that consumption be held back in the name of accumulation and investment. The country could not go on burning the candle at both ends forever, particularly if it was going to try to meet everyone's demands. Sooner or later some fundamental decisions had to be made; whatever they were, they were bound to have serious political and/or economic repercussions.[22]

The economic situation between 1952 and 1956 was a mixture of positive and negative aspects, but was essentially dynamic. The same can be said of the political situation. The chief negative aspects were the creation of a crisis atmosphere, and the attendant ad hoc, decision-making style. In like manner, the shattering of party unity and the growing threat of an FSB-led, middle- and upper-class counter-revolution created difficulties. However, the revolution was taking clear shape and moving in a specific direction. Whether one considers the direction good or bad depends on personal ideology. The point is that the center-left coalition, driven by the COB, gave the revolution a clear forward thrust backed by a formidable power base. The long-range price, no doubt, would have been the progressive replacement of the MNR middle-class elite by the emerging labor-left elite, and, ultimately, a more radical and essentially socialistic revolution.

In 1956, Siles stepped into this fluid situation and sought to put on the brakes, both economically and politically. By making

monetary stabilization the keynote of his economic policy, and by
accepting the U.S.-I.M.F. monetary strategy, Siles, of necessity, put
himself on a collision course with the labor left. Whatever his personal goals might have been, the fact remains that Siles adopted
a political strategy designed to weaken the power of the labor left.
Thus, by extension, it became his goal to reverse, or at least deflect, the forward thrust of the revolution. Under him, the previously displaced MNR rightists staged a comeback, reopening
the old MNR labor-left elite struggle for control of office and the
power to define the course of the revolution.

Siles achieved his first goal of monetary stabilization. However, the economic price was the blunting of the positive as well
as the negative trends in the economy. The inflationary spiral was
brought to a halt, but so was the entire economy. Consumption
was reduced, but so too was investment. Money became stabilized
and the economy became immobilized.[23]

As far as the social allocation of costs were concerned, the
stabilization introduced a rough equalization of the economic
situation. Pressure was taken off the middle sector, but it was
shifted to labor and, in particular, to the miners. At the same time,
labor-left solidarity, always precarious, was shattered. Labor agitation thereby increased and went beyond strikes to widespread violence, inter-sindicato war, the taking of hostages, and a general
defiance of governmental authority.[24]

The government had to fight to gain any semblance of order
in the mines. In the end, unwilling or unable to crush opposition,
Siles achieved a shaky standoff. In any event, labor support for the
national MNR was permanently weakened. Labor, as a support
public, divided. The left-wing POR and the PCB increased their
control at the local and regional levels among worker groups;
again the greatest inroads were made by these organizations in
the mines.

The first apparent political result of the Siles policy was a
dampening of the FSB threat, and the spectre of an urban-based
coup d' état. But while the urban middle was neutralized, the
MNR did not regain positive support from them. The MNR's
inability to control the all-imporatnt mining camps was all too

obvious. The threat of an open clash with the left eventually moderated, but, here again, positive support gave way to sullen and temporary passivity. Both segments had come to view the MNR core elite with new distrust.

In terms of the two historic social bases of the revolution (the urban middle and the workers), the situation had come to a negative standoff. Neither group actively opposed the MNR, but neither were they actively supporting it. Neither segment was able to impose its interests on the other nor on the revolution; but each was now able to protect itself up to a point. Neither had defining power, but both had definite measures of veto power. The revolution thereby lost its dynamic thrust and turned into a blocking operation. As the economy ground to a halt, so too did the revolution. Bolivia fell into political and economic immobilism. The ability of the national elite to initiate any major positive moves dwindled even further.[25]

The third and newest member of the revolutionary family, the campesino, remained a question mark. Given the obvious power potential of the peasants, however, the question of which way they would move became critical.

By the late 1950s, peasants were developing a very independent political game in which specific regional and local demands were the most important. Increasingly aware of their strength, they pressed these demands directly on national decision-making bodies. In all cases, the demands were backed by the threat of organized force, implemented at different times by the invasion of local party offices, the threatening of towns, or the blockage of an area and the restriction of all traffic through it. The same techniques were used to resist any government requests for taxes, land payment, or the like.

The much talked of peasant loyalty to the MNR was more myth than reality. There was a generalized gratitude for the land reform; but this was something extremely difficult to channel in concrete directions, other than a simple determination to hold on to the land. Peasant concerns were mainly local and there was little awareness of national issues. Most of the peasants of the countryside used their land and new sindicato organizations to solidify their isolation from the national reality: a development which, from the point of view of establishing a national order, was clearly negative.

In those areas where a national orientation and concern were slowly developing, it was under the sponsorship of local bosses, not the MNR. The emergent pattern was one of organized and potent demand groups showing a rather voracious appetite. The result, from the point of view of achieving a working basis of order, was the addition of another potent source of demands to the already complex equation. The problem of balancing demands and pursuing support became even more difficult. While the other groups had vestiges of loyalty born of common struggle, the peasants entered without this legacy. From the beginning, they placed a high price on their support. Actually, no overall peasant support which could be courted existed. The largest number of peasants were inert and essentially unavailable to support any national regime or order. Those available were so on a regional, not a group basis, and even here problems of inter-regional and local disputes made the support questionable. In reality, while the organized peasant centers were able to make demands and disruptions, their viability as a support group was problematic, to say the least.[26]

During his power struggle with Lechín, Siles made an open bid for campesino support. He made the Valley peasant leader, José Rojas, minister of peasant affairs. Rojas was the first Indian peasant in Bolivian history to hold cabinet rank, and his elevation was both a recognition of new power realities and a bid to win the peasants to the center-right position on the revolution.

While serving in La Paz, Rojas' control of the Valley was challenged by a rival leader, Miguel Veizaga. Consequently, an intra-campesino civil war began in the Valley which the government was powerless to stop. In 1959, Siles finally did intervene in the war, but not as a sovereign authority putting a halt to an intolerable situation and thereby demonstrating its effective control. As part of his strategy to win peasant support, Siles intervened on the side of Rojas, who was identified with the MNR, while Veizaga was identified with the POR. The intervention was successful, and

Rojas consolidated his hold on the Valley in the name of Siles and the MNR.[27] Veizaga remained isolated in the town of Cliza.

The MNR's hold on the Valley was based not on any real party or governmental control but on the feudal-like fealty of Rojas and his lieutenants, a loyalty which, as the future would show, was negotiable. An important aspect of the Valley drama was the fact that Siles had intervened on Rojas' behalf through the army.

Quietly, Siles had begun, with United States assistance, to rebuild the national regular army. The use of this "new" army in the Valley pacification effort marked a critical new political trend. Siles slowly began to remake the army's public image and to revive its strength and former control functions.

While the Valley apparently had been converted into a pro-MNR, anti-labor-left bastion, the situation on the altiplano was different. There, the boss of Achacachi, Salas, threw his considerable weight behind Lechín and the leftist COB. In lining up on different sides of the fence, these two bastions of independent peasant power, in effect, reinforced the political standoff and national immobilization.

The maneuverings of these powerful caciques reflected less of an ideological commitment than the emergence of another aspect of the complex patterns of leadership in revolutionary Bolivia. There were really two levels of elite struggle. One was national, and the dimensions of it were discussed above. The second level was local and involved intra-segmental and regional struggles by local elites for control of organizations and territory. The two levels converged in a complex process of factions and alliances in which national contenders sought to buttress their positions by arrangement with local power controllers, while local contenders sought alliances with national faction leaders to consolidate their hold over local power centers. Rojas, for example, was, at one point or another, identified with different national groups and positions. Salas likewise flirted with many groups, and Veizaga, who in 1958 was identified with the POR, was in 1960 identified with the MNR right-wing splinter group led by Guevara.[28] Sandoval Moron and Ruben Julio also made and remade alliances with national power contenders and factions. The full implications of these complex ideological and power interest combinations involving different elite levels and changing tactical situations were to become most apparent in the second and third governments of Víctor Paz.

Summary

In this chapter, I have attempted to analyze in terms of structure and process the outline of Bolivian politics which developed after 1952 and was solidified during the government of Hernan Siles. This pattern eventually froze Bolivian governments into an extremely negative position, vis-à-vis the goal of institutionalizing the revolution in a framework hospitable to state-sponsored economic development. The dynamics of the pattern can be summed up in the following terms.

After 1952, there was a rapid introduction into the political arena of new and significant demand groups—particularly peasants and miners. These groups began pressing an increased volume of demands on a national elite struggling to bring a new system into existence within an environment characterized by extremely limited resources for immediate demand satisfaction.

In facing the problem of generating support for national initiative, the national elite had to rely on the method of demand satisfaction. The situation was complicated because it would appear that affective commitments were monopolized compartmentally by localized structures and elites. Those segmental local elites articulated the demands of their sectors and pressed them on the national system. The result was that the national decision-making structures received, on the one hand, a steady stream of often contradictory demands unfiltered by an affective screen, and, on the other hand, supports, contingent on the immediate and continuing satisfaction of demands: a situation we might term "pure interest" politics.

I am suggesting that, in Bolivia, the pattern of interactions which developed within this process was such that the national decision-makers could generate only enough support for the contingent occupancy of office. They were not able to launch development programs which would divert resources from demand satisfaction or be perceived as threatening to the interests of any significant internal group (particularly peasants and miners). At the same time, the process consistently diverted potential developmental energies and resources, and resulted in a "vicious circle" of underdevelopment.

The political manifestation of this vicious circle was an increase in the dispersal of power to localized centers, increasing social gaps both horizontally among localized groups and vertically between local groups and national structures, and causing a concomitant increase in social conflict and political instability.

Floating above this general framework, the MNR national government ended by simply reacting now to this thrust, now to that. The MNR party functioned not as traditional Western theories of democracy describe a party, that is, as the connecting link between government and populace, nor as modern theory describes parties in the new one-party states, i.e., as a mechanism for mobilizing support for government initiatives. Rather, the party became an instrument through which various sectors could legitimately assault the system's meager collective surplus. The party came to have little or no control over its constituent parts, and, as a result, both party and government became the captives of shifting local and segmental power combinations. Relevant forms of power, in turn, were primarily reduced to direct control over sectors of the economy, and, ultimately, to the capacity to threaten the government with autonomous force. Beneath the single party veneer was a society in a state of incipient civil war. Forced by the situation to rely on demand satisfaction, but lacking a resource base capable of meeting fully the various demands made on it, the various MNR governments had to maintain themselves through a complex process of "robbing Peter to pay Paul." It was a self-defeating process which, although allowing the government to cling precariously to the symbols of power, blocked any real national development by draining the country's already limited capital resource base, as well as most of the capital which entered in the form of foreign aid.[29] Similarly, the political aim of gaining a solid base of support was negated in the end. The nature of the agrarian reform, increasing wage demands, the maintenance of subsidized stores, etc., all bit deeply into the country's economic capacity. At the same time, the devolution of power, authority, and status to some groups at the expense of others bit into the country's limited psychological capital; the result was a continually deteriorating political situation on the national level.

During the MNR's reign, this process became a style of public life. Organizations proliferated as each sector sought to build a solid front with which to protect what it had, while it assaulted the system for more. The MNR, in turn, proliferated into factions, and factions within factions, through which each group sought a legitimate "in" at the national level, while guarding its local power base. Very few people at the national level belonged to the MNR per se, but were, rather, the railway workers' representative, the miners' representative, the bank employees' representative, etc. One group or another partially got its way, depending on how the factions coalesced at any given point. When this preferred mechanism for pressing demands failed to be effective due to the coalitions formed at that moment, the weakened group took to the streets in strikes, work stoppages, or partial uprisings. Thus, the system was continually in crisis.

We can almost say that, under Siles, this style became so institutionalized that it won a kind of acceptance among some sectors. Alone, no single sector could take over, and by this time no group trusted another enough to enter into a permanent alliance. So, rather than risk all by rupturing the circle, most groups either came to perpetuate it actively, or did so by default. The myth of the national revolution and its popular instrument, the MNR, was strengthened; deals and counter-deals were made and broken.

I referred to this emergent political style as one of "pure interest" politics; a style which can be contrasted with a system based on pure force or pure mobilization of commitment. None of these forms of political control ever appears in pristine purity; there is always a mix. At varying times, however, one or the other becomes dominant, and there is more than enough evidence to support the hypothesis that political stability varies inversely with the degree to which either force or interest satisfaction become the dominant bases of political loyalty. Bolivia, under the MNR, supports the hypothesis and is partially explainable in terms of it. In Bolivia, interest satisfaction became the dominant basis of loyalty, and when important sectors failed to have their perceived interests satisfied, their previous support was converted into hostility, and potentially into rebellion. Beyond this, particular governing elites had to face the fact that contending elites who could project themselves as better demand satisfiers could "buy" the basis of their rule out from under them.

Pure interest politics, as well as the politics of relative force, are endemic to revolutionary situations, which, in turn, are inherently zero sum conflict situations: that is, a situation in which one contender's gain is perceived as the loss of all others. Zero sum politics occurs in other contexts as well. The job faction politics of prerevolutionary Bolivia, for example, was an intra-elite perceived, zero sum situation which later began to spread to other groups, such as labor, when the prerevolutionary system denied them admittance on an equal basis to the game.

Behind a zero sum political situation is a general perception, aptly labeled the "world as limited good"; that is, when actors view the available stock of valued things as limited and static, for example, a nonexpanding economic pie.[30] As we have seen, this view, from the late 1920s on, was a rather accurate perception of the situation on the part of relevant Bolivian political actors. I have interpreted the revolution, in part, as a complex reaction to this fundamental socio-economic fact. The Bolivian situation was worsened because it took place in a world where elites experienced the demonstration effect of the general expansion of other national state units, while non-elites experienced the demonstration effect of the increasing levels of consumption of their counterparts in other such countries. The drive for national state development (even if the full implications of the commitment are only dimly perceived) can be interpreted as a reaction at a number of societal levels to a real problem of situationally bound "limited good" in a wider world context of "expanding good."

The history of Bolivia indicates the tragic reality, however, that the ideological commitment to development (expansion of the pie) clashes with the reality of a tenaciously recalcitrant local situation of limited good. The desire to develop, reinforced by a desire to share certain life styles, stirred counter-elites to create a revolutionary situation. Their ability to make such a situation real arose from the frustrated demands of support publics who, because of the situation of limited good, could not advance to the desired level (labor and, later, peasants), or were experiencing the reduction of a previous level of sharing (the urban middle). The appearance of a revolutionary situation in post–Chaco War Bolivia and its persistence until 1952 increased the scope, tempo, and intensity of the demands on the store of collective good. Due to the structural factors previously discussed, the store of good not only remained limited but was actually declining. The reality of a steadily declining store of good in relation to increased demands became mutually reinforcing factors in a continually deteriorating political and economic process, culminating in the insurrection of 1952.

The successful insurrection, followed by the spilling over of the revolution into the agrarian system, served to increase further the scope, tempo, and intensity of demands on the collective store of good. The pre–Chaco War, zero sum, intra-elite game was generalized in terms of participants to the point where it was almost totalized. The previous situation of declining good became, after 1952, a real situation of plummeting good. After an initial period of relative gain by new groups (at the expense of old), the situation deteriorated so badly (reflected in the inflation) that all groups were forced to adopt a defensive stance to protect their newly won gains or to prevent further deterioration. The political game became not simply a zero sum game but, in reality, a declining sum game. The various social segments reacted accordingly, leading to internal fragmentation, political instability, and economic regression. By the late 1950s, the best the revolutionary government was able to achieve was a politically and economically immobilized standoff.

This is not to say that questions of ideology and new images of Bolivia became irrelevant. The question of a new order continued and added a moral tone which served to intensify even further the nature of conflict. But the question of ideology was intertwined with and, in part, subsumed under the more pressing problem of distribution; a problem which, in turn, was becoming less a question of distributing value than of allocating costs. Thus, in any attempt at a reorganization and push toward development, the basic issues that any elite had to face were the allocation of costs and the accumulation of the necessary power to make its allocation decisions stick.

13 *The Problem of Development*

As stated before, the various counter-elite groups in Bolivia, including the MNR, saw themselves as developers and modernizers. For this reason, I have conceived of the Bolivian Revolution as a manifestation of a more global phenomenon which I term the "modern developmental revolution." Common to all modern revolutions is the desire to push aside previous political orders deemed "responsible" for underdevelopment and to establish in their place new orders which will be hospitable to the rapid economic development of national state units. In this context, political structures come to be seen almost exclusively in instrumental terms, that is, as means to the developmental end. Therefore, it has become common in this context to conceive of various projected political frameworks as "political models" of development. In the post-insurrectionary phase of the revolutionary process, one of the most important sources of conflict is the struggle among revolutionary elites over alternative definitions of a new order. In the modern revolutionary situation, that conflict is primarily a battle over alternative political models of development.

280

Political Models of Development: An Ideological Struggle

Political models of development are formally expressed in ideologies, symbols, and programs. In Bolivia during the period of 1952–64, the ideological struggle eventually settled around two alternative courses expressed in the concepts of a *sociedad democrática burguesa* ("democratic bourgeois society") and a *gobierno obrero-campesino* ("government of workers and peasants"). It is interesting to note that the first concept developed out of the PIR ideological tradition, and that the second concept emerged out of the formal thinking of the POR. Eventually, however, the battle between the two was fought within the post-insurrectionary MNR party, with the center-right MNR supporting the former and the COB-based labor left supporting the latter.[1]

The first challenges of significance to be raised against the old order appeared with the movement of students and young professionals beginning in the late 1920s. Two counter-tendencies, one reformist and one revolutionary, appeared at this time. Both of these tendencies reappeared after the Chaco War and a process of formalization and evolution began within the unfolding revolutionary situation of Bolivia. In the early 1940s, the two were more or less solidified and given organizational expression within the MNR and the PIR.

In those early days, the contrasts between the PIR and the MNR appeared to be quite stark. The PIR projected a major reorganization of the society, including nationalization and agrarian reform based on a strategy of mass revolution from below. The MNR, on the other hand, projected a vague and programmatically ill-defined reformation of society based on a strategy of elite reform from above, and a coup rather than a mass insurrection power tactic. Despite these differences, it must be remembered that both positions sprang from the same generation of oncoming elite and sub-elite youth facing essentially the same life problems. Thus, both were urban bourgeois reactions. Despite strategic and tactical differences, both saw themselves as the agents destined to lead their respective movements and design the new society. Likewise, it should be remembered that the driving force in the revolutionary situation between 1935 and 1946 was the progressively disaffected urban middle segment; labor functioned mainly as a boundary setter to the central conflict: the peasant mass played no role to speak of.

Between 1940 and 1946, two factors of importance entered the situation: the increasing politicization of the labor movement, and the demonstration by the status quo elite that it would not accept the reformism of the MNR. The first factor assured that a key component of a potential MNR base would be labor; the second factor eventually drove the MNR to seek this broader mass base. Labor was available as a support base, but on its own terms. By the late 1940s, most of the original overt Fascist, corporatist, or Peronist aspects of the MNR were dropped. The critical turning point came after 1946 when the MNR sought a mass revolutionary base, and labor emerged as the key motor of the unfolding revolutionary situation. In effect, the MNR adopted the strategy and tactics of the PIR. Having made this move, it eventually adopted its program as well. Thus in 1951, the MNR unfurled its battle flag, waving the concepts of nationalization, agrarian reform, and universal suffrage. After 1946, the PIR was eliminated as a power contender, but its general image had been incorporated into the MNR. The two original bourgeois counterpositions had been more or less molded into one.

The marriage of the two tendencies was made clear in the Agrarian Reform Law of 1953 which, as I pointed out previously, drew heavily on the thinking of the former PIR member, Urquidi Morales. The key operative notion behind the law and the concept of *sociedad democrática burguesa* was the belief that Bolivia had to pass first through a full capitalist stage before any attempt to establish a socialist society could be made. Hence, the aim of the revolutionary state was to bring about a controlled capitalist society. This thinking was also behind the nationalization decree, which carefully avoided attacking the concept of private property itself. Monopolized property was brought under state control in order to assure national investment of tin proceeds, to assure the viability of small- and medium-sized private operations, and to see to it that production would serve a national, socially productive purpose. The measures were not socialistic but, rather, envisioned state-sponsored and controlled capitalism. In effect, the MNR core proposed using the state to fulfill the original liberal promise. It was from this understanding of the MNR's aims that the United States threw its support behind the revolution.[2]

Behind this merged MNR-PIR image was the belief that the defining and directing role in the new order would fall to a progressive elite sprung from the middle class. This attitude ran deep in bourgeois counter-elite writings, dating at least as far back as the original works of Tristan Marof. The idea was that, though the workers and peasants deserved a better life, they had neither the power, vision, nor capacity to lead the redefinition and reordering of the country.[3] This outlook is not surprising when we consider that the MNR and PIR elites sought to change prerevolutionary Bolivia, but were themselves products of the old order elite and sub-elite strata. They carried with them, therefore, the deepest attitudes of a conquest society which viewed itself as the paladin of Western culture, born to rule and civilize the essentially inferior, conquered Indian society. These attitudes were strengthened by the elitist components of Leninist and Stalinist thinking in the PIR, and the various Fascist, corporatist, and Peronist concepts of the early MNR. In later years, this orientation has received further encouragement from technocratic, elitist thinking based on most Western democratic development models. As the previous generations had brought various "Europes" to America, they, the progressive elite, would bring the latest twentieth-century industrial phase of Europe and the United States to the high Andes.

I stated before that the MNR elite was actually a reluctant band of revolutionaries. Whether reformist or revolutionary, the pragmatic nationalist MNR core's chief goal was not primarily political or social, but economic. Political and social changes were seen as means to the goal of economic reorganization. When this elitist core looked for a concrete example of what it was they wished to accomplish, and how, they looked to Mexico and the Mexican Revolution.

The final theoretical image that came out of all this was the idea of the "national revolutionary movement": a multi-class alliance led by a progressive middle-class elite which would push away the negative features of the old society and put in their place a mirror image of the modern European nation-state, the foundation of which was a strong economy. The two new bases of the movement (workers and peasants) were seen not as participant creators in the new society, but as objective sources of political motor power and as "human capital" to be nurtured, trained, and allocated.[4] Through an increased standard of living, the worker would be a healthier, more contented being and, therefore, more productive. The agrarian reform would "liberate" the Indian peasant politically and socially, but, more important, it would help him to become a producer and a consumer. This modern developmental paternalism was most apparent in the MNR conceptualization of the Indian mass. The Indian was to be "integrated" or "incorporated" into the national society: he was not seen as a creative force in his own right, involved in making a new "national" society. As the older elite spoke of "civilizing" the Indian, the new, younger elite spoke of "integrating" him. In either case, the assumption was that there was a given society which was good, and that the task of the leaders of that given society was to make the peasant mass over in its own image.[5] In this case, the leaders who would do the job of image-defining were those who made up the progressive MNR elite.

This rather idyllic picture floundered rather quickly after the insurrection of 1952. One thing that had never really been grasped by the MNR elite was the cost of the developmental process upon which it wished to embark. As both leaders and followers became aware of the costs, it became apparent that no one was willing to pay them; all would rather someone else did. After the resources of the old elite had been wrung dry, there was not enough left to meet everyone's consumption demands and to invest in development as well—someone in the revolutionary family was also going to have to pay. Thus began the degeneration of revolutionary harmony and the start of "intra-familial" war.

The second developmental model (*el gobierno obrero-cam-*

pesino) evolved from a different source. The POR tendency began in the same way as the other counter-elite tendencies, but quite early in the game a different path was chosen. While the MNR and the PIR sought to widen their bases across class lines, the POR consciously sought to confine themselves to one class. During the early 1940s, the POR burrowed deeply into the labor movement, with particular interest in the mines. In this process, the POR became progressively more proletarianized. At the leadership level, the MNR and PIR were basically from the middle and upper sectors, while the POR leadership was increasingly made up of working-class types. The POR in a real sense became the only specifically working-class political group to appear in pre-insurrectionary Bolivia. Although the POR was a true expression of an important tendency within the increasingly political working class, it was too localized in influence—it had almost no strength among the railway workers, for example—to dominate the movement, let alone to spearhead a working-class revolution.

In 1944, the MNR made its first real organizational contact with the labor movement. The powerful FSTMB was founded, and, by dint of his control over it, Lechín became destined to be the most influential national labor leader. Lechín and the other FSTMB leaders, while nominally members of the MNR, owed their positions of power to their labor base, not to the party. While Lechín was not a worker per se, he was clearly from a lower and much more marginal social stratum; the other FSTMB leaders were definitely workers. Therefore, this group, which began to gain prominence after 1946, represented a newly emergent, segmentally based counter-elite. Moreover, as I pointed out previously, this segmental elite had, for some time, shown growing suspicion of the bourgeois-based, counter-elite PIR and MNR.

After Villarroel's fall, the MNR temporarily lost contact with the FSTMB. During this period, Lechín and the other federation leaders drew increasingly closer to the POR, which was lodged securely in the local sindicato structure. The great influence of the POR in forming the political orientation of Lechín and the FSTMB became evident in the Lechín-endorsed *Tesis de Pulacayo*. When the MNR finally reestablished contact, it did so with a movement that was increasingly more powerful and organizationally independent, having its own leadership and a definite, independent political orientation. The MNR again succeeded in becoming the political expression of labor, but the alliance was fraught with mutual distrust.

While the FSTMB was politically aligned with the MNR, it was much more like the POR in ideological orientation. Furthermore, after 1946 the labor movement would no longer accept a passive role in which it would be led by middle- and upper-sector intellectuals in return for bread-and-butter rewards. Labor, through the POR and the FSTMB, was now demanding an active and eventually controlling role in the redefinition and remaking of Bolivia.

The FSTMB eventually split with the POR. The POR itself then split in three directions. The split was over issues of timing and tactics rather than over fundamental concepts. One large segment of the POR entered the MNR and became allied with Lechín. The second splinter group formed from basic personal antagonisms. It lasted only a short time and today is virtually extinct. The remainder of the POR original group continued to play a dominant role in individual mining unions and also played an important role in the first few years of Lechín-dominated COB activity. Members of both the COB and the POR played critical roles in fomenting the agrarian revolution. Even after their influence waned in the Valley, they continued to exert influence on the altiplano. This push for the totalization of the revolution sprang directly from the concept behind the COB-POR thrust, *gobierno obrero-campesino*.

By incorporating the COB, the MNR incorporated the POR concept as well; thus began the battle between the rival projections: the MNR-PIR concept of *sociedad democrática burguesa*, and the COB-POR concept of *gobierno obrero-campesino*. The former projected a state capitalist society dominated by a progressive middle-class elite; the latter, a state socialist society dominated basically by a mixed elite partly derived from, and mainly based on, the working class. In the former, an essentially middle-sector image would dominate. The worker and peasants would benefit with increased wages and benefits for workers and independent free-hold status for the peasants. As far as the second concept was concerned, this middle-sector image would give way to a working-class definition, particularly on questions of property. The peasants, through progressive collectivization, would be transformed into a rural proletariat. The former concept followed the Mexican orientation, while the latter presaged Cuba.[6]

Given the unanticipated consequences of the insurrection, neither concept could hope to realize itself fully. For this reason, the MNR pragmatic core pulled away from its right wing, and the Lechín wing of the COB pulled away from its radical left wing. A center-left coalition developed in which both bowed to realities, but sought to maintain their basic positions. Also at work was the fact that the MNR elite was less aware of the inherent ideological conflicts in the revolutionary movement than the COB.[7]

In facing the immediate problem of demand satisfaction, the MNR elite, locked in its image of a multi-class movement based on a commonality of interests, struggled valiantly to meet everyone's demands. The labor-left wing, on the other hand, indicated clearly its realization that in that situation, its claims on control would have to be at the expense of the MNR right wing, and its claims on available resources would have to be at the expense of the urban middle, in general. Thus, while the COB accepted the MNR lead, it immediately sought to establish itself as the pivot of the party, from where it would build for its eventual emergence as the controlling and defining power faction of the revolution.

The COB did not get all it wanted, but, at first, it did get what was considered essential to the ultimate emergence of its ideological model: (a) a mass peasant base, (b) co-gobierno, and (c) control obrero. Likewise, the COB succeeded in making its claims on the nation's available resources dominant. As it became more and more apparent that the labor left was making its immediate control and gratification demands stick, the MNR right wing withdrew from the party. The general middle segment, in search of an instrument to defend its interests, drifted to support of the FSB.

By 1956, the worker-peasant model was not dominant, but all

portents pointed to its impending triumph. During the 1956 convention, the COB forced the congress to censure Guevara Arze, one of the most prominent original MNR leaders. At the same time, the COB dominated the party's electoral lists, had more than parity in the national political committee, placed its choice for the vice-presidency, and upped the number of labor ministers from three to five.

During the period from 1952 to 1956, then, it can be said that an elite identified mainly with labor was gaining the major defining role in the continuing revolution. The social costs of the process up to that point had been effectively pushed off onto the politically weak urban middle sector. Labor, as a whole, was the chief apparent gainer, but in real terms, the big gainer was the peasant mass. Given the peasantry's extremely particularistic orientations, however, leaders of the peasant mass did not enter directly into the central battle over definitions and models. The peasants, as a whole, adopted a defensive stance based on protecting gains, especially property rights. Peasant elites expended their greatest energies in gaining and holding local territorial controls. Peasant power figured into the central power struggle as a potential ally of one or the other rival position. But no new or different ideological models were forthcoming from this new and potentially critical source of power. Peasant demands were articulated mainly at the level of resources and had not, as yet, risen to the level of national control and ideological definition.

The problem which confronted the MNR elite and its preferred model was to find a social base sufficiently powerful to become the basis of its imposition on the rest of the society. Having relied on demand satisfaction to gain support, the MNR by default had lost its middle-sector base and had strengthened the long-range power of the labor left. Hence, when Siles sought to deal with the inflationary crisis through a set of economic policies which assumed the United States-favored democratic bourgeois model, he was forced, at the same time, to attempt a reordering of the basic structure of power in the country. This political need, in turn, demanded that he form a coalition strong enough to dominate the labor left so as to push it in the direction of this preferred model. As we have seen, Siles managed to stop the movement toward the worker-peasant model, but he did not succeed in mobilizing a base powerful enough to impose the democratic bourgeois model. The result was the immobilized standoff discussed previously. It is important to review the political moves made by Siles; for they were to be revived and expanded later by Paz in his attempt to develop a power base to force development within the United States-approved state capitalist or democratic bourgeois model.[8]

At first, Siles sought to eliminate the labor-left elite from national control positions and force them back into their segmental bases. Concomitantly, he returned many of the previously bested MNR rightists to national positions in both the government and the party. He sought further to split the labor left itself by playing on old ideological disputes and courting those labor groups which had not benefited from the revolutionary reforms to the same extent as the miners.[9] The historical affinity of the MNR and PIR ideological models became apparent in this maneuver. It was the unions, previously dominated by the PIR, which lined up with Siles.[10] Lechín and the POR again drew close. The COB members supporting Siles referred to themselves as the *bloque reestructuradora del COB* ("bloc for restructuring the COB"), while they dubbed the Lechín wing *Trotcobistas*, with contempt.

These moves reflected shifts in the existing power structure rather than any new configurations. The same can be said regarding Siles' approach to the important question of social costs. Siles simply reversed the previous trend by shifting costs off the urban middle and back onto labor—particularly the miners.[11]

The innovative, and, in the long run, more important moves of Siles came when he sought to forge a new power base. Central here was Siles' attempt to drive a wedge between the peasant mass and the labor left. He sought to shift the focal point of mass support for the MNR image of the revolution to the countryside. The MNR "seized" power with the aid of labor, but it sought to make a particular kind of revolution with the aid of the peasants. This new tactic had partial success when Siles won the Valley organizations to his side. The move carried with it the emergence of the peasant leader, José Rojas, into a position of national authority. These events marked a significant development in the political reality of Bolivia. The full implications of this development are just beginning to be felt, for it brought about the first shift of the peasants from a defensive to an offensive political position. We will consider the implications of this shift later in this chapter.

Another component of his search for a new power base led Siles to revive—with United States aid—the previously discredited national military force. The move here was obviously an attempt to regain for the MNR elite-controlled state some measure of that critical capacity which Max Weber called "the legitimate monopoly of force." The army was increased in size and its image as a new revolutionary army was bolstered. It retained its "developmental" functions and partially regained its traditional control functions. The revival of the army and the courting of peasant support added two new important components to the national struggle. The stage was set for a dramatic recasting of the power dimensions of the entire ongoing revolutionary situation. However, although Siles added these new ingredients, he did not manage to put them into an effective formula. It was at this point that Paz took over.

Although it is difficult to speculate on the personality and ambitions, good or bad, of Víctor Paz Estenssoro, it is my contention that when Paz reassumed power in 1960, his overriding commitment was to go down in history as the man who built the new Bolivia. Paz made economic development the keystone of his adminstration. Moreover, he conceived that development in terms of a revised and updated version of the democratic bourgeois model. Paz set out to make real the image of a dynamic economy growing within the structure of a state capitalist system that was dominated by a middle-class elite.[12]

An important factor creating what almost became an obsession over economic development with Paz after 1960 was the ascension of John F. Kennedy to the presidency of the United States. Under Kennedy, a previously discreet desire to keep the revolution from going Communistic was turned into a positive aim to make Bolivia, along with Venezuela, a showcase of guided "democratic revolutionary" change. Previously high aid commitments were increased and broadened.[13] The taboo on aiding the state-run mining company was dropped and a pro-revolution ambassador, Benjamin Stephansky, was sent to La Paz. Víctor Paz was convinced that the United States at last "understood" what the revolution was about and that Kennedy was willing to go all the way in aiding it. Paz then decided to go all the way with the United States and to shape his regime in close accordance with the expectations of the Alliance For Progress.[14]

To achieve his goal, Paz had to face squarely the issues of leadership, power, and social costs. Above all, he had to create a social base powerful enough to break the existing stalemate and provide a foundation upon which to assert national initiatives. Inherent in any such move was the breaking of the negative standoff finally achieved under Siles, and the reopening of a full-scale, inter-sectoral struggle over both resources and control.

When Paz assumed the presidency for the second time in 1960, the general situation of the national authorities was nothing short of absurd. It is not too much of an exaggeration to say that national authority was roughly conterminous with the city limits of La Paz. Sandoval Morón and Ruben Julio effectively ruled almost half the existing territory of the country between them. The bulk of the altiplano was under the thumb of Toribio Salas. José Rojas held sway in the Valley, although, due to the persisting challenge of Veizaga, his hold was still tenuous. Northern Potosí was in a state of anarchic inter-tribal warfare. The major mining camps were indisputably controlled by local sindicatos. The overall situation had deteriorated to such a point that national officials, including the president, could not safely travel throughout large sections of the country without the express permission and protection of local bosses.

Beyond this, the country was, as we have seen, immobilized at the level of inter-class (or inter-sectoral) power. But the manner of Paz's return and Lechín's ascension to the vice-presidency seemed to augur a return to the center-left drive of 1952–56, and the eventual dominance of the interests and image represented by the labor left.

Within the party organization, power was fragmented and dissipated. During its more than eight years in power, the MNR had not established rigid party membership criteria, nor had it ever really thoroughly purged any major factions. Guevara's defection lessened the absolute size of the party, but there still remained a large and heterogeneous number of patronage-hungry members at all levels. As I indicated previously, traditional office-seeking faction politics carried over into the new MNR regime. As the size of the party swelled relative to patronage positions, so too did the number of personalized party factions. These factions adopted ideological designations, but, in reality, were more often coteries lined up behind those second-level party notables who appeared to be in line for an office from which patronage could be spread. Each ambitious leader, in turn, used his office to build discrete bases of support in which primary loyalty was to him and his ambitions.[15]

Any developmental strategy which hoped for success had to concern issues of power and interest at each of three levels—regional, sectoral, and intra-party. At each level, questions of both ideology and short-term personal, group, or regional self-interest were at stake. Often, interest and preferred ideological positions were, in the short run at least, in direct conflict. In brief, the collective reality of the country was extraordinarily tenuous. The context of politics was complex in the extreme. To do more than occupy office demanded a decisive move; but he who embarked upon such a course would of necessity open a political Pandora's box. Paz chose to open the box.

On the level of sovereign control, the Paz government moved cautiously, but with resolution. Paz's strategy combined two policies: (a) a divide-and-conquer policy in which he sponsored pro-government (really, pro-Paz) local caciques against less reliable leaders, and (b) the slow but steady establishment of a specific national governmental presence.

In order to gain national control of the vast tropical east, Paz directed his attention to gaining control of the strategically important department of Santa Cruz. Those who dreamt of a developed Bolivia had always looked to the east, and especially to Santa Cruz, as the most promising frontier. Since the completion of the road from Cochabamba to Santa Cruz in 1954, Santa Cruz has become Bolivia's political and economic frontier. Under Paz, programs to develop the agricultural potential of the region—in particular, rice, sugar, and cattle—were given high priority. Simultaneously, the government made a concerted effort to induce the population of the altiplano to move east. Under this dual push, Santa Cruz received large injections of capital and a steady influx of new population. As a result, relative to the rest of Bolivia, the area began to boom economically. The economic push led to the steady economic integration of the region into an incipient, but real, national market structure.[16] To complete the process, Paz had to be certain of political loyalty in the area. Paz moved to break the power of Sandoval Morón.

Unable to simply subdue the area, Paz at first sought to weaken Morón by sponsoring rival local factions, and, more important, by sponsoring Morón's major rival, Ruben Julio. Tensions between the rival leaders resulted in repeated acts of large-scale violence. The tempo of violence eventually reached dangerous proportions; but this had the desired effect from the national point of view. Morón's grasp on the area was weakened considerably.[17]

In approaching other important areas, Paz utilized the same tactic of playing local power off against local power. He helped to finish off Veizaga in the Cochabamba Valley, and, in so doing, helped Rojas consolidate his position. But the situation was not quite so clear-cut. At one point, Paz appeared to be sponsoring the young leader, Julian Chavez, another challenger to Rojas. Rojas' hold on the Valley proved too strong, however, and Chavez's star declined. Paz then began to support Rojas, who, in turn, publicly declared his support for the government and later provided important armed support against miners' strikes. However, perhaps remembering Paz's enmity, Rojas let it be known that he considered Siles, not Paz, to be the great leader of the revolution. More important, in late 1963 and early 1964, his name became associated with a new rising political figure, General

Rene Barrientos Ortuño,[18] the popular head of the air force and the man who was to overthrow Paz, his mentor, in 1964.

Paz also directed his attention to the altiplano and the pro-COB power base of Achacachi, from which Toribio Salas controlled the important Lake region. Here, Paz encouraged rival power centers, particularly sindicatos around the towns of Huarina and Huatahata. A pro-Paz faction was created in this region from which a potent rival to Salas, Felipe Flores, emerged. Salas, as expected, responded with violence. Intra-campesino civil war broke out in the deparment of La Paz. The struggle for control of the altiplano led to a number of deaths. Felipe Flores himself was killed in a daylight gunfight in downtown La Paz. Throughout the country, individual incidents of politically motivated violence increased as Paz pressed his offensive. The regional caciques were very much on the defensive and they fought back bitterly.

Paz did not restrict his efforts against the caciques to the purely regional level. While he attacked the pro-COB Salas on a regional level, for example, he sought to form a pro-government campesino coalition capable of dominating the national campesino confederation. Paz also sought to convert the confederation from a council of regional bosses into a truly national body friendly to the government. Success in this endeavor would have meant, in the long run, that future leaders of the confederation would have been partially dependent on the government for their position as national, rather than simply regional leaders.

It appears that Paz was following a long-range strategy, first to defeat certain regional bosses and then to "nationalize" those who remained. As long as Rojas, for example, aspired only to regional leadership, his local power base was sufficient to his ends and in this way, he was rather independent. To become a national leader, however, unless he could conquer the country, he had to transcend his local base and form higher level alliances. In that context, he needed allies among other bosses—he and Flores forged such an alliance—but he also needed national government sponsorship to legitimate the confederation and to provide the economic resources to make it effective. To become a national leader, he would become more dependent on sources of power outside his control. At the same time, he would develop a stake in the effective existence of national mechanisms, such as the party.

In the case of Ruben Julio, a similar process is apparent. Julio appeared first as a leader in the Senate and then as a major contender for the vice-presidential nomination in 1964. This apparent movement toward the "nationalization" of regional bosses tended to make national-regional power relations more symmetric. The national government continued to need the regional bosses, but the caudillos, in order to realize ambitions of national scope, also came to need functioning national organisms. We can hypothesize that had all things been equal, a national arena eventually would have been formed in which the ability to manipulate national organizations would have begun to supplant control of regional force as a basis of leadership. The caudillos would have been progressively converted into leaders more akin to the ward bosses of the early urban United States political scene. The success of this potential trend, however, depended on the resolution of a series of other clashes at a variety of levels. For the moment, the effect of Paz's various regional moves was to introduce a fluidity, punctuated by violence, into the relations between national and local decision-making centers.

The second dimension of the drive to establish a meaningful sovereignty over the geographic reality of the country involved the establishment of a national institutional presence in all areas. This presence was established by means of the national military. Paz followed and built upon the course opened by Siles. He not only continued to rebuild the army, but also the air force, and at a much more rapid pace.

When Siles first intervened in the Valley, he declared it a military zone. Paz left that order in effect, and when he intervened in Santa Cruz (August 1962), he declared it a military zone. In both interventions in which Barrientos played a significant role, national military power was used to buttress one side against another in regional struggles.[19] In so doing, a national focus of force capability was in evidence in both critical regions. Thus, while an independent regional force capacity outside direct national control was not eliminated, it now existed alongside a nationally based force capacity. Uniformed soldiers and militias now existed side by side. Given United States military aid commitments, the growth potential of the national army was obviously superior. National authority at least was beginning to get its foot in the door of major regional areas with the hope of pulling them under sovereign command.

The establishment of a military presence in Santa Cruz was only one facet of the increasing role delegated by Paz to the military in his multifaceted drive to rule and organize Bolivia for national development. Even as the military regained its control function, its developmental functions also were greatly expanded. Through *acción cívica* ("civic action") programs, militarized labor battalions built roads into new regions, established communications links, built bridges, transported and settled colonists, and built innumerable rural schools.[20] The military, now numbering about ten thousand officers and men, came both to administer and to execute a large part of the government's development program. Furthermore, a large part of United States economic aid reached the populace through the military. Very often, soldiers distributed Food For Peace shipments among the peasants and inhabitants of remote towns.

With the reestablishment of compulsory military service, the military took on the added function of being one of the nation's chief educational institutions. It was in the army that scores of Indian peasants first learned to speak Spanish, to read and write, and to acquire modern functional skills. The military was rapidly becoming the most multi-functional and "national" institution in the country. In one form or another, large portions of the rural population had their first and often only connection with a national governmental reality through the new *ejército revolucionario* ("revolutionary army").

Opposing ideological models of development were clearly in evidence when Paz reopened the problem of the relative standing of the society's key sectoral groups. To the chagrin of the labor left, the return of Paz did not presage a new center-left thrust that would at last consolidate the revolution in the left's image. Instead, Paz ended by raising the most fundamental challenge to the COB's standing to date. Paz questioned labor's standing at the level of control as well as at the level of social costs. Given his subsequent actions, it can only be concluded that Paz at some point decided to eliminate labor as a national power contender and to impose on labor (mainly the miners), for a while at least, most of the burdens of economic development.

There are both important differences and similarities between Paz's struggle with the labor left and that of Siles. The most important difference lies in the impetus behind the specific actions. The Siles action took place in the context of the need for stabilization. The belief was that rising wages and price controls fed the inflation, hence the tactic was to scale down labor's benefits. This entailed a clash; but there was no desire to break the movement as such. Stabilization accomplished, the Paz action was driven by a desire to break political and economic immobilization and to initiate economic development. Development became the single factor in judging and justifying action. Labor productivity was defined as the root obstacle to development. Labor power and "indiscipline" were defined as the major causes of low productivity; therefore the aim became that of breaking the power of the labor left and of submitting labor to a new form of control.

An important element in the ambience surrounding these moves was the decline of the counter-revolutionary threat. There was a subtle shift from the concept that major enemies were those on the political right to the concept that the major enemies were those on the political left. Under the development-productivity syllogism, the left emerged as counter-revolutionary. Paz publicly defended his activities as part of a general move against communism and "infantile leftism" in Bolivia.

A number of factors led to Paz's clash with labor. Among the most important were: (a) the historical orientation of the MNR, which had always been a middle-class elitist orientation directed toward adjusting the previous order, rather than totally reconstructing the society; (b) the decision to accept the United

States Alliance For Progress strategy, and to eschew the Soviet bloc as a legitimate aid source; and (c) the unavoidable realities of the Bolivian economic situation. To develop, Bolivia needed capital, and no outside source was willing to underwrite the total bill. Hence, some capital had to be wrung from internal economies, which meant that the consumption demands of at least some groups had to be denied.

In his long-run view, Paz saw the future of Bolivia in the east, in agriculture, and in oil. During his first four years, Paz had pushed for diversification in the east. In that period, the government had emphasized development and consumption at the same time. The bill was paid by stripping "old Bolivia" through inflation, a systematic decapitalization of COMIBOL, and exhaustion of reserves. In the 1960s, for both internal and external political reasons, an inflationary policy was no longer viable. More seriously, the COMIBOL was broke; old Bolivia no longer had anything to give to the new. Paz's aim remained the push to develop the east, but to carry that out, he had to save COMIBOL. As Cuba was later to discover, a country cannot escape from a mono-export economy by fiat. To finance diversification, a steady ingress of foreign exchange is needed, which, in turn, creates a continued reliance on the prime export. Bolivia was still chained to *el metal del diablo* ("the metal of the devil").[21] Like it or not, saving COMIBOL as a source of investable capital became the touchstone of Paz's second government.

In approaching the problem of COMIBOL, the issue which immediately loomed large was that of the position of labor. In 1956 the Siles government engaged the New York engineering firm of Ford, Bacon, and Davis to analyze the general situation of the state mining company. In the resultant nine-volume report, the ills of COMIBOL were presented as being legion: lack of capital, dilapidated plants and equipment, exhaustion of ore deposits, failure to develop new mines, and so on. But the report concludes: "It was generally found that technical problems are surmountable, within reasonable limits, but the real problems facing the industry are those of a human nature." This study goes on to say that the "human" problems to which it refers are actually labor problems; namely, the high cost of labor, social services offered to labor, and the lack of labor discipline.[22] Since that early study, both the various Bolivian governments and the U.S. aid missions have consistently held that the root problem of COMIBOL, and by extension the entire economy, was labor.

The salvation of the COMIBOL was projected as an international effort to be mediated through the so-called Triangular Plan in which the United States, West Germany, and the Inter-American Development Bank would provide the capital and expertise to reorganize the industry. The plan envisaged heavy capital investment, the pioneering of new mineral resources, and a "rationalization" of the existing administrative structure. The latter concept was a catch-all which concerned a variety of questions, including the labor problem.[23] The plan proceeded from the assumption that, to become solvent, COMIBOL had to scale down the labor component of its cost input. Translated, this meant (a) an abandonment of purely "social" activities, for example, unproductive mines, pulperías, etc., (b) an adjustment of wages to productivity levels, and (c) a cutback in the work force. In addition, the plan demanded that the principle of management authority be established, which, in effect, meant putting an end to control obrero. Given the extant zero sum political game, such aims demanded that either the power of the miners to press demands be reduced or a superior counter-power be created.

Even if the MNR's basic orientation had been different, the logic of the developmental program embarked upon by Paz demanded that he reduce the miners' share in the limited collective good available for distribution. To achieve this end in that situation he had to break the political back of the FSTMB. Central to such a political aim was the negation of control obrero. But control obrero, along with co-gobierno, was central to the labor left's entire image of the revolution and to its strategy for the revolution's future development toward the worker-peasant ideological model. Therefore, to assault control obrero was to assault the entire position of the labor left. This fact became patent when Paz later began a subtle negation of co-gobierno as well. The economic strategy, therefore, brought with it a political strategy which aimed at the elimination of the COB as a determinate political force.

Power Shifts: Conflicting Development Models

Critical to an understanding of the ensuing battle between Paz and the COB is an understanding of the basic contextual shifts which took place in Bolivia between 1952 and the early 1960s. Between 1952 and 1956, the political context was such that the labor left was the power pivot of the developing revolutionary situation. Between 1956 and 1960, the relative power capacity of the labor left peaked and then leveled off. During this important period, the power spectrum was changed fundamentally: first, when the campesinos began to appear as an offensively oriented national group; secondly, when the decision was made to rebuild and modernize the military.

These fundamental political shifts took on added significance when the logic of long-range economic thinking began to take hold. The MNR image of development was predicated on diversification, which meant a fundamental reorientation of the country away from the old tin-based national reality of Bolivia to the hitherto dormant non-tin Bolivia. In any such shifting of the national focus, the Indian peasant mass was, in the long run, the critical human group. By the same logic, the single most important national institution in the shift to this new reality was the development-oriented military. Therefore, by the early 1960s, Bolivia was beginning to experience a fundamental shift in its historical locus. All the factors in that historic shift operated to render old labor groups, especially the miners, politically weak, and economically anachronistic. The same factors operated to put both the campesinos and the army on the economic frontier. In the early 1960s, their political relevance rose as that of the miners declined.

The tension between Paz and the labor left escalated steadily throughout 1962–63. Defining the chief goal of the revolution as development, Paz branded the labor left "counter-revolutionary," and then added to that image the spectre of Communist subversion.[24] The Communist charges were not simply exercises in rhetoric. Continuing the policy of driving wedges between the peasants and workers, the government played on the theme that a society based on the labor-left ideological model would mean a collectivization of agriculture and, thereby, a negation of the individual property rights granted by the revolution. This image became an important factor in mobilizing peasant groups against the left. In any event, as the struggle escalated, the left was first pushed out of the government and then out of the party. Ultimately, the labor left had little choice but to break from the MNR and fall back on its now relatively weak primary organization base.

The threat of massive layoffs, the final discontinuance of the pulpería, and the threat to control obrero, set off mounting resistance in the major mines. Local sindicato chieftains, largely Trotskyites and Communists, accused not only Paz but also Lechín of selling out to Yankee imperialism. Lechín, again threatened from the rear, began to shift toward an opposition stance. In a move to avoid the political cross fire, he accepted an ambassadorial post to Italy in 1962. But the tension mounted and he was forced to return or face political extinction.

On his return, Paz elected to ignore Lechín. At the same time, rumors began to circulate that Paz would seek another four-year term. As the truth of the rumors became apparent, both Lechín and the labor left were put in a bind. In a scurry to regain their power base, they began vying with the more radical union leaders in hurling epithets at Paz and the triangular plan. The tension between Paz and Lechín escalated so rapidly that the two titans were put on a collision course.

In the fall of 1963, the government ordered massive layoffs in the mines; in Cataví Siglo XX alone, about one thousand miners received notices.[25] The directive brought the tension between the Paz government and the labor left to a head. When the unions urged violent protest, the government, on December 7, 1963, arrested two mine leaders, Federico Escobar and Ireneo Pimentel. In retaliation, the miners seized seventeen hostages—three of whom were United States citizens. The miners declared their intention to execute the hostages if necessary and to march on La Paz.

This crisis was, in many respects, the swan song of the labor left. In the drama surrounding it, the chief aspects of the new power context came into play. Lechín, once the second most powerful man of the revolution and, at that time, vice-president of the nation, was powerless to avert the crisis or to negotiate a settlement favorable to the embattled miners. He had little choice but to join the miners in their camp. The camp stood as the last vestige of the once independent power of the left. There they stood, Lechín and his miners, isolated and completely encircled by a combined force made up of the new military and units of the Cochabamba campesino sindicatos. An open battle was averted, but only at the price of miner capitulation to a superior force coalition. On December 15, Lechín and his miners agreed to an unconditional surrender. Sympathy strikes by other unions and demonstrations by the COB were to no avail; the labor left was in eclipse.

The battle between Paz and the labor left indicated that Paz sought to break inter-sectoral immobilism by bringing a new power coalition into being based on the military and the peasants, a coalition that could dwarf the power of the labor left and provide the muscle to jolt Bolivia off a dead-center line and into an entirely new thrust toward the establishment of a state capitalist-type system. Keeping in mind the variables derived from the previous discussion of demands and supports, the strategy of Paz at the inter-sectoral power level can be described as follows:

1) An attempt to win more solid peasant support by guaranteeing peasant demands at the expense of other groups, especially the miners.
2) Reassertion of a national ability to exercise forceful sanctions by rebuilding and modernizing the military.
3) By a combination of one and two, to break the power of other groups and stimulate state-sponsored development through a policy of selective demand satisfaction and a selective application of force, where necessary.

The strategy translated itself into public policy in a variety of ways. The government stood fast on the issue of wage increases in the name of monetary stability. It also made it clear that there would be a steady reduction of the labor force in the mines, that pulpería privileges would be withdrawn, and that other aspects of wage and bonus procedures would be reexamined. The same principles were carried over into other areas of labor management relations, with the general import being that, henceforth, economic considerations would outweigh social or political considerations in government labor policy.

At the same time, the government increased general investment in agricultural development. Efforts were also stepped up in meeting concrete rural demands, such as for schools, potable water systems, and Food For Peace distribution. Many of these efforts were mediated through the military civic action programs. To assuage any lingering fears of insecurity regarding land tenure, Paz notably speeded up the process of formal grants of land titles. The process of courting peasant support was topped off by an increasing public identification of the revolution with the peasant. More and more national attention and rhetoric was devoted to the peasant and his problems. The image of the peasant was raised to a national symbol, and every effort was made to convince the peasant that the government saw in him the future of Bolivia.[26]

As the peasants were courted, so was the military. A school of high military studies was created, and around it the image of a new officer, skilled not only in war, but also in the modern social and technical sciences. The military was no longer painted as a symbol of oppression but now was considered to be one of the most important components of the country's drive toward progress. As might be expected, the "defense" component of the national budget increased yearly.[27] Military men began to appear as prominent national personalities.

The costs of meeting the consumption demands of peasant groups and the military, while, at the same time, maintaining a high level of development investment, were forced upon the much-weakened labor sector. On the purely economic side, the strategy soon began to pay off. The economy started to grow again. Agricultural production went up, oil production gained, and the overall national G.N.P. showed quite respectable yearly increases.[28]

It was at the third level of conflict—intra-party faction struggles—that Paz hit perhaps his greatest stumbling block. Unlike

Siles, Paz did not shift back to the old party right when he clashed
with labor. The reason was partly because, since Guevara's break,
large sectors of the political right were no longer in the party.
However, there were other, more important, considerations. It is
most interesting to note that when he broke from the party,
Guevara issued a statement which clearly defined the democratic
bourgeois development model and assailed Paz for selling out by
capitulating to the left. Why didn't Paz then mend his fences
with Guevara when he made his push against labor?

In one sense it was due to the antagonistic personal ambitions
of the two leaders. Another reason was the cumbersome fact that
there were simply too many office-hungry party members in relation to jobs available. On a number of occasions, Paz publicly
complained that the government simply could not employ all the
party members, and that any attempt to do so would hurt the
country economically.[29] A more fundamental reason began to
come to light, however, in a series of public statements in which
Paz stated that one of the country's greatest developmental needs
was that of technocrats.[30]

Paz's views on development undoubtedly were derived from
the original MNR conception of a progressive middle-class elite
leading the country to the promised land, through the democratic
bourgeois model. One contemporary theorist on the question of
political models of development has posited two ideal, typical
models in which middle-class elites play the dominant role in
fostering development. One, which he calls "national capitalism,"
involves an entrepreneurial middle class cooperating alongside a
development-oriented state. The second, "state capitalism," has a
middle-class technocratic elite, using the state to foster development. The author, Helio Jaguaribe, characterized Bolivia under
the MNR as an example of the latter model.[31]

The state capitalist model, according to Jaguaribe, is one in
which "development is promoted by a middle-class technocracy
that generally installs itself by a golpe de estado and exercises
power in alliance with peasants and workers by means of a revolutionary party."[32] This statement coincides directly with the MNR's
self-image, and is, in my opinion, the image which framed the
strategy of Paz Estenssoro.

Granting that Paz was consciously attempting to establish a state capitalist model, it then becomes important to note that, aside from all his other problems, he confronted a disturbing fact: the Bolivian middle sector, in general, and the MNR elite, in particular, were surely not entrepreneurs, nor were they technocrats. Beyond this, given the era in which it arose and the circumstances to which it reacted, the MNR elite, while rhetorically committed to development, held a deeper set of values and pursued a life style which was, in the Bolivian context, negative to a true developmental commitment.

The original MNR was only one manifestation of a general nationalist wave which surged across Latin America in the 1930s. Invariably, the leaders of this wave were déclassé upper-class types or young middle-class intellectuals. These "counter-elites" primarily reacted to situations of status incongruence—the inability to achieve life styles they had been trained to expect. When these elites later linked with lower social groups who reacted to frustrations of rising expectations, a number of "national popular movements" appeared in Latin America. As Aníbal Pinto has pointed out, the nationalism of these middle-class-led movements was more an expression of outraged patriotism and a desire to eliminate foreigners from desired social positions than a commitment to grapple with the fundamental problems of development.[33] In countries such as Bolivia where these nationalists could express their aims officially, they drafted documents, e.g., the Busch constitution, which granted state-sponsored welfare schemes often in far more advanced forms than the economically developed states. Such documents were commitments to generalized levels of consumption far beyond the resource capacity of the Latin American states. This legitimation of consumption aspirations has created severe problems ever since. The more immediate point is that the first concern of elites, as well as support publics, tended to be toward distribution of wealth and consumption. However, as is generally conceded, the critical problems of development involve the adoption of new values and the restriction of consumption.

It must be remembered that the Bolivian middle sector which I previously called the petite bourgeoisie, was, in a sense, a poor relation to the national bourgeoisie—La Rosca—to whose position it aspired, but, for lack of resources, pedigree, or race, could not achieve in the old system. Moreover, this middle sector was dependent on the national bourgeoisie, either through direct employment or by providing services.[34] It was this grouping, plus elements of downward mobility from the national bourgeoisie, that produced the leadership and first bases of the MNR core. The development of the original MNR was not an antagonistic class reaction, but an intra-grouping reaction on the part of those excluded from the ability to share in the common set of values held by them, the elite, and the sub-elite of the system.

For this reason, I have argued that the MNR was never really revolutionary. It projected changes, but only those changes that would allow these excluded elements to increase their participation in the values they shared with the older traditional elite. This orientation of the MNR core was reflected in the fact that even as they went about promulgating, under pressure, revolutionary changes, they resisted attempts to change either the public or private styles of the old regime. Those changes which did occur drove the MNR's original middle-sector support base away, but the MNR elite core persisted in trying to replicate the style of the old bourgeoisie. Likewise, they continued to hold a basically negative view of the lower classes, a view which they sought to rationalize in the democratic bourgeois ideological concept.[35]

Within this elitist view was a willingness to raise the standards of living of mass groups, but, I contend, always within the framework of an elite life style which assumed a continuance of the old relations of dominance and submission on the part of the lower groups. When, as under Siles, the elite was willing to talk of production, worker sacrifice, etc., they were fundamentally unwilling to change the traditional elite life style. This fact was not missed by the labor left, who bitterly assailed the MNR elite for living a bourgeois elite life style while they were forced to suffer.[36] Beyond this, it can be argued that if traditional elite values were in part responsible for a lack of development (which is generally agreed), the persistence of this life style under the MNR was an impediment to development.

In this context, I believe that the MNR elite, upon achieving power, sincerely wanted to develop Bolivia, but its basic orientation was redistributive, both for themselves and for the general population. They had little awareness of the "costs" of development. When the inflation brought home this awareness of costs, they attempted to push them off on other groups so as to maintain their own life style. The elite drive to live the traditional style put more and more pressure on the government's patronage base and fostered a continual fragmentation of the party into job-hungry factions.[37] The major general results were the emergence of an elite who, because of past training and values, had very few development skills to contribute, but who made great claims on needed resources; and a continual fragmentation of party leadership which further negated the party's viability as an institution of national integration and mobilization. In fact, the party elite had become an impediment to development.

At the third level of conflict, we can detect in Paz's second term a decided movement away from the party and the "traditional" middle class. This shift partially reflected Paz's need to create his own personally loyal faction. Yet, in my opinion, it also reflected a deeper change in Paz's vision of the future. Inspired, in part, by United States advisors and current Western theories of development, he felt the need to create a new technocratic elite which could truly lead the country to development.

Almost all the people I interviewed in Bolivia agreed that in his second term Paz paid less and less attention to party affairs. In place of the old party leadership, he assembled around him a brain trust of aggressive post-1952 young men to whom he gave wider and wider responsibility in the form of top party command posts, personal staff positions, and governmental positions. In addition, he began to bring non-party members into technical positions. Simultaneously, Paz created a planning ministry and constantly cajoled government bureaucrats to adopt modern efficient values. He continued to maintain his grip on the national party but devoted most of his energies to the government apparatus. Moreover, he established the norm that the simple fact of being an old party member, or of being a party member at all, was no longer sufficient to secure the plum of government office. Not unexpectedly, this approach set off protestations within the party. Lower level party groups began to charge that Paz's policies diminished party democracy. With increasing boldness, rival party faction leaders made public criticisms of Paz and his *camarilla* ("personal clique").

There were also more general components of this drive to create a new technological elite. As I indicated, Paz established the *Escuela de Altos Estudios Militares* ("School of High Military Studies"). This school was part of the wider attempt to create the "very model of a modernizing military" in Bolivia. Young, aggressive, and, at least in rhetoric more technical-minded national figures began to emerge from this military school. In other words, in addition to the other functions delegated to it, Paz was also relying on the military to provide technical leadership skills.[38]

Even more dramatic was the establishment under Paz, of the *Institúto Tecnológico Boliviano* (ITB). The most important aspect of this new school, designed to produce civilian technicians, was the fact that it was established independently of the existing university system. The very creation of the Institute was a slap in the face to the existing engineering schools. More important, by making this school independent of the university system, the government openly rejected the values and quality of education as offered in the universities. Since the university in post-1952 Bolivia was the bastion of the middle sector, the new Institute was, by extension, a challenge to it and its way of life.

Previously, entrance to the university was a guaranteed ticket to graduation and middle-class existence. Professional self-interest and student pressure safeguarded a regime which put more weight on the status value of the diploma than the professional content of education. With the establishment of the new Institute, this would no longer be the case. Graduation was to be based on strict achievement. The daily rhythm of the school was to be that of any technical school in more advanced industrial cultures. Foreigners, among them, American Peace Corps volunteers, made up a significant portion of the faculty. These teachers sought to shape young Bolivians to the mold in which they themselves had been forged.

From its beginning, the ITB was met with bitter and widespread resistance. Resistance was particularly strong among the faculty and students of the existing universities. The ITB and the related question of university autonomy became major public issues. On the day that the Paz government fell, the first thing that the university students did was to invade the ITB and incorporate it into the existing university system. The American Peace Corps volunteers in the building had to flee through back alleys as the students vented their anger on all associated with the experiment.

Three points are relevant here. First, during his second term, Paz persistently alienated the bulk of the existing MNR membership. As far as I was able to determine, a full 60 percent of the party was by 1964 either actively plotting against Paz or passively hoping for the end of his rule. Secondly, Paz alienated the always critical university community. The universities became important centers of anti-Paz activity. Finally, by eschewing rule through the party, Paz became dependent on his small coterie of young leaders, government bureaucrats, and the army.

In summary then, under Paz the attempt was made, with heavy United States assistance, to achieve a solution to the revolution and begin a drive toward development in the image of an updated version of the older democratic bourgeois model. This drive included a power strategy directed at the regional, intersectoral, and intra-elite levels. First there was an attempt to replace anti-Paz caudillos with pro-Paz caudillos. Simultaneously, there was an attempt to "nationalize" the pro-Paz caudillos and the regions under their control, and to establish a national institutional presence through the military. At the inter-sectoral level, there was an attempt to make the peasants the mass base of the revolution by meeting both their objective and subjective (identity) demands. The peasants were then to be used in conjunction with the army to deny labor's demands for control and to push off onto that sector, at least temporarily, the major social costs of development. At the elite level, the attempt was to push aside the entrenched factionalized party elite and to bring into existence a new party elite. At the same time, the groundwork was laid to create a general middle-class elite trained for, committed to, and capable of presiding over a state capitalist developmental system.

Within this overall dynamic, two groups obviously became dominant: the peasants and the military. Of the two, the most immediately crucial to the Paz government was the military. First, because it was performing critical functions in the realms of control and development; and, secondly, because it was strategically relevant at all three levels of conflict (regional, intersectoral, and intra-elite). The long-range potential of the peasant mass was unmeasurable, but in the immediate picture they were crucial as an anti-labor power component, as an important production group, and as a basis for energizing and legitimizing the Paz version of the revolution. In addition, the always-pragmatic Paz was relying on the armed peasants to act as a check on any ambitions the military might develop. This latter assumption, however, depended on the willingness of the peasant mass to heed a call by Paz to come to his aid.

The Fall of Paz and the MNR

To many foreign observers, Paz's fall in November 1964, came as a shock. The general image of Bolivia was of a much-chastened military devoted to building roads and dominated by a revolutionary party based on a mass of armed peasants ready to respond to the least threat against "their" revolution.[39]

In reality, as should be apparent by now, the situation was quite different. One on-the-scene observer succinctly expressed the situation to me in these terms: "Paz had too many balls in the air and unfortunately they all came down at the same time."[40] There was a deep irony in Paz's fall, for as I pointed out above, the economy had begun to grow again after 1960. Bolivia was surging forward at a relatively rapid rate. But in the type of situation which confronted Bolivia, there was obviously much more at stake than GNP growth rates.

Precipitant to the coup of 1964 was Paz's decision to seek another term. There is a time-hollowed tradition in Latin America that presidents do not succeed themselves. This tradition is rooted in the old intra-elite circulation battles. Politicians rotate factions, and hence offices, by rotating presidents. *Continuismo* is the term used to denote the attempt by one faction to stay in office too long. This is intolerable from the perspective of the "outs."[41]

Paz's announcement in 1963 to seek another term set off a generally negative reaction throughout the country. Most immediately it put Lechín and the labor left against the wall, leaving them little choice but to get out of the party. Lechín and the bulk of the old COB formed a new party, *Partido Revolucionario de la Izquierda Nacional* (PRIN). Siles exhorted Paz to reconsider his decision to seek another term and when he refused, he openly broke with him also. On the eve of the 1964 elections, then, of the original big four of the revolution (Paz, Siles, Guevara, and Lechín), there remained only one inside the MNR, Víctor Paz Estenssoro. The original revolutionary party alliance had split into three separate parties—the PRA, PRIN, and MNR. The two original support publics of the revolution, the urban middle sectors and the labor movement, had, in the main, turned into either passive or active enemies. The MNR rump led by Paz relied on the campesinos, the military, and the United States government for its existence and continued ability to foment development.

By his continuismo, Paz upped the stakes in the party intrafaction battle. This was seen clearly in the intense struggle for the vice-presidency. At one point there were no fewer than seven individuals with well-mounted personal factions pursuing the prize. Paz, in firm control of what was a basically rigged convention, rammed through his personal choice, Federico Fortun Sanjines. Shortly after the convention, however, the military forced Paz to change his decision and appoint the popular head of the air force, Rene Barrientos Ortuño, as his running mate. The military had come a long way since 1952.

By seeking to continue in office, Paz pushed all those on the negative end of his developmental program against the wall; for by the end of another four years, there might well have been no turning back to previous options. Hence, the challenged caudillos, the labor left, the bulk of the party, the universities, and all those opposed to the revolution in any way had no choice but to act or go under. The complex lines of conflict at all levels drew together into a coalition in which contradictory personal ambitions, ideologies, and sectoral interests gave way for the moment to the overriding common goal of bringing Paz down.

The details of Paz's fall are still unknown. On the face of it, the picture is fairly clear. Demonstrations and strikes in the mines in the fall of 1964 over wages and layoffs turned into a general assault on the government by the labor left. These were followed by student demonstrations and violence which added to the general air of crisis and confusion. At that point, a national teachers' strike, ostensibly over wages, but obviously part of a political drive, was launched.

The country was on the brink of anarchy, and Paz had little choice but to order the military and the police into action. In the midst of the crisis Barrientos made a personal bid for power and began to attack the beleaguered Paz publicly. Reading the situation accurately, the ambitious general then left the capital for Cochabamba where he declared himself a rebel. The spectacle of the vice-president assailing the government in Cochabamba and of the government firing on workers and students shattered the public image of the Paz government. All the opposition groups exhorted the army to intervene. The army wavered, partly due to internal dissension, partly because it was still unsure of its power.

At one point, Víctor Paz was almost literally one man versus everyone. An anti-Paz alliance developed which ran the full ideological gamut. It embraced every political party, including large sections of the MNR. The obvious power supports in the situation were the military and the peasants. The opportunity was too enticing for the ambitious to pass up, and large sections of the military declared against Paz. The loyalists in the military had little choice but to join them or be crushed. Paz was left dependent upon the legendary peasant armed hordes who, it was said, would never allow the man who gave them their land to be overthrown. The legend turned out to be a myth; the peasants never materialized.

The turning point came when it became clear that no mass of armed peasants would appear to save their leader. The reasons for the failure of the peasants to mobilize were many. The most critical factor was that in those areas where the peasants were a potentially combative force, their political behavior was structured not by national directives, but by local caciques. Hence, the key to their support was the loyalty of the local caciques. It is now apparent that in the most important areas, and especially the Cochabamba Valley, Barrientos had managed to strike deals with the top leaders, including José Rojas.[42]

A few days before his actual fall, Paz had managed to bring a small force of altiplano campesinos into La Paz for a show of force, but the group was not large and, once disbanded, was difficult to reassemble. Moreover, it was reported to me that an attempt to remobilize them on November 3 was hampered by the threat that pro-Barrientos sindicatos would sack their homes during their absence. In the Valley, the powerful sindicato of Punata declared their loyalty to Paz, but the area around it, including Cliza and Ucureña, supported Barrientos. No peasant units fought openly on the side of Barrientos, but, then, they did not have to. In Paz's situation, a neutral peasantry was tantamount to a hostile force. As in 1952, most of the peasants did little beyond observe the national drama which, as in 1952, was resolved in La Paz. Thus, surrounded by a hostile society with only a few loyal militia units, Paz had little choice but to capitulate once the army finally declared against him.

On November 4, 1964, Paz deemed it prudent to withdraw from the country. He was escorted to the airport by his chief of staff, General Alfredo Ovando Candia. Paz did not discover until days afterward that Ovando had been one of the key conspirators. With Paz out of the country, the MNR fell apart. A military government was established and in the confusion, Barrientos, in a remarkable quick-change act, disavowed all previous connection with the MNR and landed on his feet as president of the new military junta.[43]

The fall of Paz did not mean the end of the revolution, but rather the temporary abeyance of the particular strategy he had

314 •   **BOLIVIA—Part III**

formulated to resolve the revolution. Basically, the coup solved nothing. The revolutionary situation remained wide open. The problem of sovereignty and minimal order remains acute to this day. So too does the problem of inter-sectoral power. The need for a viable developmental model remains pressing. Beneath it all, the bitter and tragic question of who shall bear the costs of any drive to development continues to plague this much plagued country.

PART IV

14 *Conclusions*

Bolivia, like many other Latin American states, did not simply glide into the twentieth century; she entered it forcefully, driven by economic growth and social and political modernization. Although this process of development was real, it was also quite limited, for it was based upon progress in one economic sphere—mining. Thus, Bolivia's developmental surge failed to stimulate a self-sustaining internal growth. In looking for economic bases for contemporary political problems in Bolivia and elsewhere in the Latin America context, it is my contention that the chief issue is not "underdevelopment" as such, but the specific effects of limited previous patterns of development.

Preconditions

The first premise advanced in this study of the phenomenon of revolution in Bolivia is that during a forty-year period (from about 1880 to 1920), Bolivia experienced a skewed and truncated pattern of development and modernization. Future growth was based upon the potential of one major industry—tin. Beginning in the late 1920s, the tin industry began to regress, leading to overall economic stagnation. Therefore, the general historical

317

hypothesis put forth here is that the Bolivian Revolution can be interpreted, in part, as a reaction to the situation brought about by this skewed development pattern; and that the failure of the MNR successfully to reorganize Bolivia either economically or politically after achieving formal power by insurrection was largely due to the persistence of the situational realities created by this previous development pattern.

In the body of this study, it was shown how this economic pattern was related to developments in the social and political structures of the country. The most important result of the economic development of tin was an internal differentiation of the country into a relatively modern urban sphere and a more traditional rural sphere. Politically, the two spheres were bound together by a thin elite stratum which dominated the apparatus of government and which had personal interests in both these urban and rural systems. Of particular importance to the dynamics of politics at this time was the appearance of private interests which monopolized the tin industry and controlled economic resources far superior to those available to the "liberal" state. Some political modernization during this period was manifested in the creation of a centralized state, modern political concepts and principles, the appearance of interest groups, and the development of political parties. As economic modernization failed to become a generalized process, however, so too did political modernization. Modern political institutions did not structure the day-to-day lives of the population of the country, and when economic regression began to set in there was a concomitant tendency toward political atrophy.

By the late 1920s, after experiencing a period of considerable economic expansion due to the development of the tin industry, Bolivia became increasingly immobilized economically, socially, and politically with the advent of this industry's decline. What existed was a society which was neither wholly modern nor wholly traditional, but neither was it transitional—in effect, the entire Bolivian economy ground to a halt. This severely arrested growth and development resulted in a number of structural strains which, in turn, began to create serious problems for significant groups in Bolivian society. In terms of the framework employed in this study, there are three preconditions to a revolutionary situation: first, the experience of multiple dysfunctions; then, the emergence of an intransigent elite; and, finally, the occurrence of accelerators.

In Bolivia, the basic source of the first precondition—multiple dysfunctions—was the chronic illness of the tin industry, whose good health had become the *sine qua non* of any societal equilibrium, be it static or dynamic. The economic immobilism which came to grip Bolivia reduced the society's surplus and created the series of financial crises which developed after 1925 and culminated in general bankruptcy in 1930. During this period, there appeared the first intimations of an inflationary spiral that was to last for over three decades.

Immobilization was also to create severe problems in various dimensions of the society. First was a generalized economic squeeze on the urban middle sectors. The hardening of stratification lines made it more and more difficult for these groups to move vertically. Their location in the service sector of the economy and their general dependence on salaries and fees rendered the urban middle particularly susceptible to fluctuations in the financial system. Thus, when the society began to experience chronic financial crises, these groups found it increasingly difficult to maintain the life style commensurate with their status and self-identity. For them, insecurity and a debilitating effort merely to remain in their present social positions became the daily reality.

Of more immediate significance in the late 1920s was the situation experienced by the oncoming generation of elite and sub-elite youth. By birthright, this generation expected high status, and through education they were prepared for entrance into appropriate roles in the liberal professions, politics, and bureaucracy. Due to its overall declining economic capacity, I believe that Bolivia, as a society, was unable to maintain a sufficient number of high status roles at the requisite level to absorb this and succeeding new generations. The result was a gap between legitimate role expectations and the ability to realize them. This problem of status incongruence (as sociologists would term it) was reinforced by two other factors: the contradiction between the official "liberal positivist" rhetoric of economic progress and the actual reality confronting the country; and the none-too-edifying comparison of Bolivia's overall position vis-à-vis that of other more developed nations (the demonstration effect). The convergence of these factors fostered a generational split in Bolivia's elite and sub-elite strata.

The third dimension of cleavage and strain arose out of the dislocation of more traditional social groupings and the problem of incorporating new groups. Economic development in a "liberal" framework resulted in downward pressure on many traditional artisan groups and, at the same time, created newer working-class groups. The former responded with demands for alleviation of economic pressure, while the latter experienced the phenomenon of "rising expectations" and pressed demands for higher wages, better working conditions, the right to organize, and political representation. The traditional artisan groups were pushed down, but not completely superseded, and new labor groups were created, though the foundations for a broad national working class failed to materialize. Hence, even in the "semi-modern" urban sector, the lower stratum of the society was a compound of traditional and modern elements. Nonetheless, this lower stratum was becoming the source of increasingly strident demands for change.

By the late 1920s the results of these structural strains were apparent. Strikes, demonstrations, and political violence were common. Even more important was the development of a combined artisan and labor movement which adopted a progressively more radical and disruptive orientation. Finally, there appeared a generalized movement among students and young professionals who began to raise serious questions about the legitimacy of the existing "liberal" order. Thus, at this early date, definite signs of two of the basic components of a revolutionary situation had appeared: counter-elites and potential counter-publics.

Immobilism was the source of other severe strains, not the least of which was the growing tendency towards factionalization within the incumbent elite. As Merle Kling has noted, in a static society in which the control of the basic sources of wealth (in

Bolivia, mines and land) becomes relatively fixed, there tends to develop a problem of the circulation of wealth among the elite.[1] Public office becomes an important means of horizontal circulation, and there is a tendency for politics to become an intra-elite struggle to control offices. This struggle became increasingly important in Bolivian politics during the 1920s. By natural processes, the incumbent elite, in effect, was outgrowing the economic basis of its own eliteness. The result was a growing factionalization of the dominant parties and a growing tendency for elite factions to employ violence against one another. At the very time that some adaptive and/or effective repressive action was needed, the incumbent elite was exhausting its energies in internecine struggles.

In the face of demands for change and reform, the incumbent elite became increasingly intransigent. The Saavedra government flirted with mild reforms, but smashed any signs of independent organization among miners or peasants. Hernando Siles, in the throes of financial crisis, raised a nationalist banner but sought to quash a university reform movement. Then Daniel Salamanca, the next president, drew a blanket of repression over the entire country.

Even if sectors of the governing elite had wanted to adapt to the pressures for the change, economic immobilism precluded the means. Ultimately, the elite's own precarious economic position and its tendency to factionalization called into question its long-range ability to control, by any method, the political pressures building up around and within it. Thus, to the developing equation was added the second critical precondition of a revolutionary situation: an incumbent elite increasingly unwilling and more and more incapable of undertaking adaptive action.

In sum, by the late 1920s Bolivia was manifesting symptoms of a serious, but probably not fatal, internal illness. Basic structural imbalance and overall immobilism were generating a series of important lines of cleavage and strain which, in turn, were generating demands from significant sectors of the society for some form of remedial action. These strains, on the one hand, were creating potentially strong foci of counter-system strength, while

simultaneously weakening the ability of incumbent elites to inno-
vate and/or resist. The most immediately critical symptom, however, was the generational fissure occurring at the elite and sub-
elite levels of society; indeed, I contend that this was the all-
important nexus between the pressures for change building in the
middle and lower levels of the society and the signs of feebleness
appearing at the top. And yet, all things being equal, the Bolivia
patient like other societies, especially in Latin America, might
have limped on indefinitely and even regained whole or partial
health. However, all things were far from being equal.

In 1929 the worldwide depression hit Bolivia with a fury
and bowled over the tenuous props of its financial structure.
Then, after scarcely enough time to assess the full damage of
the depression, the repressive Salamanca regime led the country
to the debacle of the Chaco War. Whatever Salamanca's intentions, we can argue that had he been successful in waging that
war of "national honor," Bolivia might have emerged from it in
a healthier state. But, as many others have pointed out, foreign
wars are double-edged swords: "Military adventures are excellent
diversions, and military successes can marvelously cement dis-
joined societies, but military failure on the evidence, can not fail
to hasten revolution in such cases."[2] On top of its other problems,
then, Bolivia experienced, within a period of less than five years,
a disastrous depression and a humiliating military disaster. These
two severely disjointing experiences functioned as accelerators,
the third precondition, propelling Bolivia into a revolutionary
situation.

Revolutionary Situation: Phase I

Bolivia entered a revolutionary situation near the close of
the Chaco War. The first phase of this condition of internal war
lasted for seventeen years, and its inordinately long duration was
an important factor in escalating both the level of violence and
the degree of change that the society was to experience eventually.
The first phase of this revolutionary situation can be viewed as

passing through essentially four stages of development defined by shifts in the possession of government by counter-elites and incumbent elites: 1936-39, counter-elites; 1939-43, incumbents; 1943-46, counter-elites; and 1946-52, incumbents.

Between 1935 and 1952, Bolivia experienced five successful coups (1935, 1936, 1937, 1943, 1951); two successful urban insurrections (1946 and 1952); at least three large-scale bloody encounters between the army and labor groups (1942, 1947, 1950); and a brief civil war in 1949. In addition, against a background of political challenge and reprisal there were untold abortive coup plots, small-scale bloody and bloodless strikes and demonstrations, numerous political murders, and uncountable jailings and exilings. Political violence was definitely not new to Bolivian public life, but the quantity and quality of the violence during this period was. Moreover, this era of mutual destruction was the first since the civil war of 1898 in which the prime issues went beyond changes in personnel to the basic values and definition of the society.

Perhaps the most important confirmation of the new situation into which Bolivia shifted after the Chaco War was the reappearance in more aggravated form of the generational split first apparent in the late 1920s. All evidence indicates that the humiliation of the war was a profoundly disassociating experience for Bolivia's upper- and middle-class youth. After 1936, there could no longer be any doubt that most of this generation was implacably alienated from the prevailing political order. A most important new element was added when the same generational and ideological cleavages tearing at the society at large spread into the nation's armed forces—a pivotal institution in any revolutionary situation.

Most students of revolution agree that the "master symptom" of a revolutionary condition in a society is the phenomenon of the "desertion of the intellectuals." Intellectuals play an important social role in developing and maintaining political values and concepts. The transference of the allegiance of the intellectuals, therefore, weakens the value structure of the existing system and opens a period in which new definitions of political structure and purpose vie for allegiance. The generational split that reappeared after the war confirmed the desertation of Bolivia's intellectuals.

The immediate post-war period was one of ideological effervescence, and the nation's young intellectuals groped for explanations of Bolivia's ills and attempted to formulate new social images. As the revolutionary situation progressed, two more or less coherent counter-orientations emerged: a revolutionary socialist position and a national renovationist position. The former was developed by those that eventually formed the PIR and POR parties, while the latter was sketched out mainly by those who were to form the MNR. Through these ideological images, the youths began to batter the prevailing pattern of political thought and to bid for the allegiance of various publics. Through their control of the educational apparatus, counter-groups were able to influence younger students in the secondary and primary schools and to convert the universities into bastions of counter-sentiment and activity.

This reinforcement and broadening of the generational split was the most critical result of the Chaco War. The phenomenon cut through the center of the existing control structure and aggravated the revolutionary situation. It strengthened the pressures building for change by providing ideological focus and a pool of leadership. Also, it weakened the already debilitated incumbent elite stratum by denying it the energies of its own younger generation. Of critical importance in this latter dimension was the destruction of the unity and discipline of the army, thereby severely reducing its effectiveness as a mechanism of defense for the prevailing order.

Therefore, in Bolivia the major source of counter-elites was not the marginal or suppressed sectors of the society, but the pre-existing elite and sub-elite sectors. This rupture of the existing elite and sub-elite strata is not unique to Bolivia. Recent observers have noted it to be a common occurrence, particularly in underdeveloped or partially developed societies. These observers argue—and the Bolivian situation seems to confirm the hypothesis—that such splits are important in generating the "populist"-type movements which are the most common form that counter-sentiment takes in these societies.[3] The Bolivian situation indicates further that these splits arise from a combination of status incongruence and the demonstration effect, and can be severely aggravated by an experience such as defeat in war.

In the body of the text, I have analyzed Bolivia's revolutionary drama between 1936 and 1952. I view the basic problems of financial instability, inflation, scarcities, unemployment, and underemployment as problems which either remained constant or deteriorated further and, therefore, set the stage for revolutionary solutions.

Economic hardship weighed most heavily on the urban middle sectors and on labor and artisan groups. Hence, it was the reactions of these groups that provided the publics for the countermovements that developed in this period. In both cases, the basis of their discontent was not absolute deprivation, but "relative" deprivation—an inability to maintain previously achieved life styles or to realize newly awakened aspirations.

The urban middle experienced ever-increasing pressure as a result of their decreasing ability to maintain the style of life commensurate with their self-image. For labor, the problem was basic economic insecurity compounded by the frustration of their attempts to realize recently acquired aspirations. In both cases, these groups came to view the incapacity and sheer malevolence of the incumbent elite as the major source of their difficulties. It is important to stress, however, that the problems to which these groups reacted were quite different; for this factor was to play an important role in post-1952 politics.

Beginning in the 1930s, these two social sectors were drawn ever more deeply into the central political struggle. As the political conflict expanded, new modes of organizing manpower became important to both sides, and it was in response to this need that formal structures of new parties such as the MNR, PIR, POR, and FSB began to take shape.

Until the mid-1940s the urban middle sector was the most relevant counter-public, and provided the base of support for the early civil military reformist efforts of Toro, Busch, and Villarroel. During the tenure of the Villarroel regime, it became increasingly apparent that the potentialities of a counter-movement largely based on the middle group had been exhausted. Moreover, it was evident by this time that the labor movement was shifting from its previous role of a more or less passive recipient of reforms to a much more aggressive political orientation. Government repression and the effective proselytization of the PIR and POR were converting labor into a much more coherent and radical political force.

The overthrow of Villarroel, and the attempt to reverse the reformist thrusts of the 1943-46 period that followed, marked an important watershed in the Bolivian revolutionary situation. Until then, the counter-forces had been divided into two mutually hostile camps. Both were led by middle- and upper-class intellectuals, but one, the MNR, was basically reformist and oriented toward the urban middle as a public, while the other, the PIR-POR, was more revolutionary and looked to labor for support. It is probable that, alone, neither coalition had the strength to achieve its goals.

The fall of Villarroel marked the end of a period in which a reformist solution was highly possible and the beginning of a period in which revolution became more and more probable. Between 1936 and 1946, the old elites had toppled two reform-oriented governments and brutally smashed labor's attempts to achieve redress within the system. However, incumbents were not capable of solving the basic structural problems agitating the society. The result was a radicalization of the reformist elites that had previously opposed a revolutionary solution, and an equal radicalization and politicization of the labor movement. Following this radicalization, the society tended to become definitively polarized as elements of both the revolutionary and the reformist counter-camps showed a willingness to cooperate in a broad counter-coalition.

After 1946 the revolutionary potential gained strength as most of the counter-activity moved under the loose penumbra of the MNR. Involvement of both the urban middle and labor increased in magnitude and intensity. Although the main struggle was carried out beneath the banner of the MNR, within the movement, the more radically oriented labor groups came to set the dominant tone of the battle. The new influence of labor was reflected most clearly in the rhetorical and programmatic radicalization of the MNR.

The situation thus far can be summarized as follows: due to a number of structural imbalances created by the economic development pattern that Bolivia had experienced, several key sectors of society began to demand basic changes in the political system as early as the 1920s. These demands were resisted by the incumbent elites. The country had developed two important preconditions of revolution—multiple dysfunctions and an intransigent and incapable elite—and the combined effects of the depression and the Chaco War accelerated Bolivia into a revolutionary situation. Between 1936 and 1952 the country slipped deeper and deeper into economic, political, and social disarray. Basic structural imbalances either remained constant or worsened. Throughout this period, the status quo elite remained intransigent; but while they were capable of blocking reform by counter-elites, they were not capable of directing adaptive changes nor of imposing an effective counter-revolutionary solution. The effect of the incumbents' behavior was to deepen the social crisis and radicalize all the elements of the equation. Of critical importance in the developing situation was the steady expansion of the scope and intensity of social conflict. The groups with the greatest power potential in this period were those which made up the relatively autonomous labor movement. Although the movement could not make a revolution alone, it set the major tone of conflict after 1946. Counter-elite groups helped to stimulate the expansion of conflict, but they were not able to control the process for their own ends. Thus, the original MNR counter-elite, for example, permutated during this period from a small cabal of middle-and upper-class elitists oriented toward reform from above, to the formal directorate of a broad populist movement. However, the directorate's control of the movement was problematic, to say the least.

It would be useful at this point to draw some general conclusions from this analysis of the first phase of Bolivia's revolutionary situation. The Bolivian case appears to confirm a number of previous hypotheses. It confirms, for example, the view that persistent generalized poverty is not the prime factor generating a revolutionary potential. The most poverty-stricken group in Bolivia, the peasantry, was the least revolutionary group prior to 1952. The two most important counter-publics, the urban middle and labor, experienced severe economic difficulties, but these problems were more complex than simple poverty. Both groups suffered from "relative" deprivation—as stated earlier, an inability to maintain previously achieved living levels or to realize newly awakened aspirations. The Bolivian situation confirms the view that the most volatile situation is one in which groups with relatively high aspirations come to believe that society offers them little chance of realizing these aspirations.[4]

The Bolivian situation also suggests that the explanation of such "frustration of expectations" lies, in part, in the nature and rhythm of the development pattern the society has gone through. This study supports the hypothesis that a society becomes most vulnerable when it experiences economic reversals after a fairly strong and somewhat long period of progress.[5] The issue here, however, appears to be the entire question of development. Many have noted that both completely modernized and very backward societies are the least susceptible to revolution and other forms of political instability. Transitional societies, on the other hand, are apparently the most susceptible to various manifestations of instability. This observation led to the notion of a general "crisis of transition." But many countries have managed to live through a transition period and to gain a higher level of development without experiencing revolution. In this context, it is necessary to ask why Bolivia fell victim to revolution.

Bolivia entered a transition period in the early part of the twentieth century, and, after an initial period of development, slowed to a prolonged standstill. Bolivian history indicates that the most dangerous situation is one in which a development spurt cannot be sustained and generalized; the most vulnerable society being one that is neither wholly modern nor wholly traditional and, for some reason, becomes immobilized in a transitional state.

A society that slips into such a transition-immobilization

bind will begin to generate a range of dysfunctionalities that result in an increasing level of demands for remedial action. However, the nature of the dilemma is such that the capacity to undertake remedial action is limited and probably declining. Thus, incumbent elites find it difficult to formulate adaptive action, and the society as a whole becomes vulnerable to the effects of major dislocating experiences, such as depressions and ill-conceived military adventures.

In addition, the Bolivian case indicates that the society in a transition-immobilization bind is less vulnerable to class-based counter-movements, especially those formed around lower classes, than to the formation of cross-sectoral alliances. This happens because the most important structural weakness of such a society is its inability to maintain cohesion at the upper and intermediate layers of stratification. Pressure here, especially along generational lines, creates fissures in the very core of the society's control structure, leading to a further weakening of the society's ability to maintain coherence, and to the anomaly that counter-elites and counter-publics are produced from within the existing elite and sub-elite strata. If these counter-groups are unable to achieve reform, they will then tend to reach across stratification lines and form cross-class blocs. In the terminology of some scholars, the Bolivian MNR may be appropriately categorized as a "national popular movement." These movements most often arise in partially developed countries, such as Bolivia, where no base exists for the "class"-type movements of Europe. National popular movements represent cross-sectoral alliances aimed at removing blockages to development and reform, and in their fully developed state they have three basic characteristics: "(1) an anti-status quo elite placed at the middle or upper middle levels of stratification, (2) a mobilized mass formed as the result of the revolution of expectations, and (3) an ideology or a widespread emotional state to help communication between leaders and followers and to create collective ethusiasm."[6]

The Bolivian case indicates that a prime base for such a movement is the transition-immobilization bind; but the actual biography of the movement will vary in specific contexts. Three factors are important here: the responses of incumbent elites to reformist efforts, the types of publics mobilized by the movement, and the manner in which such a movement achieves formal power (if it does).

Holding socio-economic factors constant, the Bolivian situation demonstrates the important role of incumbent elites in sustaining national popular movements and bringing about revolution. The elite most likely to bring about such action is one that is capable of blocking reform efforts, but which cannot or will not solve basic structural problems and lacks the strength or will to destroy counter-movements effectively. In Bolivia this type of elite style led to a continual expansion in the scope and intensity of conflict, it radicalized the tactics and attitude of the originally reformist MNR, and it induced the MNR leadership to pull into its orbit the more radical labor movement over which it previously had had only tenuous control. Thus, by the late 1940s the originally reformist MNR cabal had developed into a loosely knit national popular movement. Then, in 1952 the MNR came into formal power by means of a popular insurrection in which armed workers (the most radical group in the movement) played a large role. The result was that the MNR leadership, whatever its original intentions, found itself presiding over a revolution.

Revolutions, as the Bolivian situation manifests, are the products of the accumulation of strength by counter-groups, but they are also the products of the declining strength of incumbent groups. One of the surprising aspects of the Bolivian case is that such a relatively weak and poorly organized movement succeeded. In this case, and I suspect in others, the weakness of the forces of the status quo was as important a factor as the strength of the rebels, if not more so. Indeed, it may be more accurate in this and some other cases to view the occurrence of the revolution as a result of the sheer exhaustion of the status quo, rather than the "seizure of power" by the revolutionary movement. Very often, there is precious little power left to seize, and we cannot help but suspect that the rebels are sometimes surprised by the ease with which their foes finally succumb.

So far, I have indicated a variety of reasons why the incumbent elite in Bolivia was weak in relation to the problems it faced. Nowhere was this weakness more manifest than in the capacity and will of the status quo to exercise repression. Since the close of the Chaco War, the Bolivian army was seriously divided, and, therefore, incumbent elites could not rely on its full strength. In fact, on occasion, they had to play one part against the other. This potentially fatal flaw was aggravated by the inablility of the elite to decide when and how it would utilize the repressive capacity it did possess.

During the regime of the PURS from 1947 to 1951, the government vacillated between attempting to smash the opposition and offering it the olive branch. It switched from apparent concessions to popular demands one day to violent negations of these concessions the next. This bumbling was an important irritant working on the revolutionary situation. The last civilian governments of the old regime followed a course which not only inflamed, and in effect encouraged the rebels, but also managed to outrage the sensibilities of those who sought to pacify. Moreover, they failed to satisfy even those who wished to crush the opposition once and for all. The army and police were caught in the middle of these vacillations, and their internal morale and loyalty to civil politics suffered accordingly (as was indicated in the army's decision to assume authority in 1951).

A unified military government might have been able to withstand the pressures for change or at least shift them in a different direction, but once in power, the military demonstrated that it was too badly split to mount a coherent policy. The junta did little more than emulate the fumbling of its civilian predecessors. It is ironic and also indicative of the feebleness of the old regime that the betrayal of a ranking member of the junta served to open the door to the revolution that was to come.

Revolutionary Situation: Phase II

A successful insurrection such as the one the MNR conducted from April 9 to April 11, 1952, is not a revolution; it is the removal of an obstacle which makes a revolution possible.

Once formal power is gained, however, the question arises as to what direction the revolution is to take and who is to lead it. With the posing of this question it is apparent that the condition of internal war is not terminated, but, instead, tends to worsen. All the differences of interests and values previously implicit in the revolutionary family now become explicit. In Bolivia, the MNR split rapidly into three warring elite factions that vied to control the party and shape the course of the revolution.

The events that took place in Bolivia point up the fact that a revolutionized society is not a ball of clay to be molded to the taste of one or another elite group. With the old guard unseated, the revolutionary proccess becomes even more unstructured and unpredictable than it was previously. Events have a way of getting out of hand, and as the missionaries of a new order battle with each other, they find themselves forced to react to unanticipated developments in the society around them. Acutally, it is inaccurate to speak of a "society," for the collective coherence of the entity is threatened when the old control structure collapses. Revolutionary insurrections set in motion a powerful centrifugal process of fragmentation. The problem of "making the revolution"—constructing a new order—will vary in difficulty depending on the degree of fragmentation that takes palce.

This disintegration of collective coherence depends on a number of factors. One of the more important factors appears to be the previous level of integration of the society prior to the revolution. It is evident that the level of integration and coherence in prerevolutionary Bolivia was low. The country was structurally bifurcated, and most of the Indian peasants did not participate in the Spanish-speaking national system. Moreover, the national state had never really extended its rule over the full territory of the country. The old elite stratum had been the major link holding the various components of the unit together; when it collapsed the link was broken and the components began to pull apart. Another apparent factor of some importance is the length of time before a new power coalition appears at the national authoritative center. The longer elite factions battle for control, the deeper the tendency will be to fragmentation; conversely, the more difficult it will be for any elite faction, or alliance of factions, to rule effectively once it has achieved some control of the national governmental apparatus.

One of the more important developments that occurred in Bolivia after the insurrection was a sharp divergence between formal power and concrete power. In 1952 the MNR took La Paz, the buildings of government, and the presidential chair, but it was evident all too soon that these formal instrumentalities no longer brought much real power. They were little more than the outcroppings of an underlying power system that no longer existed. Since 1952, one of the most persistent obstacles hampering the termination of the revolution and the formation of a new coherent national order has been the problem of closing the gap between the formal national decision-making center and the de facto segmental decision-making centers that sprang up in the wake of the insurrection and during the events that followed. Despite the formal facade of single party rule, there was a steady dispersion of effective power from the national authoritative center to autonomous intermediate and local units.

Divergence between formal and concrete power (and a process of national disintegration) was not unique to the Bolivian Revolution; it was an important factor in the development of many revolutions, including the French, Russian, and Mexican revolutions. Although the Cuban Revolution demonstrates that this phenomenon does not necessarily have to take place, it seems safe to predict that most "developing" countries in the throes of revolution will experience a definite tendency toward internal fragmentation. In any event, it is an important area for further comparative studies of revolution. For example, it would be useful to know under what conditions fragmentation may take place; what factors may reinforce or retard it; and what effect it will have on the further course of revolutions.

If any conspiratorial plans existed for the Bolivian Revolution, they were obsolete before the first day of street fighting was over. From that point on, the leaders played the game by ear, reacting now to this event and now to another, attempting to harness random actions to their benefit. Perhaps the most unexpected consequence of the insurrection was the degree to which lower-class groups, particularly workers and peasants, became directly involved in shaping the course of politics. Before 1952, the scope of conflict had been expanded considerably, but the insurrection stimulated the process until it became almost totalized. An important development within this process of mobilization was the considerable capacity shown by these groups to generate effective leaders. From its earliest days, the MNR elite looked upon the workers and peasants as an inert mass to be shaped according to the MNR image; the insurrection opened a period in which the elite had all it could do to keep itself from being swept aside by this same mass.

The fact that workers came to play a political role was not in itself a surprise. What was unexpected, however, was the rapidity with which a coherent labor bloc was formed and the skill with which it pressed its demands. The MNR leadership was completely unprepared to deal with an autonomous labor bloc which tenaciously pressed its demands for revolution, and there is little doubt that this bloc played the largest role in radicalizing the revolution in its early days.

By far the most unexpected result of the insurrection was the unleashing of a nationwide peasant movement that, in a few months, swept aside Bolivia's archaic rural structure. The mobilization of the peasantry was in itself a revolution. In view of the predominantly rural nature of Bolivia, we might even claim that it was the revolution; at the least, it was a second revolution, and in the long run, probably the most profound. The urban revolution that culminated in the nationalization of the three major tin companies altered the face of Bolivia; but the rural revolution, ratified by the Agrarian Reform Law, transformed the country totally. No longer could there be any doubt about the degree to which the old order had been destroyed.

The peasant movement in Bolivia is so complex and important that it deserves a study in itself. However, some general conclusions seem to be quite significant. Whatever might have happened in the rural sphere before 1952, the peasant revolution was dependent on the urban revolution. The predispositions to counter-activity that worked on peasant groups were continually reinforced by urban unrest. A number of elements stimulated the peasants of certain regions to a consciousness that they could do more than periodically indulge in anomic outbursts of rage. Direct contacts with members of bourgeois and labor counter-groups were certainly among the more important feedback effects from the urban realm. Yet, there is little evidence that, prior to 1952, the mass of the peasantry was either ready or able to do anything about their plight.

The insurrection of 1952 and the events that followed acted as accelerators in the rural sphere. The psychological impact of these momentous weeks must have been significant in itself, but even more important was the shattering of the old control structure and the appearance in positions of power of groups sympathetic to peasant demands. Thus, both the means and the opportunity for the peasants to move were created. Despite the fact that there was a certain spontaneity to the peasant movement that followed, and though it eventually spun out of the control of the urban groups, the advent of the rural revolution is difficult to conceive of without the urban precedent.

The Bolivian case lends credence to the view advanced by many, including, most recently, Barrington Moore, Jr., that, although peasant involvement in a more generally revolutionary context will no doubt accelerate the tempo and broaden the changes a society will go through, it is doubtful that a peasantry can either initiate or accomplish a broad revolutionary process by itself.[7] Whether it is stimulated by a guerrilla movement that leads to an insurrection, or by an outburst following an insurrection, the revolutionary potential of the peasantry is dependent upon contact with other social sectors and a weakening of the existing control structure by counter-groups in the urban sphere.

The insurrection and the great revolutionary reforms of 1952 and early 1953 set off a tremendous process of mobilization in Bolivia. Groups excluded from the old political order were now in a position to act as significant demand groups on the government and the resources of the country. The concomitant dispersion of armed power from the state to the populace at large was also significant. The dual processes of mobilization and the appearrance of a populace in arms was perhaps the most profoundly important factor structuring Bolivian revolutionary politics over the next decade and a half.

These processes acted to reinforce and solidify the disintegration of national coherence and the gap between formal and effective power. Through their control of weapons, segmental interest groups were able to assume sovereign-like autonomy in their dealings with the national government and the party. This fact was to complicate tremendously the problem of establishing any national pattern of rule.

These factors take on even more importance when we consider the Bolivian case in the context of modern developmental revolution. The Bolivian National Revolution must be viewed within the complex worldwide drive toward economic development and modernization. The MNR (and other counter-groups as well) has been interpreted in this study as a movement born from the structural problems created by an arrested developmental spurt. Certainly, the leaders of the MNR saw their movement in this way and looked upon themselves as developers and modernizers. They justified their violent seizure of government as the only means of breaking their country out of the retarding grip of a backward and non-national "oligarchy." Taken purely on its own terms, therefore, we must conclude that the MNR was at least in part, a failure: it dismantled the old order, but neither it nor any other group has thus far been able to construct a new political order within which the dream of rapid development can be achieved. It is in this sense that the revolution continues.

The kinds of elite-level faction disputes that broke out in the Bolivian revolutionary family after 1952 are observable in all revolutionary contexts. These battles involve personal ambition and group interest, but are most fundamentally struggles over varying images of the new order. This basic struggle is becoming increasingly a battle over what has been called "political models" of rapid economic development. In the Introduction, I argued that these disputes center around the interrelated problems of elite control and social costs, and that they are complicated by the inherent tension between economic and political logics in environments characterized by extreme scarcity and high levels of mobilization. The first step to solving these problems is the formation of a coalition of elites and publics powerful enough to allocate social costs and to impose on the society a political model embodying their values and interests.

Viewed in this light, therefore, and focusing specifically on the MNR, it is possible to suggest a number of factors which help explain why the Bolivian revolutionary situation remains open-ended. All revolutionary contexts are in many respects unique, but it is my contention that the factors important in the Bolivian context will also have importance in other modern developmental revolutions. While it is not possible to formulate precise hypotheses, we can at least pinpoint a set of common problems with which revolutionary groups in various contexts will have to come to grips.

In Bolivia, the clash between the imperatives of the elite's developmental aims (accumulation) and the demands of the supporters of the movement (consumption) came almost immediately after the insurrection of 1952. This clash was severely exacerbated by three unanticipated results of the insurrection: (a) a fragmentation of national coherence, (b) a speed-up in the breadth and intensity of mobilization, particularly when the revolution spilled into the rural sphere and, (c) the divergence between formal and effective power brought about by the appearance of a populace in arms.

The first elite reaction to this reality was the formation of a center-left coalition that attempted to meet the consumption demands of workers and peasants, and to invest at the same time. The thrust of this coalition was toward a state socialist political model which imposed costs on the old elite and the urban middle. Due to both external and internal reasons, this policy weakened the already infirm tin industry, set off a wild inflation, and alienated the urban middle. In 1956 the center-left coalition was terminated and a center-right coalition was attempted. However, the policies of this new alliance resulted in economic stagnation and the alienation of important worker groups when social costs were shifted onto them. By 1960 the MNR's hold on all its support publics was tenuous in the extreme, and the country was locked in political and economic immobilism. The MNR continued to hold office, but found it almost impossible to govern.

From 1960 to 1964 a new center-right coalition, supported enthusiastically by the United States and committed to the Alliance For Progress, attempted to impose a state capitalist model. This new thrust sought to base itself on the combined power of a revived military and the peasant masses. The coalition broke the economic and political immobilism, but it provoked violent opposition from a diverse coalition made up of remnants of the old elite, the urban middle, and the entire labor left. Violence flared once more, and the revived military, sensing that they now had both capacity and opportunity, became the political pivot in Bolivian internal affairs. Driven by a mixture of personal ambitions, institutional self-interest, and ideological commitment, the military toppled the MNR with astonishing ease.

The Bolivian experience confirms a phenomenon that has become increasingly evident in many contexts: the nature of the modern developmental revolution is such that at some point, a military organization (new or modified) will come to play one of the major roles in shaping the process of change. This is no simple Thermidorian reaction. Be it led by a Bonaparte, a Boumediene, or a Barrientos, the army seldom plays a counter-revolutionary role in the strict sense of the term. It seems, rather, that in a situation where force is a principal dimension of political conflict, ambitious military men will find it hard to think up reasons not to take over, or at least they will be sure to become the power behind the throne. But the military can not turn back the clock (they seldom want to), for they too must cope with the Pandora's box of the modern revolutionary situation.

Their role as the managers of force will give military men a tremendous potential in any revolution. The modern developmental situation is such, however, that their potential is considerably magnified. As we saw in Bolivia, there is a tendency in the developmental context to broaden the range of functions performed by the military. Through "civic action"-type programs, the military assumes the added tasks of mobilizing human and material resources and providing a pool of technical expertise for development plans. Unless a strong vertical organization, such as a political party, can assert primary control over the populace, the military may become the only institution with a true national scope. If this happens, there is little to block the military from assuming open control. Recent cases, such as in Cuba, indicate that even when a strong party organization is established, the "modernizing military" will still be able to assert itself as a preponderant force in any ruling coalition.

The Bolivian experience further indicates that the inevitable clash between political and economic logics in the modern revolutionary setting is exacerbated by the nature of the national popular movement itself. MNR rhetoric had it that the problem of Bolivia was not exploitation of class by class, but the pillage of the "nation" by the "anti-nation." Thus, the rhetoric continued, all the classes of the nation (middle, labor, peasant) should gather behind a progressive bourgeois elite and march forward to the millennium. Central to this concept is the belief that, as the nation itself is oppressed, all its constituent parts (excepting the agents of the anti-nation) have a common set of interests. This argument is common to most Latin American national popular movements. The Bolivian experience demonstrates that whatever the merits of the nation versus anti-nation theory, the assumption of a common set of interests is overly optimistic in the extreme. This is particularly true when the segments are so diverse as to include the economically dependent and racially conscious urban middle, the workers in industries at various levels of development, and the Indian peasants with little or no previous contact with a national society.

Before 1952, Bolivia was not a "nation" in the modern sense of that term. Its constituent parts lived in radically different worlds closed off from any understanding of each other's reality. Even before 1952, tension and mutual distrust within the revolutionary movement were evident as different groups reacted to different problems and expressed different aspirations. When the economic environment was fraught with extreme scarcities, these

inevitable differences were exacerbated. Once La Rosca was unseated, the precarious unity of the MNR was shattered by the
issue of the distribution of rewards and, later, by the more
critical problem of the distribution of costs.

The two points of contradiction discussed—accumulation
versus consumption and the different interests in a national popular movement—are inherent in any contemporary development
situation in which modernizing elites seek to organize change
through national popular movements whether or not these movements achieve formal power by means of insurrection. As discussed
previously, widespread scarcity is the principal characteristic of
the underdeveloped context. Scarcity generates the contradiction
between investment and consumption and exacerbates the tensions arising from the different interests and aspirations of the
multiple support publics of national popular movements. Bolivia
was an extreme case of this general problem.

One observer has aptly referred to the Bolivian experience
as the "revolution at starvation level."[8] Before the revolution of
1952, Bolivia was, with the exception of Haiti, the least-developed
Latin American country. Aside from a few families, even the
legendary Rosca was only moderately wealthy when compared to
the ruling elites of Bolivia's sister republics. Old Bolivia, therefore, had very little to contribute to the new. After it was stripped,
there just wasn't enough to meet the demands of social justice and
economic development. As the saying current among the Bolivian
middle class has it, "All this revolution did was to socialize poverty." Moreover, as the Cuban experience demonstrates, dependence on a single export product cannot be banished by revolutionary fiat. But whereas the Cubans could eventually (although
with difficulty) fall back on a reorganized sugar industry, the
Bolivians had little beyond empty mountains, antiquated mining
equipment, and an inflated work force.

Poverty and backwardness may create conditions which moti-
vate men to rise up in violence. Such violent uprisings may successfully destroy the fabric of a pre-existent social order. But the
question of "making the revolution" in the modern developmental context is a different kind of problem than the process of

destroying the old. The modern revolution is a process of stripping previously dominant social groups (in some cases, not so dominant groups as well) and reorganizing them and their resources within a new political and economic framework with the avowed aim of national development. The ability to complete the process successfully depends, at least in part, on the previous level of development. The relative success of the Mexican and Cuban revolutions in institutionalizing new political economic models is undoubtedly related to the fact that both societies were among the more developed of Latin America when the revolutions occurred. The Bolivian case appears to demonstrate, on the other hand, that the prospects of completing a development-oriented revolution in countries below a certain level of development are, at best, extremely difficult.

NOTES

GLOSSARY

INDEX

NOTES

Introduction

1. Harry Eckstein, "On the Etiology of Internal Wars," *History and Theory*, Vol. 4, No. 2 (1965), p. 133.

2. Chalmers Johnson, *Revolution and the Social System*, Hoover Institution Studies No. 3 (Stanford, 1964).

3. Alexis De Tocqueville, *The Old Regime and the French Revolution* (Garden City, 1955).

4. *Revolution and the Social System*, p. 13.

5. The concept of scope of conflict is taken from E. E. Schattschneider, *The Semi-Sovereign People* (New York, 1960).

6. Hannah Arendt, *On Revolution* (New York, 1965).

Chapter 1

1. For discussions of the formation and importance of the hacienda, see Charles Gibson, *Spain in America* (New York, 1967), pp. 153–56; and José Medina Echavarria, "A Sociologist's View," in *Social Aspects of Economic Development In Latin America*, UNESCO (Belgium, 1963), pp. 33–41.

2. As part of a continent generally obsessed with the phenomenon of the caudillo, Bolivia is noted for having been dominated by some of the wildest of these nineteenth-century figures. One of the most flamboyant of Bolivia's caudillos was the infamous Mariano Melgarejo. For an account in English of Melgarejo and the style of nineteenth-century Bolivian politics, see Richard Patch, "Bolivian Background," *American University Field Staff Reports* (October 10, 1958).

3. The "free" Indian community *(comunidad indígena)* was a legally recognized

345

entity based on the Inca ayllu (basic communal unit of Inca Empire) in which communal lands were organized on a usafruct basis. The legal and not so legal methods by which these communities were despoiled is recounted in Abraham Maldonado, *Derecho Agrario* (La Paz, 1956), esp. chs. 27–32. The major legal redefinition came in 1866 during the government of Melgarejo. The takeover of Indian lands increased markedly after that date. See George M. McBride, *The Agrarian Communities of Highland Bolivia* (New York, 1921), p. 10.

4. The best discussion in English of the changes which occurred in Bolivia after the 1860s is in Herbert Klein, "The Impact of the Chaco War on Bolivian Society" (unpub. thesis, University of Chicago, 1963), esp. ch. 1.

5. The point to be made here is that Bolivia began a transition from one mode of political struggle which I consider pre-modern to another which I consider modern. The specific pre-modern mode which was experienced by the bulk of Latin America in the nineteenth century was that of *caudillaje* (in effect, a private irregular force used to pacify territory and people). Wolf and Hansen have recently defined this mode in terms of four characteristics: "1) the repeated emergence of armed patron client sets, cemented by personal ties of dominance and submission and by a common desire to obtain wealth by force of arms, 2) the lack of institutionalized means for succession to offices, 3) the use of violence in political competition, and 4) the repeated failures of incumbent leaders to guarantee their tenures as chieftains." The transition then was to a more institutionalized form of politics in which the form and nature of combat changed. This transition in Bolivia, however, was ultimately only partial. As I hope to point out in later chapters, elements of the *caudillesque* mode reappeared within the new mode. Thus, the pattern became mixed and from the developmental point of view the reappearance of older elements within the new mode was essentially regressive. Moreover, their reappearance had important and basically negative implications in relation to the new elite's ability to maintain their control when challenged by reform- and revolutionary-oriented groups. On *caudillaje*, see Eric R. Wolf and Edward C. Hansen, "Caudillo Politics: A Structural Analysis," *Comparative Studies in Society and History*, Vol. 9 (1967) , pp. 168–79.

6. Enrique Finot, *Nueva Historia de Bolivia* (La Paz, 1964), ch. 13.

7. For the best analysis of the Indian's role in the civil war see Ramiro Condarco-Morales, *Zarate: El "Temible" Willka* (La Paz, 1965).

8. Klein, "Impact of the Chaco War," ch. 2. The political ideas of this period are spelled out quite clearly in Guillermo Francovich, *El Pensamiento Boliviano en El Siglo XX* (Mexico, Buenos Aires, 1956), pts. 1 and 2.

9. Between 1897 and 1899, tin exports jumped from 3,749.5 metric tons to 9,279.4 metric tons and then climbed as follows: 1901–05, 13,163; 1906–10, 19,333; 1911–15, 23,282; 1916–20, 27,158; 1921–25, 29,219. Data are from Luis Peñaloza, *Historia Económica de Bolivia*, Vol. 2 (La Paz, 1964), p. 213; and *Analisis y Proyecciónes Del Desarrollo Económico IV: Desarrollo Económico de Bolivia* (Mexico, 1958), p. 7.

10. The most exhaustive study of government finances, taxes, and trade balances is in Eduardo Lopez Rivas, *Esquema De La Historia Económica de Bolivia* (Oruro, Bolivia, 1955) .

11. *Analisis y Proyecciónes*, p. 41.

12. For a biased but thorough account of Bolivia's financial position during the first three decades of this century, see Margaret A. Marsh, *The Bankers in Bolivia* (New York, 1928).

13. Klein, "Impact of the Chaco War," p. 69.

14. Due to the paucity and low quality of Bolivian census data, it is extremely difficult to get a clear picture of the demographic growth of Bolivia in the twentieth century. Only two national censuses were taken in this period—one in 1900 and the other in 1950. According to experts, both are of questionable value but the 1900 count appears to be particularly unreliable. There is, however, general agreement that, from the 1890s on, the city of La Paz experienced very rapid growth outstripping all other population centers. See, for example, Olen E. Leonard "La Paz Bolivia: Its Population and Growth" in eds. O. Leonard and C. Loomis, *Readings in Latin American Social Organization and Institutions* (Ann Arbor, 1953), pp. 173–78.

According to a study of the Bolivian population by Averanga Mollinedo, based upon statistical corrections of the 1900 census, the departments of Bolivia which showed major growth between 1900 and 1950 were La Paz, Oruro, Potosí, Pando, and Beni. Actually, Beni had the highest rate of growth, but as the department was almost deserted in 1900 (32,300 people), its absolute rise (to 119,770) still leaves it as an insignificant population area. The same holds true for Pando, which grew from 9,000 to 19,804. Moreover, both these areas are still accessible only by airplane. The growth of the other departments which had major populations previous to 1950 is clearly more important.

Another section of the study indicates a trend which might be very significant. It appears that between 1900 and 1950 there was a definite regional shift in the racial composition of the country. In 1900 the racial composition of La Paz was 18.59 percent non-Indian and 74.20 percent Indian. In 1950 the percentages had shifted dramatically, e.g., to 32.87 percent and 67.13 percent respectively. In other areas of traditional Indian concentration, the only area to show a similar shift was Oruro from 25.65 percent and 68.13 percent respectively, to 38.95 percent and 61.05 percent. The other major Indian departments experienced dramatic shifts in the opposite direction: in Chuquisaca, 57.36 percent was non-Indian in 1900 and 36.87 percent was Indian. By 1950, the ratio shifted to 28.43 percent and 71.57 percent, respectively. In Cochabamba, it shifted from 70.44 percent and 22.59 percent to 24.77 percent and 75.23 percent; in Potosí, from 34.05 percent and 57.44 percent to 22.88 percent and 77.12 percent. These shifts in racial composition could reflect a shift of focus by dominant non-Indian social groups, resulting in a confirmation of La Paz and Oruro as places in which it was best to pursue careers at that time. In any event, it confirms a general shift in dominance from the older regions, which dominated Bolivia in the nineteenth century, to La Paz and its major satellites. (Data from Averanga Mollinedo, *Aspectos Generales De La Población Boliviana*, [La Paz, 1956], pp. 28–88, 89.)

Another mode of clarifying developments is to focus on comparable rural and urban growth rates. According to Olen Leonard, during the period from 1900 to 1946, the rate of urban growth was higher than the rate of rural growth in only La Paz, Cochabamba, and Oruro. In all other departments the rural rate was higher than the urban. Thus, it seems that in overall terms the development process of the early twentieth century had its greatest effect on La Paz, Oruro, and Cochabamba, making them the dominant population areas, with Potosí holding roughly the fourth position. La Paz and Oruro were important as the urban links of the mining system, while Cochabamba became the only general area where some degree of commercialized agriculture developed. The rest of the country stagnated and regressed. Still, within this picture, we cannot overstress the general dominance of the city of La Paz. In all forms of political, social, and economic activity, it dwarfed all other urban areas of the country. For data on rural-urban growth and the role of La Paz, see Olen E. Leonard, *Bolivia: Land, People, and Institutions* (Washington, D.C., 1952), pp. 41–42, 196–97.

15. For further discussion of the manner in which the country was internally separated, see Harold Osborne, *Bolivia: A Land Divided* (New York, 1964). An early traveler in Bolivia conveyed the situation quite well in this observation:

> The important role that transportation plays in the development of a country is strikingly demonstrated here; for many staple articles can be brought from five or six thousand miles away and placed in La Paz cheaper than the same things could be bought from the rich and fertile valleys a hundred or so kilometers to the east. For example, the heavy timbers used in the mines are all imported from the distant Oregon woods, when not fifty miles away as the crow flies are forests whose timber could be just as well used were there any easy way of getting it over those fifty miles. Rice and sugar, too, are imported to a country that could grow enough of both to supply from twenty-five to thirty million people; and in the cities and the mining camps one pays a dollar and a quarter gold for a pound can of butter, or a dollar for a can of peaches, when not a day's journey distant is land capable of pasturing countless cows and of raising peaches enough to feed an army. (Alicia Overbeck, *Living High* [New York, 1935], p. 12)

16. For support of this analysis, see *Analisis y Proyecciónes*, pp. 8–9.

17. The problem of establishing population groupings in Bolivia is rather complex. According to the census of 1900, fully 75 percent of the population was rural and only 14.3 percent lived in centers of five thousand or more. In 1950, according to estimated figures, the distribution of the work force was as follows: of an estimated economically active population of 1,835,827, 78.9 percent (1,448,595) were in the agricultural sector; only 2.5 percent (45,330) were in the extractive industry; 3.1 percent (58,550) in manufacturing; 3.0 percent (55,800) were urban artisans; and 12.4 percent (227,552) were in service activities. If we take urban growth into consideration and the fact that manufacturing developed mainly in the late 1930s and 1940s, we can assume that the magnitude of differentiation was even greater in the earlier decades of the century. It is also of interest to note that over 70 percent of the meager manufacturing sector was located in La Paz. See *Analisis y Proyecciónes*, p. 15.

18. There was also some commercial activity in the Yungas valleys near La Paz, especially in selling coca leaves and some commercial vine cultural in the southern regions, particularly the Cinti Valley.

19. According to a United Nations study conducted in 1956, as late as 1950 only from 2 percent to 3 percent of available agricultural space was under cultivation.

Of the cultivated areas, fully 90 percent was on the altiplano and adjacent valleys. *Analisis y Proyecciónes*, p. 254.

20. Rodolfo Stavenhagen, "Seven Fallacies About Latin America" in eds. James Petras and Maurice Zeitlan, *Latin America Reform or Revolution* (Greenwich, Conn., 1968), pp. 13–31.

21. An extensive analysis of internal problems in the mines and Bolivia's difficult competitive situation can be found in Martin Sobrados, *Influencia de la Mineria en las Económias de Chile y Bolivia* (Madrid, 1953).

22. President Montes and a close ally, the Goitia family, for example, established a number of haciendas at this time. The most well known were Taraco and Pillapi.

Chapter 2

1. Andrew N. Cleven, *The Political Organization of Bolivia* (Washington, 1940), p. 213.

2. *Ibid.*, p. 212. As a result of these restrictions, as late as 1951 out of a population of close to four million, Bolivia had an electorate of about one hundred thousand persons.

3. Bolivia, at this point, corresponds to the Latin American political stage which Germani and Silvert call *Democracia representativo con participación limitado* ("Representative democracy with limited participation"). Gino Germani and Kalman Silvert, "Estructura Social y Intervención Militar en America Latina," *Argentina Sociedad de Masas* (Buenos Aires, 1965), p. 234.

4. See Herbert Klein, "The Creation of the Patiño Tin Empire," *Inter-American Economic Affairs*, Vol. 19, No. 2, pp. 3–25.

5. The differences between the tin barons and the silver magnates are clearly stated in Herbert Klein, "The Impact of the Chaco War on Bolivian Society" (unpub. thesis, University of Chicago, 1963), pp. 34–35.

6. In 1897, La Paz was a city of about 44,620 persons; then the population leaped as follows: 1909: 78,856; 1928: 142,549; 1942: 287,097. See *La Paz en Su Centenario 1548–1948*, Vol. 4 (La Paz, 1948).

7. One of the more illustrious members of the new elite who followed a pattern of this sort was Benedicto Goitia. Goitia was born in the southern town of Camargo in 1851. From there he worked his way to La Paz where, in 1867, he was a clerk in a commercial house. He made his first major move upward when he enlisted in one of the regiments that helped overthrow the flamboyant caudillo, Melgarejo, in 1871. By 1875 he held important elective and appointive governmental posts in the provinces. In the war of the Pacific he gained prominence by raising his own regiment of fighting men. By the 1880s, Goitia was holding important posts in La Paz where he became associated with the Liberals and their demands for progressive economic policies and for making La Paz the permanent seat of the national government. In the civil war, he commanded a Liberal regiment. With the close of the war, the name of Goitia rose to a position of prominence along with that of President Montes. He came to hold a wide variety of top elective and appointive

public posts including senator, president of the chamber of deputies, minister to Peru, secretary of the treasury and minister of foreign relations. At the same time, he became owner of extensive land holdings around Lake Titicaca, one of the most famous being the Hacienda Pillapi. An advocate of economic growth through the Liberal formula, he was also founder and president of the Industrial Bank, which later became the Bank of Bolivia (*Banco de la Nación Boliviana*). Goitia's name was well known in the public realm as well as among landowners. (Information taken from *Bolivians of Today*, Hispanic Notes and Monographs [New York, 1922], pp. 125–29.)

8. In 1922, the Hispanic Society of America put out a volume entitled *Bolivians of Today* (see above), which lists the biographies of 132 prominent Bolivians. While disclaiming to have exhausted all possible names, the book is presented as a list of "the more notable persons of Bolivia." A brief analysis of some of the salient data in the biographies will give us a fairly clear picture of what the makeup of the Bolivian elite was at this time. Of the 132, a full 58 are classified simply as public men, 25 as authors, 22 as educators, 21 as lawyers, 18 as men of affairs, 10 as physicians, 10 as soldiers, and a few working in other activities. Of the 132 only 3 are classified as businessmen, and another 3 as bankers, mine-owners, and capitalists. A closer look at individual educational backgrounds gives an even more revealing picture. Of the 92 for whom degrees are listed, 78 had backgrounds in law, 8 in medicine, 2 in political science (a branch of law) ; there were 2 bachelor's of arts and sciences degrees, 1 arts and letters degree and 1 simply listed as bachelor's degree. It is evident from this sample that public life was the major distinguishing activity. Overwhelmingly, they were liberal professionals, and law was by far the chief educational channel. Technical and entrepreneurial activities and backgrounds were almost nonexistent. Thus, as late as 1922 "traditional" roles and activities were still clearly dominant defining characteristics of the Bolivian elite. In terms of geographic distribution, the picture is also interesting: 49 were born in La Paz, 23 in Cochabamba, 23 in Sucre, 7 in Potosí, 7 in Tarija, 5 in Oruro, 4 in Santa Cruz, with the remaining scattered. Closer analysis allowed the conclusion that at least 81 of the sample pursued their primary careers in La Paz. In 1922, then, La Paz was clearly the primary source and major arena of this cross section of prominent Bolivians.

9. The melting of the old and new groups and the outlook of this amalgamated national elite is clearly stated by Klein, "Impact of the Chaco War," pp. 38–39.

10. The pervasive literary imitativeness of the Bolivian national elite is forcefully analyzed in Murdo MacLeod, "Bolivia and its Social Literature Before and After the Chaco War: A Historical Study of Social and Literary Revolution" (unpub. Ph.D. thesis, University of Florida, 1962). The non-national stylistic orientation of the elite became one of the major points of attack by later counter-groups. In fact, one of the most influential nationalist political tracts zeroes in on the non-national mentality of this elite. See Carlos Montenegro, *Nacionalismo y Coloniaje* 3d ed. (La Paz, 1953, first appeared circa 1942).

11. For a further description of the middle class and its values, see *Area Handbook for Bolivia* (Washington, D.C., 1963), p. 103.

12. Materials on the Bolivian middle class are scanty; for material supporting my analysis, see *Area Handbook for Bolivia*, p. 103; and "La Clase Media en Bolivia: Nota para el Estudio y Comprehensión del Problema," ed. Theo Crevenna,

Materiales para el Estudio de la Clase Media en Latino America III, mimeographed, Washington Pan American Union (n.d.).

13. The early pattern of taxation on tin exports is detailed in the following table.

BOLIVIA: TAXES ON TIN EXPORTS, 1900–1920
(In Thousands of Bolivianos)

Year	Commercial Value of Exports	Taxes on Exports	Taxes as Percentage of Value of the Exports
1900	14,608	293	2.0
1901	17,533	397	2.3
1902	15,847	401	2.5
1903	19,540	450	2.3
1904	17,064	468	2.7
1905	26,250	661	2.5
1906	35,248	1,564	4.4
1907	29,892	1,402	4.7
1908	30,929	929	3.0
1909	31,654	1,104	3.5
1910	37,007	1,455	3.9
1911	52,640	2,269	4.3
1912	60,238	2,767	4.6
1913	67,784	3,761	5.5
1914	42,480	1,949	4.6
1915	44,885	2,159	4.8
1916	42,652	2,539	6.0
1917	85,258	4,910	5.8
1918	129,611	7,381	5.7
1919	99,924	5,951	6.0
1920	112,282	6,208	5.5

SOURCE: *Analisis y Proyecciónes Del Desarrollo Económico IV: El Desarrollo Económico de Bolivia* (Mexico, 1958), p. 10.

The tax structure regarding tin was somewhat more complex, especially after 1936. For a more detailed analysis of this tax situation, see Rene Ballivian, *Tasas E Impuestos Sobre La Industria Mineria en Bolivia* (La Paz, 1946).

14. For a comparison of public financial power versus that of the big companies, see Klein, "Impact of the Chaco War," p. 84.

15. As early as 1922, Patiño was clearly the largest single financial power in the country. The following paragraph gives some idea of the breadth of his holdings as of 1922.

Señor Patiño's activities are not confined to the field of mining; he is also the sole owner of the Mercantile Bank of Bolivia, which has a capital of four million dollars. In addition to his banking and mining activities he is connected with the company administering the monopoly of alcohol and spirits, the importance of which is indicated by the fact that over 400,000 pesos have to be paid annually to the Government for the privilege. He has a large interest in the Colonizing Company of Isoboro, which owns extensive estates in the Department of Cochabamba, and in the Machacamarca-Uncía Railway which will connect the mining regions of Huanuin, Uncía, Llallagua and Amayapampa. He has, moreover, secured a concession for constructing a railroad from Cochabamba to the Mamore River, which, when finished, will give the products of Bolivia an outlet to the Atlantic. *(Bolivians of Today,* p. 214)

16. Under Saavedra, the government's tax bite rose from 5.5 percent to 13.3 percent. *Analisis y Proyecciónes,* p. 10.

17. Klein, "Impact of the Chaco War," p. 184.

18. Merle Kling, "Toward a Theory of Power and Political Instability in Latin America," ed. John Martz, *The Dynamics of Change in Latin American Politics* (Englewood Cliffs, N.J., 1965), p. 138.

19. Personalist-based clique politics was not new to Bolivia. In various forms it was the style of nineteenth-century Bolivian politics, as it was in most Latin American countries. I would argue that the question here is one of a reappearance of personal clique politics after a movement to a different form of political organization apparently had taken place. From the point of view of a concept of political development, the issue is the reappearance of this phenomenon in modified form and in a different context. Given the apparent advancement from cliques to parties, this reoccurrence can be judged as regressive. It is not a question of either party or job clique; factions and personalized ties exist in all parties no matter how highly developed. But it is a question of which is primary, job clique or party.

Where modern parties have developed, job clique politics has been controlled within the framework of the interaction among parties, interest groups, and publics. My argument is that as economic development in Bolivia was only partial and eventually arrested, so too was political development. One of the more important manifestations of this stunting of political development was the fact that personalized job clique politics again became more and more primary, with parties becoming increasingly secondary. Given its makeup, the small elite which controlled Bolivian public life was predisposed to intra-elite job faction politics. This was the case mainly because it was not a group which controlled hard forms of wealth other than land—a form of wealth which, in that context, was definitely limited in possibilities for extension and transfer. The development process created new factors—new private wealth and interests, parties, new bases of power, etc.— which, in part, reshaped and reflected that basic predisposition. The development process did not become a generalized self-sustaining process, however, and when the growth impulse began to abate, the predisposition to job faction politics began to reassert itself.

In this new context, this "regressive" development would create increasingly severe political questions. For example, without further growth how long could the splintering into factions accommodate ambitious sections of an elite which would continue to grow in numbers through the biological processes, if no other? What of the new urban middle sector created by the development process? What of the demands which would be made by new working class groups? Would not a number of points of strain begin to develop in the new structure? In discussing development in the late 1910s, Klein notes, for example:

> Given the long period of Montista rule, there had developed a large body of professional politicians who thirsted for office. Thus the classic pattern of "ins" versus "outs" set the stage for the growth of a large opposition party, and the traditional *personalismo* pattern of nineteenth- and twentieth-century politics only exacerbated the climate. So long as Montes seemed to be producing economic miracles, these combinations of patterns could be prevented from coalescing. But once this thrust of progress was stopped then the inevitable splintering was the result, as Salamanca so clearly recognized. (Herbert S. Klein, "Parties and Political Change in Bolivia 1880–1952" [unpub. manuscript, p. 86, forthcoming publication by Cambridge University Press])

20. Increasing violence, party factionalization and the formal style of political debate is described clearly in Klein, "Impact of the Chaco War," p. 90.

21. Hernando Siles was one of the founders of the Republican party. He was Saavedra's hand-picked successor, but once in power he broke from him and formed his own faction which later became Bolivia's first nationalist party. One of Siles' sons, Hernan, was a founder of the MNR and one of its most prominent leaders. For a biography of the elder Siles, see Benigno Carrasco, *Hernando Siles* (La Paz, 1961).

Chapter 3

1. The relatively simple pattern of stratification in interior towns is pointed out by Harry Hawthorn in "Stratification in a Latin American City: Sucre," eds. C. Loomis and O. Leonard, *Readings in Latin American Social Organization and Institutions* (Ann Arbor, 1953), pp. 212–17.

2. The 1942 census of the city of La Paz estimated "urban floaters" *(población flotante no censada)* to be 14,353. *Censo Demografico De La Ciudad De La Paz 15 de Octubre de 1942* (La Paz, 1943), p. 7.

3. Of an estimated city population of 301,450 in 1942, 82,856 whites, 86,202 mestizos, and 64,565 Indians were from the department of La Paz. *Ibid.*, pp. 22–25.

4. The reaction of artisan groups to the first effects of modernization is analyzed at length in Guillermo Lora, *Historia Del Movimiento Obrero Boliviano, 1848–1900* (La Paz, 1967), pt. 3.

5. Data on the Bolivian labor movement is still rather fragmentary. The two best sources in English are Robert J. Alexander, *The Bolivian National Revolution* (New Brunswick, 1958) and Herbert Klein, "The Impact of the Chaco War on Bolivian Society" (unpub. thesis, University of Chicago, 1963). The most detailed

study in Spanish is Augustin Barcelli, *Medio Siglo de Luchas Sindicales Revolucionarias En Bolivia* (La Paz, 1956). Another more recent general study is Jaime Ponce G., et al., *Breve Historia del Sindicalismo Boliviano,* IBEAS Monograph (La Paz, 1968). Besides these works, I have relied for my analysis on interviews with Bolivian labor leaders and an interesting unpublished history of Bolivian leftist movements authored by Guillermo Lora, head of the POR (see glossary).

6. Klein, "Impact of the Chaco War," pp. 99–100.

7. Barcelli, *Medio Siglo de Luchas,* p. 108.

8. After a certain hour, taxis were the only means of public transportation. Therefore, this ban not only made it difficult for meetings of the opposition to take place, but also made it easy to spot unofficial cars on the virtually empty streets. Saavedra's friends could get about in officially sanctioned vehicles. This practice is common in Bolivia and other Latin American countries even today.

9. Klein, "Impact of the Chaco War," p. 105.

10. The battles between the anarchists and socialists are recounted in the above-cited works. In addition, thanks to the generosity of Robert J. Alexander, Department of Economics, Rutgers University, I was able to get a further feel for anarchist thinking by examining the rich interview collection which Professor Alexander has accumulated since 1946. Regarding the anarchists, the most interesting interviews are those with the late anarchist leader, José Mendoza Vega. In these, Mendoza stresses the desire of the anarchists to remain free of all political parties and governments and he attacks other unions for being unprincipled in their pursuit of political power.

11. Data on the graficos was collected from a compendium of documents contained in the pamphlet *Primer Congreso Nacional De Trabajadores Graficos* (La Paz, 1952); and extensive personal interviews during 1966 in La Paz with Waldo Alvarez, longtime head of this union and Bolivia's first minister of labor.

12. Klein, "Impact of the Chaco War," p. 170.

13. In a most interesting study of the economic possibilities of early twentieth-century Bolivia, a French visitor, Paul Walle, makes much of the new spirit of nationalism and the desire for development being fostered in Bolivia by the liberals. See Paul Walle, *Bolivia* (New York, 1914).

14. A sense of "backwardness" became rather pervasive in the educated sectors of Bolivia from the 1920s onward. In the ideological outpouring that begins in this period, there is continued play upon the visible backwardness and poverty of Bolivia vis-à-vis other nations. This theme was so important among change-oriented youth groups that it seems legitimate to argue that the young and educated had begun to experience the so-called "demonstration effect" of the advanced states.

15. *El Norte,* Oct. 4, 1927, p. 1–1.

16. See for example *El Norte,* Oct. 20, 1927, p. 5–5, and *El Diario,* Nov. 23, 1928, p. 7–3.

17. As we saw with the sample of 132 prominent Bolivians (chapter 2, note 8), whatever the final career designation, the basic educational preparation was in law. Moreover it appears that the study and practice of law was a particularly important career channel for the urban middle sector. One group of observers have noted for example: "By some time around 1920 professional training had been sought as a path to socio-economic advancement by so many upwardly mobile urban *cholos*

that the practice of law had fallen into disesteem among members of La Rosca ('upper class') in many provincial cities as being the mark of the *arribista* ('climber')" *(Area Handbook for Bolivia* [Washington, D.C., 1963], p. 119).

18. There is no accurate data on the development of the Bolivian public service. However, an analysis of the overall situation conducted by the United Nations in the late 1940s gives a picture of an inflated civil service whose problems had been developing over a period of years. According to this study, the public service was excessively large, ill-trained to perform its tasks, and generally a drain on an already pressed economy. The reason for the situation was the long-standing habit of creating and dispensing offices on a political basis. *Informe Keenleyside* (reprinted in La Paz by La Universidad Mayor de San Andres, 1952) pp. 31–33.

19. The dominance of foreigners in top positions in the mines became a matter of some bitterness. In a 1927 article "Nationalize the Personnel of Patiño Mines," it is argued, "Various publications dealing with the development of the labor force in Patiño mines assure us that we will encounter there personnel foreign to the country camping in the prinicipal posts and having the dominant influence; with comfortable work and an excessive luxury; while nationals are always in subsistence jobs of inferior status and with half pay" *(El Norte,* Nov. 23, 1927, p. 5–3).

20. The dominance of foreigners in almost all commercial and entrepreneurial activity is noted with surprise by Walle, *Bolivia,* p. 58.

21. The problem of a politics dominated by the pressure of a job hungry middle class also began to be a national concern. In one daily, for example, the country was characterized as suffering from a new sickness which was called "Empleomania" and was said to have been reaching crisis proportions. *Renovación,* Jan. 23, 1926, p. 1–1.

22. Crane Brition, *The Anatomy of Revolution* (New York, 1938).

23. *La Calle,* June 23, 1936, p. 3–3.

24. *La Calle,* July 18, 1936, p. 6–1. Later that month job faction politics was again attacked and dubbed *"política criolla,"* slang for "crass office-seeking." *La Calle,* July 30, 1936, p. 7–1.

25. Many years later, a prominent revolutionary born from that generation, Walter Guevara Arze, reminded his peers of the situation that had confronted them:

> At that time the professional or employee that was not in the direct or indirect service of the oligarchy had to vegetate in economic and occupational mediocrity, since the only ones who could pay regularly did not need more than a limited number of doctors, lawyers, or engineers. Besides, to fill the jobs of true importance in those activities they generally imported foreigners. . . . (Speech entitled, "Hay que Reconciliar a la Clase Media con La Revolución," text reprinted in *El Diario* [July 28, 1959], p. 6–1)

Taking into account that the indigenous upper and middle sectors neither valued nor pursued entrepreneurial or technical careers in great numbers, but rather clustered in the liberal professions, it is relevant to note that the 1942 census of La Paz reports over eight hundred lawyers (versus 269 in the city according to the 1900 census) servicing a permanent population of around 287,097. That would be an overbalanced situation in a developed economy, but when we take into account the small number of that total population who could afford to pay reasonable fees, it seems safe to conclude that the lawyers' market in La Paz, the principal arena of the country, was rather overcrowded. The problems confronting the young during this period were not confined to La Paz. According to one historian of the Cochabamba Valley, "The young people who had no opportunity to follow industrial or commercial activities left for the mining centers or have gone out of the country. Agriculture was in decline due to the regressive system of *Latifundio*" (Rafael Peredo Antezana, *La Provincia de Quillacollo* [Cochabamba, 1963], pp. 141–42).

26. Klein, "Impact of the Chaco War," p. 176.

27. The best chronicle of the national reformist group in these early days is Augusto Cespedes, *El Dictador Suicida* (Santiago de Chile, 1956). A chronicle of the socialist group appears in Miguel Bonifaz, *Bolivia: Frustración y Destino* (Sucre, Bolivia, 1965).

28. Cespedes, *El Dictador Suicida*, p. 82.

29. "We were vacillating between mental anti-culture and a strong but confused feeling of the negative work realized by the oligarchy with liberal ideas." *(Ibid).*

30. *Ibid.*, p. 83.

31. Many figures associated with the movement managed to appear in most every government despite its ideological coloration up to 1952.

32. Early ideological statements of this group are contained in Ernesto Ayala Mercado, *Critica Del La Reforma Universitaria* (Sucre, 1938, reprinted in La Paz, 1955). Their first formal declaration was announced with the formation of the *Federación Universitaria Boliviana* ("Bolivian Federation of University Students") and is reprinted in Alberto Cornejo, *Programas Políticos de Bolivia* (Cochabamba, 1949), p. 297.

Chapter 4

1. In 1925, 32,598 tons returned a value of 27,123 bolivianos (bs); in 1930, 38,722 tons could return only 26,967 bs. See *Analisis y Proyecciónes Del Desarrollo Económico IV: El Desarrollo Económico de Bolivia* (Mexico, 1958), p. 12.

2. Herbert Klein, "The Impact of the Chaco War on Bolivian Society" (unpub. thesis, University of Chicago, 1963), p. 154.

3. In the all-important Cataví Siglo XX complex, for example, the amount of fine tin mined in 1925 was 7 percent. By 1929 it dropped to $3\frac{1}{2}$ percent and from that point dropped steadily until it is less than a half of one percent today. The quality of tin is a profoundly serious problem, for as quality drops, recovery problems increase significantly, continually compounding the production problem. (Data taken from unpublished materials of C. Blott, ex-director of Cataví Siglo XX, presently technical advisor to the Banco Minero, La Paz, Bolivia.)

4. *Analisis y Proyecciónes*, p. 13.

5. Klein, "Impact of the Chaco War," p. 167 and previously cited unpublished materials of Guillermo Lora (chapter 3, note 5).

6. General disorder during this period is recounted in Klein, "Impact of the Chaco War," pp. 190–205.

7. The reason for Argentina's support of Paraguay is a matter of debate—some say it was due to a desire to safeguard foreign oil interests; others, that it was based on a desire to weaken the Bolivian political state as a matter of policy.

8. There is a huge amount of Bolivian literature on the Chaco War. One of the most interesting relatively scholarly accounts is Roberto Querejazu Calvo, *Masamaclay* (La Paz, 1965). There is also an excellent account in English by David H. Zook, Jr., *The Conduct of the Chaco War* (New Haven, 1960).

9. These accounts are analyzed at length in MacLeod, "Bolivia and Its Social Literature, Before and After the Chaco War: A Historical Study of Social and Literary Revolution" (unpub. Ph.D. thesis, University of Florida, 1962).

10. A fairly sizeable colony of Bolivian deserters developed in northern Argentina during the war. According to Zook, the Bolivian army suffered approximately ten thousand desertions. Zook, *Conduct of the Chaco War*, p. 240.

11. Klein, "Impact of the Chaco War," p. 218.

12. *Ibid.*, p. 333. It appears that the influx of the people into La Paz was great enough that the government felt compelled to issue compulsory work decrees.

13. One school of thought is associated mainly with Professor Richard Patch, Department of Anthropology, State University of New York at Buffalo. He has done the major groundbreaking work on a variety of contemporary Bolivian questions, and puts great emphasis on the Chaco War as a causative factor in explaining later Indian peasant activities. While I do not reject this interpretation out of hand, I do feel that the direct causal effects of the war have been overemphasized and that a variety of other equally or more important factors must be taken into account to formulate an adequate explanation. See chapter 10, and chapter 10, note 12, this volume.

14. The reformist paper, *La Calle,* reported the developments in Cochabamba as an effort by the Toro government to carry out reform on estates owned by corporate entities such as the Catholic church. (The Toro government was a coalition of young army and civilian reformers. See chapter 5 for more on Toro.) The clear implication is that the effort was at least in part initiated by those elites who controlled the government after the coup of 1936. *La Calle,* November 7, 1936, p. 4–1.

15. In his account, Zook stresses over and over the complete mismanagement of the war by the Bolivian authorities. See Zook, *Conduct of the Chaco War.*

16. The loss to Bolivia of skilled workers, particularly miners, in the war is stressed in a most important study of Bolivia conducted in 1940–41 by the U.S. Embassy staff. The report is entitled *The Bolivian Report* and is available in typescript in the U.S. Embassy, La Paz, Bolivia.

17. By 1952, more than 70 percent of the country's manufacturing was located in La Paz.

18. The minimal impact of the growth in manufacturing was stressed by the United Nations Technical Mission in its Keenleyside report as this quote from a Bolivian reprint indicates:

> The number of establishments grew from 1,000 in 1941 to 2,000 in 1947. The number of employed in the same period grew from around 12,000 to 20,000. Nevertheless, the size of the establishments remained small and on the average employed ten persons each. In 1950 total invested capital was

estimated at 2,000 million bs [bolivianos], thus averaging about 1,000,000 bs per establishment. According to these figures, the level of capitalization and mechanization is small and many establishments classified as industrial are really artisan shops. (*Informe Keenleyside* [reprinted in La Paz by La Universidad Mayor de San Andres, 1952], p. 257).

For a detailed analysis of manufacturing in La Paz, see *La Paz en Su Centenario,* vol. 4, pp. 31–127.

19. For an analysis of inflation in this period, see *Analisis y Proyecciónes,* pp. 57–63. During this time, paper circulation went from 60.4 million bs to 863.1 million bs. For an interesting general historical analysis of inflation in Bolivia, see: Guillermo Alborata Velasco, *El Flagelo De La Inflación Monetaria En Bolivia, Pais Monoproductor* (Madrid, Spain, 1963).

Chapter 5

1. The army was one of the chief means of mobility for the lower groups and its perception as such by the upper class is stressed in Harry Hawthorn, "Stratification in a Latin American City: Sucre," eds. C. Loomis and O. Leonard, *Readings in Latin American Social Organization and Institutions* (Ann Arbor, 1953), p. 215.

2. The debilitating effects of personal politics to the war effort is stressed over and over by David H. Zook, Jr., *The Conduct of the Chaco War* (New Haven, 1960).

3. For excellent accounts of the makeup of the Toro regime, see Augusto Cespedes, *El Dictator Suicida* (Santiago de Chile, 1956), ch. 11 and Herbert Klein, "David Toro and the Establishment of Military Socialism in Bolivia," *Hispanic American Historical Report,* Vol. 65, No. 1 (1965), pp. 25–52.

4. The attitude of the nationalist elite toward workers was expressed frequently in the editorial pages of *La Calle.* In one such editorial, for example, it was noted: "We sincerely believe that the workers do not have a clear idea even of the duties of unionism and its activities." Because this is true, the editorial goes on, unions must be controlled by the state. *La Calle,* July 7, 1936, p. 4–3. The manipulative view is even clearer in the following: "The unions will be under the guidance and permanent control of the socialist government and the union organization will be incorporated as a mechanism of the state as a base of its constitution." *La Calle,* July 23, 1936, p. 5–4.

5. Toro expressed his view of the Indian problem in the following way:

One cannot pull the Indian from his actual atony raising him immediately to spiritual spheres for which he hasn't begun to be ready; nor can one give him intellectual factors foreign to his origin. . . . This, far from being a good policy, is for the moment an idealistic, empty, and futile effort: First, it is necessary to teach him to read and write. (*La Calle,* November 6, 1936, p. 1–1)

6. Interview with General David Toro, La Paz, Bolivia, 1966.

7. For an account, see Herbert Klein, "American Oil Companies in Latin

America: The Bolivian Experience," *Inter-American Economic Affairs*, Vol. 18, Autumn (1964), pp. 47–72

8. In a personal interview in La Paz, 1966, Toro related that his relations with Patiño were always bad, but he felt that Aramayo and Hochschild understood what he was trying to do. At the same time, he related that he came to find the young nationalists much too radical and that he removed them from the government to slow down the pace of change.

9. See Herbert Klein, "German Busch and the Era of Military Socialism," *Hispanic American Historical Report*, Vol. 67, No. 2 (May 1967), pp. 166–84.

10. Tristan Marof, *La Justicia del Inca* (Brussels, 1926). Another important work was *La Verdad Socialista En Bolivia* (La Paz, 1938).

11. Quoted in Miguel Bonifaz, *Bolivia: Frustración y Destino* (Sucre, Bolivia, 1965), p. 129.

12. *Ibid.*, p. 140.

13. The battle between Marof and Gainsborg and the formation of the POR is recounted in Guillermo Lora, *José Aguirre Gainsborg: Fundador del POR* (La Paz, 1960).

14. The rising influence of proletarians in the POR is symbolized in the emergence to prominence of Guillermo Lora, son of a Siglo XX miner. Although Lora himself devoted his life to political and intellectual activities, his brother Cesar and other working miners came to play important roles in the party.

15. The FIB was launched with the document entitled ¡*Hacia La Unidad de las Izquierdas Bolivians!* (Santiago de Chile, 1939).

16. The first program of the PIR is reprinted in Alberto Cornejo, *Programas Politicos de Bolivia* (Cochabamba, 1949), pp. 181–86. The present position of the PIR is expressed in *PIR y Desarrollo Nacional* (La Paz, 1961).

17. There is hardly a party document or a book written by a member which does not go into education in minute detail. Both Arce and Añaya devoted great effort to the construction of elaborate education curriculum schemes.

18. The role of the school and the influence of PIR teachers in preparing political attitudes in the Valley is treated at length in Jorge Dandler-Hanhart, "Local Group, Community and Nation: A Study of Changing Structure in Ucureña, Bolivia," University of Wisconsin Monograph (1967), ch. 3.

19. Statements of FSB thinking can be found in Rodolfo Surcou Macido, *Hacia La Revolución Integral* (La Paz, 1961) and a program in Cornejo, *Programas Politicos de Bolivia*, pp. 131–41.

20. During the period from 1936 to 1940, the major public source of nationalist thinking was the newspaper *La Calle*. The developing nationalist ideology was expressed both in editorials and lengthy polemical essays. In one such essay signed by a Sargento Yujra, most of the basic concepts which formed the group's thinking and attitudes were spelled out. The article begins with an attack on "infantile leftists," both for their commitment to "internationalist" theories and, interestingly enough, their failure to support the war effort. It then argues for the concept of "Socialismo del Estado" which the author insists is a new nationalist ideology suitable for all the emerging colonial countries. Each country, however, must develop its own autonomous form of the ideology and, hence, he refers to a "Bolivian socialism." In terms of solving Bolivia's problems, the author opines

that "the semi-colonial condition of Bolivia obliges that the white and mestizo minority first battle against imperialism before entering the social revolution. Only the economic sovereignty of the nation will make possible an eventual economic equality of individuals." He goes on to argue that in the Bolivian context, both La Rosca and the leftist extremists are agents of imperialism. Given this, the task is to aid the army in its battle against La Rosca, communism, and caudillismo by working for a disciplined Bolivian socialist position. In that task, the most important group is the Excombatientes. *La Calle,* August 22, 1936, p. 4–2.

21. Because it was a secret society, there is little material available on the RADEPA. The following, taken from a late pamphlet of the organization, gives some idea of what this organization stood for:

The aims of the organization are:

a) to create a robust spirit of nationality locked in the desire to enrich Bolivia
b) to encourage every Bolivian tendency and free the country of international influences
c) to combat and destroy all who go against the higher interests of the country
d) to raise the moral values of the people
e) to raise military behavior toward a single thought and doctrine. (Albert Candia Almaraz, *Razón de Patria Ante La Historia* [Cochabamba, 1957])

22. *Sindicalismo dirigido* as used here means "unionism directed by the reformist elite." From the beginning of this period, labor, while supporting the reformers, complained that little concrete change was filtering down to them. Typical was a complaint of the miners of Colquechaca printed in *La Calle,* August 27, 1936, p. 4–1.

23. Quoted in Augustin Barcelli, *Medio Siglo de Luchas Sindicales Revolucionarias En Bolivia* (La Paz, 1956), p. 155.

24. Using 1931 as a base of one hundred, the cost of living between 1936 and 1940 jumped from 214 to 865; food alone went from 201 to 716; combustibles from 186 to 722; clothing from 238 to 941; services from 140 to 388; and rent from 253 to 1,347. *Analisis y Proyecciónes Del Desarrollo Económico IV: El Desarrollo Económico de Bolivia* (Mexico, 1958), p. 61.

25. Although the data are fragmentary, there is reason to believe that anti-Semitism was rife among the Bolivian middle. The anti-monopoly capitalism and anti-Semitism then common in Germany appeared in Bolivia and centered around Mauricio Hochschild (a German Jew) who became a generally hated figure in Bolivia.

26. Again, data are fragmentary, but there is reason to believe that the average person concerned himself more with municipal than national politics. By all accounts, regionalism was a more potent force in Bolivia before 1932 than nationalism. People identified much more with their *municipalidad* than with the state. Although the state was unitary in form, muncipalities were independent. Women could vote in muncipal elections, but not in national elections. In all departments of Bolivia, municipal governments were stronger than the national prefects and municipal budgets dwarfed department budgets considerably. Municipal

government was one of the major sources of middle-class jobs. The importance of localism, municipal finances, etc., is stressed over and over in the *Informe Keenleyside* (reprinted in La Paz by La Universidad Mayor de San Andres, 1952), Section III, pp. 23–52

Chapter 6

1. Luis Peñaloza, *Historia del Movimiento Nacionalista Revolucionario: 1941–1952* (La Paz, 1963), p. 35.

2. In a personal interview with German Monroy Block who was one of the founders of the MNR and held the post of minister of labor under the Villarroel government, La Paz, 1966. Another founder of the party also stressed the middle-class nature of the group and its lack of contacts with significant publics: "The fight against the restoration government, even after the formation of the *Movimiento Nacionalista Revolucionario,* was developed by a minority of the middle class. Contacts were not made with the people, who on their part, were ill-informed and had little awareness of their rights" (Augusto Cespedes, *El Presidente Colgado* [Buenos Aires, 1966], p. 46).

3. Interview with German Monroy, La Paz, 1966.

4. Peñaloza, *Historia del Movimiento,* p. 39.

5. The first formal ideological statement of the MNR was a pamphlet entitled simply *Movimiento Nacionalista Revolucionario* (June 7, 1942). In Bolivia this statement is often referred to as *El Libro Verde.* Unfortunately, there are very few copies of the document still in existence. Luckily, I was able to locate one and a microfilm of it is available at the University of Pittsburgh Library. The quote in the text is from p. 40.

6. *Movimiento Nacionalista Revolucionario,* p. 40.

7. I might add that the emphasis on foreigners in top Bolivian jobs tends to substantiate the point that this younger generation found meaningful outlets in short supply. In *El Libro Verde,* they demand prohibition of foreign employees and, in a most interesting point, demanded the retirement of all military officers over fifty-five years of age. *Movimiento Nacionalista Revolucionario,* pp. 41–42.

8. In a recent personal interview, La Paz, 1966, the important MNR leader, Augusto Cespedes, stated that on his part and that of others, anti-Semitism was mainly tactical. It should also be pointed out that between 1936 and 1939, *La Calle* disavowed fascism and often attacked its doings in Europe; for example, *La Calle* supported the Loyalists in the Spanish Civil War.

9. Paz Estenssoro's parliamentary speeches during this period were later collected and published. They are an invaluable source on the early thinking of the MNR. See *Víctor Paz Estenssoro Discursos Parlimentarios* (La Paz, 1955).

10. The importance of technical requirements related to the grade of ore mined was pointed out by C. Blout, chief manager of Catavi Siglo XX in the early 1960s, and, presently, advisor to Bolivia's mining industry. Personal interview, La Paz, 1966.

11. *Labor Problems in Bolivia,* Report of the Joint Bolivian–United States

Labor Commission, International Labor Office (Montreal, 1943), see esp. p. 17.

12. Tensions in the Villarroel regime are discussed in Peñaloza, *Historia del Movimiento*, ch. 5.

13. In Article 107, the constitution declares that the main function of the economy is to "assure for all inhabitants an existence consistent with human dignity." Article 108 gives the state previous title to all land, minerals, and water, and the power to regulate private use. Article 109 makes the state the pivot of the economy: "The state will be able to regulate by law the exercise of industry and commerce when it is required by the needs of security or the public good. It can also in such cases assume the direction of the national economy. This intervention will be exercised in the form of direct control or stimulation" (Ciro Felix Trigo, *Constitución Política Del Estado* [La Paz, 1945]).

14. Inflation dropped from 23.74 percent to 7.7 percent under Villarroel. *Analisis y Proyecciónes Del Desarrollo Económico IV: El Desarrollo Económico de Bolivia* (Mexico, 1958), p. 62.

15. For details of the measures, see Peñaloza, *Historia Del Movimiento*, chs. 6 and 7.

16. That these organizing efforts had an important impact is attested to by a recent anthropological study of the region of Nor Yungas in Bolivia. One of the first vivid memories of national political life among the Indians of this region was the congress and the organizers that preceded it. See Barbara Leons, "Changing Aspects of Social Stratification in an Emergent Bolivian Community" (unpub. Ph.D. thesis, U.C.L.A., 1966).

Chapter 7

1. Luis Peñaloza, *Historia del Movimiento Nacionalista Revolucionario: 1941–1952* (La Paz, 1963), p. 123.

2. The document in question declares the party to be an organization oriented toward "scientific evolutionary socialism"; it also accepts the Marxist analysis of society, but rejects any concept of "violent revolution." In discussing revolution, the document argues, "There is no revolution that is absolutely necessary or indispensable, Schomoller tells us. All revolutions can be avoided with an opportune reform and all historical progress is based upon making reforms in place of revolutions." It goes on to argue that only the resistance of a ruling class to desires for change brings on revolutions. The document further develops an analysis of Bolivia strikingly similar to that of the MNR. It points out the backwardness of Bolivian workers and peasants and, therefore, the need for the middle class to lead a multi-class reform movement. It then sets down a relatively radical program which, in terms of specifics, was more elaborate than anything the MNR had previously identified itself with. Among other things, the program calls for planning for economic development, suppression of monopolies, nationalization of public utilities, control of mining profits for purposes of development investment, many planks favorable to labor, and a program for the rural areas. *Declaración de Principios y Programa De Acción de La Unión Socialista Republicana* (La Paz, 1949).

3. Between 1940 and 1943, about 40 percent of the value of tin exports made its way to the Central Bank. Under Villarroel, the figure climbed to 60 percent. Under the PURS, it dropped again to around 50 percent. *Analisis y Proyecciónes Del Desarrollo Económico IV: El Desarrollo Económico de Bolivia* (Mexico, 1958), pp. 34–35.

4. Throughout the period, *El Diario,* in editorial after editorial, complained of severe economic problems in La Paz. For example: "In no period has the Bolivian people suffered more hunger and deprivation than the present . . . not a month goes by without scarcity, the absolute lack of bread and now it is going to begin again" (*El Diario,* March 3, 1950, p. 4–1). That this comment was not made simply for political maneuvering is substantiated in the *Informe Keenleyside* (reprinted in La Paz by La Universidad Mayor de San Andres, 1952), which documents at great length the abysmal state of the Bolivian economy by 1951.

5. This development is noted with some glee by Peñaloza, *Historia Del Movimiento,* p. 127.

6. A somewhat popularized account of the rise and fall of the PIR can be found in "Historia del PIR la Muerte del Primer Partido de Masas de Bolivia," *Primera Plana,* No. 7 (August, 1965).

7. Estimates run from seven hundred to seven thousand.

8. By now, somewhat concerned for its public image, the Patiño company published a lengthy collection of documents and texts presenting its side of the violence in the mines during 1947. *Los Conflictos Sociales En 1947* (La Paz, 1948).

9. Labor's side of this clash is presented in Augustin Barcelli, *Medio Siglo de Luchas, Sindicales Revolucionarias En Bolivia* (La Paz, 1956), pp. 227–31.

10. The hunger strike and other activities by MNR women is recounted in Lydia Gueiler Tejada, *La Mujer y la Revolución* (La Paz, 1959), see esp., ch. 4.

11. *El Diario* brought out its January 22, 1951, edition with a headline lamenting that never before had Bolivia seen such a large and sad mass of political deportations and jailings.

12. For pro-rebel accounts of the war, see Peñaloza, *Historia del Movimiento,* ch. 18, or Jose Felman Velarde, *Victor Paz Estenssoro: El Hombre y La Revolución* (La Paz, 1955), pt. 3, ch. 4.

13. Peñaloza, *Historia del Movimiento,* p. 128.

14. The middle-class composition of the MNR leadership is made clear when reading Peñaloza's party history. In one passage, he describes the Cochabamba leadership, with pride, as "all of the youth of the middle class, distinguished in Cochabamba society and in some cases in national arts and letters" (*Historia del Movimiento,* p. 49). For data on this organization, see chs. 10, 11, 12.

15. *Ibid.,* p. 134.

16. These conclusions are based on Peñaloza's *Historia del Movimiento* and numerous personal interviews with MNR leaders then on the scene and other labor and political leaders important at the time.

17. The average factory in La Paz employed no more than ten persons. Only two or three operations employed more than a hundred; the largest factory, S.A.I.D., employed a number varying between two and three hundred.

18. This pattern of workers from one factory living together is evident even today. In many cases, the factory union has bought a building or set of buildings

and the group rents from the union. These concentrations tend to be the primary, and in a sense total, community of the workers.

19. The analysis is based on data appearing in Paul Walle, *Bolivia* (New York, 1914) and *The Bolivian Report* (available in the U.S. Embassy, La Paz).

20. *Labor Problems in Bolivia,* Report of the Joint Bolivian–United States Labor Commission, International Labor Office (Montreal, 1943), p. 8. It is important to note that the miners' cash wage was supplemented by subsidized food stores, housing, and medical care. None were particularly excellent, but they did increase the miners' real standard of living.

21. In news reports of miners' demands after 1946, protection against layoffs, demands for cost-of-living increases, and demands for organizational rights are the most frequently noted issues.

22. The inability of the MNR actually to incorporate labor and control it was stressed as an important factor in understanding the revolution by Víctor Paz Estenssoro in personal interviews, Lima, Peru, 1966.

23. One of the most important leaders of the railway workers, Juan Sanjines Obando, was generally recognized to be a PIRista. The cautious attitude the ferroviarios maintained toward the MNR was stressed to me in a personal interview with another union leader, Ramon Claure, La Paz, 1966.

24. The *Tesis* also demanded nationalization, agrarian reform, the immediate occupation of the mines by workers, and, eventually, a government based on the proletariat. The *Tesis* is reprinted in Alberto Cornejo, *Programas Políticos de Bolivia* (Cochabamba, 1949), p. 314.

25. This POR strategy was stressed in personal interviews with Edwin Moller, then a PORista, later a member of the MNR, and now an important figure in Lechín's new party, the PRIN, in La Paz, 1966.

26. Interviews with Paz Estenssoro, Lima, Peru, 1966.

27. Peñaloza, an ardent enemy of Lechín and a leader of the MNR core recounts with distaste the situation in the mines:

> In the mines, especially in Uncía and Chocaya, there appeared a miners' bloc controlled by Communists and Trotskyite leaders. The group was under the protection of Lechín and it refused to accept the MNR list of local candidates delivered to them by the party agent, Augusto Cuadros. (Peñaloza, *Historia del Movimiento,* p. 123)

28. *Ibid.,* p. 150.
29. *Ibid.,* p. 145.
30. The predisposition of the MNR leadership to the coup tactic and their continuing fear of mass involvement, especially on the part of campesinos, is pointed out by Augustin Barcelli as one of the keys to the failure of the civil war:

> But the fundamental error lay in the lack of confidence of the men of the party in the masses and their fear of the involvement of the masses. Obsessed by the idea of a golpe, they failed to recognize that the insurrection had to mobilize a mass base and, to achieve that, demanded a revolutionary program. A program calling for nationalization of the mines, banks, railroads, and insurance companies; and agrarian reforms, the suppression

of personal services, and the unionization of the campesinos would have assured mass support. (Barcelli, *Medio Siglo de Luchas,* p. 219)

31. *El Diario,* November 7, 1950, reported a MNR-Communist pact and printed a document containing these specific goals. Months later, the MNR disavowed the pact, but not the goals. In any event, most sources agree that the MNR ran on this platform in 1951. This news report, however, was one of two pieces of documentary confirmation of this generally held view that I was able to locate. However, after numerous personal interviews, I do agree with the general view that the MNR did indeed associate itself in the public mind with these goals after 1951. In addition to the news accounts, I did locate a one-page mimeographed sheet which dealt specifically with the question of agrarian reform. The sheet was published by a local MNR group in Santa Cruz and was less a statement of policy than an exhortation by one group to the rest of the party concerning what the party's position should be. The sheet argues that "personal land for all has to be the slogan of the MNR in its long fight of sacrifice for the people." It is interesting to note, however, that the manner of achieving this goal, as spelled out in the sheet, is much less radical than the positions taken by the leftist parties. The program first emphasizes a plan based on the opening of new lands and the distribution of government-owned lands. Only then does it go on to attack *latifundios,* indicating that some lands may have to be redistributed. Such redistribution, however, was to be based on just compensation. This sheet was published late in 1950 and indicates two things about the core party's views on agrarian reform at that point: (a) agrarian reform was not a generally held view in the party, but still a question of debate and exhortation, and (b) this particular plan, at least, was not as radical as that put forth by the left, and it emphasized non-confiscatory measures over a program of expropriation and redistribution. It seems fair to speculate, then, that even as the MNR became publicly identified with a more radical program, it did so hesitantly and with a somewhat restricted view as to what the program would entail. The pamphlet in question was entitled *Tierra Propia Para Todos Ofrece El MNR* (Santa Cruz, December 8, 1950), and is signed by Ovidio Barbery Justiniano.

Chapter 8

1. *El Diario,* May 9, 1951.
2. Results printed in *El Diario,* various days, May 1951.
3. *El Diario,* January 30, 1952, p. 4–3.
4. One particularly bitter attack on the United States sponsored by the tin companies began with the title, "The Diminution of the Income of a Poor Country in Order to Benefit Another Country of Enormous Economic Power." *El Diario,* October 9, 1951, p. 1–7.
5. After offering $1.06 a fine pound (pure ore), the United States eventually set the price of $1.12. *Analisis y Proyecciónes Del Desarrollo Económico IV: El Desarrollo Económico de Bolivia* (Mexico, 1958), p. 31.

6. Luis Peñaloza, *Historia del Movimiento Nacionalista Revolucionario: 1941–1952* (La Paz, 1963), chs. 21 and 22.

7. This line of speculation arose mainly out of personal interviews with various MNR, labor, and leftist party leaders. It gains some definite validity in a reading of a violent attack on the MNR by a former leader of the FSB who joined the MNR right wing in 1950. See Alfredo Candia, *Bolivia: Un Experimento Comunista En America* (La Paz, n.d.). See especially chs. 2, 3, 4, 5, 6.

8. The best information on Los Grupos de Honor is in Lydia Gueiler Tejada, *La Mujer y la Revolución* (La Paz, 1959). Miss Gueiler (now the wife of the former PORista, Edwin Moller) was one of the chief organizers of Los Grupos in 1950, 1951, and 1952. The data in her book were amplified considerably in several personal interviews with her in La Paz, 1966.

9. Peñaloza, *Historia del Movimiento*, p. 149.

10. Gueiler stresses the emotional approach and almost total lack of specific goals among this group. *La Mujer y La Revolución*, ch. 6.

11. Gueiler, among others, stresses the desire for jobs as a motivating factor in this group. *Ibid.*, p. 98.

12. From the early days of Tristan Marof, those goals were, above all, nationalization of the mines and agrarian reform. After 1946, they were escalated to the demand for a leading role for labor and its leadership in shaping a new Bolivia.

13. The names of both were associated with projected agrarian reform programs in the late 1930s. Klein, "Impact of the Chaco War," p. 403. Paz later presented a mild reform project to the national assembly in the early 1940s: the project envisioned mainly the introduction of wage labor and was restricted to his home department of Tarija. See *Victor Paz Estenssoro Discursos Parlimentarios* (La Paz, 1955), p. 297. It should be stressed, however, that in neither *El Libro Verde* nor the latter MNR program reprinted in Alberto Cornejo, *Programs Políticos de Bolivia* (Cochabamba, 1949), p. 143, was fundamental agrarian reform mentioned. Agrarian reform, as far as I can make out, was not publicly associated with the MNR as such until 1951.

14. The distrust of Paz by the in-country leaders is made clear by Candia in *Bolivia: Un Experimento Comunista*.

15. Jose Felman Valarde, *Víctor Paz Estenssoro: El Hombre y La Revolución* (La Paz, 1955), p. 228. MNR right wing resistance is also stressed by Richard Patch in "Bolivia: U.S. Assistance in a Revolutionary Setting" in Richard Adams et al., *Social Change in Latin America Today* (New York, 1960), pp. 108–76.

Chapter 9

1. Robert J. Alexander, *The Bolivian National Revolution* (New Brunswick, 1958), p. 46.

2. Personal interview with Walter Guevara Arze, La Paz, 1966. The economic thrust of the revolution was also stressed by Paz, who argued that "the country lingers in a permanent state of economic backwardness which extends itself into the social field" (Victor Paz Estenssoro, *La Revolución Boliviana* [La Paz, 1964], p. 9).

3. In later years MNR theorists indulged in post hoc attempts to reconcile the contradictions between official and revolutionary justice. One of the more interesting examples is in Alipio Valencia Vega, "Teoretica Sobre Política Nacional," *Abril* (July–August 1964), pp. 18–35.

4. For a summary of the right-wing position at this time, see Alfredo Candia, *Bolivia: Un Experimento Comunista En America* (La Paz, n.d.) ch. 5. An important source of public manifestation of the intra-party disputes can be found in the pages of the official MNR newspaper *La Nación;* selected articles more or less giving the MNR pragmatic center's view of events are contained in Saturnino Rodrigo, *Diario de La Revolución Nacional* (La Paz, 1955).

5. According to Armando Arce, one of the founders of the MNR, this limited view was his own and that of many other older members. Personal interview, La Paz, 1966. This view was also expressed by a prominent figure in the party right wing, Hugo Roberts. Personal interview, La Paz, 1966.

6. Reported in *Hispanic American Report* (May 1952).

7. Quoted in Alexander, *The Bolivian National Revolution,* p. 103.

8. Quoted in *Bolivia: 10 Años de Revolución* (La Paz, April 1962), p. 35.

9. A case of a purged, jailed, and then rehabilitated officer is that of General Alfredo Ovando Candia. After his rehabilitation, Ovando swore loyalty to Paz and the MNR. Through adroit maneuvering, he emerged in the 1960s as chief of staff of the army. In 1964, he was one of the chief figures in the overthrow of Paz and the MNR. After a period as co-president and then president of a junta, he is again chief of staff of the army.

10. Under the junta which ruled after Paz's overthrow in 1964, the military minister of peasant affairs was a full-blooded Aymara Indian. One student of the military holds that there was little change in the composition of the officer corps after 1952. He estimates that in 1956 fully 80 percent of the corps were members previous to 1952. William Brill, *Military Civic Action In Bolivia* (unpub. Ph.D. thesis, University of Pennsylvania, 1965), p. 132.

11. *El Diario,* June 5, p. 4–3.

12. The speed of organization of workers' militias was pointed out in a personal interview with one of Bolivia's most knowledgeable students of labor affairs, Señor Daniel Bracamonte, Instituto Boliviano de Estudios y Acción Social, La Paz, 1966.

13. In all COB documents, this concept of independence, usually expressed in the idea of "Fuero Sindical," is stressed. See, for example, *Programa Ideologico y Estatutos de la Central Obrera Boliviana* (La Paz, 1954), pp. 24–25, in which the following points are made:

Only the proletariat supported by the peasants can avoid an abandonment of the revolution by the petty bourgeoisie. . . .

The proletariat wishes to push the revolution to its ultimate consequences. . . . .

The best guarantee of the defense of these conquests consists in the participation of the worker in government, worker control with a veto and the unionization and militarization of workers and peasants.

Chapter 10

1. These developments are fully reported in *El Diario* during the period.

2. This concern was reflected in increasing taxes on tin in the thirties and forties and the attempt by the Urrialagoitia government to take over the exchange earned by the companies in 1950.

3. Robert J. Alexander quotes old guard exiles favorable to the nationalization measure in *The Bolivian National Revolution* (New Brunswick, 1958), p. 102.

4. Many have stressed the pivotal role of the hacienda institution in practically all Latin American countries. See José Medina Echavarria, "The Sociologist's View," *Social Aspects of Economic Development in Latin America II* (United Nations, 1963) p. 33, and Frank Tannenbaum, *Ten Keys to Latin America* (New York, 1963), ch. 5.

5. It is generally agreed upon by students of Latin America that the hacienda was not simply an economic institution but rather a total multifunctional community.

6. From independence to the 1920s, the story of land in Bolivia is punctuated by the continual ruthless expropriation of Indian land. This story is recounted in many studies, among the most important of which are Abraham Maldonado, *Derecho Agrario* (La Paz, 1956); Arturo Urquidi Morales, *El Feudalismo En América Y La Reforma Agraria Boliviana* (Cochabamba, Bolivia, 1966); and Rafael Reyeros, *El Pongueaje* (La Paz, 1949). For a detailed study of how one community of Indians was dispossessed in the early twentienth century, see Edmundo Flores, "Taraco: Monografía de un Latifundio Boliviana," *El Trimestre Económico*, Vol. 22, No. 86 (1958), pp. 209–29.

7. There are many novelistic portrayals of mutual racial hatred and suspicion in Bolivia. One of the most moving is the famous novel by Alcides Arguedas, *Raza De Bronce* (Valencia, 1923).

8. One of the most remembered recent uprisings took place in 1924 when the Indians of Jesús de Machaca invaded an altiplano town killing and burning the majority of its inhabitants.

9. One has only to spend a brief time in Bolivia and speak to city people to hear the Indian characterized as dirty, treacherous, ill-tempered, thieving, stupid, vengeful, and so on. To be called an *"indio"* in Bolivia is to be delivered one of the highest insults. For this reason, the revolutionary government banned the term and the Indian is today called campesino ("countryman").

10. This limited concept of reform was, according to Señor Hugo Roberts, then an important right-wing MNR figure, the position he and the majority of the right wing held. Personal interview, La Paz, 1966.

11. As the debate was mainly behind the scenes, I was forced to base this account on personal interviews. However, I should make it clear that no one appeared hesitant to express his opinion and the various stories told to me coincided with each other to a remarkable extent.

12. The first studies are: Richard Patch, "The Social Implications of the Bolivian Agrarian Reform," (unpub. Ph.D. thesis, Cornell Univ., 1959); Edmundo Flores, "La Reforma Agraria En Bolivia," *El Trimestre Económico*, Vol. 20, No. 79 (1953), pp. 480–506; Dwight B. Heath, "Land Reform in Bolivia," *Inter-American Economic Affairs*, Vol. 12 (1959), pp. 3–27; William E. Carter, *Aymara Communities and the*

Bolivian Agrarian Reform, Univ. of Florida Monograph Series, No. 24 (Fall, 1964); Barbara Leons, "Changing Patterns of Social Stratification in an Emergent Bolivian Community," (unpub. Ph.D. thesis, U.C.L.A., 1966). Important works in progress are a comparative study of Bolivia and Peru by Mr. Melvin Burke, University of Pittsburgh; a study by the Land Tenure Institute of the University of Wisconsin; and a just-completed three-year study by the Research Institute for the Study of Man, New York.

13. The data is based on a census conducted in 1950 which was not a complete census but did account for 86,377 landowners. *Censo Nacional Agropecuario De 1950,* Oficina Nacional de Estadísticas y Censos Sección Agropecuario (La Paz, 1950).

14. For more extensive data, see any of the works in Note 12, above. It should also be noted that in the eastern regions, there were large land tracts but they were not classic haciendas. There, labor was usually paid for. In addition, the government owned large tracts in these areas. However, the vast bulk of the Indians did live on haciendas.

15. The extremely defensive behavior of the Indians is stressed in the first systematic study of rural relations in Bolivia published in English, Olen E. Leonard, *Bolivia: Land People and Institutions* (Washington, 1952), pp. 96–97.

16. In one important study of the Lake area, it was noted, for example, "During the last years of the previous century and the first of the present there began the massive establishment of latifundios. The community of Chivo along with others was incorporated as a hacienda into the holdings of the Goitia family" (Francisco, Baluarte Garay, *Tierra y Reforma Agraria en Chivo,* Estudios de Communidades Bolivianos, No. 4 [Lima, 1964], paging of manuscript unclear).

17. Paul Walle in his study noted, for example:

In the departments of Chuquisaca and Potosí, the Indians who live on haciendas or great rural properties work gratis two days a week. In the departments of La Paz and Oruro, this servitude is more onerous, for they must build their houses, plough, sow, reap the grain, and carry it to market, to say nothing of the compulsory duty or corvie known as pongueaje. . . . (Paul Walle, *Bolivia* [New York, 1914], p. 374)

Rafael Reyeros throughout his *El Pongueaje* (see note 6, above) makes much of the onerous conditions in the Cochabamba Valley. In personal discussions with knowledgeable Bolivians, the view that the regimen was more difficult in the Valley and around the Lake was generally agreed upon. Particularly informative were two ex-landowners, Mr. Hugo Ernst from La Paz and Mr. Percy Aiken from the region of Potosí.

18. In 1950 the density of population per square kilometer by departments was Chuquisaca, 5.49; La Paz, 7.08; Cochabamba, 8.82; Potosí, 4.52; Oruro, 3.92; Santa Cruz, 0.77; Tarija, 3.37; Beni, 0.56. In the province of Omasuyos where Achacachi is located, the concentration was 31.37, while in the Valley province of Jordán where Ucureña is located, the figure was 76.91. *Censo Nacional,* pp. 7–10.

19. The problem of man-land ratios in the Valley is vividly elucidated in the important study, Olen E. Leonard, *Canton Chullpas: A Socio-Economic Study of an Area in the Cochabamba Valley of Bolivia,* U. S. Dept. of Agriculture (1948).

20. The psychological importance of the visibility, or lack thereof, of the two cities is made quite convincingly in an excellent general article on Bolivia. See Christopher Rand, "Letter from La Paz," *New Yorker* (December 31, 1966), pp. 35–56.

21. In the Valley province of Quillacollo, for example, it was observed that "the division of large properties took place before the agrarian reform by means of direct purchases by peasants that returned from the salt fields and the mines with enough capital to acquire a small plot" (Peredo Antezana, *La Provincia de Quilla-collo*, [Cochabamba, 1963] p. 186).

22. Patch, "Bolivia: U.S. Assistance in a Revolutionary Setting," p. 137.

23. Reyeros, *El Pongueaje*, p. 127. For a discussion of the variability of tenure patterns, see Leonard, *Bolivia: Land, People, and Institutions*, p. 113.

24. The *indigenismo* ideology is a Latin American ideology glorifying the Indian culture, especially the early Aztec, Mayan, and Incan civilizations. For a fascinating account of the school, see Elizardo Perez, *Warisata: La Escuela Ayllu* (La Paz, 1962).

25. An important recent study of the development of peasant activities in Ucureña is Jorge Dandler-Hanhart, "Local Group, Community, and Nation: A Study of Changing Structure in Ucureña, Bolivia," University of Wisconsin Monograph (1967).

26. PIR influence in this period was stressed in interviews in Cochabamba, 1965, with two persons intimately familiar with events in the area: Señor Walquer Humerez (former PIR member), and Señor Roberto Carvajal who was an agricultural engineer on the hacienda of Santa Clara in the 1940s. Dandler-Hanhart also points out the influence of the PIR and, in particular, its influence through the new school built at Ucureña. He notes, for example:

> During this time the colonos became increasingly dependent on the leadership of Juan Guerra, the newly appointed school director. As most rural teachers of his generation, he strongly felt that he was called to defend the Indians against exploitation. In addition Guerra became a member of the Leftist Revolutionary Party (PIR), the militant Marxist party that had a detailed program of land reform, Indian education, nationalization of the mines, and other measures. ("Local Group, Community, and Nation," p. 71)

27. This claim is made in the previously cited interviews with the anarchist leader, Mendoza Vega, conducted by Robert J. Alexander (chapter 3, note 10).

28. Among the considerable number of campesino leaders I spoke with, all mentioned this event as important in their memories.

29. The peasant leader referred to is Macedonio Juarez, present boss of Cliza. He expressed this view in a rather heated exchange with the now deposed José Rojas. Dual interview, Cliza, 1965. The foreign scholar referred to is M. Jean Pierre Bernard, Attaché de Recherches a la Foundation Nationale des Sciences Polítiques, who is preparing a book-length study of the history of the agrarian movement.

30. An important MNR leader notes, for example, that in Cochabamba during the civil war of 1949, "there was hesitation among MNR leaders on the wiseness of unleashing a campesino movement whose consequences were unpredictable" (Jose

Fellman Velarde, *Víctor Paz Estenssoro: El Hombre Y La Revolución* [La Paz, 1955], p. 228).

31. In the opinion of Chavez, these miners played a critical role in organizing sindicatos. He indicated that when he took office in 1952, unions headed by ex-miners were in a position to make demands on him, and that they later helped spread organization in other areas. Personal interview, La Paz, 1966.

32. For example, on the altiplano, the Casa Cural of Santiago de Huata was attacked and religious artifacts destroyed. *El Diario,* August 20, 1953, p. 7–4.

33. For example, in February 1953, armed campesinos invaded the city of Cochabamba. *El Diario,* February 2, 1953, p. 5–3. Again on July 1, 1953, campesinos from Ucureña invaded the town of Tarata and sacked it completely. In this action, four were killed and twenty wounded. *El Diario,* July 3, 1953, p. 5–1.

34. This perception is reported over and over again in news accounts. The numerous leaders interviewed by Professor Robert J. Alexander during the period in question conveyed the same perception.

35. In interviews with Indian leaders from relatively nearby but isolated regions, I was told that they did not know a revolution was going on. Later they heard some vague reports, but the first real knowledge came when MNR organizers arrived.

36. His own personal account, news accounts, and reports of other persons leave little doubt that Chavez Ortiz played a prime role in fomenting the agrarian movement.

37. The previously mentioned invasion of Cochabamba (note 33 above) was motivated by the arrest by local police of important peasant leaders. In December, an MNR group in Oruro demanded that the peasant activity be smashed. *El Diario,* December 14, 1952, p. 7–1. Also in December there were reports of police helping a landowner control his rebellious colonos. *El Diario,* December 31, 1952, p. 7–3.

38. According to Chavez Ortiz, the battle in the cabinet on the issue was quite bitter and the decision carried by only one vote. Personal interview, La Paz, 1966.

39. This *proyecto* by Urquidi is reprinted in *Revista Jurídica,* Universidad Mayor de St. Simon (Cochabamba, 1953), pp. 154–220.

40. For example, in relation to development Urquidi argues,

> But such development would not be possible without adopting progressive forms of production, without moving from small peasant exploitation to capitalist agriculture on a grand scale, that would permit the application of modern techniques and a better organization of work . . . within the actual stage of our evolution it is then important to recognize the progressive character of capitalism in the campo. (*Revista Jurídica,* pp. 204–05)

The Urquidi *proyecto* also called for indemnification (stated in principle in the reform). By way of contrast, the POR member, Ayala Mercado, called for no indemnification and, while he accepted the allotment of individual plots to the Indian, he concludes:

> Finally, in certain rural zones, on federal lands or on expropriated latifundios the state ought to organize pilot collectivized farms in order to stimulate general rural progress and to avoid the absorption of capitalist

type methods and to demonstrate the advantages of collectivism under state direction. (Ernesto Ayala Mercado, *Revista Juridica,* p. 294)

41. It is generally believed that the campesinos were armed by the MNR. While this is probably true in some cases, many peasant leaders claimed to me that they bought their own weapons. Moreover, in regions where organization is strong today, the campesino is taxed by the sindicato and portions of the funds are used to buy weapons and ammunition.

42. In one study of a region around the Lake, the exodus of mestizos and whites is stressed. See Instituto Boliviano de Estudios y Acción Social (IBEAS), mimeographed study (La Paz, 1965). Numerous ex-hacienda owners interviewed by me complained bitterly of their inability to return to their lands. This process is also pointed out in a study by William E. Carter, to be published in James M. Malloy and Richard Thorn, eds., *Bolivia Since the Revolution* (Pittsburgh, 1971).

43. The Research Institute for the Study of Man team in Bolivia reported that the town of Sorata which they studied was taken over by Indians after 1952. Thereafter, the town administration was held by local sindicato officials. Many other rural towns had the same experience.

44. After numerous fruitless visits to the confederation office in La Paz, I concluded that the only time it was near to functioning was when the present leader of the Valley, Jorge Soliz, was in town. During other periods, it was seldom open and when it was, it was attended only by a none-too-busy secretary. There were no visible signs of organization records, etc., in the bare office. A further indication of the weakness of the confederation was the way in which campesino funds were allocated. According to one early report, 50 percent of funds went to the intermediate level, known as central, 40 percent to the department federations, and only 10 percent to the national confederation. *El Diario,* January 26, 1956, p. 4–4.

45. This pattern was described to me in private discussion with Dr. Barbara Leons, Department of Anthropology, University of Pittsburgh. Dr. Leons worked in the Yungas region for sixteen months.

46. Recounted in detail in an excellent study done under the auspices of the Research Institute for the Study of Man. Victor Novick, "Revolutionary Change in a Bolivian Hacienda Town," paper presented at the meeting of the American Anthropological Association, Pittsburgh, Pa., 1966.

47. It should be noted that centralized regional organizations on the altiplano appear to have collapsed since the coup of 1964. In the Valley, however, organization is as powerful, if not more powerful, than ever.

48. I personally visited one campesino *cuartel* ("barracks") in Punata where the local leader Gregorio Lopez proudly had his men give a demonstration of close order drill. During one of President Barriento's trips to Cochabamba, I saw a display of campesino militia might which included rifles, hand grenades, machine guns, and mortars. In interviews with individual campesinos, the power of the sindicato to tax and punish was related in many vivid stories.

49. Shortly after the reform, campesinos from Achacachi blocked truck traffic along the Lake in a demand for higher food prices. *El Diario,* August 19, 1953, p. 7–1. In 1954 armed peasants invaded Achacachi and freed peasants held in the

local jail. *El Diario,* May 5, 1954, p. 7–3. On January 27, 1959, campesinos stopped, held for eight hours, and then robbed Víctor Paz Estenssoro. *El Diario,* January 28, 1959, p. 7. Again in 1961, altiplano peasants blocked traffic and cut transport to the city. *El Diario,* November 8, 1961, p. 4–6. Shortly thereafter, the city was totally cut off and Salas forbade all persons except the president, the minister of peasant affairs, and newsmen to enter the campo under threat of "arrest." *El Diario,* January 13, 1962, p. 5–1.

50. Leons, "Changing Patterns of Social Stratification," ch. 5.

Chapter 11

1. The fear was first stated in 1935 by Augusto Cespedes and was used at that time as a "realistic" argument for rejecting the "infantile" projections of the more radical socialists. *La Calle,* series of articles beginning July 25, 1935.

2. It is interesting to note, for example, that in most official MNR documents, the tri-class nature of the party is always expressed as an alliance of the "clase media, obreros y campesinos," in that order. In most labor-left documents, however, it is expressed as "obreros, campesinos y clase media revolucionaria," in that order. Lechín's personal view of the MNR right was expressed as follows: "The right of the MNR allied with the most reactionary elements of the Army has attempted to stab the revolution in the back" (*Lechín y La Revolución Nacional* [La Paz, n.d.], p. 72).

3. The idea of entrismo and the battles it started on the left were clarified for me in an interview, in La Paz in 1966, with Edwin Moller, a former POR member and one of the best-known exponents of the idea.

4. The mental outlooks of those in Los Grupos de Honor and, in particular, their lack of a program was stressed to me in a number of interviews with Lydia Gueiler Tejada, one of the founders of Los Grupos. La Paz, 1966.

5. The leftist perception of Paz as a pragmatist with whom they could work was spelled out for me in the above-noted interview with Edwin Moller. The deep distrust that the MNR right wing held toward Paz is spelled out in the previously cited Alfredo Candia, *Bolivia: Un Experimento Comunista En America* (La Paz, n.d.) which is, by and large, a systematic indictment of Paz.

6. Elitism and the belief that only progressive sectors of the upper and middle groups could direct a viable solution in Bolivia ran deep in all the counter-tendencies that emerged from the Bolivian bourgeoisie after 1929. The famous Marof, for example, argued: "It is understood that a revolution is not possible unless there is a clear consciousness and unless there is an elite, be it called republican, democratic or Communist" (Tristan Marof, *Ensayos y Critica* [La Paz, 1961], pp. 10–11). In an important speech in the 1940s, Paz expressed the same view:

> But my respected colleague forgets or doesn't want to mention who are the
> ones who make the great transformations of history. It is a general law that
> the men of the oppressed class never are the ones who achieve gains for

their own class and this is for a simple reason; those of an oppressed class do not have the economic means to even raise themselves culturally and develop their personality, let alone be able to make a great reform or a revolution. . . . (*Victor Paz Estenssoro Discursos Parlimentarios* [La Paz, 1955], pp. 316–17)

In an early ideological statement, Walter Guevara Arze argued: "It is certain that in Bolivia the conditions do not exist to create class consciousness and revolutionary capacity in the proletariat" (Walter Guevara Arze, *Teoria, Medios y Fines de La Revolución Nacional* [Cochabamba, 1946], p. 12). There seems little doubt that the MNR core saw itself as an elite destined to lead a backward people to modernity.

7. Quoted in Lydia Gueiler Tejada, *La Mujer y La Revolución* (La Paz, 1959), pp. 119–21.

8. *Ibid.*, pp. 122–24.

9. *Ibid.*, p. 124.

10. This long-range view of the Lechín labor left is clearly expressed in Ernesto Ayala Mercado, *¿Ques e la Revolución Boliviana?* (La Paz, 1956).

11. Gueiler, *La Mujer y La Revolución*, p. 125.

12. Candia, *Bolivia: Un Experimento Comunista*, p. 53.

13. Among the many who have pointed out the importance of jobs in the dispute, Gueiler notes: "But the desperation of the people to get a public job; that is to say the revolution could not immediately free itself from the classic 'job-mania' so common to all underdeveloped countries that lack solid industries and sufficient commerce" (*La Mujer y La Revolución*, p. 98).

14. The fact that the first blow was struck at the man credited by the right-wing with starting the peasant movement seems hardly coincidental.

15. In actuality, the formal call for the commission was made on January 10. *El Diario*, January 10, 1953, p. 4–5.

16. *El Diario*, January 7, 1953, various stories.

17. As might be expected, the events surrounding the quixotic coup attempt were cause for deep personal bitterness among many MNR leaders who had worked and plotted together for years. Not wishing to fan these flames, I will leave names out, but will note that many of the golpistas whom I interviewed launched emotional personal attacks upon old comrades who they claimed betrayed them at the eleventh hour because of job hunger and/or fear. To a man, all spoke with venom of Paz Estenssoro.

18. For an analysis of labor's position after the revolution, see Anna-Stina Ericson, *Labor Law and Practice in Bolivia*, U.S. Dept. of Labor, B.L.S. Report No. 218 (November 1962).

19. In 1952–53, the cost of living jumped from a base figure of 100 percent to 173.0 percent; in 1953–54, it jumped another 99.6 percent; and in 1955–56, another 196.4 percent; the value of the boliviano, meanwhile, dropped from 60 to the dollar to 12,000 to the dollar. *Analisis y Proyecciónes Del Desarrollo Económico IV: El Desarrollo Económico de Bolivia* (Mexico, 1958), p. 62.

20. The coup attempt was made on November 9, 1953. *Control Politico*, especially under the direction of Claudio San Roman, became one the FSB's most hated symbols of MNR rule. Since the fall of the MNR in November 1964, there

have been a spate of publications attacking the MNR and, in particular, Paz and San Roman. One rather macabre account is "San Roman Biografia de Un Verdugo," *Primera Plana Numero Especial* (1965).

21. For the somewhat different FSB view of the revolution see Enrique Acha Alvarez and Mario Ramos y Ramos, *UNZAGA: Martir de America* (Buenos Aires, 1960) and Hernan Landivar Flores, *Infierno en Bolivia* (La Paz, 1965).

22. Stated to Professor Carter Goodrich, then head of a U.N. mission to Bolivia, by Walter Guevara Arze. Related to me in personal conversations at the University of Pittsburgh where Professor Goodrich is presently Mellon Professor of Economic History.

23. Results published in *El Diario,* various days in June 1956.

24. In his speech, Guevara made an important ideological point, namely that he was, "a partisan of free enterprise within the limits of the nation's realities." This view I would argue was shared by the MNR pragmatic center. However, for reasons of personal ambition, among others, Paz and Siles were not inclined as yet to openly clash with Lechín. For a report of the convention, see Lois Deicke Martin, *Bolivia in 1956,* Hispanic American Studies Series (Stanford, 1958), p. 2.

25. In his violent reply to Guevara, Lechín laid down the gauntlet to the party. He attacked the MNR leaders around Guevara as nothing more than middle-class thieves, seeking to enrich themselves from the revolution. At the same time, he reaffirmed his attachment to the *Tesis de Pulacayo* and called for a "permanent revolution." Finally, he warned the MNR that "the workers will be loyal to the party only so long as it remains the vanguard of them" *(El Diario,* January 18, 1956, p. 4–3).

26. The POR received the nomination of Siles with disdain. They argued that it was proof that the MNR right wing wished to stall the revolution and give it over to the U.S. Reported in *El Diario,* June 11, 1956, p. 4–4

27. For details of the plan, see *Analisis y Proyecciónes,* pp. 80–82.

28. The pulperias were a real financial boost to the miners in this inflation-ridden country. The miners did not feel the brunt of the inflation since the subsidized stores kept prices stable. Furthermore, the miners were able to resell goods at enormous profits.

29. This is emphatically the view of Señor Quadros Quiroga who argues that Siles missed a golden opportunity to do Lechín in once and for all. Personal interview, Cochabamba, 1965.

30. Their loss of congressional control and its negative effect on their position was related to me by Edwin Moller in the previously cited interview.

31. Significant U.S. military aid was renewed in 1958 and went up steadily from that year. Report Submitted to the House Committee on Appropriations, 90th Congress, 2d Session, p. 624.

32. Siles also began to use the military in other "control" operations. According to the *New York Times,* of ten "major" disturbances between 1956 and 1960, the military was used to quash seven, including one that involved a coup attempt by members of the national police. *New York Times,* March 20, 1960.

33. In this attempt, which began with an abortive assault on a military *cuartel* ("barracks") in Sucre, the long-standing leader of the FSB, Unzaga de La Vega, was killed. Unzaga's appeal was more potent to the new young Bolivian

Falangists than to the by now middle-aged, original members. His removal from the scene introduced a new kind of leader to the FSB and is probably a contributory factor to the more moderate position the FSB has since taken. The younger members hold the belief (not totally unfounded) that Unzaga was murdered in cold blood. They continue, therefore, to hate the MNR, in general, and Walter Guevara Arze (then minister of government), in particular, with a fierce passion.

34. The newsmen covering the convention reported that the Lechín faction was the strongest in the meeting. *El Diario,* February 16, 1959, p. 7–3.

35. The old guard MNR, now behind Guevara, began to blast Paz in a series of pamphlets. These pamphlets express the long-standing MNR view of the need for a middle-class, elite-run state which would achieve development through a system of state-regulated capitalism. The failure of the aim to succeed is attributed to the designs of Paz and Lechín. In my view, this basic ideological position which we can call state capitalism continued to be the preferred view of Paz and the remaining MNR core. The break came not over ideological images, but over tactics and personal ambition. Indeed, many close to Paz, and Paz himself, indicated that during 1963–64, Paz sought to bring back Guevara as the only man other than himself capable of besting Lechín. For the Guevara wing's view, see *Acusación Contra Víctor Paz Estenssoro Los Auténticos Se Dirigen A La Nación Desde El Destierro* (June 1961) and *P.M.N.R.A. Exposición de Motivos y Declaración de Principios* (April 1960).

36. Election results in *El Diario* beginning June 9, 1960.

Chapter 12

1. The understanding of organized "legitimate" power used here follows that developed by Talcott Parsons and brought into the theoretical problem area of revolution by Chalmers Johnson. The following quote of Parsons by Johnson illustrates the concept.

> Power, as a generalized medium, operates in a way analogous to the func-
> tioning of money. The money held by a social unit is, we may say, the
> unit's capacity, through market channels under given rules of procedure, to
> command goods and services in exchange, which for its own reasons it
> desires. Correspondingly, the power of a unit is its capacity, through invok-
> ing binding obligations (e.g., civic obligations such as military service,
> contractual obligations, the obligation to follow vested leadership, and
> so forth) to contribute to collective goals, to bring about collective goal
> inputs that the constituents of the collective action in question desire. . . .
> Once units are brought within the relevant context of collective organiza-
> tion, power is the medium of invoking their obligations to contribute to
> collective functioning. . . . (Like monetary systems, power systems) depend
> on the continuing willingness of their members to entrust their status in
> and interpretations of the collective interest to an impersonal process in
> which binding decisions are made without the members being in a position

to control them (directly). (Chalmers Johnson, *Revolutionary Change* [Boston, 1966], p. 29)

2. Another concept which would express the idea meant here is "entropy," a reversal of "collective" organizational maturity, resulting in a declining capacity to perform collective work or pursue collective goals within the organizational state unit.

3. The developing situation was expressed by Lechín in a statement in which he defines his views on government and representation. "It often happens, I say, that governments forget the old fights and promises and therefore the *Central Obrera Boliviana* must control the government. I represent the workers in the cabinet and not the cabinet to the workers" (*El Diario*, March 16, 1958, p. 5–3).

4. *New York Times*, November 8, 1964, p. 26.

5. The dominance of municipal governments over their areas and the corresponding weakness of nationally appointed departmental officials is stressed in *Informe Keenleyside* (reprinted in La Paz by La Universidad Mayor de San Andres, 1952), p. 30.

6. In 1965, I sat in on a session of the Agrarian Reform Commission in which representatives from various departments reported on the situation in their areas. The representative from the department of Pando described one town, situated close to both the Peruvian and Brazilian borders, where, of eighty-five inhabitants, only three (the mayor, police chief, and local cop) were Bolivians.

7. The separatist sentiment of Santa Cruz is legend in Bolivia. It stems, in part, from the racial differences between the people of Santa Cruz and those of the highlands. Due to the location of the Indian peoples in the highlands previous to the Spanish conquest and to the long isolation of Santa Cruz there has not been as much miscegenation in this area. As a result, the people of Santa Cruz tend to be more purely European racially and, indeed, take great pride in their "direct" Spanish lineage. These people now refer to themselves as *Cambas* ("Lowlander") and refer to the highlanders derogatorily as *Collas*. Since the completion of the Cochabamba-Santa Cruz highway, there has been a large migration of *Collas* into the region. This, in turn, has led to a great deal of tension within the department. In a recent trip to Bolivia, the depths of the sentiments involved was brought home to me quite graphically. Due to engine difficulties, my plane for Lima was cancelled and the seventy-odd passengers who had been waiting aboard for five hours had to return to La Paz to spend the night at the airline's expense. None of us was too happy with the situation. One young lady from Santa Cruz was particularly angered by the situation and upon arrival at the hotel began to inform the airline's representative of her feelings on the matter. Visibly shaken by her outburst, the representative attempted to deflect her anger by appealing to her patriotism. After a lengthy explanation he concluded with the observation that after all, *"Somos todos Bolivianos"* ("We are all Bolivians") to which she made the furious reply *"¡Yo no soy Boliviana— yo soy Camba!"* ("I am not a Bolivian—I am a *Camba!"*).

8. Inter-mine camp wars were particularly frequent under Siles, especially in 1959.

9. William Kornhauser, *The Politics of Mass Society* (New York, 1959), ch. 3.

10. After fourteen months in Bolivia, I feel I can say with confidence that every person who attends to politics sees *cargos* or *puestos* ("jobs") to be central to

Bolivian politics. Moreover, they structure their political behavior around that perception.

11. Given the fact that general life expectancy in Bolivia is agreed to be about thirty-three years of age and even less in the mines, this statement does not seem to be an exaggeration.

12. Pierre Noel Lenoir, *Revolución Altitud 4,000 Metros* (Buenos Aires, 1958), p. 97.

13. In a very important speech to the FSTMB by Lechín's long-standing right-hand man, Mario Torres, a number of critical points regarding worker independence, the workers' suspicion of the MNR, etc., are made. Torres then listed the benefits which the miner had gained and made the following critical statement on the functions of COMIBOL:

> . . . The mine companies before 1952 were commercial enterprises. . . . If the price of tin dropped, they closed mines, fired workers, and cut wages in order to cut costs. COMIBOL is not a commercial enterprise. If imperialism does not pay us well; if imperialism does not permit the satisfaction of the desires of the people—that are actually rights; if imperialism does not pay what it owes us, the corporation ought to take upon itself and accept this tremendous responsibility. The corporation and above all the control obrero must work with a social criterion and the latter with a union criterion.

In other words, the COMIBOL must follow a social logic and the unions, a class logic. Mario Torres, *Informe a FSTMB* (1954, mimeographed, available at the U.S. Embassy, La Paz.) An even more radical view was expressed by the miners of the San José mine during the stabilization fight. "Now the mines belong to us just like the land belongs to the peasant." *(El Diario,* June 5, 1957, p. 7–2).

14. One study indicates that over thirty-eight agricultural enterprises were taken over due to peasant action since 1953. Enrique Levy Merrivia, "La Ejecución de La Reforma Agraria en El Departamento De Cochabamba," *Revista Juridica* (Cochabamba, circa 1956), Nos. 67–70, p. 138.

15. See Abraham Maldonado, *Legislación Social Boliviana* (La Paz, 1957).

16. For an analysis of the relationship between these factors, see *Analisis y Proyecciónes Del Desarrollo Económico IV: El Desarrollo Económico de Bolivia* (Mexico, 1958), p. 68.

17. For a detailed analysis of labor's early social and economic position, see Anna-Stina Ericson, *Labor Law and Practice in Bolivia,* U.S. Dept. of Labor, B.L.S. Report No. 218 (November, 1962), and *Area Handbook for Bolivia* (Washington, D.C., 1963), ch. 20.

18. For breakdowns of inter-sectoral benefits which indicate that the peasant was the biggest long-term gainer, see *Analisis y Proyecciónes,* p. 19, and "Ideas Preliminares Para La Elaboración de un Diagnostica De La Económia Boliviana," *Planeamiento,* No. 1 (La Paz, 1960), pp. 68–69.

19. According to one source, between 1952 and 1965 there was a five-fold increase in the number of rural schools and a 250 percent increase in enrollment. Lambros Comitas, "Education and Social Stratification In Contemporary Bolivia," *Transactions of the New York Academy of Sciences,* Series II, 1 of 29, No. 7, p. 943.

20. Between 1952 and 1960, per capita income declined over 20 percent. Gross

income of COMIBOL declined from $84 million in 1953 to $43 million in 1961. Between 1958 and 1962, COMIBOL was losing between $10 million and $12 million per year. Aside from previously cited studies, the best studies available on the recent Bolivian economy are Carter Goodrich, *The Economic Transformation of Bolivia*, New York School of Industrial and Labor Relations, Cornell University, Bulletin 34 (October 1955); David Green, "Revolution and the Rationalization of Reform in Bolivia," *Inter-American Economic Affairs*, Winter, 1965, pp. 3–27; Cornelius Zondag, *The Bolivian Economy 1952–1965* (New York, 1966); the most up-to-date and compact statistics are in *Economic and Program Statistics*, U.S.A.I.D. (Bolivia, yearly).

21. See *Analisis y Proyecciónes*, pp. 32–36.

22. *Analisis y Proyecciónes*, pp. 21–24, shows how simultaneous consumption and investment policies, despite massive United States economic aid, depleted the national capital base.

23. The stultifying effects of the stabilization are pointed out in Richard Patch, "Bolivia: U.S. Assistance in a Revolutionary Setting," in Richard Adams et al., *Social Change in Latin America Today* (New York, 1960), and Green, "Revolution and the Rationalization of Reform in Bolivia."

24. During the battle over stabilization, Lechín made it clear that the makeup of the leadership of the MNR and the allocation of social costs were the real issues at stake. In one speech, for example, he blasted Siles for bringing back to office the *golpistas de 6 de Enero* (those involved in the coup attempt of January 6) and went on to warn that the revolution would consume those who tried to hold it back. He then discussed the issue of social costs, arguing that starving workers could not be asked to sacrifice further. Also, he bitterly observed that the workers produced the wealth, but the speculators lived off of it. The MNR, Lechín argued, could not just be a party of founders, but had to be refurbished with true revolutionaries. He concluded by arguing that the way out for Bolivia was to strip the rich in favor of the poor, who would then, through their buying power, stimulate growth. Reported in *El Diario*, June 15, 1957, p. 4–3.

25. The negative economic effects of what was an obvious political standoff are gone into at great length in a United Nations analysis of planning and development problems in Bolivia. See *Informe Sobre Bolivia*, Hecho por Expertos de Naciones Unidos, I.P.E. (La Paz, 1966), pt. 2. This report was a confidential office memo which was made public by the I.P.E., a private group which issues reports on the Bolivian economy, causing a major furor in Bolivia.

26. One problem of the peasants as a support public, especially from the point of view of armed force, was their lack of mobility. On numerous occasions, I was told of cases when peasants of one area marched out for one reason or another and returned to find that their neighbors had sacked their homes. Thus, in many regions, the peasants feared to leave and preferred to stay home and guard their homes and lands.

27. A leftist description of the intervention appears in Amado Canelas, *Mito y Realidad De La Reforma Agraria* (La Paz, 1964), pp. 197–205. Veizaga, who now is restricted to the town of Cochabamba where he works as a laborer in the university's agricultural station, complained bitterly to me of his political eclipse at the hands of, first, Siles and then Paz. Personal interview, Cochabamba, 1965. Although

admittedly biased, these reports gained credence in other interviews with MNR leaders and by a careful reading of the national newspapers which clearly show that Veizaga was being harassed by the government.

28. After 1952, rural areas turned in overwhelming vote returns for the MNR. Indeed, in most towns the vote was completely for the MNR, with none at all for other parties. In the 1960 elections, the pattern in the Cochabamba Valley was similar, except in Cliza, Veizaga's stronghold. Cliza turned in all its votes for the PMNRA (the PMNRA was later changed to the PRA, the Guevara group which broke from the MNR). The lesson is obvious: the peasant voted as he was told to by his cacique. Therefore, the cacique was the key to control. Election returns in *El Diario,* June 9, 1960, p. 6.

29. For a breakdown of foreign aid to Bolivia, see Zondag, *The Bolivian Economy, 1952–65,* ch. 16.

30. This concept has been used by a number of anthropologists, particularly G. M. Foster, in analyzing exchange system patterns in peasant societies. See, for example, George M. Foster, "Peasant Society and the Image of Limited Good" in eds. Jack M. Potter et al., *Peasant Society: A Reader* (Boston, 1967), pp. 300–24.

Chapter 13

1. I am not saying that all political rhetoric was cast formally in these terms, but that these ideas influenced the positions of the critical groups struggling for power. However, it should be noted that Mario Alarcon, a close confidant of Siles, expressly defined the battle between Lechín and Siles in terms of these concepts. Personal interview, La Paz, 1965.

2. One anti-MNR spokesman grasped the thrust of the MNR thinking in regard to the revolution when he pointed out, "For that reason the decree of October 31 (nationalization of tin) corresponded to the democratic bourgeois character of April 9 and revealed that it was essentially a bourgeois nationalization" (Amado Canelas, *Mito y Realidad De La Reforma Agraria* [La Paz, 1964], p. 165).

3. See Note 6, Chapter 10.

4. *Capital humano* ("human capital") is a concept which pervades post-1936 Bolivian writings.

5. Víctor Paz Estenssoro expressed this view in the following statement:

Another feature of our political economy was the agrarian reform. The reform signified not only a reparation of centuries of injustice from the human point of view, but also a liberation of productive forces, the creation of conditions for national economic development, the incorporation into the money economy of the peasants so as to increase the internal market for possible industrial development. *(El Pensamiento de Paz Estenssoro* [La Paz, 1954], p. 72)

6. Important expressions of the POR's views include *¿Que Es y Que Quiere El POR?* (La Paz, 1959) and Guillermo Lora, *La Revolución Boliviana* (La Paz, circa 1965).

7. Among the many expressions of the transformed labor-left view, the most developed and clearly expressed is Ernesto Ayala Mercado, *¿Que es La Revolución Boliviana?* For variations on the MNR core's view, see Hernan Siles Zuazo, *Mensaje Al Honorable Congreso Nacional* (La Paz, August 6, 1959); and Víctor Paz Estenssoro, *La Revolución Boliviana* (La Paz, 1964).

8. For reasons of space and controllability of the study I have focused mainly on internal variables in analyzing the development of the revolution. This still seems to me a viable approach, but it is obvious that a "total" study of the revolution would have to take into account external variables and, in particular, U.S.–Soviet relations. From the beginning, the MNR core rejected any definition of the revolution that would alienate the United States. Then, under Siles and later under Paz, the Soviet Union was rejected as a source of aid. This made Bolivia reliant on the U.S. as the only source of aid, and it also made it subject to the conditions attached to that aid. The U.S. made it clear, in turn, first in the stabilization plan and later in the triangular plan for tin, that its continued aid was predicated on the establishment of a state capitalist economic system within a formal constitutional political framework. U.S. economic aid to Bolivia has been very significant. Between 1952 and 1966, commitments under the U.S. AID program alone totaled $313 million; from 1952 to 1965 commitments under the Social Progress Trust Fund were $14.6 million; Food For Peace, $69.1 million; import-export bank loans, $39.4 million; Peace Corps, $16.9 million. (Sources: Statistics and Reports Division, "Worksheet" [May 4, 1966], U.S. Economic Assistance Programs [April 3, 1948–June 30, 1965 (1966)] p. 28, Operations Report as of June 30, 1967–69, Proposed Foreign Aid Program FY 1968, Summary Presentation to Congress [1967] p. 284, U.S. AID/Washington.)

9. The differential impact of the stabilization was pointed out by Baltomero Costell, a leader of the construction workers, to Robert J. Alexander during a personal interview with him in La Paz, 1957. Costell noted that the construction workers, factory workers, and railway workers had about the same buying power after the plan went into effect as before. From his point of view, the situation was actually better for these worker groups because things were easier to get and they did not have to stand in endless lines. He noted that the miners were the ones to be hit by the plan. He argued that the crisis under Siles was fomented by the POR which was also powerful in the COB. He noted further that he and other leaders were against the "POR-dominated executive committee of the COB" and that is why they backed Siles.

10. The union most important in backing the Siles tactic was that of the railway workers which, since the early 1940s, was more influenced by the PIR than the POR. The leader of the railroaders, Juan Sanjines Obando, backed Siles and later Paz in their battles with Lechín. The anti-Lechín position of Sanjines and the railroaders was conveyed to Robert J. Alexander in a personal interview with Feliberto Gutierrez, a member of the economic committee of the union, La Paz, 1963.

11. The issue of social costs was paramount in this battle. Lechín constantly assailed the MNR for depriving the miners while party bureaucrats became rich. See, for example, *La C.O.B. y La Estabilización Monetaria* (La Paz, 1957). During the stabilization battle, Siles argued that the basis of future development turned on three factors: (a) to obtain and amplify U.S. aid; (b) to pay external debts so as to

be able to get credits from the world bank; and (c) to encourage private capital investment. *El Diario,* June 14, 1957, p. 6.

12. The basic aims of Paz's second government are spelled out in *Movimiento Nacionalista Revolucionario Programa de Gobierno 1960–1964* (La Paz, 1960).

13. Of the previously cited $313 million in U.S. AID commitments, fully $215.9 million in commitments were made between 1960 and 1966. All the Social Progress Trust Fund support and most of the Food For Peace support were given after 1960 also. The same, of course, holds true for the Peace Corps, and, as we shall see in note 27 below, for the bulk of military assistance as well. Previously cited sources in note 8, above.

14. The tremendous influence of Kennedy on Paz was made evident in my interviews with the Bolivian ex-president in Lima, 1966. Paz's image of the American president was painted with deep personal emotion. Paz saw Kennedy as a kind of personal ally who would give him the support to achieve his dreams and goals. Paz himself indicated, and others close to him at the time believe, that Kennedy's death so disoriented the Bolivian leader that he almost lost his will to go on with what he had begun.

15. The most popular post for the ambitious was that of minister of peasant affairs. During this period, ministers came and went, but while in office each sought to use the position to line up peasant support behind his own personal ambitions.

16. See Colen J. Crossley, *Santa Cruz at the Cross Roads: A Study of Development in Eastern Bolivia* (Leicester, United Kingdom, 1961).

17. Between 1961 and 1964, there are constant reports in *El Diario* of fighting in Santa Cruz.

18. Barrientos was a military man before the insurrection of 1952 and had been associated with many attempts to overthrow status quo governments. However, after 1952, he joined the MNR and cultivated a close relationship with Paz, becoming an active propangandist for Paz's policies. He climbed quickly within the political power structure and was eventually made head of the Bolivian air force and then vice-president of the short-lived Paz government of 1964. The public linkage of Rojas with Barrientos began immediately after the first of many attempts on the life of Barrientos. *El Diario,* February 27, 1963, various stories.

19. It is by no means coincidental that General Rene Barrientos Ortuño played an important leadership role in both interventions. It was during these actions that Barrientos first emerged as a figure of national prominence. Perhaps more important, it was during these actions that Barrientos forged critical personal contacts with local peasant and party leaders. This turn of events was to prove rather important in regard to the Cochabamba Valley and to José Rojas, in particular.

20. The only general study of military civic action in Bolivia written in English is William Brill, "Military Civic Action in Bolivia" (unpub. Ph.D. thesis, University of Pennsylvania, 1965).

21. The phrase was first created as the title of an important historical novel by Augusto Cespedes, *El Metal Del Diabo* (Buenos Aires, 1960).

22. See *Report on the Mining Industry of Bolivia,* Vol. I, Summary (La Paz, 1956), p. 12.

23. The two chief concepts to shape the new approach are spelled out in the decree establishing the plan and in a companion explanation of it. ". . . National

development must necessarily start from the strengthening and diversification of the mining industry, as the only sector capable of generating internal savings, capitalizing the country and creating the conditions for a balanced mobilization of other sectors." To achieve this, the plan aims specifically to "reestablish the principle of authority and of labor discipline" (Reprinted in *Estaño*, No. 8, [1964]).

24. This redefinition of the concept "counter-revolutionary" began in a speech by Paz entitled, "La Revolución es un Processo que tiene Raices, en El Pasado" to a sector of the MNR, La Paz, 1961.

25. The magnitude of the layoffs and the ensuing battle over them was related to me in interviews in La Paz in 1966 with C. Blout, then general director of the mine.

26. Paz developed this line in a series of important speeches. During one of his crises with the miners, for example, he went to Cochabamba to address a mass assembly of campesinos. He told the peasants that for the good of Bolivia, the mines had to be controlled. He then identified the peasant as the key to the future of the revolution. "The national revolution will go ahead because Cochabamba wants it to." After Paz, Rojas spoke and flayed the "Communists" and "leftists" as the source of all Bolivia's ills. He ended by pledging that the campesinos would save the revolution. *El Diario*, August 25, 1963, p. 4–5. In addition, Paz considerably stepped up the process of granting land titles to peasants. Between 1955 and 1960, a total of 47,746 signed titles were given. Then, in a rush of activity, Paz granted the staggering number of 200,413 between 1960 and 1964. James W. Wilkie, "Bolivian Land Reform Since 1952: A Statistical View of Title Redistribution," mimeographed, (Speech to the Conference on Political Parties and Political Stability in Latin America, State University of New York at Buffalo [1968], Appendix A).

27. The budget outlay for defense climbed from 1.7 billion bolivianos in 1953 to 75.2 billion bolivianos in 1963. *United Nations Statistical Yearbook* (1963), p. 559. The decline and rise of the military is recorded in the fact that its proportion of the budget fell from 23 percent on the eve of the revolution to a low of 6.7 percent in 1957; thereafter, it climbed steadily to 12.4 percent by 1963. The reversal of the trend reflected the policy begun under Siles and broadened under Paz of rebuilding and refurnishing the military. See James A. Wilkie, "The Finance of the Bolivian Revolution," mimeographed, Department of History, U.C.L.A. (1968), p. 38 and Appendix N. An important factor in the military's new budget picture was U.S. military assistance, which was resumed in 1958. Of the $10.5 million recorded by U.S. AID sources, fully $10.1 million was granted between 1961 and 1965. U.S. AID/Washington, Statistics and Reports Division, "Worksheet" (May 4, 1966). According to another U.S. source, Bolivia received $18.7 million in military assistance between 1958 and 1967. Report submitted to the House Committee on Appropriations, 90th Congress, 2nd Session, p. 624.

28. In 1961, the G.N.P. rose 3.5 percent, then, in 1963 and 1964, it jumped to 6 percent.

29. Reported in *Presencia* (January 18, 1964), pp. 5–6. During my interviews with him in Lima, 1966, Paz constantly argued that he ran into his worst opposition inside the party and that it came from disgruntled office-seekers.

30. In an important speech in January 1962, for example, Paz attacked the existing university system. He argued that the universities had put themselves outside the mainstream of Bolivian history and, therefore, did not fulfill the needs of

the country. The basic need of Bolivia, he argued, was for technocrats. Paz stated that to insure a rapid creation of a group of technocrats, the *Instituto Tecnologico Boliviano* was being organized. *El Diario*, January 25, 1962, p. 5–5.

31. Jaguaribe, *Desarrollo Económico y Desarrollo Político* (Buenos Aires, 1962), p. 101.

32. *Ibid.*, p. 87.

33. See Aníbal Pinto, "Political Aspects of Economic Development in Latin America," ed. Claudio Veliz, *Obstacles to Change in Latin America* (New York, 1965), pp. 9–47.

34. Víctor Paz and other MNR leaders, for example, actually worked for Patiño and others in the early 1930s.

35. While in Bolivia I was struck constantly by the distinct impression that MNR leaders, as well as other elites, live much as the middle and upper classes did before the revolution, i.e., large well-walled-in houses, numerous servants, cars, etc., etc. Their basic values as expressed in their life style appeared to me to have changed little. Indeed, on more than one occasion, I was given graphic descriptions by well-known MNR leaders of the problems of hiring decent servants in Bolivia.

36. When Paz fell, urban mobs burned and looted many of the elaborate homes in which prominent MNR members lived. A particular target of fury was the ultra-modern home of Guillermo Bedregal, head of COMIBOL.

37. It also led to what all, including those friendly to the MNR, agree was a very high level of corruption among public officials.

38. The school was for officers of field rank and above. One of its first and most illustrious graduates was Rene Barrientos Ortuño.

39. The only real exception to this view previous to the fall of Paz was in a very perceptive article by C. A. M. Henessey, "Shifting Forces in the Bolivian Revolution," *World Today* (May 1964), pp. 197–208.

40. Due to his position, the observer requested his name be withheld.

41. Paz was given the capacity to succeed himself (historically denied in all constitutions of Bolivia) by the adoption of a new constitution in 1961 (the first since 1952).

42. Barrientos was able to gain the support of peasant leaders such as Rojas because of his prominent role in civic action programs and also because his mother was an Indian from Cochabamba. Furthermore, he spoke the language of the Quechua area, and made a personal effort to win peasant support in the 1960s.

Previous to the coup, Rojas was publicly identified as a Barrientos man. Other important leaders such as Jorge Soliz told me that they had made alliances with Barrientos at least three months before Paz's fall. In April 1964, the Valley unions and the army entered into the *Pacto Anti-Comunista Militar-Campesino*. At this point, the Valley leaders were openly identified with Barrientos and the military to such an extent that Rojas attacked Paz and called for Barrientos to assume the presidency.

43. After a stormy year in which Barrientos ruled for a time alone and later with Ovando as co-president, he was elected to the presidency (July 1966). Throughout the next three years, Barrientos governed Bolivia with a strong hand. He continued the general policy thrust of Paz and actually succeeded in breaking the

political back of the labor movement. His forceful pursuit of the state capitalist model won him the support of the United States, but created bitter enemies in Bolivia. By 1968 internal political pressures had built up to crisis proportions and Barrientos' hold on power became dependent on the support of Ovando and the army. By 1969 rumors of a coup were rife and Barrientos appeared to be in deep trouble. On April 27 the flamboyant general's career was brought to an abrupt end when he was killed in a helicopter crash. A brief and politically chaotic period followed under the caretaker government of Luis Adolfo Siles, vice-president under Barrientos. Siles never really gained complete control of the government and the army, under Ovando, ousted Siles and assumed control on September 26, 1969. Ovando announced that his government would follow a national leftist line similar to that adopted by the military regime in Peru. To show that he meant business, Ovando nationalized the Bolivian holdings of the Gulf Oil Corporation. At this writing, this is where the Bolivian Revolution stands–nineteen years old and as yet uncompleted.

Chapter 14

1. Merle Kling, "Toward a Theory of Power and Political Instability in Latin America," ed. John Martz, *The Dynamics of Change in Latin American Politics* (Englewood Cliffs, N.J., 1965).

2. Harry Eckstein, "On the Etiology of Internal Wars," *History and Theory*, Vol. 4, No. 2 (1965), p. 155.

3. See, for example, Torcauto Di Tella, "Populism and Reform in Latin America," in Claudio Veliz, *Obstacles to Change in Latin America* (New York, 1965), pp. 47–75.

4. For a discussion of the relationship of aspirations and expectations to revolutions, see Raymond Tanter and Manus Midlarsky, "A Theory of Revolution," *Journal of Conflict Resolution*, Vol. 11 (Sept. 1967), pp. 264–81.

5. This relationship was first pointed out by James C. Davis in "Toward a Theory of Revolution," *American Sociological Review*, Vol. 27 (1962), pp. 5–19.

6. "Populism and Reform in Latin America," p. 53.

7. Barrington Moore, Jr., *Social Origins of Dictatorship and Democracy* (Boston, 1967), ch. 9.

8. Stanislav Andreski, *Parisitism and Subversion: The Case of Latin America* (London, 1966), p. 232.

GLOSSARY

Terms

CACIQUES   Regional bosses or strong men who controlled rural *sindicato* organizations after 1952

CAMARILLA   Clique of loyal followers formed around a political strong man

CAMPESINOS   Countrymen—official term for Indian peasants adopted by the government after 1952

CAMPO   Rural areas or the countryside

CAUDILLISMO   System of rule by *caudillos* similar in many respects to the Chinese warlord system

CAUDILLO   Chief or leader who rules through a combination of armed might and personalized control

CO-GOBIERNO   Co-government—a concept through which the COB was recognized as holding co-governmental status with the MNR after 1952

COLONOS   Indian peasants who work on haciendas and contribute a number of free days of labor per week in return for a subsistence plot of land

CONTINUISMO   The attempt by an office-holder, usually the president of the government, to remain in office longer than the stipulated term

CONTROL OBRERO   Worker controller—provided by the nationalization decree to give labor some participation in the management of the COMIBOL

DIVISAS   Foreign exchange—as in the *divisas* decree

EMPLEADOS   Employees or white-collar workers, usually in bureaucratic positions

ENTRISMO   Infiltration—used in reference to the infiltration of leftists into the MNR in order to radicalize the party from within

387

FABRILES   Factory workers

FERROVIARIOS   Railway workers

FUERO SINDICAL   A pro-labor decree affording labor special legal status

GOBIERNO OBRERO-CAMPESINO   Government of workers and peasants—concept of labor left wing of MNR projecting a state socialist society dominated by a mixed elite based on the working class

GOLPE DE ESTADO   "Blow against the state"—Latin American equivalent of *coup d'etat*

GOLPISTAS   Slang for those who attempt a *golpe de estado* or *coup d'etat*

GRÁFICOS   Typesetters and printers

HACENDADO   Owner of a hacienda or large landed estate

INDIGENISMO   Ideology glorifying the Indian, seeking to better his status

LA ROSCA   Literally, "screw and nut"—pejorative term for pre-1952 upper class connotating a group that exploited the country and drained its wealth

LATIFUNDIOS   Large unproductive landholdings

LOGIAS   Secret military societies

MINEROS   Mine workers

MINIFUNDIOS   Small subsistence peasant land plots

PERSONALISMO   System of governance in which loyalty is given primarily to individuals, not parties, and patronage is distributed to family and friends

PONGUEAJE   System in which free personal services are rendered by *colonos* to landowners

PULPERÍAS   Originally, company stores; later, state-subsidized stores selling goods at stable prices to miners and other labor groups

SEXENIO   Period of Six Years—refers to the period from 1946 to 1952 when the MNR leaders were persecuted and driven into exile

SINDICALISMO DIRIGIDO   Directed or controlled unionism—state-controlled labor organizations

SINDICATO   Labor union

SOCIALISMO DEL ESTADO   State Socialism—political doctrine associated with the regimes of Toro and Busch

SOCIEDAD DEMOCRÁTICA BURGUESA   Democratic bourgeois society—concept of center and right wing of MNR projecting a state capitalist society dominated by a progressive middle-class elite

Organizations

COB	Central Obrera Boliviana	Bolivian Labor Central. After 1952, the only legitimate national labor organization.

COMIBOL	Corporación Minera de Bolivia	Bolivian Mining Corporation. State mining corporation founded after the nationalization of 1952.
	Comité Político Nacional	National Political Committee. The executive body of the MNR.
CSTB	Confederación Sindical de Trabajadores Bolivianos	Confederation of Bolivian Workers. The first nationwide organization of workers.
FIB	Frente de la Izquierda Boliviana	Bolivian Left Front. Short-lived organization of left-wing groups formed in 1939.
FOL	Federación Obrera Local	Local Labor Federation. Anarcho-syndicalist organization formed in the early 1920s.
FSB	Falange Socialista Boliviana	Bolivian Socialist Falange. A right-wing party modeled after the Spanish Falange.
FSTMB	Federación Sindical de Trabajadores Mineros de Bolivia	Bolivian Mine Workers Federation. The first miners' federation in Bolivia, formed in 1944. Became the most powerful and radical labor organization under the COB.
	La Concordancia	The Concordance. An alliance of traditional political parties formed in 1939.
	Legión de Excombatientes	Legion of Veterans. Veterans' organization formed after the Chaco War.
	Los Grupos de Honor	The Groups of Honor. Paramilitary organizations of the MNR.
MNR	Movimiento Nacionalista Revolucionario	National Revolutionary Party. The party which initiated the revolution of 1952 and led the government from 1952 to 1964.
PCB	Partido Comunista de Bolivia	Bolivian Communist Party. Founded in 1950 by a splinter group of the PIR.
PIR	Partido de la Izquierda Revolucionaria	Left Revolutionary Party. Marxist party formed in 1940; played an important role in the radicalization of the labor movement.

PMNRA	Partido Movimiento Nacionalista Revolucionario Auténtico	Authentic National Revolutionary Party, later called the Partido Revolucionario Auténtico (PRA) or the Authentic Revolutionary Party. This party consisted of the MNR right-wing splinter group formed by Walter Guevara Arze in 1960.
POR	Partido Obrero Revolucionario	Workers Revolutionary Party. A leftist party affiliated with the Fourth International, which had important influence in the mines.
PRA		See PMNRA.
PRIN	Partido Revolucionario de la Izquierda Nacional	National Left Revolutionary Party. This party consisted of the left-wing MNR splinter group formed by Juan Lechín in 1964.
PSOB	Partido Socialista Obrero Boliviano	Bolivian Workers Socialist Party. A short-lived left-wing party of the late 1930s.
PURS	Partido de la Unión Republicana Socialista	United Republican Socialist Party. A group of factions developing out of the Republican party which supported the status quo governments of 1947–51.
RADEPA	Razón de Patria	Reason of the Fatherland. Secret organization of young military officers which spearheaded the coup of 1943.

INDEX